Friends and Enemies

MODERN AMERICA

A series edited by

Barton J. Bernstein and David M. Kennedy

Friends and Enemies

THE UNITED STATES, CHINA, AND THE SOVIET UNION, 1948-1972

GORDON H. CHANG

Stanford University Press   1990
Stanford, California

Stanford University Press, Stanford, California
© 1990 by the Board of Trustees of the
Leland Stanford Junior University
Printed in the United States of America

CIP data appear at the end of the book

TO MY MOTHER AND
THE MEMORY OF
MY FATHER SHU-CHI

Preface

There are many people I would like to acknowledge for their assistance in the completion of this work. Bart Bernstein and David Kennedy provided encouragement and support throughout the entire project. Alex Dallin, John Lewis, Rebecca Lowen, and Michael Salmon were generous with their time in reading the manuscript at various stages. Phil Ethington was also kind to read several early chapters. The book is improved because of the comments and criticisms of my friends and colleagues. I am responsible for inaccuracies and infelicities.

Capable and enthusiastic archivists and staff at the National Archives and the presidential libraries of Harry S. Truman, Dwight D. Eisenhower, John F. Kennedy, and Lyndon B. Johnson provided invaluable guidance to my research. The staffs at the Seeley G. Mudd Library of Princeton University, Sterling Library of Yale University, Rockefeller Archive Center of Rockefeller University, Bancroft Library of the University of California, Berkeley, the Hoover Institution Library and Archives, and the Green Library of Stanford University all contributed significantly to my research efforts. My friends and colleagues at the International Strategic Institute of Stanford were helpful in both large and small ways. I also wish to thank colleagues in China for their help in arranging a research visit and introducing me to specialists and government officials who provided insights into Chinese foreign policy. My thanks go especially to Wang Tieya, Yuan Ming, He Di, Zhang Zhifang, Zi Zhongyun, and Zhang Xiaoming. I am also appreciative of the New China News Agency for allowing me to spend a fascinating morning with some of its photograph archives, and for providing a number of the illustrations in this book. Muriel Bell and Barbara Mnookin of Stanford University Press provided wise and diligent counsel throughout the preparation of the manuscript.

There are also several organizations whose support made this study possible. A fellowship and research fund, administered by the Center for International Security and Arms Control at Stanford for the MacArthur Foundation, enabled me to complete my research and writing in a timely fashion. Stanford's Center for Research in International Studies supported a visit to China. I would also like to thank the Office of Graduate Studies and Research and the History Department of Stanford, the Harry S. Truman Institute, and the Lyndon Baines Johnson Foundation for providing research grants. The warm support and understanding of a number of friends and relatives sustained me through this endeavor. To them, I give heartfelt thanks. I also want to thank Carmen for her patience and thoughtfulness.

In writing this book, I have relied on the large amount of previously classified material the U.S. government has released in recent years concerning its conduct of foreign policy in the Truman, Eisenhower, Kennedy, and Johnson presidencies. Over the coming years more material will be released that will permit further insights into U.S. policy, especially in the 1960s. But it will surely be a much longer period of time, even with the dramatic political changes now occurring in the Soviet Union and China, before something approaching an "equilateral" study of the history of triangular relations can be completed. Policymaking archives in Moscow and Beijing are not likely to be open any time soon. Because our understanding of Chinese and Soviet policymaking is limited largely to what can be gleaned from published materials and reminiscences, this study is necessarily heavily weighted toward understanding the American side, and in particular to official and elite opinion.

An earlier version of Chapter 4 was published in the Spring 1988 issue of the journal *International Security*. An earlier version of Chapter 8 appeared in the March 1988 *Journal of Ameri-*

can History, after receiving the Lewis Pelzer Memorial Award for 1987. In both cases new material not available when the articles were written has been added to the text and notes.

Chinese personal names, place names, and sources are given in *pinyin*, with a few exceptions. Chiang Kai-shek, Hong Kong, Kuomintang, Sun Yat-sen, Taipei, Yangtze River, and Yenching are used because of their familiarity to American readers. Over the years the Chinese rendered Mao's name in different ways in their English-language publications. I have standardized to Mao Tsetung in the Notes.

The following abbreviations are used in the text:

ACDA   Arms Control and Disarmament Agency
AEC   Atomic Energy Commission
CCP   Chinese Communist Party
CFR   Council on Foreign Relations
CPSU   Communist Party of the Soviet Union
KMT   Kuomintang (Guomintang)
NATO   North Atlantic Treaty Organization
NLF   National Liberation Front (Viet Cong)
NSC   National Security Council
PPS   Policy Planning Staff (U.S. State Department)
PRC   People's Republic of China
ROC   Republic of China
SEATO Southeast Asia Treaty Organization

For the abbreviations used in the citations, see the list at the beginning of the Notes, pp. 297–98.

G.H.C.

Contents

Eight pages of photographs follow pages 90 and 178

Friends and Enemies

One of the first requirements in a state's foreign policy [is] to be able to distinguish your friends from your enemies.

—Dean Acheson, 1971

Who are our enemies? Who are our friends? This is a question of the first importance. —Mao Zedong, 1927

Introduction

For those of us who lived through the 1950's, one of our most vivid collective memories must be of a map of the world dominated by an immense, uninterrupted red mass representing the extensive lands of Communist Russia and China. Before our eyes, the color of revolution seemed ready to inundate the other countries of the world, in weak hues of blue, green, pink, and yellow, reflecting—so we thought—the geopolitical realities of the Cold War.

The map gave color to America's popular belief in the existence of what was then known variously as "international communism," "the Sino-Soviet bloc," or "monolithic communism." If there seemed to be one incontrovertible assumption about international affairs in the 1950's, it was that the United States faced not just a united but a seamless communist threat. Communism had no national identities.

That map ill-prepared us for what was unquestionably one of the signal events of the post–World War II era: the fracturing of the Sino-Soviet alliance. Beginning at least as early as 1960, China and the Soviet Union split into hostile camps, soon to fight bloody battles along their common border in the wilds of Siberia and Central Asia. Their split altered the entire complexion of international politics: the bipolar division of international power was replaced by a "diffusion of power" (in the words of Walt W. Rostow) that demanded a more sophisticated and complex diplomacy. Henry Kissinger and Richard Nixon, and Zhou Enlai and Mao Zedong, would rise to meet the challenge. They would free their countries from what had been one of the most hostile and rigid relationships in modern international history.

The demise of a united international communist movement also profoundly transformed the revolutionary challenges to capitalism in both the Third World and the capitalist countries themselves. What did socialist revolution mean when the conflict between the two most prominent examples of "existing socialism" loomed greater than their conflict with U.S. imperialism? The split even had profound implications for the political economy of the socialist countries. The radical political and economic transformations occurring today throughout the socialist world could not have been launched without polycentric communism. It is difficult to conceive of what the world would be like today if there had been no Sino-Soviet split.

How did such a complete turn of events in the socialist world come about? What had changed in the Communist relationship? Had there been different hues all along in that red blot on the map? The question intrigued Western scholars, and they produced an extensive literature in the 1960's and 1970's. They dissected Marxist-Leninist polemic, speculated on the psychology and bureaucratic habits of Communist leaders, and reassessed the history of Russian-Chinese relations since imperial times.

Yet for one who had studied the twists and turns of the history of the Chinese Communist movement and the Sino-Soviet split, the story seemed incomplete, if not wrong. Most specialists in Communist affairs and historians of American foreign policy had concluded that the United States was tardy in detecting the tensions that produced the split, and had done little, if anything, to divide the Communists. Evidence for this conviction was that Washington had apparently treated the Chinese Communists as mere adjuncts of the Kremlin. John Foster Dulles, Dwight D. Eisenhower's secretary of state, was certain Mao Zedong was "at the beck and call of the Kremlin," according to Dulles's own historian cousin.[1] The public comments of American leaders of the time—presidents and secretaries of state alike—betrayed little interest in trying to create rifts within what was supposedly the enemy camp. But it was difficult to believe that the top policymakers of the United States had been so obtuse. Could they have been so blind, so insensitive to the possibilities, so uninvolved in such a historic development as the breakup of international communism? This study began as an effort to examine those questions. What I learned went far beyond what I had even suspected: at no time since 1949, when Mao Zedong's armies triumphed on the Chinese mainland, have the top policymakers of the United States ever assumed that communism was monolithic, that China was irretrievably "lost" to the Soviet Union, or that the United States was not without means to encourage Sino-Soviet frictions, if not an eventual split. Without access to Chinese and Soviet archives, it is impossible to determine the extent of U.S. responsibility for the split, but it at least can be said that American leaders since the late 1940's pursued policies that had as their deliberate objective the aggravation of Sino-Soviet differences. Moreover, the United States sought to exploit the differences as they appeared, all considerably before Richard Nixon's historic trip to China in 1972 dramatized the possibilities of what is now known as triangular politics, the interactive pursuit of the strategic interests of the United States, China, and the Soviet Union.

The thoughts American policymakers had from the late 1940's to the early 1970's about how the United States might divide its Communist adversaries, and then exploit the division, were never consistent or unified. In fact, devising a strategy of division itself divided American leaders and the United States and its closest allies and friends. These ideas did not remain untested—they influenced U.S. actions in the Jinmen-Mazu crises of 1954–55 and 1958, the U.S. response to China's development of nuclear weapons, and the U.S. decisions to intervene in Korea and Vietnam. Ironically enough, then, a policy that appeared obvious in its advantages, and that may stand as perhaps one of Washington's signal triumphs in the postwar period, ultimately came at great cost to America.

This study attempts to show how the Sino-Soviet alliance figured in the development of U.S. policy, especially toward China, from 1948 to Richard Nixon's historic journey to Beijing in 1972. It seeks to understand how the United States tried to undermine the alliance, and then how the United States tried to exploit the rupture when it came.[2]

Before Mikhail Gorbachev's assumption of power in the Soviet Union, Ronald Reagan frequently condemned the Soviet Union as an "evil empire" and identified its policy as Russian "imperialism." His intemperate language recalled the hyperbole of the Cold War years of the 1950's. But Reagan's anticommunist tirades only superficially resembled the earlier rhetoric, for his anticommunism was not indiscriminate. Reagan censured the Soviets, and those he deemed their surrogates, the Sandinistas in Nicaragua, the rebels in El Salvador, and the Cubans. The Chinese Communists, though, were another matter entirely. After a shaky start, Reagan settled down to a comfortable relationship with Beijing and continued the efforts of his Democratic predecessor to try to construct an alliance against Moscow. But just as it now appears that Washington's noisy official opposition to "international communism" in earlier years obscured a more nuanced understanding of world affairs, perhaps Ronald Reagan's simple anti-Soviet rhetoric also inadequately reflected the complexities of his foreign policy. Understanding how the United States tried to divide two of its most important enemies in the recent past may provide some historical perspectives that a bilateral approach (Soviet-American) to the Cold War might not provide. It may also help give us some new insight into U.S. policy objectives today, when the communist world, China in particular, is in turmoil and transition.

ONE

Old Friends and New Enemies

You and I were long friends: you are now my enemy,
and I am   Yours, B. Franklin
—1775

On August 8, 1945, when the Soviet Union formally entered the Pacific War, Russians joined Americans, Chinese Nationalists, and Chinese Communists as allies in the fight against Japan. All were ostensible friends against a common enemy. Yet just four years later almost to the day, the Truman administration released its famous China White Paper, characterizing the Nationalists as corrupt and unworthy of further U.S. military aid, the Soviet Union as an expansionist power subjugating China, and the Chinese Communists as contemptible agents of the Kremlin. Congressman Walter H. Judd, a leading Republican supporter of the Nationalist leader Chiang Kai-shek, lamented the change in attitude toward the Nationalists and Japan, the new pivot of American interests in Asia. In a bitter note to himself, Judd wrote: "How much better it was to be an *enemy* of the US, rather than a *friend*."[1]

Indeed, World War II had profoundly changed international politics. The United States emerged from the war a triumphant superpower, virtually unscathed and economically invigorated. The vast empires of the British, French, and Dutch were passing into history as more and more of their subject states sought to become independent actors in world affairs. The Soviet Union, with its tremendous military and political might, loomed as America's only challenger for global hegemony.

Making new determinations of which countries were friends and which enemies was not always easy for policymakers in Washington in the late 1940's. Not only did the United States now have to look on the former axis powers—Germany, Italy, and Japan—as important friends, albeit in need of reform; it also had to deal with countries that refused to take sides in the new East-West confrontation and with regions in flux whose orientation was as yet unsettled. China in revolution fell into the last category.

The United States had once had great plans for China. During World War II President Franklin D. Roosevelt envisioned a united, stable, and friendly China as the anchor for American interests in the postwar Far East. Hundreds of millions of U.S. dollars went to support Chinese resistance against Japan, and Roosevelt promoted Chiang Kai-shek to the rank of world leader, entitled to join Stalin, Churchill, and him at the 1943 Cairo Conference as one of the "Big Four" to help determine Asia's peacetime future.

But as the end of the war approached, China's military, political, and economic weaknesses eroded hopes that it could play a major postwar role. Instead, China itself threatened to become a battleground for big power rivalries. In the hope of preventing that, Roosevelt consented to Stalin's proposal at the Yalta Conference in early 1945 to enter the war against Japan and conclude a treaty of friendship and alliance with Chiang Kai-shek's government in exchange for territorial concessions and privileges in Northeast Asia.

The Yalta agreements failed, however, to prevent the steady growth of Soviet-American suspicions, which mounted as the war drew to a close. After Harry Truman assumed the presidency on Roosevelt's death in April 1945, American officials became convinced that the Soviet Union's efforts to consolidate its influence in Eastern Europe presaged wider expansionist efforts, which would include Asia. The Yalta agreements also did little to resolve the contest for power within China between the ruling Nationalist Party (Kuomintang, or KMT) and the Chinese Communist Party (CCP). Soon after the surrender of Japan on August 14, 1945, the two parties resumed in earnest the intermittent civil war they had waged for almost twenty years.

This conflict created an immense quandary for the United States. What could it do to help its longtime friends, the Nationalists, stop the Communists? What kind of Communists were Mao Zedong and his comrades, and what kind of relationship did they have with Moscow? And what were the ramifications of the struggle in China for the global contest with the Soviet Union? By the start of 1946, the Cold War had begun in Asia,[2] and the Truman administration was grappling for answers to these difficult questions.

I

On taking up his post as consul general in Shanghai, John Moors Cabot, of the venerable Boston family, promptly reported his early impressions of the Chinese Communists to his friend and superior in the State Department, W. Walton Butterworth, director of Far Eastern Affairs. They were not "coming with gilded halos and wings to save and modernize China," as some Americans naïvely believed, he wrote in February 1948; they were mouthing the same sort of promises he had heard at his previous post in Yugoslavia—promises they would inevitably ignore. "It seems to me probable," Cabot observed, "that if the Communists do succeed in winning all of China they will install in China a tyranny as subservient to Russia and a terror as brutal as Tito's."[3]

Cabot could not know how ironic his words would sound in just a few months. On June 28, 1948, the Cominform, successor to the Communist International, announced the expulsion of socialist Yugoslavia from its ranks and charged its leader, Marshal Josip Tito, with "nationalist" deviations. The development stunned Washington, still convinced that Tito was one of Europe's most dedicated and loyal Stalinists, despite hints over the months of serious discord between Belgrade and Moscow. Convinced that Tito was irrevocably antagonistic, the United States had given him no comfort, let alone encouragement. Washington's attitude had been tough and unfriendly right up to the break with Moscow. When Cabot learned of the split, he confided in his diary that the news was "one of the most incredible and significant in many a day." "What comes next?" he asked himself. "Titoism" became synonymous with schism in the Communist world, and many in the West wondered if China's Communists would be next to break with the Kremlin.[4]

The State Department immediately appreciated the implications of the Tito-Stalin rift. In the face of the intensifying Cold War, Washington had already adopted the Truman Doctrine, which pledged active support for anticommunist resistance in Europe, and the Marshall Plan, which bankrolled the reconstruction of capitalism on the continent. The United States also undertook the revitalization of Germany and Japan, prompted the formation of what became the North Atlantic Treaty Organization (NATO), and assembled a growing nuclear arsenal. All these steps aimed to strengthen the Western home front and contain the perceived Soviet threat. But now, with the unexpected schism in the Communist world, the United States seemed to gain a weapon to erode the enemy camp from within: if one Communist state could break with Moscow, why not others? The veteran diplomat and strategist George Kennan, author of the policy of containment, suspected that Tito's defection was "as important for Communism as Martin Luther's proclamation for the Roman Catholic Church."[5] Kennan relished the fragmentation of the Moscow-dominated international Communist movement.

Yet, American policymakers were not at all certain how to exploit, let alone duplicate, their windfall. Cautious accommodation and support of Tito, despite his commitment to the construction of socialism in Yugoslavia, might encourage further Eastern European estrangement from Moscow by demonstrating American tolerance for "national communism," a lesser evil, in the eyes of Washington policymakers, than Soviet hegemony. On the other hand, too obvious an American approach toward Yugoslavia might produce the opposite effect by seemingly validating Moscow's accusation that Tito was a stooge for the West and force Moscow to weld the Eastern bloc even more tightly to prevent further defections. Thus, the United States proceeded cautiously, delaying an offer of economic assistance to Belgrade until a year later in the fall of 1949.[6]

Throughout the rapprochement, the United States insisted that Tito make the overtures. Kennan, who formulated the State Department's response to the events, counseled that the United States, while welcoming Tito's independent stance, should base its policy on Yugoslavia's actual behavior toward the West. Tito did not have to become anticommunist but he did have to "prove" himself a friend, if he wanted a positive response from the United States. The American handling of Tito set a critical precedent: American policymakers would invariably refer to this experience when they considered what to do with other potential defectors from the Soviet camp.[7]

The impending victory of the Communists in China inevitably became linked with Tito's defiance of Stalin in the minds of many Americans. Just days after the Cominform announcement, Ambassador Walter Bedell Smith cabled the State Department from Moscow that the criticism of Tito had "extremely interesting implications for Chinese C.P." Tito and Mao, it seemed to him, advocated similar heretical, "common front" approaches with "non-proletarian" elements. Though Smith did not think that Stalin would soon chastise Mao for his deviation, he urged Washington to seize the opportunity to shake the Chinese Communists' confidence in their Soviet ally. His counterpart in China, John Leighton Stuart, heartily agreed. Stuart, who knew the country well as a missionary and educator there for some fifty years, thought the United States ought to use the Cominform denunciation to promote divisions between pro- and anti-Stalinist Chinese Communists and foment suspicion of Moscow. According to John Melby, second secretary in the American embassy in Nanjing, the Yugoslavian developments "most assuredly" would help the United States in any attempt "to split the Stalinists off from other Communists" and create anxiety among the "Non-Communist left and liberal groups." It was simply "a heaven sent opportunity." From then on, American diplomatic personnel throughout China carefully monitored signs of Sino-Soviet friction or rifts among the Chinese Communists over the Party's relationship with Moscow.[8]

Even though the Chinese had joined in denouncing Tito's deviation, the State Department was receptive to the idea that serious discord might develop between the CCP and Moscow. For one the history of the Chinese movement seemed to parallel that of Yugoslavian communism. Like Tito's party, the CCP was indigenous politically, organizationally, and ideologically, and determined to retain its autonomy from Moscow. Strong national sentiments had propelled both movements, and the

Communist groups had gathered power through their own efforts. These features distinguished them from other ruling Communists in Eastern Europe, most of whom were installed by the Soviet Red Army.

Moreover, American curiosity about whether the CCP-Soviet relationship was manipulable was long-standing. Foreign service officers like John Paton Davies, John Emmerson, and John Service, who had made contact with the Chinese Communists in 1944 at their wartime capital in Yanan (Yenan), were aware of the rocky history of their relations with the Soviets. Although Comintern agents from Moscow had helped organize the CCP in 1921 and develop its early revolutionary strategy, the Kremlin had also meddled in its internal affairs. Moscow had been ambivalent about Mao's ascendancy into the Party's top position in the 1930's at the expense of Soviet-trained leaders. Davies and his colleagues found Mao and the other top leaders pragmatic and beyond Moscow's control. They even appeared interested in continuing amicable relations with the United States after the defeat of Japan. At one point Davies dangled what he called the vision of "capitalist benefits" to interest the Party leaders in an American alternative to Moscow. His ploy was unsuccessful, and his superiors in Washington continued to favor the KMT after the defeat of Japan, despite ample evidence that Chiang Kai-shek's regime was unpopular and venal.[9]

Following the war some leading American officials had argued that the CCP's independence from Moscow favored the Nationalists against the Communists. Major General Patrick J. Hurley, ambassador to China from 1944 to 1945 and an ardent supporter of Chiang's, concluded after talks with Stalin in 1945 that the Soviet leader disdained the Chinese Communists. "Margarine communists" is what he called them. Convinced that Mao and his comrades were not authentic Marxist-Leninists, Hurley helped popularize the notion that the Chinese Communists were simply democrats and "agrarian reformers."[10] If the United States fully supported the Nationalists against them, Hurley argued, the CCP, lacking Moscow's backing, would have to come to terms with Chiang. Hurley helped produce a brief ceasefire in the civil war, but fighting resumed at the end of 1945. On his return to the United States, he charged that pro-Communist elements in the State Department had sabotaged his effort to save the Nationalist government. Nevertheless, he continued to insist that the Communists in China were on their own. On that point Truman agreed with Hurley.[11]

The CCP-Soviet relationship had also occupied the attention of the former Chief of Staff and war hero George C. Marshall, sent to China by Truman in late 1945 after Hurley's failure to mediate between the warring sides. During his famous yearlong mission, Marshall, unlike Hurley, concluded that Mao and the other top CCP leaders were genuine Marxist-Leninists, not mere rebels. But like Hurley, Marshall found the Chinese Communists independent of the Soviets. There was "no concrete evidence," he reported, that they were being supported by "Communists from the outside." In fact one of the reasons Marshall sought an end to the civil war was to keep the CCP autonomous of the Kremlin. He feared that continued fighting would force the Communists to seek help from Moscow and make the country more vulnerable to Soviet penetration. But by January 1947 Marshall recognized the futility of his efforts to negotiate a coalition government and returned to Washington to become secretary of state. He left China accusing both the KMT and the CCP of intransigence and expressing pessimism about Chiang's ability to reverse the deteriorating situation. His sole consolation was his conviction that China would be a morass for whoever was on top.[12]

The experience of Hurley, Marshall, and other American officials in China helped persuade Truman, whose anticommunism was ordinarily visceral and impatient, that the CCP might be a different sort of Communist Party. He talked about the "so-called Communists" of China and privately said he agreed with Stalin that the people of North China would "never be Communists."[13] As with many other Americans at the time, Truman's attitude toward the Chinese was also condescending—he believed the Chinese people were simply uninterested in politics. This view in turn encouraged the belief that communism was an unnatural doctrine for the Chinese, one that was incompatible with their society and would eventually alienate them. Such assumptions underestimated the extent to which the CCP had come to represent powerful aspirations in China and sustained the hope that Chinese communism, at least in a pro-Soviet form, had a dubious future.

Finally, the prospect of Titoism in China intrigued many in Washington because it seemed to offer one last, desperate chance to salvage something from the looming debacle. By late 1948 the Communist armies were sweeping to victory over the KMT, even with its three billion dollars of U.S. military and economic aid since the end of the war. If the United States could not have a friendly China under the KMT, perhaps a communist China could be prevented from joining the Soviet camp. But while this prospect tantalized many who believed that the Nationalist cause was hopeless, it was not at all clear what, if anything, the United States could do to realize such an ambition. As it turned out, an Asian Yugoslavia was a chimera.

II

Late 1948 was a turning point in U.S. China policy. Chiang's armies suffered spectacular setbacks and were about to lose Manchuria and all of North China. The economy in KMT-held areas threatened to collapse momentarily. The Communists vilified America for its imperialistic support of the Nationalists and intervention in Chinese affairs. Faced with these depressing conditions, the Truman administration decided it had no choice but to cut its losses and begin distancing itself from the apparent loser in the civil war.

On August 12 and 13 Secretary of State Marshall rejected urgent requests from Ambassador Stuart for new military aid for the Nationalists. Just four months earlier, Truman had signed a $450,000,000 Congressional appropriation for arms and economic aid for the KMT. Now Marshall informed his envoy that Washington wanted to avoid providing "ammunition in China for propaganda alleging that the United States was encouraging and prolonging the civil war." The United States, Marshall wrote, could not "formulate any rigid plans for our future policy in China. Developments in China are obviously entering into a period of extreme flux and confusion. . . . This Government plainly must preserve a maximum freedom of action."[14] Even a personal visit to Washington by America's favorite Asian heroine, Madame Chiang Kai-shek, failed to extract further U.S. funds. Madame Chiang, sensitive to Washington's preoccupation with Moscow, bluffed that if the Nationalists did not get more aid from the United States, her husband might have to make "an accord with the Soviets." Truman, fed up with the Nationalists—that bunch of "grafters and crooks"— gave little credence to her threat. The Nationalist leaders were not about to jeopardize the billion dollars of U.S. aid he believed they had socked away in New York bank accounts by making a deal with the Soviet Union. By January 1949 a demoralized Chiang Kai-shek prepared to flee to Taiwan (Formosa), his last redoubt.[15]

Meanwhile, as the Nationalists' fortunes had declined, the State Department had prepared a comprehensive review of China policy. Responsible for the daunting task was the department's new Policy Planning Staff (PPS), directed by George Kennan. Kennan believed that Americans wildly overestimated the importance of China, and that sentimentality colored the issues. European issues preoccupied him, as they did the rest of the upper reaches of the State Department.

The policy review, labeled PPS 39, was remarkably frank, deliberately vague, and delusory, all at the same time. Its evaluation of the deplorable China situation was candid and accurate: the Nationalists were admittedly "on the verge of losing their long struggle with the Chinese Communists." To the question Might not the Nationalists "yet save themselves?" PPS 39 bluntly answered: "No." To the question Might not "American aid reverse the course of the civil war?" PPS 39's response was equivocal: possibly, "but only if the U.S. would provide as much aid as was necessary for as long as necessary." And to do that, PPS 39 made abundantly clear, was foolish. What happened in China was a result of "deep-flowing indigenous forces which are beyond our power to control." China was not for anyone to win or lose—its destiny, said the PPS, was largely "in its own hands." "The salvation or destruction of China lies essentially with the Chinese—not with foreigners."[16]

This candor was immediately followed, though, by policy

recommendations that revealed the PPS was unreconciled to its own cold analysis: the United States should maintain its ties with the Nationalists and try to manipulate Chinese affairs. The PPS reaffirmed America's traditional "open-door policy" for China, namely, territorial integrity, "equal opportunity" for all potential trade partners, and the development of a "friendly and unified China." But since these goals were unattainable in the foreseeable future, the PPS advanced other, more immediate aims: to continue recognition of the Nationalist government; to consider the recognition of any future Chinese regime "in the light of circumstances at the time"; and "to prevent so far as is possible China's becoming an adjunct of Soviet politico-military power." One thing the PPS did not suggest was that the United States accept the verdict of the struggle in China.

Finally, in an effort to minimize the impending U.S. policy defeat, the PPS encouraged new illusions about China and its relationship to the United States and the Soviet Union. The Chinese Communist triumph, though "regrettable," would not be "catastrophic" to American interests. Soviet power would not be substantially increased, and China might actually burden Moscow. The Kremlin probably viewed China as little more than a "vast poorhouse," ungovernable and another potential Titoist headache if the Communists actually consolidated their position. The Russians would face "the passive drag and sly resistance of Chinese individualism," if not outright revolt. China, in other words, would be just as much a quagmire for Moscow as it had been for Washington. Moreover, according to the PPS, the conventional view of U.S. interests in China— "trade and idealism"—had been sorely misguided. Trade was never substantial, Christian converts disappointingly few, and the social and political emulation of the "American way of life" insignificant to nonexistent. It seemed from the PPS paper that the long American attachment to China had been either slightly naïve or foolish.[17]

There was some foundation for the PPS's low assessment of China's importance for American business. U.S. assets in China in 1949 were valued at somewhere between $100,000,000 and $200,000,000, compared with British holdings of over

$840,000,000, and trade in the postwar period did not exceed
4.8 percent of total U.S. exports, 2 percent of imports.[18] But in
geopolitical terms the PPS grossly misassessed both the potential impact of the Chinese revolution on international politics and the ability of the Communists to consolidate their victory. Kennan and other top State Department officials had not
wanted China to divert strategic or political attention away
from Europe, the locus of American global interests, but they
ill-prepared Washington for the consequences of Mao's triumph.

Although the PPS believed its proposed program was flexible, its underlying assumptions indicated that the United
States did not intend to accommodate itself to the new political realities in China. The PPS assumed that the Chinese revolution was inimical to American interests, that the future relationship with revolutionary China would not be friendly, that
the United States might still manipulate China's future, and,
perhaps most important, that the Chinese needed the goodwill
of the United States more than the United States needed
China's. This imperial view of things would fundamentally
clash with the Communists' national liberation objectives and,
ultimately, with the Truman administration's own aspiration
of denying China to the Soviet Union.[19]

PPS 39 was transmitted as virtual State Department policy
to its new chief, Dean Acheson, who assumed office in January
1949. Acheson, an imperious foreign policy professional from
the Eastern elite, had been assistant secretary of state during
the war years and undersecretary from 1945 to 1947. He had
helped plan George Marshall's mission to China but never had
an abiding interest in the Far East.* Moreover, Europe more

---

*No doubt in part because of his little-disguised prejudices against colored
peoples. Edwin Martin, who worked with Acheson in the State Department,
recalled that Acheson made "remarks about people of Southeast Asia" that he,
Martin, was too embarrassed even to repeat. In 1971, while discussing Nixon's
trip to Beijing, Acheson concluded his comments about China's leaders with
this bit of free verse: "I still cling to Brete [sic] Harte's aphorism / That for ways
that are dark / And for tricks that are vain / The heathen Chinee is peculiar /
But no more so than the heathen Japanese." Acheson also staunchly defended
the apartheid regimes of southern Africa in the 1960's and 1970's. Edwin Martin oral history, June 1975, p. 114; Acheson to Roy Welensky, Aug. 30, 1971,
Acheson Papers, Yale, box 34, folder 432.

than ever preoccupied him in early 1949. The Soviets' Berlin blockade in 1948–49, a Communist coup in Czechoslovakia, and Western steps to form the NATO military alliance were splitting the continent into armed camps. In Acheson's view, the challenge of China for Washington was to develop policies that would weaken Soviet power while not committing the United States to a debilitating Asian sideshow.

News of the ongoing policy debate surfaced in the *New York Times* soon after Acheson took office, when C. L. Sulzberger reported on the speculation in government circles that, "devout Marxist" though Mao was, he still might become a "Titoite" heretic. According to Sulzberger, some administration officials suspected that all was not well between the CCP and the Kremlin but were unclear whether Mao's ideological commitment would "serve to keep him the abject political tool of Moscow." Since that remained to be seen, Sulzberger said, Washington had adopted a watchful attitude. The American public widely believed that the administration was generally "waiting for the dust to settle" before developing a new China policy.[20]

Washington, though, did not wait passively for events in China to unfold. In late February and March Dean Acheson oversaw the development of a series of policy papers based on the premises of PPS 39. These papers, which would guide the Truman administration through the rest of 1949, formally shifted the emphasis of U.S. policy from direct involvement in China and support of the KMT to more subtle economic and political methods, including covert activities, to undermine the Chinese revolution and preserve American interests. Confidence, or perhaps wishful thinking, that China was not irrevocably lost to the Soviets ran throughout the policy papers, a distillation of the highest-level American thinking about China on the eve of Mao's victory.

"U.S. Policy Toward China," a paper issued under Acheson's imprimatur, established the administration's basic position. In it Acheson acknowledged the virtual defeat of the KMT but still saw possibilities for U.S. involvement in China and the eventual alienation of the Chinese Communists from Moscow. "The fruits of victory in a revolution are responsibility," he wrote. Certain that neither the CCP nor the Soviets could solve China's immense problems, he predicted that the Communists would eventually have to seek help from the West. Moreover, the force of Chinese nationalist sentiment, which was then directed against the United States, would also turn against Moscow. Soviet intrigues in Manchuria and the border regions would inevitably stir Chinese rancor. Acheson comforted policymakers with the thought that the positions of the United States and the Soviet Union would be reversed one day: the Soviets would find themselves in the China tangle, and "we shall be seeking to discover, nourish and bring to power a new revolution," Acheson wrote. Although he admitted it might take years before his vision could be realized, Acheson was certain that the loss of China to the Soviets was not permanent.[21]

What was not clear, though, was what kind of "new revolution" Acheson expected. It might take the form of an armed rebellion against the Chinese Communists, he suggested, but it might also be a movement that saw the CCP transformed into "a truly independent government, existing in amicable relations with the world community." For Acheson, the predicted future upheaval in China would not necessarily be anticommunist, only anti-Soviet.

To position the United States for that "new revolution," Acheson proposed reducing American visibility in the Chinese civil war. Though he did not rule out support for anticommunist resistance that appeared promising, he was opposed to direct involvement: plainly "any rifts between the Chinese Communists and the USSR and between the Stalinist and other elements in China" should be exploited, but only by "indigenous Chinese elements." "Because we bear the incubus of interventionists," Acheson observed, "our official interest in and support of these elements, a vast and delicate enterprise, should not be apparent and should be implemented through appropriate clandestine channels." Acheson adopted what the Chinese call "two-handed policies"—giving the appearance of one thing (disengagement) while doing another (covert intervention). In fact the "most important" reason for ending military aid was because it was helping to "solidify the Chinese people in support of the Communists and perpetuate the delusion that China's interests lie with the USSR."[22] The unpopular Chiang

Kai-shek and his KMT already appeared to be a liability for the strategy of driving a wedge between revolutionary China (communist or otherwise) and Moscow. Acheson's position paper betrayed no eagerness to reach an understanding with the top leaders of the CCP or any confidence that they were potential Titos.

Although Acheson recognized that the United States had limited options, he believed that the manipulation of trade might place some pressure on the Communists. He was unsympathetic to waging open economic warfare against China, since that would alienate Britain and Japan, both of which had extensive commercial interests there. In any case he believed that economic warfare would have only a minimal effect on China's "subsistence economy" while tending to drive the Chinese into "complete subservience" to Moscow. He proposed instead that Washington control nonstrategic trade through a licensing system and make clear to the Communists that the application of more stringent controls depended on their behavior. Trade, Acheson argued, would "augment such forces as might operate to create serious rifts between Moscow and a Chinese Communist regime." Some trade might even encourage the Chinese Communists to "develop a sense of dependence on the west."[23]

And then there was the difficult problem of Taiwan. At the end of the Pacific War, China had resumed control of the island that had been a Japanese colony for fifty years. Although the Cairo and Potsdam conferences had acknowledged Taiwan as Chinese territory, Washington now wanted to find a way to deny it to the Communists, which meant in effect detaching it from the mainland once again. But the Pentagon, though it fully appreciated the island's military worth, opposed a commitment to "go to war" to stop a Communist takeover because of other demands and limited resources.[24] Kennan, Acheson, and Truman all agreed that "crude unilateral intervention" was unwise and favored promoting a "Formosan autonomy movement" that could deny the island to the Communists if the mainland fell.[25] Such an approach could "lead to an agreement in the UN for a new deal for Formosa," Acheson remarked at a meeting of the National Security Council (NSC) on February 4, 1949. "This way," he observed, "we could get international sanction for U.S. intervention." But, he cautioned, "we must carefully conceal our wish to separate the island from mainland control," for fear of prompting "an American-created irredentist issue just at the time we shall be seeking to exploit the genuinely Soviet-created irredentist issue in Manchuria and Sinkiang."[26]

What the Truman administration conceived as an adaptable China policy, designed to meet any number of possible developments, in fact contained contradictory aims and tactics. The United States wanted to deny Communist China to the Soviets. To that end Acheson recommended reducing the U.S. profile in China to minimize the Communists' ability to stir up anti-Americanism among the people. There was never any serious thought, in or out of government, about committing the United States to a land war against nearly half a billion people; the U.S. armed forces remaining in China would be withdrawn. But the United States was unwilling to abandon Taiwan or the use of covert involvement in Chinese internal affairs. And it would not end its association with the Kuomintang, the Communists' implacable enemy.[27]

The administration's "wedge-driving" strategy itself involved two contradictory tactics. One implied that the United States might try to *entice* the Chinese Communists away from Moscow (as against aggressively attempting to "wean" them from the Soviets, something that Acheson never recommended), offering some bait in the form of trade. Acheson also did not dismiss out of hand the possibility of a future accommodation with the Communists. But the other element in Acheson's approach was coercive. It assumed that the Chinese Communists would seek rapprochement with the West only after they experienced Moscow's bear hug, the difficulty of running China, and popular dissatisfaction. By carefully creating problems for them, the United States might help stimulate internal discord. An example of this approach was the termination of American food and other economic aid to Communist-dominated areas in early 1949. Officials of the U.S. Economic Cooperation Administration had argued that continuing the supplies would help "prevent Russian-domination in China by demonstrating the continued friendship of America for the

Chinese people," and interpreted the decision to end the aid as based on the U.S. government's determination to make it "just as difficult for the Communists as possible, in order to force orientation toward the West."[28]

These obvious conflicts in goals and methods were explained in part by the administration's reluctance to surrender any advantage. If the United States could produce Titoism in China as well as retain Taiwan, so much the better. There were also tensions between short-term demands and long-term objectives. Encouraging Sino-Soviet estrangement was a long-term aim—Acheson was skeptical that the United States could soon induce such a rift. After all, the West had done nothing to attract Yugoslavia away from the Soviets. One week after the approval of the NSC papers, Acheson told an executive session of the Senate Foreign Relations Committee that as the Chinese Communists gained power, they would probably "go out of their way to show their sympathetic attitude of cooperation with the Russians," so the West should expect CCP hostility in the "initial period." But farther down the road, Mao's forces might turn out to be "more Chinese" than "Communist," and the United States might then be able to exploit Sino-Soviet frictions. His colleague W. Walton Butterworth, director of Far Eastern Affairs, agreed that counting on Titoism in China was "premature." "Things happen in China," he told the committee, "with great slowness."[29]

Beyond all this, finally, it was not even clear by what route China might be detached from Soviet power. The top CCP leadership could split, with anti-Soviet elements triumphing over pro-Moscow ones. Or a united CCP leadership might break with Stalin and chart an independent course. An anti-Soviet uprising by the Chinese people could force a reorientation of, or perhaps even topple, the Communist regime. Because it seemed that these possibilities were not yet mutually exclusive, the United States wanted to keep its options open. However, the events of 1949, and America's own actions, as will be seen, steadily led the United States toward reliance on fomenting a futile "new revolution" from below to achieve the anti-Soviet end.

Washington faced a challenge unlike that it faced in East Europe, where most of the Communist regimes had at best weak support from the people they ruled. The "basic dilemma for U.S. policy," an administration paper on China later admitted, was the fact that the "Chinese Communists are both adjuncts of the Kremlin and the popularly preferred leaders of the Chinese Revolution." These "twin properties of Kremlin domination and popular acceptance" vexed U.S. policymakers. Both active antagonism and accommodation would work against the central objective of preventing China from becoming bound to Moscow. At the same time, the administration also refused to cut its links to the Nationalists. Small wonder, then, that American actions confused many and generated controversy. Conservatives charged that the administration was "selling out" Chiang Kai-shek. Liberals condemned the continuing ties with the Nationalists and the failure to reach an understanding with the new Communist regime. It is hardly surprising that these many years later historians are still arguing about whether the Truman administration followed a "tough" or "soft" line on the Communists. Events in China were complicated, and the Truman administration was attempting to pursue what it believed to be a sophisticated policy, but this policy was fatally flawed by conflicting purposes.[30]

III

Sino-Soviet relations and the prospects for Titoism in China continued to be a hot topic among American officials throughout the spring of 1949. Although there were some exceptions, the reports and advice Acheson received reinforced the belief that a CCP-Kremlin split was possible only in the long term, and that efforts to reach an understanding with the Communist leadership would not hasten it.

The CIA and other top intelligence bureaus concluded in mid-April that, for at least the next two years, the Chinese Communists would support Soviet foreign policy and engage in anti-Western diplomacy. As in Eastern Europe, the Soviet Union would attempt to use the CCP "as its chief instrument" to consolidate control in China. While the CIA predicted that the Soviets would encounter "considerable difficulty" in that endeavor, there was no evidence of effective opposition to Moscow within the CCP and consequently, for all practical purposes, "the CCP will remain loyal to Moscow."[31]

The U.S. embassy in Moscow also considered an early Sino-Soviet break unlikely. In fact, the top man at the post, Foy Kohler, thought Tito's defection might have made a rift even less likely. "Unquestionably Soviets feel keenly overriding necessity prevent Tito-like defection China," he cabled Acheson in January, "and therefore proceeding cautiously." In April, Kohler reported that all indications pointed to "Stalin-Mao solidarity and uncertainties of CCP-USSR relations are uncertainties of future and not of present." Kohler encouraged Acheson to "work as hard to develop Soviet-CCP rift as [Soviet Foreign Minister V. M.] Molotov must be working to prevent it." Although Kohler gave no specifics, Acheson valued his understanding of the Soviet Union and soon brought him back to join the PPS.[32]

Acheson received a similar assessment from Ambassador Stuart in China. Though Stuart thought the "apparent lack of Soviet enthusiasm for the success of the Chinese Communists" suggested troubles in the relationship, he disabused Washington of the notion that the top Chinese leaders could soon be separated from Moscow. By June he felt the Chinese Communists deserved an "excellent" rating for their cooperation with the Soviet Union.[33]

The principal dissenters from these perspectives were the consuls general in Shanghai and Beiping (Peiping), John M. Cabot and O. Edmund Clubb. Both were inclined to believe that an early Titoism was possible and favored more active, immediate efforts to break the CCP-Soviet relationship. Cabot, who had not anticipated the advent of Titoism during his tour in Yugoslavia, now seemed to see signs of it all around him in China. He suggested that a promise of aid to the Chinese Communists might induce them to break with Moscow. "Without our help," he wrote the State Department in December 1948, "it is doubtful whether the Chinese Communists can run the country." Again, in April, he suggested that the time had come

for a "positive approach to [the] Communists," using the promise of trade and diplomatic relations as an inducement. On June
14, 1949, Cabot wrote in his diary, "the more I see of this picture [China] the more I think Titoism is inevitable—but when?
How violent? How successful? *Essential thing to remember is
that we can influence results.*"[34]

The soundness of Cabot's reading of the situation is questionable, however. He was new to China and unfamiliar with
its people and politics. He was also strongly influenced, perhaps unduly, by his close contact with the Shanghai foreign
business community and Chinese social democrats. Both elements, for their own reasons, eagerly hoped that China's relations with the West could be maintained and desperately tried
to find ways to reduce frictions between the United States and
the Communists.[35]

Clubb, by contrast, was one of the most knowledgeable
American observers on the China scene. His parents had been
missionaries in China, and Clubb himself had served as a foreign service officer in the country since the 1930's. Early in his
diplomatic career he came to despise the Nationalists for their
corruption and incompetence. Clubb was one of the first field
officers to urge a halt to the support of armed resistance against
the Communists; in November 1948 he suggested that "the
main American hope would seem to be one of fostering Titoism." Still, Clubb, who was later to be pilloried by Senator
Joseph McCarthy for his advocacy of accommodation with the
Chinese Communists, was cautious in his specific recommendations. He had no concrete evidence to show that a moderate
policy toward the Communists would produce the desired split
between China and Moscow. "Until such time as there may be
actual break with USSR," he wired Acheson in early June 1949,
"Communists must be assumed remaining in Soviet political
camp." Like the NSC he thought that in the meantime the
Chinese Communists should be made to pay for their friendliness with the Soviets. "So long as Communist China is run
for political benefit [of] USSR," he advised Acheson, "let it pay
on barrel head for what it receives, either in economic equiva-
lent or in terms political concessions designed [to] break up its
alliance with USSR."[36]

Domestic politics exerted a different sort of pressure on the administration. During the war years Chiang Kai-shek had cultivated a coterie of American supporters both in and out of government. At the end of 1947 this so-called China Lobby began raising a public outcry against the growing anti-Chiang sentiment in the Truman administration. Powerful figures like the publishers Henry Luce of Time-Life and Roy Howard of the Scripps-Howard newspaper chain, columnists Joseph and Stuart Alsop, Air Force General Claire L. Chennault, and the former ambassador to France and the Soviet Union William C. Bullitt vociferously opposed reducing backing for the Nationalists. In Congress Republican Senators William Knowland, Styles Bridges, Kenneth Wherry, and H. Alexander Smith, and Democrat Senator Pat McCarran prominently carried the Nationalists' torch. At times the activities of these Chiang proponents bordered on the fanatical. As the Truman administration began to disengage from the Nationalists, the China Lobby and its congressional bloc charged that the Nationalists' defeat was a result of sabotage, even treason, within the State Department. In April 1949 Senator Bridges accused Acheson of selling out the Nationalists and called for an investigation of the government's China policy. Within a year Senator Joseph McCarthy picked up the China Lobby's complaint and launched his anticommunist witch-hunt against the State Department. Although Acheson later claimed that the conservative attack did not significantly affect China policy, the right wing's inflexible ideological opposition to communism undoubtedly complicated the debate about the value and likelihood of a CCP-Soviet division. The legacy of the "who lost China?" acrimony tainted the American political landscape for decades to come.[37]

Chiang's backers detested the thesis that a Communist split was possible or even desirable, since the idea undercut support for the KMT. In July two Chiang stalwarts, Stanley Hornbeck, a former top official in the State Department's Division of Far Eastern Affairs and onetime ambassador to the Netherlands, and George Taylor, a prominent China scholar, attacked the administration's China policy on national radio. Taylor openly sneered at the Titoist theory, saying it had little chance in China, and Hornbeck questioned whether Titoism would even make any difference. "Communists are Communists, no matter where you find them, or what nationality they are," he declared. "They are all sworn to the idea of world victory for communism." He doubted whether the Chinese and Soviet Communists could be kept apart over "a critical issue."[38]

Walter Judd of Minnesota, a former missionary doctor in China and perhaps the most famous of the KMT boosters in Congress, also rejected the idea of pursuing Titoism in China, but for different reasons. Unlike Hornbeck, he accepted the possibility of an independent communist China, but he dreaded that development as potentially more ominous than even the Soviet threat:

Imagine a dissident Bolshevism loose in Asia. It would be free to renounce Russian influence, drop the onus of Russian influence. It would pick up the slogan of Asia for the Asiatics. It would have Manchuria, half the base of Jap war industry. It would have in prospect the resources of Indonesia, not only for its side [but] as a denial to us. It could rally half of humanity.

It could turn the "underprivileged" line from focus on the underprivileged *class* to the underprivileged *nations*. It could renew the conflict of *haves versus have-nots* on international lines.[39]

Like the State Department Judd rejected the notion of a "monolithic communism." Where he violently parted with the administration was over the significance of the Chinese revolution. Its threat to American interests in the Third World weighed more heavily on Judd's mind than on those of the Atlanticists who dominated the State Department. From their point of view Judd's argument was alarmist and distracted attention from the Kremlin. For Judd, however, the enemy was not so much a specific country, the Soviet Union, as it was revolutionism itself. Furthermore, the concept of Titoism profoundly disturbed Judd, who was concerned with America's moral vigilance. "The mind of the west," he wrote, "seeking a way out of unpleasant conclusions, lazy to face fresh strains and problems, eager for self-narcosis, has seized on Titoism as a hope." Judd warned: "The Kremlin knows among other things that an appearance of Titoism can quiet our fears, that it can be a new stalking horse."[40] Evangelical language aside, Judd's viewpoint became commonplace among policymakers, liberals and conservatives alike, when it had become evident, after the Korean War, that the United States had grossly under-estimated the practical and ideological significance of Mao's revolution.

Even more extreme than Judd's were the words of a young congressman from California named Richard M. Nixon. Nixon inflamed the China issue by impugning the patriotism of those who flirted with the thought that China might go the way of Yugoslavia. From the floor of the House of Representatives, Nixon charged that the "apologists for the Chinese Communists in the United States, both in and out of the State Department," had been deceived by the "fallacious theory that Chinese Communists somehow are different from Communists in other countries and will not owe their allegiance to the Russian bloc in the event they come to power in China." In May 1949 Nixon read into the *Congressional Record* an article entitled "Mao No Tito; United States Must Act," by David J. Dallin, a Russian émigré and former Menshevik. Dallin demanded, "Who originally planted the idea that Mao Tse-tung may become a Chinese Tito? Was it, perchance, Moscow itself?" The article, Nixon contended, exploded "the myth of the independence of the Chinese Communists effectively and completely."[41]

Still, though partisan politics certainly complicated the debate, American observers of all political stripes sharply disagreed over the possibility of Chinese Titoism. Indeed there was little consensus on the principal threat facing the United States, let alone what tactics would most effectively reduce it. Dividing one's enemies, the dictum of power politics, proved to be a far more elusive task for American policymakers than they wished. The opaque CCP-Kremlin relationship did not make the task any easier.

IV

"The radiance of the October Revolution shines upon us," wrote Mao in a November 1948 tribute to the 31st anniversary of the Russian revolution. His article was published in the news organ of the Comintern, intent on eradicating other potential Titoist deviations. In it he both affirmed that the Chinese revolution against the KMT reactionaries and U.S. imperialism was part of an international "anti-imperialist united front headed by the Soviet Union" and acknowledged Stalin's leading contributions.[42]

For Richard Nixon and other conservatives in the United States, such rhetoric was indisputable evidence of Communist solidarity. Officially, there was no question that the CCP was allied with the Soviet Union and considered U.S. imperialism the premier enemy of the people of the world. That had been repeatedly made explicit by Mao, Liu Shaoqi, Zhou Enlai, and other leaders. The CCP-Kremlin relationship, however, was considerably more complex than many Americans appreciated at the time. The Chinese Communists were neither pliable agents of the Kremlin nor potential defectors from the socialist camp.

As their victory approached, the CCP leaders, like the Truman administration in its China policy, tried to pursue a foreign policy that retained some maneuverability. Certain fundamentals were fixed, to be sure: the Communists identified themselves with the socialist world; they demanded respect of Chinese sovereignty and an end to foreign privileges; they opposed any ties with their principal enemy, the remnants of the Nationalist Party; and they wanted to secure their revolutionary victory. "New China," as it would be called, would base its conduct of foreign affairs on those fundamentals. But though the CCP leaders were not sanguine about quickly establishing normal relations with the Western powers, they did not assume that hostilities were inevitable. On April 30, 1949, they publicly announced their interest in establishing trade and diplomatic relations with all other countries.[43]

Of the Western powers, the CCP was most concerned about the United States because of its long support of the KMT, and because it was the leader of the capitalist world. By 1949 it was also clear that the United States was helping to rebuild Japan, China's recent brutal invader, to become the anticommunist bulwark of Asia, a shift from the previous emphasis on reform and democratization.[44] Still, in mid-1949 the pragmatic Chinese Communist leaders had not precluded the possibility of establishing a working relationship with Washington.

As for their relationship with the Soviets, despite their expressions of fraternity, the Chinese Communists were not entirely happy. The Soviets had carted off whole factories from Manchuria at the end of World War II. But what irritated the CCP leaders most in 1948 and 1949 was Stalin's conservatism. Washington may have believed that Moscow was inciting communist revolutions around the world, but the CCP saw Stalin as overcautious and lukewarm in his support of their own revolution. Several of Mao's essays written in the late 1940's implicitly criticized the Soviets for being intimidated by the United States and not appreciating the full revolutionary importance of former colonial areas like China.[45]

As late as 1949 the Soviets apparently advised the CCP leaders to avoid provoking U.S. intervention by stopping their advance at the Yangtze River, to reach an accord with the Nationalists, and perhaps even to accept a partition of the country. Stalin, too, wanted to keep his options open in China. His main concerns in the postwar period were reconstructing the Soviet homeland and creating a security buffer around its borders. In China, as elsewhere, Stalin subordinated the interests of local Communists to the needs of the Soviet Union. Thus he continued his relations with Chiang Kai-shek's government long after Washington had recognized its defeat on the mainland, and he privately disparaged the ability of Mao's forces to achieve complete victory. The Soviet press devoted scant attention to the Red Army's sweep across China—*Pravda* did not even run a front-page article on the Chinese revolution until the founding of the People's Republic of China in October 1949. The Soviet Union, like the United States, was preoccupied with European tensions and with the possibility of a military conflict with the United States. And like Washington, Moscow wanted no distracting conflagration in China.[46]

At the same time neither the Chinese Communists nor the Soviets wanted a further splintering of the Communist movement in the aftermath of the Tito affair, a development that could only help their mutual adversary, the United States. Both worked to improve their relations. In April 1949 the CCP joined other Communists in denouncing the formation of NATO and pledging support to its "ally, the Soviet Union," even in the event of war. At the Party Congress in Czechoslovakia in June, the CCP representative openly rejected the possibility of Titoism in China. And as the CCP approached its final victory, Stalin, while remaining suspicious of the loyalty of the independent-minded Chinese Communists, suddenly became uncharacteristically solicitous of them. When Liu Shaoqi traveled to Moscow in July to discuss the founding of the People's Republic of China, Stalin took the unprecedented step of criticizing himself for past interference in CCP internal affairs, which had led to devastating setbacks in the revolution. "We had been in the way of a hindrance to you," Stalin admitted, during one of the five meetings he had with Liu, "and for this I feel compunction."[47]

Despite these efforts CCP-Kremlin relations retained an element of strain. In the recollection of one Chinese Communist leader, Stalin continued to suspect that China might take the "road of Yugoslavia" and turn to the West. Moscow took "an indifferent and skeptical attitude towards us" on various issues, according to the director of Soviet and Eastern European Affairs of the Chinese Foreign Ministry after the founding of the PRC. Not until the Korean War did Stalin fully accept the CCP. The Chinese were not so fully committed either. Some interest in remaining distant from the Soviet Union was clearly being shown within the CCP, witness Mao's apparent need to quash such hopes in June 1949. In his famous address "On the People's Democratic Dictatorship," otherwise known as his "lean to one side" speech, he categorically declared that China would align itself with the Soviet Union and the socialist world. "We also oppose the illusions about a third road," Mao stated. The CCP had no intention of surrendering its hard-fought independence to Moscow, but it was equally convinced that the Soviet Union was a valuable friend.[48]

V

At midnight, April 20, 1949, after a month of unproductive negotiations between the Nationalists and the Communists, the Red Army staged a dramatic crossing of the Yangtze River. Nationalist officials fled south to Guangzhou (Canton) in humiliation. Within days Nanjing, the national capital, fell to the Communists. Shanghai, the country's commercial center and most powerful city, soon followed. In the United States such prominent figures as the China Lobby's Claire Chennault demanded U.S. action to stop the Communist advance. The renowned commander of the Flying Tigers, which had supplied Chinese armies during World War II, immediately called for a $700,000,000 program to sustain anticommunist resistance in Southwest and Northwest China. The State and Defense departments rejected Chennault's scheme as unrealistic.

But the administration's refusal to make a major new commitment to the KMT or to other anticommunist resistance in China was not matched by any indication of an interest in seeking accommodation with the Communists. Despite the administration's objective of denying Communist China to the Soviets, its actions in the spring and summer of 1949 gave the CCP no incentive to consider distancing itself from the Kremlin.

On the contrary. In late March, just before the crossing of the Yangtze, the CCP charged that the U.S. military had helped the Nationalists destroy the country's largest warship, the *Chungking*, whose officers and crew had deserted to the Communists in North China. The loss of the heavy cruiser had upset Acheson, who saw it as a dangerous weapon against the tens of thousands of Nationalist supporters fleeing across the Taiwan Strait. The Communists verbally blasted the United States, charging that the sinking of the *Chungking* "once more discloses [the] evil of American imperialists' military intervention in [the] Chinese civil war." When Washington ignored the Communists' accusation, a Communist newspaper declared that the silence was an admission of guilt. American foreign service officers throughout China, and Ambassador Stuart himself, repeatedly urged the State Department to respond. Clubb reported from Beiping that the Chinese Communists were even rallying schoolchildren to denounce the crime. Not until two weeks after the first accusation did Acheson finally instruct Stuart to deny the charge.[49] Whether the United States was actually involved, Acheson's dilatory reaction reaffirmed the CCP's conviction of U.S. culpability. What is more, at the end of April the United States suddenly increased its military activities at its base in Qingdao (Tsingtao), a move that the Communists took as a possible prelude to direct military intervention in the revolution.[50]

Despite Acheson's avowed wish to prevent Taiwan from becoming an irredentist issue for the Chinese, he continued his efforts to detach the island from the mainland even after his machinations were exposed. In February Livingston Merchant, counselor of embassy at Nanjing and later deputy assistant secretary of state for Far Eastern Affairs, arrived in Taiwan to make contact with the Taiwanese anticommunist underground and promote an independence movement.[51] His mission was supposed to be secret, but it did not remain so for long: in a March 16 radio broadcast, the Communists denounced the United States for coveting the island. An appalled Consul General Cabot in Shanghai wrote in his diary that the exposé was "awful" and wondered if there had been a security leak. Even the Nationalists saw what the United States was up to. Foreign Minister Wang Shijie, in a speech in Taipei, affirmed that Taiwan had legally and physically reverted to China with Japan's defeat and condemned any "future direct or indirect attempts at imperialistic control." Acheson's press secretary disputed Wang's claim: the "final status" of Taiwan was not settled; its future would be determined by a peace treaty with Japan, "if and when we get one," he told journalists.[52] After Merchant finally left Taiwan in early May, Washington decided to pursue "vigorous secret spadework" to place the island under U.N. trusteeship if the KMT failed to hold the island; it also continued to maintain confidential ties with independence leaders.[53]

Washington's obvious interest in retaining control of Taiwan was hardly conducive to weakening CCP-Kremlin solidarity. Likewise, the administration continued its support of the Nationalist government: nothing was done to prevent Chiang from preparing Taiwan as his final fortress, and U.S. economic and military aid poured into the island. In late June the administration also acquiesced in a Nationalist blockade of mainland ports under CCP control, even though this hindered Acheson's proposed policy of using trade for leverage against the Communists. The administration transferred more ships to the Nationalists, helping their blockade. Truman informed Chiang's ambassador to the United States that his mind was not closed to supplying new funds if the Nationalists strengthened their resistance against the Communists and stopped their political infighting. While it may be that Truman was just being diplomatic with the KMT envoy, the administration in fact never abandoned its political support of the Nationalists.[54]

In contrast American official contact with the Communists appeared both uncooperative and manipulative. In March the Communists declared that until their future government established diplomatic relations on "the principle of equality," they would not recognize the official status of diplomatic personnel in China; they then abolished all the "treasonable treaties of the Kuomintang period."[55] The CCP was serious about these measures, since one of its paramount goals was the ending of foreign privileges in China. Nationalist agreements with the United States alone included large loans and permission for the stationing of military personnel on Chinese soil. (In May 1950 an internal U.S. government study found that China owed the United States almost $800,000,000—$157,500,000 for economic rehabilitation and $642,000,000 for "financial assistance primarily of a political character.")[56]

The Communists' withdrawal of recognition outraged the United States more than any other country, and Washington persisted in challenging the action. When local Communist representatives approached some of the Americans still in China in the spring of 1949 about reviving trade with Japan and the United States, Acheson tried to use the overture to prod the CCP into restoring some official functions to the U.S. consulates. The Chinese, however, would exchange neither their pride nor their principles for some commerce.[57]

Ugly clashes between American consular officials and Communist authorities seemed to confirm even further that the United States remained unreconciled to the new order in China. The Communists' treatment of Americans was generally restrained, but in late 1948 in Shenyang they arrested the U.S. consul general, Angus Ward, for alleged espionage. (They apparently had some foundation for the charge—the British chargé d'affaires in Nanjing reported to his home office that there was suspicious activity in the U.S. consulate in Shenyang, and that "it was certainly no ordinary consular post.") In Shanghai in July 1949 Vice-Consul William Olive violently resisted detention after he drove his jeep through a Communist parade. In both cases the Communists believed the Americans were arrogant and contentious. Washington interpreted the incidents as deliberate affronts to the United States.[58]

As it turned out, fundamental differences over diplomatic relations became the formal obstacles on which U.S.-CCP relations foundered. In his memoirs Acheson cited the Ward affair as one of the principal reasons why the United States could not establish diplomatic relations with China in 1949. But the conflict was not over the violation of traditional diplomatic practices themselves. It was about basic attitudes. For Acheson the Chinese Communists' attitude toward their "international obligations," which included the treaties and debts of the KMT government, showed whether they would be an "evolutionary regime" or a "revolutionary one." The United States, Acheson told the British ambassador to the United States, would do all it could to prevent the latter development. The contention over international obligations, in fact, was really about revolution and counterrevolution. American diplomatic personnel gradually left the mainland, not to return for thirty years.[59]

Two further incidents illustrate Washington's uninterest in actively pursuing the possibility of encouraging Chinese Titoism through an accommodation with the Communists. The first concerned what appeared to be an extraordinary demarche from Zhou Enlai, relayed to the State Department in early June 1949. Zhou supposedly wanted the United States to know that the CCP was divided into a "radical wing," which favored an alliance with the Kremlin, and a "liberal wing," including Zhou, which disliked the Soviets and wanted aid from the United States. Consul General Clubb, who received the communication in Beiping and was one of the people most interested in Chinese Titoism, urged the State Department to respond positively. For two weeks he heard nothing from Washington, and when he was finally allowed to pursue the lead, Zhou's "spokesman" had disappeared. Although it now appears that the demarche was fabricated, all American officials in 1949 accepted it as genuine. Washington's slow response reflected the administration's wariness about developing a relationship with the Communist leaders.[60]

Then there is the famous case of Ambassador Leighton Stuart's invitation to visit Yenching University in Beiping, the school he once headed. Huang Hua, head of the CCP's "Office of Alien Affairs" in Nanjing, extended the invitation on behalf of some school alumni in late June. In earlier discussions Huang had spoken of Chinese interest in establishing formal relations with the United States. Now he intimated that if Stuart made the trip, Mao and Zhou would meet him during his stay. Stuart strongly favored accepting the invitation, since the CCP's leaders had till then remained aloof from American officials. He urged the State Department to approve the journey in the hope of improving mutual understanding and suggested, among other things, that it might "strengthen more liberal anti-Soviet element in CCP." This time Washington did not dawdle. Within a day of receiving Stuart's report and after consulting the president, Acheson cabled Stuart that he was "under no circumstances to make visit Peiping." Acheson cited considerations that Stuart himself had given in his report of the invitation: domestic American criticism, damage to Western unity against the Chinese Communists, confusion of Chinese politics, and enhancement of the Communists' prestige.[61]

A darker assessment about contact with the Chinese Communists had come from Foy Kohler in Moscow. Just two days before Stuart's message about the Beiping invitation arrived in Washington, Kohler warned against naïveté about the Chinese Communists. His views were representative of those American professional foreign service officers experienced in communist affairs. Kohler observed that the Chinese Communists were "intelligent, hardheaded realists," who at present could not "be weaned away from the Soviet Union." He suspected that Huang Hua's friendliness with Stuart in Nanjing had been a ploy to fish for U.S. trade concessions. U.S. policy, Kohler urged, must be "firm, patient and impervious to temptation." Only after the Soviets failed to provide sufficient help to industrialize China might "Mao and company . . . toy with idea [of] following independent path from Soviet teachers." But for now the United States must realize that "Mao is not for sale." Later, after reading Kohler's cable and Mao's "lean to one side" speech, Stuart conceded to Acheson that the "long view is only view US Government and its friends in west can take on China." He ruefully concurred with Kohler that for the time being the United States could not buy Mao's favor.[62] Stuart did not see Yenching again; he left China soon thereafter, never to return.

Was the aborted trip a "missed opportunity" to forge an early rapprochement with the Communists? Probably not. The Truman administration and the CCP leadership were familiar with each other's views. If Mao and Stuart had met, they would not have had anything new to say beyond what had already been communicated publicly and privately. The gulf between the two sides was too large, and there was no compelling reason for them to put aside major differences.[63] For all that American officials thought they had tried to avoid a rigid policy, the United States was not about to cut its ties with the Nationalists. Truman himself had established the American stance in his response to the supposed Zhou Enlai demarche. The president had directed his people "to be most careful not to indicate any softening toward the Communists but to insist on judging their intentions by their actions."[64] It was the same position the United States had taken with Tito only a year earlier. On their part the Chinese Communists were not about to distance themselves from the Soviet Union to please the United States. The Chinese Communists, by reason of both ideology and the actual political support they got, still considered the Soviet Union their most helpful foreign friend, despite its failings.

VI

Soon after Stuart left China the Truman administration issued *United States Relations with China*, better known as the China White Paper. It was released to the public on August 5, 1949, less than two months before the formal founding of the People's Republic of China. Truman and Acheson hoped the thousand-page study would quiet domestic critics by showing that the United States had done everything possible to support the Nationalist government, and that the responsibility for its defeat was Chiang's, not America's. But the White Paper not only failed to silence the conservative clamor for more aid for Chiang; it incited a fierce anti-America propaganda campaign in China. It also nudged the Nationalists toward administrative reform on Taiwan, which ironically later improved the KMT's prospects for receiving new aid.[65]

Acheson's fourteen-page letter of transmittal to the president provoked the most public attention. It summarized in clear and lively language the tedious history set out in the White Paper, and concluded with a diatribe against the activities of the Chinese and Soviet Communists in China. The letter was the administration's most substantive public comment to date on the Chinese revolution and presented its basic stand, even though it was not meant to be a full statement of what future U.S. China policy would be.

The traditional policy of the United States, according to Acheson, was one of helping the Chinese people resist foreign domination. Unfortunately, he declared, "the heart of China" had fallen into "Communist hands":

The Communist leaders have foresworn their Chinese heritage and have publicly announced their subservience to a foreign power, Russia, which during the last 50 years, under czars and Communists alike, has been most assiduous in its efforts to extend its control in the Far East. . . .

We must face the situation as it exists in fact. We will not help the Chinese or ourselves by basing our policy on wishful thinking. We continue to believe that, however tragic may be the immediate future of China and however ruthlessly a major portion of this great people may be exploited by a party in the interest of a foreign imperialism, ultimately the profound civilization and the democratic individualism of China will reassert themselves and she will throw off the foreign yoke. I consider that we should encourage all developments in China which now and in the future work toward this end.

In the immediate future, however, the implementation of our historic policy of friendship for China must be profoundly affected by current developments. It will necessarily be influenced by the degree to which the Chinese people come to recognize that the Communist regime serves not their interests but those of Soviet Russia and the manner in which . . . they react to this foreign domination.[66]

The White Paper generated immediate controversy. The columnist Walter Lippmann questioned Acheson's defense of

America's long attachment to the disreputable Chiang Kai-shek. From the right, conservatives condemned the White Paper as an apology for America's betrayal of the KMT—Patrick Hurley branded the paper "a smooth alibi for the pro-Communists in the State Department who have engineered the overthrow of our ally . . . and aided in the Communist conquest of China." The White Paper helped convince Congressman Nixon that Dean Acheson headed a "Cowardly College of Communist Containment." [67]

The language of Acheson's letter of transmittal was provocative, but it was neither gratuitous nor a ploy to "shame" the Chinese Communists into becoming anti-Soviet. Acheson was not one to tailor his words to placate domestic conservative critics, and he had characterized Chinese communism as a "tool of Russian imperialism" in at least one confidential session with the Senate Foreign Relations Committee and later with Truman himself. [68]

The White Paper was a serious effort to close the door on further aid to the Nationalists unless they reformed, but it hardly opened the way for a modus vivendi with the Communists. The Communists reviled the White Paper; within a matter of weeks Mao pronounced it a "counter-revolutionary document which openly demonstrates U.S. imperialist intervention in China." [69] The previous sporadic expressions of anti-Americanism on the mainland became a nationwide campaign vilifying the United States. Mao Zedong himself took the unprecedented step of writing five public commentaries on the document ridiculing the professed friendship of the United States for China and Washington's admission that it had fully backed Chiang Kai-shek. The White Paper, wrote Mao, reeked of anticommunism, distorted Chinese history, and turned logic on its head with the base slander that the Chinese people had come under a new "foreign yoke." "The Chinese people should thank Acheson" for his revelations, he noted sarcastically. [70]

Acheson's letter of transmittal in fact eliminated any possibility that the CCP leaders would soon distance themselves from the Kremlin. The White Paper made the issue Manichaean: either friendship with the evil Soviet empire or friendship with democratic America. Acheson would not let the

Communists have both, and the CCP would not jettison its Soviet comrades for what was at best a dubious relationship with
Acheson and Truman. Acheson's letter, seeking to incite the
Chinese people against the CCP's leaders allied with the Soviet
Union, was an open expression of the aim of promoting a "new
revolution" in China. "The policy on China is the same policy
that it has always been," Truman told reporters soon after the
release of the White Paper. "We have never been favorable to
the Communists."[71]

As the *New York Times* observed at the time, the White
Paper was a turning point in China policy. The *Times* editorial-
ized, "There has been a complete change of attitude on the part
of the United States toward the aims and objectives of the Chinese Communists and the Soviet Union. What is now quite
clear is that President Chiang's estimate of those aims was
right and that the State Department's estimate was wrong."
The State Department had conceded this by admitting that the
Chinese Communists had not been honest, "indigenous" elements, and that the Soviet Union had not acted in good faith
toward American mediation efforts. As to future China policy,
the *Times* saw American "opposition" to a regime acting in the
interests of a foreign power as "an immediate problem in implementation." The newspaper recommended a tough policy: if
Washington was rejecting Chiang, as seemed to be the case,
then "at the very least" it should adopt a policy of "equal dis-
sociation from the Communist regime." The conclusions of
the editors, several of whom were personal friends of the secretary of state, were logical and consistent with his transmittal
letter.[72]

Although the White Paper was not the complete reversal
that the *Times* claimed, its tone was more militantly anticommunist than previous U.S. statements about China. The administration's heightened belligerence toward the Soviets was
one reason for the change. An NSC paper written about the
same time on Eastern Europe reflected this: the United States
was locked into a "two-world struggle" with the Soviet Union;
the West should seek to undermine Soviet control over the satellite nations by encouraging anti-Soviet "nationalism" among
the enslaved people; and the time had come to take the "offen-

sive" against the Soviet empire.[73] In addition the top Chinese Communist leaders, in Acheson's view, had proved themselves loyal followers of Moscow. In the spring he held a faint hope that they might moderate their pro-Soviet policies. Nothing they had done, though, had given any indication that they were interested in distancing themselves from the Kremlin in favor of the United States in the near future. An actual split in the CCP leadership over the Soviet Union also seemed remote. For all practical purposes, from Acheson's point of view, the top leaders of the CCP *were* acting in the interests of a foreign power. "The grasp of the USSR upon China and of the Chinese Communists on the Chinese people will, for the foreseeable future, grow more firm," the CIA had concluded even before the White Paper's release.[74]

Acheson's closest advisers—Walton Butterworth, George Kennan, Dean Rusk, John Paton Davies, and Philip Jessup—all had moved toward a harder line on China. The State Department's Far East Research Division in late July had concluded that "no early change in the current strongly pro-Soviet orientation of Communist China is to be anticipated." Ideology, the researchers claimed, not a cold "calculus" of national interests, appeared to be the dominant force in CCP policymaking. By August 24 Davies was even ready to recommend the use of "punitive" air strikes to end the "intolerable state of affairs" on the mainland, referring to the rampant anti-Americanism. Davies wanted to "compel [the Communists] to respect the United States and moderate their behavior." By then Kennan, one of the most hopeful about Titoism in China in late 1948, was also of a different mind. "George wants a crackdown [on China]," Cabot wrote in his diary after a meeting with Kennan in Washington, "but I favor promoting Titoism."[75] Cabot was a lonely voice in the State Department by this time.

Weighing heavily on the heads of policymakers, too, was the growing impact the Chinese revolution was having on the rest of Asia. About the time Acheson drafted his letter of transmittal, he directed the U.S. ambassador in London to impress on the British government the seriousness of American concern about the "Communist domination not only of China but remainder [of] Asia as well." According to John Foster Dulles, Republican senator from New York and future secretary of state, Acheson agreed in late August that the United States had to stop the Chinese Communists "somewhere and sometime," and it was better to do so "early" before they "go beyond China."[76]

Whereas Tito's Yugoslavia had minimal capabilities to expand beyond its borders, the Chinese Communists were assuming control over a vast, populous nation, influential in its region of the world. It was becoming clear to the State Department that a militant Communist China, whether or not it was independent of Moscow, would be a profound problem for the United States in Asia.

If the United States had adopted a more positive policy toward the CCP in 1949, might it have succeeded in inducing a Titoist deviation? Most likely not, if the price for Washington's favor was to turn against Moscow. As long as the United States required an either/or choice between friendship with Moscow and friendship with Washington, as the China White Paper presented it, there was no possibility of reconciliation. But if Washington had ended its ties with the KMT and accepted a China that had cordial relations with the United States and the Soviet Union simultaneously, there very well could have been at least functional, if not normal relations. In late 1949 the director of the CIA sent a report to Truman and Acheson quoting a major statement issued by Zhou Enlai:

The Chinese Communist Party has to have allies, and, if Chiang and the reactionaries are allied with the United States, the Communist Party (China) must ally with the U.S.S.R. It would be a dream on the part of the American Government to expect the Chinese Communist Party to split with the U.S.S.R., but they can expect that the Chinese Communist Party will not always be anti-American. The Chinese Communist Party cannot afford two enemies at one time, but there is nothing to keep them from having more than two friends.[77]

There is no evidence that the administration seriously considered the possibility of developing a relationship with China on the basis described by Zhou. In fact Acheson specifically opposed the CCP's effort to get the "best of both worlds" in its diplomacy.[78]

The distance between the CCP's attitude toward foreign relations, as exhibited by Zhou, and American assumptions of the importance of the United States to China was profound indeed. That contradiction was symbolized by John Leighton Stuart's apparently unauthorized attempt sometime in 1949 to offer the Chinese Communists tens of millions of dollars in loans for economic construction if they broke with Moscow. His crude effort insulted the Communists, full of pride over their epic victory. Stuart learned, in his own words, that "Mao was not for sale." Years later Huang Hua, Stuart's Party contact in Nanjing, associate of Zhou Enlai, and eventual foreign minister of China, still condemned the attempted payoff. With all the suffering caused by American support for the KMT in the civil war, recalled Huang, the attempted bribes were a "mockery" and an affront to Chinese dignity.[79]

On October 1, 1949, Mao Zedong, atop Tian An Men gate, entrance to the old Forbidden City of China's emperors, declared the founding of the People's Republic of China. "The Chinese people have stood up," he proclaimed. The next day the Soviet Union became the first country to recognize the new regime. More than thirty years would pass before the United States would do so.

TWO

Alliances Weakened, Alliances Forged

Alliances [are] held together by fear, not love.
—Richard Nixon, 1989

In August 1949 the Soviet Union broke the American monopoly on atomic weapons with its first test explosion. The news thoroughly shocked the Truman administration, which had thought that a Soviet breakthrough was at least two years away. The Soviets, Ambassador Alan Kirk glumly reported from Moscow at the end of the year, were "rather cocky over their successes in China, elsewhere and their own atomic bomb."[1]

Though the United States could do little to stop further Soviet developments in nuclear weaponry, Washington still entertained hopes of keeping China out of the hands of the Kremlin. But the forging of a coherent, wedge-driving strategy was complicated by conflicts with Great Britain, disunity within the State Department, pressures from the Pentagon and conservatives, among others, and a hardening of Cold War attitudes, and those hopes were dashed even before the outbreak of fighting in Korea in June 1950. By then Sino-American relations had already deteriorated into hostility, and top U.S. officials had begun to advocate taking decisive steps to deny Taiwan to the Communists.

I

As the Chinese Communists swept to victory in 1949, British and American policies increasingly diverged, to a large degree over the question of how the West could prevent China from falling completely into the Soviet sphere. By late 1948 London had already decided against any attempt to detach Taiwan from the mainland, was unconvinced that the CCP could soon be separated from the Soviets, and believed the Communists were prepared to tackle China's problems without any economic and administrative help from the West. To the Foreign Office it seemed that the "best hope" lay in simply "keeping a foot in the door." Specifically, that meant establishing de facto relations with the Communists and trying to maintain Britain's substantial economic interests in China.[2]

For a time London and Washington largely succeeded in suppressing their differences, but the policy conflict threatened to break into the open when, on May 3, the British ambassador to China informed Ambassador Stuart of London's interest in extending de facto recognition to the Communists, who had just taken Nanjing. Stuart's report of the news arrived at a delicate moment for the administration. The Senate Foreign Relations Committee had just begun hearings on the North Atlantic Treaty, which Acheson had recently concluded with eleven European nations. Europe was "the keystone" to U.S. national security, Acheson told the Senate committee.[3] But Senate ratification of the treaty and passage of a related $1.4 billion military assistance program were not foregone conclusions. Congressmen spoke darkly of "entangling alliances" and attacked the administration for emphasizing Europe at the expense of Asia. Were Britain to be seen as undermining the U.S. position in Asia, the volatile China bloc in the Senate might create problems for the entire Atlantic program.[4]

Acheson wasted no time after receiving Stuart's news. He immediately sent a cable to U.S. diplomats in the Atlantic treaty countries instructing them to discourage any thought of recognition or "giving the impression" of interest in relations with the Chinese Communists, and advising them to urge the adoption of a "common front." He sent a special aide-memoire to British Foreign Secretary Ernest Bevin expressing the U.S. government's concern. And he informed Stuart that the United States should "oppose hasty recognition [of the] Commies either as *de facto* or *de jure* authority by any power" and obtain "full agreement" of other powers, "particularly Brit[ain]," to work in concert. London, bending to Acheson's pressure, agreed on May 19 to consult frequently and postponed its advance to the CCP. The immediate rift was healed before word leaked out.[5]

Still, even as Acheson worked to keep the Western allies in line with the United States, he tried to prevent U.S. policy from veering too far from that of the British. He had Leighton Stuart remain in Nanjing to try to influence the other foreign missions, the most important of which had not accompanied the Nationalist government to Guangzhou. But at the same time he sought to accommodate the British by moderating U.S. trade restrictions against China, appreciating that an economically distressed Britain could hardly be dissuaded from adopting a conciliatory policy toward the Communists when it had so much to lose in China.[6]

The Chinese Communists were sensitive to the differences between Washington and London and tried to turn them to their own advantage. In July, after the Nationalists began blockading Communist-held ports, CCP officials, including Zhang Hanfu, director of Shanghai's Foreign Affairs Bureau, approached the British consul general for help in running badly needed supplies into the city. The Communists understood that the Nationalists' action especially hurt the large British business community in China. At the same time the Communists did nothing to disguise their continued hostility toward American officials and businessmen. Both parties saw through these tactics. The U.S. consul general in Shanghai, Walter P. McConaughy, thought it regrettable that the Communists were "up to their old device of playing one group of foreigners against another," and the British embassy in Nanjing similarly concluded that the Communists were set on splitting Anglo-American unity. The Foreign Office responded positively to Zhang's overture nevertheless.[7]

If inciting Anglo-American conflict bore some marks of traditional Chinese statecraft, it was indelibly stamped as well with Mao Zedong's analysis of the postwar international alignment of forces. During his long revolutionary experience Mao devoted considerable attention to the problems of distinguishing principal and secondary enemies, winning direct and indirect allies, forging united fronts, and exploiting contradictions among adversaries. Japan had hardly been defeated before Mao concluded that the United States had become the principal enemy of the world's peoples. As early as August 1946, in his famous interview with the American journalist Anna Louise Strong, he described the world as divided into three zones, or forces. At one extreme was the Soviet Union, at the other the United States. In between was "a vast zone which included many capitalist, colonial and semi-colonial countries." What characterized this range of nations in the "intermediate zone" was their various conflicts with the United States. American imperialism not only oppressed the nations of Asia, Africa, and Latin America, but also trampled the interests of the less powerful capitalist nations. The United States, said Mao, sought "to control the whole of the British Empire and Western Europe."*

As he had done so often during the twisting fortunes of the Chinese revolution, Mao selected the "principal contradiction"—Chiang Kai-shek's KMT backed by U.S. imperialism—and encouraged the formation of a "united front" to isolate the enemy. Thus even the British, with their own ignominious history in China, might become a "friend" against the United States. British and Communist forces had violently clashed in April, when the British gunboat *Amethyst* tried to make its way up the Yangtze River, but the Communists had toned down their anti-British denunciations about the incident shortly afterward. In contrast, as Consul General McConaughy noted, a virulent "anti-American propaganda campaign" and "discriminatory treatment" persisted and undermined any tendency toward a "united front among [the] various western communities" in Shanghai.[8]

Though Washington was persuaded that Britain's conciliatory policy toward the Chinese Communists was due to its

---

*Mao, "Talk with Anna Louise Strong," Aug. 1946, in *Selected Works*, 4: 99. At first blush Mao's worldview may seem bipolar: he acknowledged the United States and the Soviet Union as opposing forces. But his emphasis on the activities of the middle zone distinguished his view from the truly bipolar views embraced in Moscow and Washington. Whereas the two big powers tended to see their contention as decisive in the various conflicts in the world, Mao believed that the struggles in the intermediate zone, which included China, would increasingly determine the course of world history.

large commercial stake in China, and not least to its concern to preserve its lucrative colony Hong Kong, that judgment was too harsh. Economic interests certainly influenced British policy, but not to the degree that the United States assumed. Foreign Secretary Bevin understood that dissuading the Communists from appropriating British property was a tenuous hope at best, and the Board of Trade concluded that recognition would probably have little effect on the amount of commerce the Communists would conduct with England.[9]

Politics may go further than economics alone in explaining the British attitude. As a trading nation, Britain had often been more responsive to political changes in the world than other Western states. It had been the first major power to recognize the Soviet Union. British accommodationism may also have been due in good part to the government's awareness of its limited capabilities. As Bevin himself pointed out to the British cabinet, the United States was "the only Power" with sufficient resources to sustain resistance against the Chinese Communists. Britain, well aware that its foreign objectives had to be commensurate with its national capabilities, and that it was not a superpower, would adopt more modest objectives.[10]

Britain's conciliatory attitude toward revolutionary China was not the only source of tension between Washington and London. Another sore point was the best way to go about undermining the CCP-Kremlin link. In August, soon after the publication of the China White Paper, Bevin gave his interpretation of the Anglo-American differences to the British cabinet. Between December 1948 and early August 1949, he said, Washington and London had followed roughly similar policies. But now, "without any prior warning, United States policy seem[ed] to have taken a sharp turn in the direction of retreat." The United States had begun evacuating its nationals, closing its consulates, and pressing Britain to tighten trade restrictions. The British consul general in Shanghai had sent a less-than-flattering description of American behavior in China: "The United States," he wrote, "has been the prima donna in China since the war. [But now] she has flown into a tantrum and is kicking the footlights out. She wants the whole company of foreigners to leave the stage with her."[11]

Bevin professed to be puzzled by the change in American policy. But he was quick to note that there was a line of thought in Washington that "Communist China should be allowed to relapse into complete chaos, which will encourage the Chinese people to overthrow the Communist regime." He reminded the cabinet that this view was "diametrically opposed" to the British view, which was "that if we are not to drive Communist China into the arms of Moscow we must do our utmost to maintain Western contacts."[12]

A conversation between Bevin and U.S. Ambassador Lewis W. Douglas a few days later confirms that major differences did indeed exist over how to drive a wedge between the CCP and the Soviets. Douglas was a friend of Acheson's and also from the same Wall Street wing of the Democratic Party. His brother-in-law was John J. McCloy, U.S. high commissioner for Germany. Douglas tried to explain the U.S. position to Bevin. "A new Communist government in China," the administration believed, "could be more forcibly convinced of its dependence on western economic assistance and normal economic and financial relationships by withholding such assistance and only granting help in consideration for specific concession." Douglas reported that Bevin said he understood the American line but restated the British belief "that it would be wiser to remain in China, maintaining trade relations and establishments in order thus to influence the Chinese Communists in our favor."[13]

Acheson himself had an opportunity to discuss China policy directly with Bevin in mid-September, when he and the foreign minister of France came to Washington for a series of meetings. At a preparatory conference on September 13, Acheson and his advisers were in a tough mood. Kennan attacked the British for "deluding" themselves in thinking that they could "profit in China from a policy of disunity between themselves and the United States." The United States should be prepared to impose unilateral sanctions on the Communists if they continued to harass its representatives and nationals. The group agreed that the Communists would have to learn that they needed the West and rejected the British idea of "keeping a foot in the door." Later in the day Acheson began his meeting with Bevin by reading portions of a recent cable from the American embassy in Nanjing that Kennan and others had strongly supported in the preparatory meeting. It endorsed the view that America's basic objective should be to prevent China from becoming a "reinforcement to Soviet power." That had to wait, however, until the Chinese learned by their own experience that the Soviet Union had "little to offer, that Soviet friendship is always one-sided, that China will lose much more than it will gain by such association, that it will receive no assistance from [the] US as long as it is [a] satellite of [the] USSR." The CCP would "have to learn these facts the hard way," the embassy concluded. In the meantime the United States should avoid making itself a target for Chinese hostility.[14]

Acheson went on to argue that recognizing the Chinese Communist regime would fail to win any favors for the West, and urged Bevin to consider joining the United States in imposing stricter trade controls. Bevin just as vehemently defended his view of the value of maintaining a Western presence in China. He feared that if the West was "too obdurate we will drive the Chinese into Russian hands." Acheson agreed that playing "for a split between China and the USSR" seemed to be the thing to do but insisted that recognizing the Communist regime would not help. He doubted that recognition was a strong card in keeping China away from Moscow. The conflict went unresolved.[15]

Just days after the establishment of the People's Republic of China on October 1, 1949, the British decided they could no longer wait and would move toward de facto recognition to the new regime. Owing to some breakdown in communications, Washington was not informed of the decision until after the British conveyed their intention to the Chinese authorities. Truman flew into a rage when he heard the news and complained to Acheson that the British "had not played very squarely with us on this matter." Resolute in his hostility to the Chinese Communists, Truman had only days before told Under Secretary of State James Webb that "we should be in no hurry whatever to recognize this regime." The United States "had waited some 12 years to recognize the Russian Communist regime."[16] A few days after the British decision, the NSC decided not to support the British in the military defense of Hong Kong.[17]

For their part the Chinese Communists continued to try to exploit Anglo-American differences. The American embassy in Nanjing reported in early November that the Communists were according "definite preferential treatments" to the British in China. "This adds up to definite effort, not only to prevent rapid American recognition by producing atmosphere in which it [is] impossible," the report noted, "but also to split US and British on this matter." The author bitterly concluded that the entire "white man's burden" to hold the Chinese to accepted international behavior had fallen on "American shoulders." Rudyard Kipling, who had dedicated his poem "The White Man's Burden" to the United States, would have been amused.[18]

Despite repeated American efforts to convince London otherwise,[19] the British government decided, on December 15, 1949, to extend formal diplomatic recognition to the new Communist regime at an "early date." On that day the cabinet met to consider Bevin's memo on the current state of affairs. He "had done his best" to forge a common policy with Washington, he reported, but it was clear that the United States Government would not follow the British. In fact he thought it might be "difficult for the United States to follow our lead, at any rate for some time to come"; the United States had not given any indication that it would change its nonrecognition policy. The next day Bevin sent a personal message to Acheson restating the reasoning behind the decision: in his government's view withholding recognition indefinitely was "to play straight into the hands of the Soviet Union."[20]

On January 5, 1950, London announced its withdrawal of recognition from Chiang's government. The following day it formally recognized the Beijing regime. The Netherlands, Switzerland, and the Scandinavian countries quickly followed the British lead. Senator William Knowland of California, one of Chiang's most fervent supporters, publicly denounced the British decision. The United States, he blustered, could not continue to aid its North Atlantic allies to resist communism in Western Europe if they failed to oppose communism in Asia.[21]

The Western front against China had been broken. It seemed that China was having more success, at least in the short run, in exploiting rifts among its adversaries than the United States.

Knowland and other Acheson critics suspected the secretary of state of secretly favoring the British in their policy of "appeasement." Years later historians sympathetic to Acheson also suggested he supported the British view.[22] In fact Acheson doggedly disagreed with London's policy. Throughout 1949 he kept constant pressure on the British to align their policy with that of the United States and rejected their approach on how best to encourage Titoism. But it is also true that, mindful of the importance of the Anglo-American alliance, Acheson tried to prevent an open rupture. As he told the British ambassador to the United States on the eve of Britain's recognition of Beijing, the Communists were clearly trying "to drive a wedge" between Washington and London, and he wanted to minimize their ability "to make capital out of an apparent difference of opinion." Acheson's effort at maintaining a semblance of unity gave the appearance to some that he was "winking" at British accommodationism. In that respect, even though Anglo-American differences over China were never reconciled, British policy did act as a restraint on Washington. As Acheson admitted to his advisers in October 1949, it was difficult for the administration to justify supporting armed opposition against a Chinese government that was going to be recognized by America's allies.[23]

II

Acheson had to contend not only with the British, but also with his own deeply divided State Department, where the question of how China was to be denied to the Soviets was even more hotly debated after the release of the White Paper. Acheson delegated responsibility for the development of policy toward China and the Far East to Ambassador-at-Large Philip C. Jessup, his close friend and adviser. In late July he directed Jessup to find ways to halt the spread of "totalitarian communism in Asia" and selected two prominent Republicans from academia, Raymond Fosdick, former president of the Rockefeller Foundation, and Everett Case, president of Colgate University, to help him. Jessup and the consultants, as the two outsiders were known, met from August through November. Acheson deliberately chose three men who had no expertise on the Far East since their effort was intended to be a fresh look at U.S. Asia policy, especially China. As Jessup observed to one of his aides just after the start of the review: "We still have not decided whether to oppose [the Communists] openly, to oppose them covertly and increase their troubles, or to try to make some deal and establish relations with them as if to woo them away from the USSR."[24]

Jessup's principal assistant, Charles W. Yost, was particularly keen on trying to apply lessons from Yugoslavia's break with the Kremlin to the China problem. Yost was one of the rising stars of the State Department, a liberal Democrat and intellectual, with a background that provided a sound foundation for his opinions. By 1949 he had already had extensive foreign service experience in both Asia and Eastern Europe, most recently in Czechoslovakia and Austria. He was soon to become director of the State Department's Office of Eastern European Affairs. Later in his career he served in the Nixon administration as ambassador to the United Nations, and then, in 1973, became president of the National Committee on U.S.-China Relations. In 1949 Yost was responsible for organizing and directing much of Jessup's review of Far East policy. That review provoked some of the most explicit government thinking yet about how the United States might stimulate Sino-Soviet discord.[25]

Soon after the consultants began their work, Yost sent Jessup an extensive memorandum outlining his own policy views.[26] "There is of course no question," he wrote, "what our fundamental attitude toward the Chinese Communists is or that we hope in the long run to see them unseated or at least split off from Moscow." The problem was in developing a strategy. Yost was against making an all-out effort "to attack and weaken the communist regime," which seemed beyond American means. But he was also against seeking a modus vivendi. The CCP's attitude toward the West, he argued, would not be improved by accommodation. The experience with other Communist re-

gimes showed that "they invariably consider a policy of compromise toward them to be motivated either by Machiavellian-
ism or by weakness." The Communists "therefore profit by
such a policy without allowing it to affect their long-term
strategy and objectives." Yost, like Acheson, did not believe in
letting the Chinese Communists have the best of both possible
worlds.

Yost saw much value in promoting divisions between the
CCP and the Kremlin, but he differed sharply with the view of
his fellow foreign service officers Edmund Clubb and John
Cabot that flexibility might help entice the Chinese Communists away from Moscow. As he put it:

Titoism does not arise because it is encouraged by the West but because pressure from the Russians becomes intolerable to the local
Communist regime. While a dissident Communist regime must receive support from the West in order to survive indefinitely, it is more
likely to become dissident if the degree of its dependence on Moscow
encourages the latter to exploit its satellite beyond the bonds of en-
durance. A satellite able to draw sustenance from the West can better
afford to remain politically loyal to the Kremlin precisely because it is
not economically at the latter's mercy.

Drawing from his recent experience in Prague, Yost explained:

For example, a Czech Communist regime strengthened by a substantial East-West trade is more likely to follow its natural bent of loyalty
to Moscow than a Czech regime confronted by unmitigated Soviet exploitation with all the inevitable consequences to the Czech economy
and people. There is every reason to believe that these observations
apply to the Chinese Communists and that a hard rather than soft policy on our part, provided it is subject to readjustment if conditions
change, is more likely to promote their ultimate detachment from
Russia.

Yost suggested that the United States minimize its dealings,
including trade, with the Chinese Communists and "wait until
the Communists have been obliged to make the approach" to
the West. He recognized that though Britain might have difficulty with this program, the United States could "afford to
wait." Yost urged continuing the policy of nonrecognition until
the Communists ended their hostility toward Westerners in
China. Although he labeled his policy "hard," he did not advo-

cate attempting to overthrow the Chinese Communists, and accepted their rule as an established fact for the indefinite future.*

Yost expounded his hard policy to Jessup and the consultants through August and September. In it he clearly tried to combine a bipolar, Cold War outlook with a sensitivity to the particular conditions of China. He harbored no sympathy for the Nationalists but also appeared tough and realistic toward the Communists, although he assumed that the overthrow of the CCP was not a viable option. Yost understood that the internal dynamics of the Sino-Soviet relationship were decisive, and that external pressures could influence but not determine the relationship. In a follow-up memo to Jessup, he stated that the policy he advocated "would be the most likely to result in (1) honorable and mutually advantageous relations between Communist China and the West and (2) the encouragement of trends toward Titoism." The "alternative policy of dealing with the Communists on their terms"

(1) would not affect their basic orientation, (2) would relieve the Chinese-Soviet relationship of certain of the strains conducive to Titoism, (3) would weaken our standing not only elsewhere in Asia but also in the long run with the Chinese themselves, and (4) would be less likely to produce conditions under which Western business could in fact operate profitably in China.[27]

Yost's reference to "Western business" reflected the pressure the administration was under from American companies with commercial interests and investments in China. Businessmen, especially on the West Coast, urged Washington to adopt positive policies toward the CCP, arguing, as the British did, that Western contact was necessary to keep China away from the Soviets. Roger D. Lapham, former Republican mayor of San

---

*Yost concluded his memo with three specific recommendations: "the United States and the Western Powers would be well advised . . . to adopt a short-term policy of obliging [the Chinese Communists] to rely wholly on their own and Soviet resources. Such a policy would involve . . . (1) reducing Western trade with Communist China to the absolute minimum; . . . (2) withdrawing as rapidly as possible all Western nationals and official representatives from Communist territories (with the possible exception of one consular office to maintain a minimum of contact); (3) not interfering with the Nationalist blockade." NA, Yost to Jessup, Aug. 15, 1949, 890.00/11-1849.

Francisco, president of the American-Hawaiian Steamship Company, and chief of the Economic Cooperation Administration in China from May 1948 to June 1949, was one of the most vocal proponents of keeping a "foot in the door" to influence the Communists. In a speech at the Commonwealth Club of San Francisco in September 1949, Lapham advocated maintaining business, philanthropic, missionary, and diplomatic ties with the Communists and recognizing their new regime. These steps were necessary if the United States was to capitalize on future Sino-Soviet antagonism. Lapham's approach to promoting Titoism in China became known as the Pacific Coast businessmen's China policy.[28]

Many American China scholars agreed with the Lapham approach. Unlike the China Lobby, with its view of a monolithic communism, academics such as Owen Lattimore and John K. Fairbank stressed that the CCP leaders were Chinese as well as Communist. During a three-day round-table conference on China policy organized by the State Department in early October, both scholars urged the adoption of a lenient U.S. policy to encourage China's reconciliation with the West.[29]

Within the State Department, however, there was little sympathy for the idea that the West could soon wean China away from the Soviets. Sentiment divided between those who favored a more "active" policy to create problems for the Communists and those who believed that internal problems would be sufficient to encourage Chinese disenchantment with communism and the Soviet Union. Both camps believed in the possibility of Sino-Soviet estrangement, but only at a distant date.

Yost was representative of the activist group. Admitting that his point of view was characteristic of diplomats with experience in Eastern Europe, he urged "vigorous political and economic warfare" against the Communists before they were able to create "a regimented and appallingly massive instrument of power." He wanted the United States to continue covert assistance to anticommunist elements so as to multiply the problems facing the Communists. A harassed Chinese Communist regime would be more dependent on the Soviets, hastening disenchantment with the Kremlin.[30]

The consultant Raymond Fosdick was typical of those who favored a benign policy. Fosdick suspected that the United States could do little to increase the problems for the Communists. The Nationalists were thoroughly discredited, and trade sanctions would be ineffective because of the likelihood of British noncompliance. Instead Fosdick believed that "of all the weapons at our disposal, the so-called psychological weapon is most important." He urged a propaganda offensive, using "radio, pamphlets, material for newspapers, agents, etc." to discredit the Soviets in the eyes of a Chinese population that continued to retain a deep fondness for America. "The Achilles heel of the CCP," Fosdick contended, "is its relation to the USSR." America's only hope was that "the development of nationalism in China will pull China away from the USSR orbit." The United States should hammer away on the theme of Soviet imperialism's threat to China and its own sympathy with the Chinese people's aspirations. Aside from propaganda, however, Fosdick had little to recommend and conceded that his view amounted to a "policy of 'watchful waiting'—never a popular policy." By the end of October Fosdick was persuaded that the United States should recognize the new Communist regime if it met certain basic conditions.[31]

Jessup appears to have taken a middle ground between Yost and Fosdick. In early September he concluded that it might not be in American interests to see the fragmentation of territory under the control of the Chinese Communists. The CCP's problems, it seemed to him, would be simplified if they could concentrate their efforts on a smaller area until they were stronger. "The inability of the CCP and the USSR to build a prosperous Communist China," he contended, "will become apparent to the Chinese people sooner if the CCP has to deal with the problem of all China." However useful local anticommunist resistance would be in complicating matters for the Communists, Jessup favored allowing "inherent centrifugal forces" to develop without visible Western interference. "An attitude of calm aloofness with the minimum of overt interference one way or the other in the Chinese civil strife would pay the best dividends. We may be charged with dallying with the Communists but may we not eventually return from the ride with a smile on the face of the paper tiger?"[32] The tentativeness in Jessup's thinking mirrored the controversy within the State Department over the extent to which the United States should actively harass the Chinese Communists.[33]

By now Dean Acheson's own views on China also seem to have combined elements of both extremes. He endorsed the consultants' advice that the United States adopt a long-term view toward events in Asia. Since communism had apparently succeeded in tapping the nationalistic feelings of the Asian peoples, the challenge for the United States was to align itself with their national aspirations and to turn this powerful sentiment against the Communists themselves. With regard to China specifically, Acheson told the Senate Foreign Relations Committee on October 12 that the Communist government was "really a tool of Russian Imperialism in China. That gives us our fundamental starting point in regard to our relations with China." But open support of armed resistance against the Communists would only "solidify the Chinese people against us and in favor of the Communist government, and will be vastly expensive and in the long run it will be futile." Acheson also suggested that no "artificial government prohibitions" be placed on nonstrategic trade with China. At the same time he supported the indirect harassment of the Communists. The United States would not challenge the Nationalist blockade of Shanghai, since it was "helpful to the West generally in creating problems for the Communists in Shanghai." The State Department was still investigating the possibilities of covert support for anticommunist resistance groups. Consequently, he did not foresee normal diplomatic relations with the Communist regime any time soon. As he told the British and French foreign ministers in November, as long as there was any opposition to the Communists in China, to accord them recognition would be to "stab [those opposition groups] in the back."[34]

During the committee hearing Republican Senator Alexander Wiley of Wisconsin directly asked Acheson about the possibility of Titoism in China. Fielding the question for the secretary, Jessup said that there were a "good many elements" suggesting such a possibility, but that it was not "safe to bank on it." Titoism, Jessup concluded, "has got to develop within the country as to its relations with [Russia]. . . . It is not a thing you can force too much or you are likely to defeat your own ends."[35] Jessup had pointed out a quandary that would continue to plague American policymakers in the months ahead: too obvious an effort to divide China and the Soviet Union could very well force them together.

Acheson tried to reconcile conflicting opinions within the State Department during a top-level two-day conference held on October 26 and 27 to receive the formal recommendations of Jessup, Case, and Fosdick. Others in attendance were Dean Rusk, Walton Butterworth, George Kennan, Leighton Stuart, Charles Yost, and John Paton Davies. Jessup characterized the consultant's proposals as based on the aim of encouraging Communist China's "deviation from Moscow" by bringing out "our interest in the welfare and independence of the Chinese people." Fosdick argued for continuing American educational and philanthropic work, and even proposed offering a rural assistance program to the Communists. "We must keep China in touch with the West and keep our ideas and ideals before the Chinese people through our contacts with them. It must not be we who draw down an iron curtain." Fosdick hoped that in such a way Washington could nurture anti-Soviet feelings among the Chinese people. Case supported Fosdick's point of view.[36] It was a point of view that reflected the popular belief in the United States that the Chinese people held a special and compelling fondness for Americans. The British were under no such illusion about themselves.

Kennan disputed the wisdom of the consultants' proposed program and suggested that the United States should avoid "either kindnesses or slights," both of which the Communists could exploit, as they had in the Soviet Union. Rather, the objective should be "to make life unpleasant for Communist China within the framework of Soviet domination." Butterworth agreed that assistance to the Communists should certainly be "a long way off." Davies suggested that a more devious selective treatment of the Soviets and Chinese Communists—alternately harder on one and softer on the other—could split them.

The consultants' program did not enchant Dean Rusk either. He proposed that the United States consider supplying aid to resistance forces in the hope of "fomenting dissatisfaction with the Communist regime." Rusk, as paraphrased in the minutes, provocatively suggested that the United States provide "arms for some guerrillas as a form of payment" and "employ whatever means were indicated . . . in the furtherance of our interests—arms here, opium there, bribery and propaganda in the third place."[37]

Acheson, aware that the CIA had just started secret support of anticommunist forces in China, appeared sympathetic to Rusk but admitted that "stirring up guerrillas must be regarded as a short-term operation." The secretary tried to minimize the importance of the recognition problem, saying that the United States should not regard establishing diplomatic relations with the Communists "as a major instrument for showing interest in the Chinese people or for winning concessions from the Communist Government." On the other hand he agreed that no obstacles should be put in the way of unofficial contacts between the Chinese people and private citizens.[38] But apart from that Acheson expressed only moderate interest in the consultants' recommendations. To him they appeared either unrealistic or little different from existing policy. The two-day meeting left sensitive questions unresolved, despite efforts to achieve agreement. Even a memorandum that tried to summarize the decisions reached by "consensus" appeared in at least two different versions. And the key difference between them was the crucial question of whether the United States should actively try to create problems for the Chinese to make life difficult "under Soviet domination" or adopt a more aloof attitude, confident that the Communists would be unable to solve their problems. Policy toward Communist China remained one of restrained hostility; as Kennan had suggested, it would be a policy of neither "kindnesses nor slights."[39]

But at this point Truman, uncomfortable with subtleties, was growing impatient with the Communists. The president insisted on "strict adherence" to his policy of permitting the Nationalist blockade of mainland ports to work effectively. At an October 19, 1949, press conference, he bluntly stated that he hoped the United States would not have to recognize the new

Beijing regime, and added that he still had undisclosed "plans" for the support of the Nationalist government. After the Communists imprisoned Angus Ward in late October, Truman directed his advisers to consider a coastal blockade of coal shipments to Shanghai to force the consul general's release. The action would show the United States meant business, the president suggested, and would make it difficult for the British to recognize the new regime. Truman said the United States "should be prepared to sink any vessels which refused to heed our warning."[40]

That impulse to action changed, however, after Truman met with the consultants on November 17 to receive their final recommendations. In a subsequent discussion he told Acheson that he had learned much about the reasons for the Communist victory from the consultants and had "found himself thinking about it in a quite new way." According to Acheson, the president said that if there had been more time during the meeting, he would have liked to discuss "what seemed to me to be a pretty basic issue of policy on which I thought the Consultants' minds were very clear." To this Acheson responded that of the two possible courses of action—"to oppose the Communist regime, harass it, needle it, and if an opportunity appeared to attempt to overthrow it," or "to attempt to detach it from subservience to Moscow and over a period of time encourage those vigorous influences which might modify it"—he and the consultants favored the second. Taking such a line "did not mean a policy of appeasement any more than it had in the case of Tito." Acheson recorded that Truman agreed "in the broad sense in which I was speaking." The president dropped the idea of a blockade of the China coast.[41]

III

Sharp as the policy differences were within the State Department, the top officials at least generally agreed that the United States should work for an eventual Sino-Soviet rift. In contrast the Pentagon saw Titoism in China as only a "faint hope or distant prospect" too far in the future, if it occurred at all, to help solve present problems with communism in Asia. Basing policy on a future Titoism was "folly," for it would "deny to the United States the moral strength of opposing communism because of its basic evil." The Pentagon-influenced NSC staff, who gave voice to these views in a draft paper submitted to the White House in late October 1949, proposed a military-oriented campaign to "roll back" Soviet gains in Asia.[42]

Influential voices outside of the administration echoed the Pentagon line. General Douglas MacArthur, presiding over the occupation of Japan, publicly advocated sending a combined force of hundreds of airplanes flown by American "volunteers" under Claire Chennault and a fleet of ships under the Nationalists to shield Taiwan and "blockade and destroy China's coastal cities." Senator William Knowland dramatized continuing resistance to the Communists by visiting territory still held by Nationalist forces on the mainland. On his return Knowland again called for new U.S. military support for the Nationalists. At a December 1 news conference, Senator H. Alexander Smith, who also visited Asia in the late fall, urged that the United Nations be asked to assume responsibility for Taiwan. In late December the Pentagon recommended that a military fact-finding mission visit Taiwan, and that the United States provide new military aid to the Nationalists.[43]

While the steady collapse of Nationalist resistance on the mainland made U.S. reinvolvement there unlikely, Taiwan was another matter. With a hundred miles of ocean separating the island from the mainland, Nationalist air and naval forces, far superior to those of the Communists, could make a Communist invasion of the island an extremely costly venture. From the State Department's view, however, overt backing for the Nationalist remnants on Taiwan would undermine any strategy of driving a wedge between the Soviets and the Chinese.

On the morning of December 29 Acheson convened a special meeting with the Joint Chiefs of Staff to argue against their proposal to aid in the defense of Taiwan. Acheson admitted that the Chinese Communists would not soon be split from Moscow but stressed that the United States had to "take the long view not of 6 or 12 months but of 6 or 12 years." Seeds of "inevitable conflict" existed in the Sino-Soviet relationship. Mao's independence from Moscow, Acheson contended, was "our one important asset in China," and the United States should not "substitute [itself] for the Soviets as the imperialist menace to China." The Taiwan matter had to be seen in this light. With the same corrupt government that lost the mainland now in control there, Taiwan was more likely to be lost through internal collapse than invasion. Providing new aid to the discredited Nationalists would insult Asians, damage American prestige by involving the nation in "another failure for all to see," and "bring upon ourselves the united Chinese hatred of foreigners." By the end of the discussion, the chairman of the JCS, General Omar Bradley, had to concede that "political considerations" might have to override military ones. Later in the day President Truman endorsed Acheson's position. The United States would continue to avoid direct involvement in the Chinese civil war.[44]

Truman's decision to side with Acheson is hardly surprising. The president may have had some reservations about an eventual Titoism in China, but he was certain that the Nationalists were losers. Only a few weeks before, on December 8, they had moved their seat of government to Taipei, and two days later Chiang himself arrived to take charge. Truman had nothing but contempt for both.* This he made abundantly clear to Walter Judd when the congressman telephoned him on December 30 to make one last pitch for the military's position. Judd suggested that the Truman Doctrine could work in Asia if the administration gave it a chance. Truman interrupted, according to Judd's note on the conversation, saying "Yes, and that is exactly what we have done in China," but the Nationalists, unlike the Greek anticommunists, had refused to accept U.S.

---

*Truman's judgment may have been colored to some extent by an antipathy toward the Chinese, assuming he had not shaken free of the attitude he expressed in a 1911 letter to his future wife: "I think one man is just as good as another so long as he's honest and decent and not a nigger or a Chinaman. Uncle Will says that the Lord made a White man from dust, a nigger from mud, then threw up what was left and it came down a Chinaman. He does hate Chinese and Japs. So do I. It is race prejudice, I guess. But I am strongly of the opinion that negroes ought to be in Africa, yellow men in Asia, and white men in Europe and America." Robert H. Ferrell, ed., *Dear Bess* (New York, 1983), pp. 52–53, as cited by Arnold A. Offner, "The Truman Myth Revealed: From Parochial Nationalist to Cold Warrior," unpublished paper, March 1988.

guidance. The conversation drifted briefly to the impending recognition of the Beijing government by India's Nehru, but Truman quickly returned to the attack. How many American soldiers did Judd want to put on Taiwan? It would take "10 divisions" to save the island, Truman said, and he was not willing to do that. Judd agreed. He had no wish to send U.S. forces to Taiwan either, he assured the president; but in his view enabling the Nationalists to fight now would prevent the need for American soldiers later. At this point, Judd noted, Truman "became intense, angry, explosive about 'rottenest gov[ernment] that ever existed.'" The United States could not help people who would not help themselves. The Nationalists had surrendered "every bit of aid we had given them," the president declared, and "had never tried to fight." Neither Truman nor Judd would give an inch. Finally Truman foreclosed further argument by telling Judd, "I know what I'm talking about—no use you arguing with me or me with you." He had tried everything possible, but, so far as he could see, nothing could be done about Taiwan. Judd closed by wishing the president a "happy and good new year."[45]

Despite Truman's decision the military and their right-wing supporters were unreconciled to the possible fall of Taiwan. Their clamor alarmed London, just then on the point of recognizing the new Beijing government. The Chinese Communists themselves charged that the United States was about to seize the island.[46] Counterattacking to save his position, Acheson succeeded in pressing Truman to announce publicly on January 5, 1950, that the United States "had no desire to obtain special rights or privileges or to establish military bases on Formosa at this time" and would "not provide military aid or advice to Chinese forces on Formosa." The announcement shocked conservatives, and Acheson's pressure tactics angered top presidential aides and military officials.* Though Acheson had won out for the moment, his policy was never on firm ground within the administration.[47] Pressures to reverse the decision began immediately.

---

*The flurry of activity and maneuvering that produced what the *New York Times* accurately disparaged as a "political impromptu" are set out in detail in note 47.

A few days after Truman dropped his bombshell, Acheson went before a secret session of the Senate Foreign Relations Committee to defend and popularize his position. He facetiously paraphrased the message his conservative critics wanted to give the Chinese people: "No, forget about the Russians. Hate us. We want to fight you. We want to send our soldiers to drop bombs on you. We want to be the foreigners who are attacking China." Acheson explained that the administration wanted to avoid providing the Chinese Communists with any pretext—military action, the seizure of Taiwan, a trade embargo—to incite anti-Americanism and rally the people behind them. At the same time the United States would not make it easy on the Communists. If they wanted loans, Acheson said he would tell them, "No, your friends are in Moscow. They are not in Washington. You go and get your loans and work these things out with the Russians." Acheson was confident that the Chinese would not be successful, and that "disillusionment [with the Soviets] will work out." The position Acheson set out here essentially reflected the line Kennan had proposed: the United States would avoid both kindnesses and slights.[48] But it was a difficult position to hold, because it seemed to leave the initiative to the Communists. Circumstances would soon demand an affirmative policy.

IV

Even before the official founding of the People's Republic in October 1949, hundreds of Russian military and civilian personnel were scattered throughout the country.[49] American reports about rising popular resentment against the Russians and Chinese Communists undoubtedly sustained the Truman administration's assumption that it could place its hopes on nurturing anti-Soviet sentiment among the Chinese people. But in the main the Sino-Soviet relationship was solidifying. British diplomats in the Far East were right to dismiss the American eagerness to see anti-Sovietism in China. The American reports, they informed London, were "full of wishful thinking."[50]

On December 16, 1949, after a long train ride from Beijing, Mao Zedong arrived in Moscow to oversee the conclusion of military and economic assistance pacts and celebrate Stalin's seventieth birthday. Other top Chinese leaders had secretly traveled to Moscow before the founding of the People's Republic to discuss cooperation, but Mao's trip was to formalize the relationship. Mao and his Party colleagues received a warm and enthusiastic reception from the Soviets. Stalin, on meeting Mao for the first time, gushed, "I never quite expected that you would be so young, so healthy and strong!" The Soviet leaders expressed their regret for their past mistakes on the Chinese revolution.[51]

Ambassador Alan Kirk reported from Moscow that the Sino-Soviet talks would probably result in "cementing China to USSR along lines conventional satellite treaties." And Consul General Clubb, still in Beijing, similarly judged that developments in Sino-Soviet relations had now made Titoism "unlikely." But Mao's unexpectedly long stay in the Soviet Union soon provoked a rash of speculation about difficulties between the two sides. The Soviet press carried no word about Mao or the discussions for two weeks. At one point Kennan thought the Soviets might be detaining Mao as a "guest" while they undermined him in China. Clubb, too, suggested that Mao might be in trouble in Moscow, and he reported that anti-Soviet resentment was on the rise in China.[52] It was not until February 14 that Zhou Enlai, who as premier handled the actual negotiations, and Soviet Foreign Minister A. Y. Vyshinsky signed a Treaty of Friendship, Alliance, and Mutual Assistance.

The heart of the treaty was the pledge by each party to assist the other in the event of aggression by a third country. Other agreements included several temporary Chinese economic concessions to the Soviets in exchange for a $300,000,000 low-interest loan and other economic assistance. The Sino-Soviet Friendship Treaty, Zhou Enlai proclaimed at the signing ceremony, utterly defeated American imperialism's attempt "to foster divisions between our two countries." On February 16 the Soviets hosted a grand banquet in the Kremlin in honor of Mao, Zhou, and the rest of the Chinese delegation. Stalin, in especially "high spirits," jovially bantered with the Chinese and their fellow guest, Ho Chi Minh, leader of the Communist movement in French Indochina, who was secretly in Moscow at the time. Sino-Soviet relations had never been as close or as warm.[53]

The Chinese, though, were not completely pleased with the results of the drawn-out negotiations. The Soviets were stingy in their aid and made them pay dear for it. Wu Xiuquan, who participated in the talks as director of Soviet Affairs in the Chinese Foreign Ministry, recalled some thirty years later that, through this experience, his comrades became aware of "Soviet big-nation chauvinism and national egoism." Nevertheless Sino-Soviet relations seem to him to have been based "on the whole on equality and mutual benefit." On balance the assessment of the British embassy in Moscow at the time is probably still sound: both parties benefited, with the Chinese as clear "winners." Mao probably turned out to be a tougher partner than the Soviets expected, the embassy concluded, and any hope that the Sino-Soviet honeymoon would soon be over was misplaced. In his departure speech at the Moscow train station, Mao saluted both host and host country: "Hail to the teacher of the world revolution, best friend of the Chinese people, comrade Stalin," and to the nation he led, which would be "the example for construction of the New China."[54]

Mao no doubt aimed by this effusive praise to please Stalin, but he almost certainly also intended to retaliate against Washington's obvious attempts to foment CCP-Soviet discord during his stay in Moscow. For months the State Department had planned a propaganda attack to encourage Chinese disillusionment with the Soviets and their allies in the CCP.[55] The Moscow talks provided the occasion to launch that attack. Ambassador David Bruce in Paris was instructed to leak a flurry of rumors about Soviet demands on the Chinese, including the demand that a million laborers be sent to work in the Soviet Union. On January 12, in a carefully planned major address to the National Press Club, Secretary of State Acheson himself denounced what he called the traditional predatory nature of the Russian state. Communism, he declared, was really the "spearhead of Russian imperialism." The Russians were "detaching the northern provinces of China from China" and "attaching them to the Soviet Union." Acheson, with Truman's January 5 statement repudiating designs on Taiwan still fresh, claimed that the United States, on the other hand, upheld the territorial integrity of China and maintained its traditional feeling of friendship toward the Chinese people. Acheson urged his audience to appreciate the enormity of the Russians' actions: they were "saddling all those in China who are proclaiming their loyalty to Moscow, and who are allowing themselves to be used as puppets of Moscow, with the most awful responsibility which they must pay for."[56]

Acheson's speech was provocative, and his charges unsubstantiated. The Chinese Communists and Soviet Foreign Minister Vyshinsky bitterly objected to Acheson's accusations, and the Communist press around the world condemned what a Polish newspaper called his effort to "force a wedge between the Chinese and Soviet nations." British officials kept their own counsel, but they privately called the speech "silly" and saw it as a confirmation of their low regard for U.S. intelligence reporting from China, so prone to exaggerate popular discontent with the Communists. The *New York Times* drew altogether different conclusions from Acheson's statements. "At the very least," his analysis suggested that the United States had to adopt "a vigorous and helpful policy. . . . Obviously we and the Chinese are not being confronted merely by a 'social revolution' or a routine 'civil war' but by a program of massive aggression."[57] The immediate practical effect of Acheson's effort was to encourage Communist solidarity and increase American public antagonism toward the Chinese Communists.

Other developments in this period exacerbated Sino-American tensions. On January 13, after months of acrimony, the Soviet delegate to the U.N. Security Council walked out to protest the continued presence of the Chinese Nationalist representative in the international body. The Soviet walkout would end only after the start of the Korean War. Several days later the State Department recalled all its remaining personnel in China in response to Beijing's seizure of some consular properties of the United States and other countries. Under Secretary of State James Webb, in recommending the action to Truman, cautioned that it might play directly "into the Russian hands." But Truman decided the move was justified, thus ending the few remaining American contacts in China.[58] Simultaneously Acheson maneuvered to stir the American public to greater hostility toward the Chinese Communists. While other affected foreign powers tended to minimize the Communists' seizure of their consular properties, for example, he told the press that the incident showed it was the Communists who did not want American recognition. Several days later, on January 27, he suggested to Truman that Angus Ward, recently returned from captivity in China, should have "ample opportunity to give his story to the American people generally." Ward's experiences quickly became a top story in the American press. Acheson was determined to burden the CCP with the responsibility for destroying the traditionally close bonds between America and the Chinese people.[59]

On March 15 Acheson delivered his harshest speech yet against Beijing. He announced that the recently concluded Sino-Soviet Treaty of Friendship was "an evil omen of imperialistic domination." Russian aid would prove woefully inadequate for the Chinese, whose Communist leaders were replacing established ties of "old friends" with those of "new-found and voracious friends." He of course knew, he said, that the "present unhappy status within the orbit of the Soviet Union" was not the choice of the Chinese people, and America would assuredly retain its deep feeling for them. Acheson's intended audience was as much the Chinese people as his fellow Americans.[60]

Acheson's press conferences and speeches upset the British, less interested in amorphous ties with the Chinese people than in mollifying the ruling Communist Party. Ernest Bevin told the British cabinet that Acheson's lecturing "China on the way in which she should conduct herself" would only embitter the Communists toward the United States and encourage them "even more to look to the Soviet Union." "Tripe" was what the British ambassador to the United States, Oliver Franks, called a U.S. State Department report suggesting there was a crisis brewing in China that had the potential of unseating the Beijing government. Even Yugoslavian officials warned that the United States was driving the Chinese into the hands of the Soviets.[61]

On the other hand Acheson's new public toughness toward Beijing pleased Walter Judd. The leader of the China bloc in

Congress praised Acheson's March 15 speech, happy to find that the secretary had at last recognized that the "objectives of the Communist conspiracy in China" were nothing less than the conquest of "Asia, then of Europe, then of ourselves." Washington, it seemed, was finally moving from an attitude of "what we cannot do to what we can do and must try to do." Despite Acheson's continuing distaste for the Nationalists, Washington's propaganda against the mainland began to sound more and more like that emanating from Taipei. The KMT also played to the nationalist sentiments of the Chinese people, hammering away at the theme that Mao was giving away China's northeastern and northwestern territories to the Soviets. In the words of one KMT slogan: "Mao Tse-tung wants to do away with our country. Stalin wants to destroy our nation."[62]

To the Communists Acheson's comments were more than just arrogant and insulting; they indicated that he had no intention of seeking a modus vivendi with Beijing. Acheson saw that the British moderate policy had not led to an appreciable improvement in relations with the Communists. Despite London's recognition of the new regime, Beijing had refused to exchange ambassadors on the grounds that the British continued to maintain a consulate on Taiwan and had not supported the PRC's efforts to oust Chiang Kai-shek's representative from the United Nations. Beijing charged Britain with conducting a two-faced policy. The stalemate in Anglo-Chinese relations helped sustain Washington's belief in the futility of trying to placate the CCP leaders. The important result was that, in openly playing for the affections of the Chinese people and trying to convince them that communism "was another name for Russian imperialism," Acheson promoted at home the notion of the monolithic threat of communism.[63] If, as he himself stated, the Chinese Communists had already reduced China to an appendage of the Soviet empire, it would be difficult to justify allowing Taiwan to fall to Beijing. Judd had a right to be pleased.

But there was still an ambiguity in American policy that Livingston Merchant pointed out to Acheson in early March: the United States was trying to straddle opposed positions. On the one hand it was anxious to avoid exciting widespread anti-American sentiment among the Chinese people, but at the same time it was attempting to deny Taiwan to the Communists and was supporting the KMT with diplomatic recognition, backing in the United Nations, economic aid, and sales of weapons and munitions. More than that, it was even supporting the Nationalists "in their war against the Mainland with the blockade and bombs." Merchant suggested a "less intimate association with Chiang" to resolve the obvious contradiction. Unfortunately, the resolution was not to be along the lines Merchant proposed.[64]

V

The administration's tough rhetoric toward China was consistent with the overall militarization of U.S. foreign policy in the spring of 1950. The focal point of this development was NSC 68, a top secret, comprehensive review of U.S. policy sparked by the Soviet development of nuclear weapons and by the fall of China. Authored by Paul Nitze, who became head of the PPS after George Kennan resigned in late 1949, NSC 68 consolidated implicit Cold War assumptions into one blunt statement.

Even though China was barely mentioned in the April 14 document, the thinking behind it had direct implications for China policy. For one thing, by insisting that power now reposed in "two centers," the United States and the Soviet Union, representing antithetical moral and political principles, NSC 68 allowed little or no possibility for U.S. acceptance of an independent national position. The growing conviction among policymakers that the United States faced an international coordinated threat had been well expressed by Loy Henderson only a few weeks before. "It should be borne in mind," the U.S. ambassador to India had said in late March, "that the United States does not pursue one set of policies with regard to the Americas and Europe and another with regard to Asia. The foreign policies of the United States by force of circumstances have become global in character."[65]

NSC 68 also affected China policy by drawing attention to the Far East as a focus of Cold War turmoil. China was no longer seen as a "strategic morass" for the Soviets, as Acheson had held the previous year, but was looked on as a "springboard" for further communist troublemaking in Southeast Asia.

Finally, NSC 68's preoccupation with the military balance of power blurred the distinction between fundamental and peripheral interests, a distinction that the administration had till then tried to maintain. Holding that any shift in the military balance could imperil America, Nitze and his colleagues favored opposing any advance of the Soviets with equal resolve. For the China area this highlighted the problem of Taiwan. As late as March 29 Acheson had still tried to minimize the island's military importance to the United States in his meeting with the Senate Foreign Relations Committee. Taiwan, he averred, was "not one of our vital security points in the Far East"; it was important only "as it relates to our hopes and our activities in regard to China."[66] However, after the appearance of NSC 68, which Acheson strongly endorsed, the State Department's thinking about Taiwan shifted. By the NSC's inexorable logic, for political, moral, and military reasons the United States had to prevent the loss of any further territory to communism. NSC 68 acted as a catalyst for resolving the contradiction that had troubled Livingston Merchant.

Not surprisingly, NSC 68 strengthened the military point of view on China within the administration. Never reconciled to Truman's January 5 policy statement, the Pentagon continued to press for a tougher position toward China. On April 27 General Bradley reiterated the JCS's opposition to recognizing the Beijing regime lest the United States undermine resistance to Communist aggression in Southeast Asia and Japan. Bradley also raised a new consideration. Recognition "would tend to increase, in some degree, the internal security problems of the United States," opening the door for Beijing to increase its pressure "on the Chinese domiciled in the United States and elsewhere to support Communist activities."[67] With national sensitivities about subversion heightened by Senator Joseph McCarthy's inquisition of the State Department, Bradley's warning could not be dismissed lightly. A week later the chairman again expressed the JCS's dissatisfaction with the ban on providing new military aid and advice to the Nationalists. Since Truman's January 5 statement, Bradley noted, several major developments had elevated the importance of Taiwan in American security interests. For one thing the Communists had taken over the mainland more rapidly than anticipated. For another, as Acheson had declared publicly, the "domination over the Chinese Communist Government by the USSR is virtually complete"; the Soviets were known to be rapidly consolidating their position in the Chinese Communist government and military. At the same time the Nationalists' military supplies were dwindling, and the situation in Southeast Asia was deteriorating. The JCS argued that the Nationalists were "absorbing the major attention and efforts" of the Chinese Communists, which would otherwise be directed beyond their borders. The continued resistance of the Nationalists was thus "in the military interest of the United States." The United States and the Soviet Union, it should be remembered, were "now, to all intents and purposes, engaged in war—except for armed conflict." [68]

Sentiment for a tougher policy was growing within the State Department as well. Edmund Clubb, once among the most hopeful of a Titoist shift and a persistent opponent of a rigid policy toward China, was now of a completely different mind, apparently because of developments in China since the signing of the Sino-Soviet Friendship Treaty. Just before he departed his post as one of the last American officials in China, Clubb bitterly wrote to George Kennan that the CCP had "oriented its own program to Moscow's and attached China to the Soviet chariot, for better or worse." At this point, he said, "the Chinese political frenzy is as perverted in some respects as that of Hitlerite Germany, but is less intelligent in even a Machiavellian sense, and there is no reasoning with that madness born of xenophobia and infatuation (contradictorially enough) for the Soviets." The Communists were prepared to risk world destruction for their goals. Clubb urged that Washington prepare for a "shooting war," and specifically recommended imposing stringent trade sanctions against Beijing, helping anticommunist elements on the mainland, and even employing Japanese agents for covert military actions inside China. Only by taking "the fight to the enemy," he concluded, could an atomic war be avoided, "or if not avoided, won." China might someday return to friendship with the West, but it was "only by the hard way that they might learn the error of their ways and swing away from Moscow."[69]

By June Clubb, back home, was considering what the United States could do to retain control of Taiwan. His proposals included sending military advisory groups or forming a "volunteer military group" to support the Nationalists. Clubb thought that the economic and political situation on the mainland had deteriorated so badly that there might even be a possibility of entirely reversing things there. "Nationalism is still the dominant theme," Clubb told a meeting of top State Department officials; "this might well be so stretched by the USSR relationship as to result in the downfall of the Chinese Communists."[70]

Paul Nitze, the author of NSC-68, also wanted to overturn Truman's January 5 policy. An armed commitment to defend the island was necessary to save Taiwan from the Communists, he believed. Moreover, military action might also dramatize America's general purpose.[71] But influential as he and Clubb may have been, it was not their arguments so much as those of Dean Rusk that prompted the shift in Taiwan policy within the State Department.

Rusk had been appointed assistant secretary of state for Far Eastern Affairs in late March, replacing Walton Butterworth, who had raised the ire of the Republican right wing. Rusk, who had been serving as deputy under secretary of state, was known to be more sympathetic than Butterworth to renewing support for the Nationalists. He no sooner took office than he began working to reverse policy toward Taiwan.[72]

In May Rusk endorsed the proposal of John Foster Dulles, a leading Republican selected by Acheson to draft a peace treaty with Japan, that Taiwan be neutralized under the aegis of the United States, thereby ensuring that it would neither be taken by the Communists nor be "used as a base of military operations against the mainland." Dulles's recommendation had several attractive aspects for the State Department. His concern with the military balance of power and the need for the United States to "take a dramatic and strong stand that shows our confidence and resolution" was drawn right from NSC-68. The plan would also restrain the troublesome Nationalists.

Their use of American planes and bombs to wreak havoc on Chinese coastal cities (and attack American and European shipping as well) was infuriating Britain as well as the Communists, and threatened broader hostilities, perhaps even involving the Russians. Moreover, the move could be carried out without sending a single foot soldier to Taiwan—the Navy and Air Force could be used exclusively. The overall attraction of Dulles's proposal was that the United States could cloak an aggressive act (detaching Taiwan from the mainland) under the pretense of peaceful intent and restraint of the Nationalists.[73]

Dean Rusk sent the identical proposal under his own name to Acheson on May 30. Ten days later he sent Acheson a longer and more detailed plan that linked the denial of Taiwan to the Communists to a "package deal" involving the development of relations with the mainland and the resolution of the U.N. impasse over the seating of a Chinese delegation. Rusk's hope, evidently, was to forge a new consensus toward China, on the thought that a policy combining an explicit commitment to the defense of Taiwan with the promise of overtures toward Beijing would address the concerns of the State and Defense departments, Congress, and Republicans and Democrats alike.[74]

The principal question mark for Rusk was what Acheson would think of this policy. China and the situation in Asia had increasingly absorbed the secretary's attention since the beginning of the year, and his frequent conversations with British officials provide insights into his changing state of mind. In late December 1949 he gloomily told Ambassador Franks that he thought Asia would be "the principal preoccupation of the State Department in 1950," and admitted that he and his advisers "had changed their views" about the consequences of China's revolution. They now thought that an "early expansion south and east beyond the borders of China" was "likely." By the following March Acheson had become even more pessimistic. He confided to Franks that it seemed to him there had been "a deterioration in our common position and a corresponding increase of strength to the Russians" over the last six months. Acheson indicated that he was searching for ways to reverse this trend, focusing on Germany and Indochina. No mention was made of Taiwan. But he came around to the matter in talks with Foreign Secretary Bevin in early May, noting that the United States had recently "assessed more highly the strategic importance" of the island. A few days later he told his British and French counterparts that "the China question cannot be separated from [the] whole question of recognition and protection [of our] interests in Southeast Asia." It seemed evident to Bevin that, though Acheson had not totally abandoned hope of an eventual Titoism in China, the United States was working toward encouraging "a general break-up of central authority in China."[75]

More telling were Acheson's comments to Ambassador Franks in an "after-dinner chat" they had on June 5. Franks relayed to the Foreign Office Acheson's report that the State Department was "wracking its brains to see whether conditions conducive to preservation of the present status [of Taiwan] could not be encouraged or possibly created." According to Franks, "Acheson had nothing to offer. . . . But it was clear that there is pressure in the administration for another look at the Formosa position and that the attitude of January last . . . is not now quite so firm." Franks did not think Acheson would agree to military intervention, but it was clear to him that the United States would try "to delay the elimination of the token anti-Communist group."[76] Only with reason would Acheson have given the British an impression of impending change in U.S. policy.

Earlier that same day the British consul general on Taiwan confidentially reported to London that thirty American military advisers had arrived in a civilian capacity. He alerted London to the possibility that the United States might be moving to prevent the Communist occupation of the island. The consul general, of course, did not know that in late May the State and Defense departments agreed to facilitate the shipment of the remaining military aid committed to the Nationalists and intensify covert actions in China and Taiwan.[77]

A week after Acheson's "chat" with Franks, Dulles hinted to the Nationalists' ambassador, Wellington Koo, that the regime could expect a change in policy toward Taiwan. Dulles, who was careful to stay in line with existing policy, told Koo that a "better attitude" in the State Department toward Taiwan had recently developed, and "he believed there was some possibility of reconsidering the question of military aid." Even John Paton Davies, the China specialist on the PPS who had earlier encouraged a flexible policy to encourage Sino-Soviet friction, now contemplated the United States sponsoring "counter-revolutionary movements in China and North Korea" with the ultimate aim of overthrowing their communist governments. His program for combating communism in Asia, he admitted, implied "American intervention."[78]

Washington was quickly moving toward finding a way to deny Taiwan to the Communists, although few called for an outright American occupation of the island. General Douglas MacArthur himself stopped short of such a recommendation in a long June 14 memorandum on the importance of holding that "unsinkable aircraft carrier." On June 22, 1950, just days before the United States learned of the North Korean invasion of the South, the State Department held a top-level interdepartmental meeting to listen to Brigadier General Robert H. Soule, who had been the military attaché at the American embassy in Nanjing for three years before his recent departure from China. In February Soule had favored ending ties with the discredited Nationalists and entertained hopes that the CCP's leaders might divide over their relations with the Soviets. But now he too painted a very different picture: Soviet influence was growing, Mao was an "international communist, first and last," and the prospects for Titoism were nil. Many Chinese hoped that Taiwan would be held at whatever cost, he said, since it represented "the only chance to save China." "China today," Soule rued, "is not the China we have known."[79]

In their review of Far East policy months earlier, the consultants had recommended that the State Department remain "opportunistically alert to take advantage of any circumstances not now foreseeable" that would allow the United States to deny Taiwan to the Communists. North Korea's attack on the South on June 25 provided the occasion. On June 27, acting on Acheson's advice (which echoed the Dulles-Rusk proposal), President Truman announced that the U.S. Seventh Fleet would "neutralize" the Taiwan Strait, and that the ultimate disposition of the island would have to await international agreement. American warships soon patrolled the waters just miles from the mainland coast. The Communists denounced what they called U.S. aggression and the American occupation of Taiwan. The United States had reinjected itself into the Chinese civil war.

VI

The North Korean attack confirmed the bleakest American suspicions about a coordinated international Communist threat. With U.N. sanction, Truman immediately committed U.S. military forces to the defense of South Korea. "This aggression was ordered by the Kremlin," Acheson wrote Foreign Minister Bevin soon after the start of the war. "There can be little doubt but that Communism, with Chi[na] as one spearhead, has now embarked upon an assault against Asia with immediate objectives in Korea, Indo-China, Burma, the Philippines and Malaya and with medium-range objectives in Hong Kong, Indonesia, Siam, India and Japan."[80]

The initial American response to the outbreak of hostilities reflected many of the old assumptions about the Sino-Soviet relationship. Just hours after the attack, for example, the State Department's intelligence division estimated that a "hard policy" on the Communists would effectively strain what would increasingly be called the "Moscow-Peiping axis." American intervention in the conflict, including the denial of Taiwan to the Communists, would dismay the CCP, damage its prestige, and shake its confidence in the advantages of the alliance with the Soviets. "As a consequence, the strength of the Chinese Communist ties to the USSR would be significantly weakened."[81]

The belief that a tough, coercive policy toward the Communists would most effectively undermine the Sino-Soviet alliance, as well as meet obvious immediate needs, now became Washington's accepted wisdom. To be sure, there were some in the administration, such as Philip Jessup, who still felt that the best wedge-driving strategy was to adopt a moderate policy toward China, which was not at this point directly involved in the fighting. But the hard line, which Charles Yost, Acheson at various times, and others had articulated over the previous months, now seemed most persuasive. In late August Charles

Bohlen, one of the State Department's senior Soviet experts, expressed this view in a meeting with British and French officials, who feared American actions were giving the Chinese no choice but to enter the embrace of the Soviets. Rifts between China and the Soviet Union, Bohlen stressed, were "not likely to be brought about by Western attempts to wean Communist China away from Kremlin control. . . . Kindness from the West will not tempt them to break away from the Soviet world. If a break should come, it may be expected to come from within." But the British in particular were not completely persuaded, and it was thanks largely to their apprehension of provoking wider hostilities with China or the Soviet Union that the United States was forced to conduct a "limited war."[82]

General Douglas MacArthur's dramatic surprise landing at Inchon, behind the North Koreans' lines, on September 15 turned the fortunes of war against them. Their forces, which had almost overrun the South, now frantically retreated to escape destruction. The Truman administration, with little difficulty, affirmed the order that MacArthur should continue his offensive, pursue the Communists beyond the 38th parallel, the boundary between North and South Korea, and seek to liberate the North from communism. It was a disastrous decision, leading directly to Americans and Chinese killing one another a month later, when American forces approached the Yalu River, the boundary between Korea and China. China and the United States became the bitterest of enemies.

The decision to have MacArthur cross the 38th parallel was tragic but also ironic. For a year and a half the Truman administration had hoped to exploit rifts between the Chinese Communists and Moscow and encourage Chinese antagonism toward the Soviet Union and Stalinist communism. But now in the fall of 1950, in deciding to "roll back" communism in North Korea, it virtually dismissed China as a Soviet surrogate and horrendously underestimated China's own vital interest in keeping the United States away from its border. Acheson believed that Moscow, stung by the strong Western response to the Soviet Union's Korean adventure, was unlikely to intervene in the fighting. And China, it was easily assumed, would follow the Soviet lead.[83]

Privately, both Acheson and Truman saw the Beijing regime,

for all practical purposes, as an instrument of Moscow. But publicly they preached to the Chinese people that it was not in their interest to become involved in a war on behalf of the Kremlin. On September 10 Acheson once again alerted them to the danger of the "imperialism coming down from the Soviet Union." As in his earlier speeches addressed to the Chinese people, his aim was to divide them from their leaders. For the Chinese people, with the ships of the Seventh Fleet patrolling the Taiwan Strait, however, the administration's professions of concern for their interests most likely sounded like "thief calling thief" and aroused greater suspicions of American intentions. The administration's belief in the CCP leaders' subordination to Moscow, the consistent underestimation of the Chinese Communists, and the fundamental misunderstanding of Chinese national interests all contributed to the ill-fated decision to cross into North Korea.[84]

The decision to move north of the 38th parallel has provoked sharp criticism from historians generally sympathetic to Acheson's China policy and to his efforts to distinguish between Soviet and Chinese communism before the Korean War. These evaluations suggest that, in some fundamental ways, the decision was an unfortunate departure from what had been a sound policy.[85] The administration, however, made the decision to go north without hesitation, without betraying any awareness that it was radically altering its assumptions about the Chinese Communists. Several continuities in the administration's beliefs and perceptions suggest that the decision may not have been as great a policy departure as some have maintained.

For one thing American policy toward China had become significantly more belligerent in the spring of 1950 before the outbreak of war, in part because the administration became convinced of Beijing's solidarity with Moscow. As discussed above, there are indications that the State Department was moving toward reinvolvement with Taiwan by May 1950. Avoiding making Taiwan an irredentist issue, a point that Acheson had emphasized in 1949 and early 1950, had receded in importance as concern with the global military balance of power with the Soviet Union came to dominate policymaking. Moreover, Acheson's decision in the spring of 1950 to aid the French colonial war in Indochina and recognize the anticommunist Bao Dai government in South Vietnam reflected the increased militarization of the entire containment doctrine, as expressed by NSC-68.

The Truman administration's policy toward China had all along been based on an exaggerated sense of America's importance and goodwill to China and, conversely, the malevolence of Moscow. Officials never appreciated the depth of Chinese animosity to America's support of, and continuing links with, Chiang Kai-shek. After a brutal four-year civil war fueled by billions of dollars of aid to Chiang, many Chinese must have found Acheson's words of friendship for them contemptible. The slights of the Soviets against China, whatever they may have been in 1950, could only have paled in comparison. No other foreign power had supported the Chinese Communists as the Soviet Union had. The Truman administration's obvious efforts to divide Beijing and Moscow only confirmed that the United States had not reconciled itself to the Chinese revolution, making the alliance with Moscow all the more valuable in the eyes of China's new leaders.

Ignoring Beijing's explicit warnings not to cross the 38th parallel was not an unexpected response—Truman and Acheson had grown increasingly contemptuous of Mao and his comrades as time wore on. Unfortunately, the United States would have to endure bitter lessons before it began to appreciate the Communists' determination to define and defend China's interests. The war dragged on for two long, bloody years after peace talks began in Panmunjom in July 1951 and fighting stabilized along the 38th parallel.

In the end hundreds of thousands of Chinese and Koreans, and 34,000 Americans lost their lives in the conflict, according to U.N. estimates.[86] But beyond this appalling human cost, the war transformed East-West relations and Cold War policies. With Chinese and Americans at each other's throats, Stalin became convinced that Mao would not soon become a new Tito. He increased Soviet military and economic aid to China, and Beijing learned the power of the modern weaponry that the United States used with such deadly effectiveness against the "people's volunteers." Although Soviet personnel did not become directly involved in the fighting and Soviet assistance was less than what the Chinese had expected, the war validated the importance of the alliance for China's security. Frictions that did emerge between the two powers were those between allies opposing a common enemy.[87]

The Soviets had undoubtedly known of North Korea's preparations to invade the South, but the actual timing of the attack, it seems, had surprised and embarrassed them, contrary to Washington's insistence that they were behind the whole affair. Throughout the war Moscow's attitude was restrained, even as it supplied its Communist allies, and its feelings mixed. The war may have helped consolidate the ties with the Chinese and North Koreans, but it also drained important resources from the Soviet Union, militarized America's containment policy, and hardened Western anti-Soviet sentiment.[88]

For the United States the Korean War seemed to provide incontrovertible evidence of the solidarity of Sino-Soviet ties (although Washington continued to look for frictions between the two countries during the war) and of a Communist design for world conquest. The Chinese, in the eyes of policymakers and public alike, became a demonic threat: they were oblivious to death, attacked in "human waves," and "brainwashed" American prisoners. On the other hand the United States radically elevated its evaluation of the Nationalists on Taiwan and of the utility of the island itself. New military aid began to flow to Chiang Kai-shek. The JCS concluded that the United States had to retain Taiwan as a potential base for "the conduct of offensive operations" against the mainland, and that the island was "essential" in the "strategic defense of our off-shore island chain" stretching from Japan through the Philippines. In late summer 1950 the United States also began supplying covert aid to Tibetan rebels. The United States led the way in getting the United Nations to brand the Chinese as "aggressors" in Korea (and subsequently led in keeping the PRC out of that body until 1971), imposed a complete embargo on trade with China, and prohibited American travel.[89]

The break between China and the United States was complete.

THREE

Strategies of Division

Instead of our making an effort to prove that we are their [the Chinese Communists'] friends, we ask them to prove that they are ours.   —Dean Acheson, 1950

On May 31, 1953, Karl Lott Rankin, American ambassador to the Nationalist government on Taiwan and self-appointed booster for Chiang Kai-shek, entered the Oval Office of the White House for a meeting with President Dwight Eisenhower bearing a personal communication from the generalissimo. Rankin expected the Republican president to be more sympathetic to the Nationalists than his Democratic predecessor had been on Rankin's trip to Washington the year before, when Truman had ranted about the ineffectiveness and corruption of Chiang's regime.

Eisenhower cordially welcomed his ambassador, who proceeded to convey Chiang's greetings and message. The generalissimo, Rankin began, expressed sympathy with the president as "undoubtedly the busiest man in the world today and carrying the heaviest responsibilities." To lighten that great burden, Chiang humbly suggested that Eisenhower seek "simple solutions." With the Soviets obviously concentrating their attention on Asia, the president should understand that China was the key to the entire international situation. Chiang advised that the "liberation of Mainland China from Communism" would solve the world's problems, including the Soviet threat to Western Europe. The Nationalists would be honored to carry out such a mission and, Chiang added magnanimously, American troops would not even be necessary, although other forms of U.S. "help" would be.[1]

"Tell old Chiang that we have China very much in mind,"

Eisenhower tartly replied. Continuing to puncture Rankin's hopes, Eisenhower pointed out that Chiang was no longer an important figure in Asia—"the two big leaders today [are] Mao and Nehru." And so far as the notion of taking action against China was concerned, such as the widely discussed idea of a blockade, the president mused that a certain amount of trade with China might even be useful in keeping Beijing from falling entirely into the arms of the Soviets.

Rankin must have listened in disbelief. Just a few months earlier during the presidential campaign, Eisenhower had threatened to "unleash Chiang Kai-shek" against the mainland to bring the Korean War to an end. Public frustrations about the war had helped sweep the Republicans into office. But here, in private, the president was not talking about overthrowing the Chinese Communists, merely about separating them from the Soviet Union. Rankin had heard this tune all over Washington during his previous trip in 1952. When he saw Chiang again in Taiwan, Rankin presented an innocuous account of his meeting with the president, saying only that Eisenhower "had China very much in mind and was fully aware of the importance of the general situation."[2]

The Nationalists were not fooled by Rankin's diplomacy. They were already less than satisfied with the new Republican administration. Despite the pro-Nationalist reputations of Eisenhower and Dulles and their firm commitment to preventing the fall of Taiwan to the Communists, the Nationalists sensed that major differences still separated them from the United States. Eisenhower's "unleashing" of Chiang had produced simply a puff of smoke—nothing substantive came of it.[3] Contrasting estimates of China's relationship with the Soviet Union also divided Taipei and Washington. Continuing rumors that the United States might accept a Communist China if it broke with the Soviet Union made the Nationalists insecure. A few months into the new administration, Taipei learned from Assistant Secretary of State Walter Robertson that Eisenhower himself was interested in the possibilities of Titoism in China.[4] The fascination with Titoism had not left the White House with the Democrats.

The Nationalists correctly understood that American interest in an independent but still Communist mainland diminished the importance of their mission. Chiang justified the existence of his regime on Taiwan with the contention that the Communists did not uphold any of China's national interests. Without roots in the Chinese earth, the Communists had to be irrevocably tied to their masters in Moscow. As Madame Chiang Kai-shek coldly proposed, a third world war was necessary to "free the Chinese and the Russian people." "I would bomb Moscow" to "help" them, she once told an American admiral.[5]

I

Secretary of State John Foster Dulles, like Eisenhower, publicly identified with the Nationalists' cause and spouted rhetoric similar to that emanating from Taiwan. Dulles also played to the public. As a State Department consultant, he had dismissed the Beijing regime as totally alien to Chinese soil in a 1951 address to the China Institute on Chinese-American Friendship in New York City, a strongly pro-Nationalist group. "By the test of conception, birth, nurture and obedience, the Mao Tse-tung regime is a creature of the Moscow Politburo," said Dulles, "and it is on behalf of Moscow, not of China, that it is destroying the friendship of the Chinese people toward the United States. . . . We should treat the Mao Tse-tung regime for what it is—a puppet regime."[6]

But Dulles, like Eisenhower, disdained Chiang Kai-shek and had his own mind about the Sino-Soviet relationship. During the 1952 presidential campaign, he wrote privately that "Chiang is bitter, arrogant and difficult for us. . . . He distrusts the British, the Communists and the Americans, in that order. He has a vested interest in World War III, which alone, he feels, might restore his mainland rule." In mid-November 1952, a few days after Eisenhower selected him as secretary of state, Dulles met with Chiang's foreign minister, George K. C. Yeh, and Ambassador Wellington Koo. The three men, according to Dulles's record of the meeting, discussed the problem of "breaking Communist China away from Russia." Yeh argued that that could happen only after the Soviet Union was "broken" through war. Dulles rejected such an appalling choice. He told

Yeh that both the United States and Great Britain shared "the main and acceptable objective" of ending the present ties between China and Moscow, although a difference of opinion existed over how this was to be accomplished. According to Dulles, the difference concerned "whether this was best done by treating Communist China kindly or keeping it under pressures which would, in turn, keep the Communists pressing Russia for more than Russia would give."[7]

Dulles had given considerable thought to the problem of dividing the Chinese Communists from Moscow. He revealed his ideas in 1952 in an exchange of letters with Chester Bowles, then ambassador to India and a leading liberal Democrat. The correspondence outlined the two strategies of division that were debated throughout the Eisenhower years.

Bowles initiated the cordial dialogue in March 1952 with a letter commenting on Dulles's recent *Foreign Affairs* article on security in the Pacific.[8] Bowles thought Dulles underestimated the importance of India and misassessed the China problem. He contended that the United States should consider ways of "weaning" China away from the Soviet Union, a goal avidly discussed among his fellow Democrats in 1949 and 1950 but dashed by Sino-American antagonisms and the Korean War. Bowles, however, had not abandoned his own hopes, even as fighting raged in Korea. In India he had listened to Prime Minister Nehru and other top officials argue repeatedly that China was not a satellite of the Soviet Union, and that the "free world" should keep the "door open" to sustain a chance to split the two Communist countries. The Indian leaders said Chinese officials bristled at insinuations that they were under Soviet control.[9]

Bowles now suggested that the United States "should carefully avoid any act or statement that would tend to strengthen Russia's grip on China and support the Communist accusation that we are planning an all-out aggressive war on the Chinese mainland," for there was "always the remote possibility that if left alone, [the USSR's and China's] varying interests and different stages of development will result in their gradually drifting apart." He hoped the United States would adopt a "moderate attitude" toward China to further this end.

Dulles quickly responded from Washington, saying that he agreed with most of what Bowles had to say, except about China. "My own feeling," he said, "is that the best way to get a separation between the Soviet Union and Communist China is to keep pressure on Communist China and make its way difficult so long as it is in partnership with Soviet Russia. Tito did not break with Stalin because we were nice to Tito. On the contrary, we were very rough on Tito. It seems to me that if China can win our favors while she is also working closely with Moscow, then there is little reason for her to change."[10] Dulles's reasoning recalled that of Charles Yost and the others who, in earlier years, had proposed a coercive policy to undermine the Sino-Soviet alliance.

Bowles in turn replied to Dulles at length. China would never accept a subservient position similar to that of the Eastern European countries, he wrote. Its size, population, history, and national experience would prevent it from becoming a Soviet appendage. "Whatever China may become in the future it will probably not be an unthinking Soviet stooge, dependable under all conditions," he said, and therefore their aim should be to give China the opportunity to develop independently. Bowles admitted that he saw no signs of such independence "at the present time," and conceded that a determined China might even go "berserk" and become impossible to deal with. But he rejected Dulles's interpretation of the Yugoslavia experience, stressing that Stalin had forced Tito to look to the United States in spite of, not because of, U.S. hostility toward Tito. Stalin would not and could not do the same with China because of the considerable power China already possessed. In any case, Bowles wrote, his point was that the United States, while fighting aggression, should "avoid needless provocation," "hold the door open for peaceful negotiations," and "give the natural forces which are working constantly for a more independent China a chance to develop." Dulles politely bowed out of the exchange. He acknowledged that much of what Bowles wrote made "plenty of sense." Although the two of them honestly differed over "tactics," he wrote, they were in agreement over the "desired result."[11]

Dulles's strategy of division may seem Byzantine in its logic or simply a contrived rebuttal. But it was neither. In some respects his view derived from the policy of containment articulated by George Kennan. In his famous article, "The Sources of Soviet Conduct," published in *Foreign Affairs* in July 1947, Kennan wrote that by increasing the strains on the Soviets and forcing them to moderate their policies, the United States could "promote tendencies which must eventually find their outlet in either the break-up or the gradual mellowing of Soviet power. For no mystical, Messianic movement—and particularly not Soviet communism—can face frustration indefinitely without eventually adjusting itself in one way or another to the logic of that state of affairs."[12] Although Kennan was addressing the problem of one particular Communist nation, his approach could be applied to China and the Sino-Soviet alliance. In his view communism was not only an unnatural and vulnerable movement in specific countries; the alliance between the Chinese and Soviet Communists was likewise aberrant. The logic of containment as applied to the Sino-Soviet alliance suggested that a policy of pressure would weaken the tie, even though Kennan himself in early 1949 proposed a benign policy toward the Chinese Communists. Frustrated international ambitions would heighten contradictions within and between the two countries. Eventually the partnership would either disintegrate or mellow, either development being favorable to the West. In this way of thinking, the sensibilities of Kennan and Dulles were not dissimilar.

It was Bowles's ideas that were unconventional and out of step at that moment when the United States was still in combat with Chinese forces in Korea. Bowles sent Dean Acheson a long letter with the proposals he had submitted to Dulles but received only a perfunctory reply. Voices in the State Department were already suggesting that the United States should follow a policy similar to that advanced by Dulles. George Kennan himself now believed that heightened American pressure on China might force Beijing to increase its demands on the Soviets, and that this would in turn strain the Communist alliance.[13] Bowles caused a stir when he tried to get his views into *Foreign Affairs*, the forum for authoritative public debate about foreign policy. "Bowles has jumped into deep water. . . . What he says about China and the Soviets is very controversial," wrote one commentator on the manuscript in an internal memo to the editor, Hamilton Fish Armstrong. Acheson would be shocked to read what Bowles had submitted, he suspected. Armstrong, expressing doubt about the likelihood of separating Mao from Moscow in the discernible future, asked Bowles to rewrite his piece, limiting it to the ambassador's experiences in India. In the published version of the article, Bowles mentioned China only in passing, commiserating with the Chinese people who toiled under a "ruthless Communist dictatorship" working in the interests of "an alien imperialism." Speculation about dividing Beijing and Moscow had been dropped.[14]

The differences between Dulles and Bowles represented more than simple disagreements between two individuals. Throughout the early 1950's those who thought about how the United States might try to separate China and the Soviet Union divided into two general schools of thought. Dulles represented a trend that believed in a "closed door" policy,[15] a policy designed in the short run to force CCP dependence on the Soviets. Confident that Chinese disenchantment and resentment of the Soviets were inevitable, Dulles believed his course of action would eventually produce the desired rupture. Lessening the pressure on China might actually damage prospects for a division, since this would give the CCP more room to maneuver. This line became dominant in the administration. The contending view, held by Bowles and other liberals, and also by some in the Eisenhower administration, believed that a flexible policy toward China was necessary to weaken its ties with the Soviets. The West should leave a door open or at least ajar, so to speak, as an option. A policy of inducement, not pressure, would produce the division.

These contrasting strategies of division were not adhered to consistently by individual policymakers—Eisenhower himself bounced back and forth between them. Neither were the two strategies totally opposed to one another; both were based on the assumption that fundamental conflicts between the Chinese and Soviet Communists lay beneath their apparent unity. As Dulles told Bowles, the difference in their views was over tactics. But neither of the two views was completely realistic.

Events in the first several years of the Eisenhower administration forced it to moderate its policy of pressure. At the same time it became clear that China could not soon be wooed or "weaned" away from its revolutionary path.

A third view, held by the Nationalists and their supporters on the right in the United States, discounted the possibility of any serious Sino-Soviet discord. In the upper levels of the administration, only Assistant Secretary of State for Far Eastern Affairs Walter Robertson held that narrow perspective. An anticommunist ideologue, Robertson was appointed to his position as a concession to the obstreperous China Lobby, which held that China's link to Moscow could be broken only through the destruction of the Communist regime and the restoration of the Nationalists to power.

These differing views of the Sino-Soviet alliance contended with one another for preeminence in Washington between the end of the Korean War in 1953 and the offshore island crisis of 1954–55.

II

Sometime during his first several months in office, Dwight Eisenhower decided that nuclear weapons might have to be employed to end the fighting in Korea. The Truman administration had contemplated their use from the very start of the war, but allied opposition to escalated hostilities and skepticism about the effectiveness of nuclear weapons under Korean conditions forced the United States to rely on conventional weapons and a strategy of "limited war." Eisenhower vowed to reject that approach and, soon after taking office, he ordered the military to renew plans for the possible use of nuclear weapons against Chinese and North Korean targets. The president sent word to the Chinese of his intention. When the breakthrough subsequently came in the ceasefire negotiations at Panmunjom in June 1953, Eisenhower presumed he had compelled the Chinese Communists to end the conflict.[16]

But Eisenhower may have been mistaken. There is some question whether the Chinese ever received his threat of nuclear destruction. Today Chinese Foreign Ministry officials and researchers, including some who were at the Panmunjom talks, maintain that China never learned of Eisenhower's confidential warnings. They claim that China entered the war knowing full well the United States might use nuclear weapons at any time, and that it was the recognition of the stalemate on the battlefield that brought about the armistice on July 27, 1953. With some chagrin Chinese officials admit that they did not appreciate the destructiveness of nuclear weapons in the 1950's, and thus a nuclear threat, even if it was received, would not have been compelling.[17] Regardless of whether or not the Chinese ever learned of Eisenhower's nuclear warning, the president believed they had, and this undoubtedly colored his handling of the subsequent crises in Asia during his administration. He so cherished this lesson in the apparent effectiveness of using massive threats to intimidate Asian adversaries that years later, during the Vietnam War, he was still urging President Lyndon B. Johnson to learn from his experiences in employing the nuclear threat.[18]

The outcome of the Korean War radically altered perceptions of China in the United States. Americans had to acknowledge grudgingly that China, which had fought them and their allies to a stalemate, was a formidable, independent power in the world. Soviet aid and backing had been significant but not decisive—Beijing could rightly claim that its successful defense of North Korea and its border was largely its own victory. A secret administration review of U.S. policy toward the Communist world, conducted during the final days of the Korean War, reflected this new estimate of China.

Eighteen top national security officials in June and July 1953 participated in this policy review, called Project Solarium after the White House room where Eisenhower had approved the project. They divided into three panels to examine alternative approaches to deal with the Soviets and, more broadly, the fundamental foreign policy orientation of the United States. After several weeks of study and deliberation, the panels presented their findings to the president. Eisenhower found the exercise immensely helpful and used the results to establish the direction of his diplomacy. The main conclusion of Project Solarium was that, with respect to the Soviet Union, the United States would largely continue the containment policies established by the Truman administration. The United States accepted the Soviet Union as a long-term challenge and would oppose Soviet expansionism firmly but not provocatively. The United States would not pursue the aggressive "rollback" or "liberation" strategy Eisenhower and Dulles promised during the presidential campaign.

Most influential in the final results was George Kennan's Panel A, whose 150-page report included an assessment of the China problem. Panel A concluded that the United States had lost "prestige in Asia vis-à-vis the Chinese Communists as a result of the Korean war." Moreover, the outlook for that part of the world was not good. China's emergent power threatened Southeast Asia and had widened the divisions among the Western nations. But interestingly, Panel A also noted that the West was not the only party disturbed about the Chinese. It was possible that China's growth in stature and independence from the Soviet Union was making Moscow uncomfortable. Panel A suggested that a tough policy toward China would create severe burdens for the regime and "perhaps even contribute to a serious split between Peiping and Moscow." But it still cautioned that "a Communist China, even independent of Moscow, predominant in the power equation in the Far East and attracting Asian support, is very much against our interest."[19]

This appreciation of China's significance had come a long way from Kennan's view in 1948. Where he had once dismissed China as relatively unimportant and saw the Soviet Union as the main danger to Asia, his Panel A now concluded that "the 'bipolarity' which distinguished the immediate post-hostilities period" was losing much of its rationale. The United States must face "a more complex and fluid international situation, in which many national entities are going to play an important part." It was clear that China was to be one of those important, and troubling, "national entities."[20]

III

Once Project Solarium was completed, the administration began to develop policy papers on specific trouble spots, such as Germany, Korea, and China. In November 1953 the National

President Truman meeting with Angus Ward (center), former consul general in Shenyang, and Secretary of State Dean Acheson at the White House, January 23, 1950. The Chinese detained Ward for months on various charges, including espionage. Photo courtesy Bettmann Newsphotos, Inc./United Press International.

President Truman conferring with (l. to r.) Under Secretary of State Robert Lovett and foreign policy advisers George F. Kennan and Charles E. Bohlen at the White House. Photo courtesy Bettmann Newsphotos, Inc./United Press International.

Zhou Enlai signing the Sino-Soviet Treaty of Friendship, Alliance, and Mutual Assistance in Moscow, February 14, 1950, as Stalin and Mao look on. Photo courtesy New China News Agency.

President-elect Eisenhower in Korea, eating with troops of the 15th Infantry Regiment, 3rd U.S. Infantry Division, December 4, 1952. Photo courtesy Dwight D. Eisenhower Library; U.S. Army.

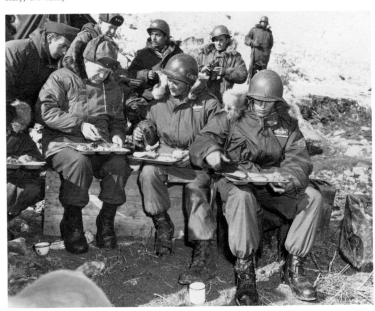

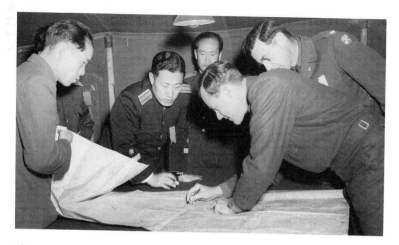

Chinese, North Korean, and American negotiators discussing the location of a ceasefire line, November 1951. Photo courtesy New China News Agency.

Chinese forces dismantling fortifications in the demilitarized zone after the ceasefire in Korea, 1953. Photo courtesy New China News Agency.

Secretary of State John Foster Dulles and President Eisenhower, Denver, Colorado, September 1954. The first offshore island crisis began on September 3. Photo courtesy Dwight D. Eisenhower Library.

PLA troops landing on Yijiang Island off the coast of Zhejiang, January 18, 1955, under naval, air, and artillery cover. Photo courtesy New China News Agency.

PLA troops landing on Yijiang Island, January 18, 1955. Photo courtesy New China News Agency.

The bombardment of Yijiang Island from the Chinese mainland, January 18, 1955. Photo courtesy New China News Agency.

Secretary of State John Foster Dulles and Representative James P. Richards, head of the House Foreign Affairs Committee, discussing the offshore islands crisis, January 24, 1955. Photo courtesy Wide World Photos, Inc./Associated Press.

Admiral Arthur W. Radford, chairman of the Joint Chiefs of Staff, and Assistant Secretary of State Walter Robertson following a meeting with President Eisenhower to brief him on their trip to Taiwan, May 5, 1955. Photo courtesy Dwight D. Eisenhower Library; National Park Service.

Left. Zhou Enlai (at right) and the Chinese delegation to the Bandung Conference, 1955. Photo courtesy New China News Agency. *Right.* Soviet Premier Nikolai Bulganin and President Eisenhower in Geneva, July 1955. Photo courtesy Bettmann Newsphotos, Inc./International Newsphotos.

Mao addressing Chinese students in Moscow, November 17, 1957. Photo courtesy New China News Agency.

Anastas Mikoyan   Mao Zedong   Oleg Rakhmanin   Nikolai Bulganin

Mao Zedong signing the final declaration of the Conference of Communist and Workers' Parties of the Socialist Countries, Moscow, November 14–16, 1957. Seated to Mao's right are Deng Xiaoping and Guo Moruo. The man standing at the far left appears to be Yang Shangkun. Photo courtesy New China News Agency.

Mao addressing the crowd welcoming the Chinese delegation to the fortieth anniversary of the October Revolution, Moscow, November 2, 1957. The banner on the building in the background reads "Long live the fortieth anniversary of the Great October Socialist Revolution." Photo courtesy New China News Agency.

Nikita Khrushchev   Mikhail Suslov   Song Qingling   Andrei Gromyko (?)   Yekaterina Furtseva   Ho Chiminh   Deng Xiaoping

Khrushchev and Mao signing the joint communiqué following meetings held July 31 to August 3, 1958, in Beijing. The Soviet delegation included Defense Minister Rodion Y. Malinovsky, Acting Foreign Minister Vasily V. Kuznetsov, and Boris N. Ponomarev. Standing in the rear behind Mao are (l. to r.) Zhu De, Liu Shaoqi, and Zhou Enlai. Photo courtesy New China News Agency.

Mao and Khrushchev at Zhongnanhai, the CCP Central Committee compound, Beijing, during the Sino-Soviet talks, July 31 to August 3, 1958. Seated between the two are (l. to r.) Zhu De, Deng Xiaoping, and Zhou Enlai. Photo courtesy New China News Agency.

Security Council started consideration of policy paper NSC 166/1, as it became known in its final form. NSC 166/1, the Eisenhower administration's first top-level paper on China, was consistent with much of the thinking contained in Dulles's letters to Chester Bowles. It stated that "the primary problem of United States foreign policy in the Far East is to cope with the altered structure of power which arises from the existence of a strong and hostile Communist China, and from the alliance of Communist China with the USSR," and called for both "weakening or at least retarding the growth of Chinese Communist power in China" and "impairing Sino-Soviet relations."[21]

In defining the challenge to the United States as a dual one, that of China itself and that of its alliance with the USSR, NSC 166/1 seemed to be ambiguous. Which would be the principal objective for the United States: weakening China or weakening the Sino-Soviet alliance? Actions to undermine Beijing, such as strengthening the Nationalist Chinese, military harassment, covert actions, or economic warfare, might only solidify Sino-Soviet relations. Conversely, actions to disrupt the Sino-Soviet alliance, such as trade inducements or overtures to draw China away from its partner, might help the Communists consolidate their rule.

But the contradiction was only apparent and not substantive for the administration. For the moment at least it believed there was no conflict between the twin goals of weakening China and damaging the Sino-Soviet alliance. Concessions would not necessarily moderate Chinese Communist hostility toward the United States and the West or help erode the Sino-Soviet alliance, cemented in common ideology and mutual interest. The ability to affect the relationship from "outside" was limited: "the potential dangers to the alliance will stem primarily from the inner workings of the partnership and only secondarily from the nature of external pressures or inducements."

NSC 166/1 sanctioned a policy of pressure on China, although it stopped short of advocating any attempt to overthrow the Beijing regime by U.S. forces or by the Nationalists. The position paper specifically directed the United States to maintain the security of the offshore islands, to prevent the territorial expansion of the Chinese Communists, to recognize and support the Chinese Nationalists, to strengthen noncommunist Asia, and to continue to exert overt as well as "unconventional and covert" pressures against China. It also called for employing "all feasible means, covert and overt, to impair Sino-Soviet relations," but as another NSC study had spelled out several months before, providing "an avenue of escape" from the Soviet relationship was "academic," since Beijing was not looking for one. The earlier NSC study had concluded that a policy of pressure would not conflict with trying either to encourage Beijing's "defection" from Moscow or to "overthrow" the regime. The objective was to impress on the Chinese that their ties with Moscow, far from bringing benefits, simply multiplied their hardships and sacrifices.[22]

The administration recognized that the Sino-Soviet relationship was a unique one, totally unlike that between the Soviet Union and the Eastern European nations. At the November 1953 meeting that discussed NSC 166/1, Allen Dulles, head of the CIA and John Foster Dulles's brother, reported that China was not a "satellite" of the Soviet Union, but "Moscow's only voluntary and genuine ally." He pointed out that there was no need for the Kremlin to exercise "direct control" because China "willingly follows the Soviet lead in foreign affairs." The elevated role of Mao in the international Communist movement since the death of Stalin in March 1953 and the recent Soviet acceptance of Beijing's clear authority over Manchuria and Xinjiang, along with other Russian concessions, convinced the CIA chief that no weakening of the relationship was in sight. Because of China's ability to extract concessions from the Soviet Union, there was almost no chance of Beijing's breaking with Moscow. "There was little prospect of Titoism in China," Allen Dulles conceded.[23] Previously, in 1949–50, many American officials had thought that China's vulnerability and deficiencies invited Soviet exploitation. The Kremlin would try to place China under its heel as it had the Eastern European countries, but Chinese nationalism and the desire for independence would clash with Soviet ambitions and a break would occur. Now, at the end of 1953, the NSC concluded that China's actual strength and its relatively independent status reinforced the bonds between the Communist countries and precluded a division for the time being.

The prospects discouraged the administration. Compared with previous assessments, NSC 166/1 was considerably less sanguine about achieving a turn of events in China favorable in the near term to the United States. Just a year and a half earlier, in February 1952, John Foster Dulles had encouraged the idea that Titoism was still possible in China, if only the United States pursued a tough line. "The essential thing," he had said publicly, "is to have action which will bring about a change."[24] But now the NSC avoided entertaining hopes for a defection of China from the Soviet Union, questioned the efficacy of efforts to split the two Communist countries, and only talked about "impairing Sino-Soviet relations."

The NSC paper did, however, contain perceptive and optimistic (for the United States) estimates of possible *future* long-term developments in Sino-Soviet relations. Further Chinese Communist success, the NSC study noted, would hurt the United States but might also produce "real concern" among the Russians. The NSC staff surmised that "the Russians could hardly view with equanimity the development of an independent China on [their] frontiers which was powerful, well armed, industrially competent, and politically united." China's success in extending its power in the Far East might actually "confront the Russians with a partner whose ambitions could be achieved at cost not to the West but to the Russians themselves." If the time came when the Chinese were "too independent and self reliant" for the Russians, and they interfered in Chinese affairs, the "alliance [would] be critically endangered." After all, the NSC staff reminded its readers, "the Chinese Communist leaders are Chinese as well as Communists."[25]

The NSC paper perceptively anticipated some of the actual future dynamics of the Sino-Soviet relationship and its later demise. The assumption during the Truman administration, impressed by the events in Yugoslavia, had been that an eventual Sino-Soviet split would occur because of Chinese desire to break away from the Soviets. But Eisenhower's NSC staff offered the novel idea that the Soviets might distance themselves from the Chinese because of Beijing's contentiousness.* If trends de-

---

*The removal of experienced China experts from Washington during the McCarthy period set back America's ability to deal with Asian problems intel-

veloped according to the NSC staff's analysis, the implications for Sino-U.S. relations as well as U.S.-Soviet relations would be profound. Might the United States have a certain stake in maintaining a Sino-Soviet bloc in order to thwart the more aggressive Chinese? Should the United States help build up a China that could threaten the Soviets? Or might the United States at some point even try to cooperate with the Soviets to control China?

IV

A big problem for the United States in the effective implementation of NSC 166/1 was that important friends, especially Britain, continued to follow a different policy toward China. Since 1949 London had held out hope for winning the CCP away from Moscow by "keeping a foot in the door." Even during the Korean conflict the divisions among the allies frustrated U.S. prosecution of the war. The British conducted limited trade with the Chinese throughout the conflict. "In general our object in the Far East," Anthony Eden told the cabinet, "must be to divide China and the Soviet Union." Not long after the end of the war, Britain and China resumed their efforts to establish full diplomatic relations.[26] The Japanese and Indians also did not fully agree with U.S. policy. The Japanese were interested in reopening trade with the mainland, traditionally their main overseas market and source of raw materials, and the Indians for the most part felt as the British did.

At a meeting of the heads of government of the United States, Great Britain, and France in Bermuda in mid-December 1953,

---

ligently. But, at least regarding the Sino-Soviet alliance, the administration's thinking as expressed in NSC 166/1 was consistent with that of one of the most prominent purged specialists, O. Edmund Clubb, the former U.S. consul general in Beijing. In a prescient essay written in late 1952, "'Titoism' and the Chinese Communist Regime," Clubb discounted the possibility of a break between China and the Soviet Union along the lines of the "Yugoslavia pattern." A split was inevitable, he believed, but it would be a broader, slower "Chinese-style" split, with the "independent evolution of China as a nation." As China grew in strength, it would demand more and more "authority" and respect for its policies and interests as a Communist power: the Soviet Union had to "prepare for an ultimate reckoning with China in Asia."

the deep differences separating the Western allies surfaced. During one session Dulles presented the administration's thinking about China and the Soviet Union to British Prime Minister Winston Churchill, Foreign Secretary Anthony Eden, and French Foreign Minister Georges Bidault. Dulles acknowledged that some strain in the Sino-Soviet relationship existed, but, he said, there were differences among the allies over how best to promote divisions among the Communists. He characterized the British view as one based on the old theory that by "being nice" to the Chinese Communists, the West could "wean them away from the Soviets." In contrast the United States believed that maximum pressure would most effectively strain the Sino-Soviet relationship. China would only have the "best of both worlds" if the West tried to compete with Russia "as to who would treat China best." Aware that Mao's stature as a Marxist-Leninist theoretician already challenged Soviet leaders, Dulles noted that the Soviet elevation of Mao to an "equal partner" in the international Communist movement since Stalin's death "may eventually give us an opportunity for promoting division between the Soviet Union and Communist China." For the time being, however, the allies should work in concert to ostracize China in the international community. A division might occur but only through united Western pressures, including a trade embargo. Finally, Dulles wanted the allies to know that the United States had been prepared to use nuclear weapons against China to end the Korean War and would employ them if fighting recurred. He concluded by defending America's support of the Nationalists on Taiwan as part of "the theory of exerting maximum strain causing the Chinese Communists to demand more from Russia and thereby placing additional stress on Russian-Chinese relations."[27]

Eden praised Dulles for his "masterly survey" and admitted that "it was a puzzling question to know how far we can by our actions help to foster a division of opinion between the Chinese Communists and the Russians." Differences might develop, he conceded, but it could take a long time. The Communists were "trying to divide the three of us [Britain, the United States, and France], just as we were trying to divide them." For that reason, Eden said, it might not be wise to break off all contacts with the Chinese, including a certain amount of trade. He ended by expressing discomfort with the U.S. tendency to regard nuclear weapons as "conventional." Eden implied that U.S. China policy was reckless and too easily discounted China's defense ties with the Soviets.[28]

Indeed U.S. policy appeared contradictory. Washington condemned international communism as the source of the world's problems, yet in its tough China policy it seemed to minimize the solidarity of the Sino-Soviet alliance. The U.S. decision to use nuclear weapons against China if there was new fighting in Korea, or if China openly intervened against the French in Vietnam, did not seem to take Soviet reaction seriously.[29] Sensing the distress of his European friends, Eisenhower tried to clarify the U.S. position on nuclear weapons. First of all, the United States would not be irresponsible in the use of these weapons, but the allies had to understand that his administration had great budgetary problems to worry about. There was strong domestic sentiment favoring reductions in military expenditures. If the United States was to supply the needed manpower in Korea and elsewhere, it had to include atomic weapons in its contingency planning. The American people had spent billions of dollars to develop the atomic bomb, and they would expect it to be used if the Communists renewed their aggression in Korea. The others must realize, Eisenhower argued awkwardly, that "any prior decision that did not recognize the need for using what we had in a limited military situation would work for our discomfiture." In any case, said Eisenhower, they "should not allow [themselves] to be cramped by trying to guess exactly what Russia would do."[30]

Eisenhower's worry about the budget and his inattention to the Soviet commitments to the Chinese did little to calm the British. The differences over China policy were never resolved and remained a constant irritant for the administration. Domestic critics cited the division with the British as a reason to modify U.S. policy and bring it in line with world opinion. Even for some in the administration, it appeared that the current policy was more successful in encouraging divisions among the Western allies than in driving a wedge between China and the Soviet Union.[31] These foreign and domestic sentiments made it difficult for the United States to maintain a rigid policy of pressure.

V

While the division with friends pushed the United States toward moderating its China policy, developments in its relationship with its main enemy, the Soviet Union, worked to the opposite effect. Evolving U.S.-Soviet relations sustained the administration's belief in the effectiveness of its policy of pressure on China as a means of straining the Communist alliance.

Stalin's death in March 1953 marked the end of an era in U.S.-Soviet relations, although Washington was not immediately hopeful about the implications of the dictator's passing. During an NSC meeting Eisenhower and Vice-President Richard Nixon agreed with John Foster Dulles that the world situation "might very well be worse after Stalin's death." Eisenhower said he was convinced that Stalin "would have preferred an easing of the tension between the Soviet Union and the Western powers" following World War II, but hard-line elements in the Politburo "had insisted on heightening the tempo of the Cold War."[32]

Nevertheless top officials in the Eisenhower administration went into action to develop plans to exploit Stalin's death. Dulles urged that the United States play up nationalism among the satellite countries. "Nationalism," he told the NSC, "is the great theme to be developed as the means of breaking down the Stalinist structure." Charles Bohlen focused on the Sino-Soviet relationship as most vulnerable, since Beijing had more opportunity for independent action than the Eastern European nations. Bohlen was convinced that Mao would "most certainly not accept willingly any subordinate role" in ideology to Georgi M. Malenkov, the apparent new Soviet leader. Going still further, Harold Stassen, director of Mutual Security for Eisenhower, composed a long list of ploys, including "dirty tricks," that the United States might adopt to exploit the Soviet Union's vulnerability. He suggested that a visit to Mao by a prominent American newspaper publisher "will cause uneasiness in both the USSR and China." More darkly, he recommended that Washington "covertly arrange" to spawn speculations around the world that "Mao Tse Tung will be the first one liquidated by Malenkov," followed by other Communist leaders.[33]

Before the United States was able to follow through on these proposals, though, Moscow took the offensive and adopted a new public attitude toward the West. On March 15 Malenkov declared that there were no existing disputes between the United States and the Soviet Union that could not be decided by peaceful means, on the basis of mutual understanding. Malenkov's speech was the beginning of a "peace offensive," which Washington later called the Soviet "new look." (This is not to be confused with Eisenhower's own "new look" in foreign policy that emphasized economy in military spending combined with a liberal use of the nuclear threat to deter enemies.) The United States was skeptical of Soviet sincerity but wanted to encourage the moderate tone from Moscow. A few weeks after Malenkov's speech, Eisenhower responded with a speech of his own, entitled "A Chance for Peace." Speaking before the American Society of Newspaper Editors, the president conjured up a vision of a world in which the United States and the Soviet Union would not have to squander their resources on armaments but would live in peace. Eisenhower called for discussions with the Soviets to settle disputes between the two countries and to explore ways to limit the arms race. Though both of these speeches were largely propaganda directed toward world public opinion, the two heads of state had signaled their interest in a new relationship, even as American and Chinese soldiers continued to shoot at each other in the hills of Korea in the last months of the war. As Eisenhower recalled, after Stalin's death "a major preoccupation of my mind throughout 1953 was the development of approaches to the Soviet leaders that might be at least a start toward the birth of mutual trust founded in cooperative effort."[34]

The conclusion of the Korean War in late July allowed the United States and the Soviet Union to pursue their mutual efforts more freely. By the end of the year the Soviets called for a four-power summit conference to discuss the problems of

Korea, Germany, and Austria. The United States welcomed the proposal, and in late January 1954 the secretary of state and the foreign ministers of the Soviet Union, Great Britain, and France met in Berlin for four weeks. The occasion provided Dulles an opportunity to investigate at first hand the new Soviet attitude toward the United States. But what especially piqued his interest was the Soviets' apparent discomfort about their ally to the east, China.

Right at the start of the Berlin summit, Molotov proposed including China in a five-power conference to settle Far Eastern questions. Outraged by this suggestion, Dulles responded with some of his most vituperative condemnations ever of Communist China:

Who is this Chou En-lai whose addition to our circle would make possible all that so long seemed impossible? He is the leader of a regime which gained *de facto* power on the China mainland through bloody war, which has liquidated millions of Chinese; . . . which so diverts the economic resources of its impoverished people to military efforts that they starve by millions; which became an open aggressor in Korea and was so adjudged by the United Nations; which promotes open aggression in Indochina by training and equipping the aggressors and supplying them with vast amounts of war munitions. Such is the man Mr. Molotov urges would enable the world to solve all its problems and to gain lasting peace and mounting prosperity.[35]

China, according to Dulles, was simply "evil."[36]

Molotov was not put off. He injected the China issue into virtually every item of discussion during the long conference, as well as in private conversations with Dulles. In one talk with the secretary of state, Molotov advised Washington to drop its "bankrupt" policy and recognize China. The United States was simply forcing China closer to the Soviet Union, "which was not to United States advantage." Dulles probably wondered whether Molotov was sincere and trying to unload China or merely dabbling in "reverse psychology." Although Dulles had expected Molotov to promote China's cause at Berlin, the intensity of the Soviet effort startled the U.S. delegation.[37]

Interestingly, the United States interpreted the Soviets' persistence on China not as an indication of well-being in the Sino-Soviet relationship, but as a sign of possible trouble. Eisenhower's close friend C. D. Jackson, the editor of *Fortune* magazine, and a Cold War specialist who attended the Berlin meeting, reported to the president that "Molotov's solicitude for the social standing of his ally went well beyond the call of either friendship or expediency. For the first time since the war—in fact, since 1918—the Russian Soviets have to look over their shoulders at 400 million Chinese when they are negotiating with the West, and this may have important implications." Jackson, who had been interested in China for years, surmised that the Chinese Communists would not be pleased "at the lack of performance on the part of their Russian ally, which always advertised itself as almost omnipotent."[38]

Dulles ultimately arrived at a similar conclusion. In private talks during the conference, he had urged the Soviets to restrain the Chinese, cautioning them that Chinese recklessness would benefit neither the United States nor the Soviet Union. But on his return Dulles told Eisenhower that he was "not at all certain as to the degree of influence which the Soviets can exert on this situation [in Asia]" or about how effective the Soviets might be as an intermediary between the United States and the Chinese. Dulles told the NSC that one of "the most interesting aspects" of the Berlin meeting was what was learned about the relationship between the two Communist powers: the Soviet anxiety about China was quite apparent. The Soviets, he believed, wanted to avoid a major war but feared China could set one off and thus had to be restrained "by persuasion and by economic pressures." Evidently, all was not well between the Communist giants. As C. D. Jackson put it, the "Soviet rulers haven't even begun to chew the Chinese mouthful, let alone swallow it—but they know they've got something big and tough in their mouths, something that may prove troublesome."[39]

These observations reinforced the administration's approach toward straining the Sino-Soviet alliance. The Soviets, it seemed, already displayed signs of indigestion. By ostracizing China internationally, the United States could keep force-feeding the Soviets an unpalatable diet. Eisenhower soon approved plans for secret CIA operations to "impair relations between the USSR and Communist China," activities that were conducted throughout the entire Eisenhower administration. Most of the information about these activities, which at least involved operations in Tibet and North China, is still classified.[40]

The Berlin Conference reached agreement on little, except to convene an international conference at Geneva on April 26, 1954, to discuss Korea and Indochina. All the parties involved, including China, would participate. The United States disliked the idea of a conference but consented in deference to its allies, especially the French, who hoped a conference would help extricate them from Indochina. In agreeing to be present, the United States made explicit it was not moving toward recognition of Beijing.

John Foster Dulles's famous refusal to shake the hand of Premier Zhou Enlai at Geneva symbolized American animosity toward the CCP.* Dulles certainly detested the Chinese Communists, but his action was not due simply to personal revulsion. The administration was sensitive to the charges of domestic conservatives that Geneva was a "Far Eastern Munich" (recalling the British capitulation to Hitler's demands in 1938), and Dulles, during his brief visit to the conference, wanted to ensure that no one mistakenly concluded that the United States was selling out noncommunist Asia or changing its China policy. The right wing believed that Dulles, because he had not "unleashed" Chiang, inadequately backed the Nationalist cause. A photograph of Dulles and Zhou shaking hands would have certainly given the wrong impression. But Dulles's refusal to acknowledge the presence of the Chinese at Geneva did not mean he neglected studying the relationships among the Communist representatives. On the contrary: he closely watched for rifts among them. Dulles may also have had the Soviets in mind when he snubbed Zhou. According to the recollection of his sister, Eleanor Lansing Dulles, the secretary of state was concerned with how the Soviets, not the American press, might use a photo of him shaking hands with Zhou. The Soviets had doctored previous pictures of Eisenhower and Soviet leaders for use in the Soviet bloc, and Dulles feared they might similarly use photos of him to create confusion about U.S. policy toward China.[41]

---

*There is some question whether such an incident ever occurred. The various accounts of it are discussed in note 41, pp. 318–21.

The Geneva Conference produced mixed results. No solution was found for the stalemated Korea problem, since neither China nor the United States was in a mood or position to compromise. Dulles returned home on May 5, and the United States withdrew from active participation in the Indochina portion of the conference. But the dramatic surrender of the French garrison at Dienbienphu to the Communist Viet Minh on May 7, and with it the collapse of the French in Indochina, made a peace accord almost inevitable. On July 21 representatives of China, the Soviet Union, France, Britain, Cambodia, Laos, and North Vietnam signed agreements that ended seven and a half years of war in Southeast Asia, recognized the sovereignty of Cambodia, Laos, and Vietnam, and divided Vietnam as a step toward future national elections. The United States and South Vietnam refused to be signatories.

The outcome of the conference deeply upset Washington. The Western allies had bickered throughout the meeting and strained their relations. Further Communist advances were confirmed. For China, on the other hand, Geneva was a grand success. Its southern border was secured, its skill in diplomacy acknowledged, and Washington's policy of isolating it punctured. A *People's Daily* editorial of July 22 exulted, "The international status of the People's Republic of China as one of the big world powers has gained universal recognition."[42]

VI

Dulles's uncompromising anticommunist performance at Geneva did not placate conservatives at home. The right wing of the Republican Party was becoming alarmed at China's growing world importance and suspected the administration was not doing enough to oppose the Communists. On July 1 Senate Majority Leader William F. Knowland announced that if China were admitted to the United Nations, he would resign as majority leader to devote his full efforts to ending U.S. membership in it. Dulles assured the public that the United States would keep Red China out of the United Nations. But persistent high-level interest in dividing the Sino-Soviet alliance continued to make conservatives uneasy about the direction of the administration's China policy.

The right-wing viewpoint was well expressed by one of the country's most prominent Korean War heroes, General James A. Van Fleet, who at the request of Eisenhower led a high-level mission in mid-1954 to evaluate the American military assistance programs in Korea, Taiwan, Japan, and the Philippines. The top secret report he submitted to the president after his several-month tour was highly critical. "United States leadership in the Far East," he wrote, "has fallen far short of the need. We now find ourselves on the defensive, militarily and diplomatically, and our position rapidly deteriorating." American policies "are pointing toward ultimate defeat" at the hands of the "relentless march of Communist power." The Chinese Communist regime was the Kremlin's "chosen instrument" to conquer Asia, Van Fleet wrote, and though Moscow was the fundamental danger, China for the next several years would be a "greater menace to the Free World than the Soviet Union itself" because of the probability of Chinese aggression. Van Fleet stopped short of recommending an immediate declaration of war against China, but he was convinced that the United States would have to destroy communism there eventually. The United States failed to seize the opportunities offered by the Korean and Indochinese wars to take the fight to China, he lamented, but the United States must now be prepared "to strike back and seize that strategic opportunity" when Chinese Communist aggression again presented itself. America's nuclear arsenal would deter Soviet intervention in "subtracting" China from the Communist orbit. Van Fleet was certain the fight with China was not far off.[43]

Many members of John Foster Dulles's Policy Planning Staff roundly rejected these views. The PPS was now headed by Robert Bowie, a Dulles appointee, fellow Princeton graduate, and foreign affairs specialist from Harvard. Bowie was a moderate Republican who favored a "soft" policy on China to try to split the Sino-Soviet alliance. It was widely known that Dulles was very close to Bowie and respected his judgment. In early 1956, over vehement conservative opposition, Dulles promoted Bowie to assistant secretary of state.[44] Another of the PPS dissidents was Louis J. Halle, a researcher who went on to become a distinguished historian. Halle strongly disagreed with the "closed door" strategy toward China as the way to undermine the Sino-Soviet bloc. When he retired in July 1954 after thirteen years in the State Department, he wrote Dulles a long evaluation of U.S. foreign policy that included a sharp reproach about the line on China. Halle charged that U.S. policy was strengthening and solidifying the Communist bloc while disrupting U.S. relations with the rest of the free world. Washington was giving no alternative to Beijing except "what must be at best an onerous dependence on Moscow, and thereby [easing] what must be a principal anxiety and dilemma of our rival policy-makers in the Kremlin." Halle rejected the argument that pressure would erode the "Moscow-Peiping marriage." History showed that pressure solidified coalitions; they disintegrated only when the common threat was removed. Look at the experience of the West and the Soviet Union during World War II, he pointed out. Halle called for steps toward negotiation with Beijing.[45]

What particularly infuriated conservatives was news that Dulles's close friend and former law partner Arthur Dean, who had been Eisenhower's special ambassador to the Panmunjom armistice talks in Korea, wanted a review of U.S. policy toward China. A press leak in early 1954 revealed that Dean favored trying to drive a wedge between Beijing and Moscow, perhaps using trade as a device. Dean was quoted as saying that while he would like to see Chiang Kai-shek back on the mainland, those who pinned their hopes on him were looking at the China problem "through rosy glasses." "In our own tough, realistic self-interest," Dean ventured, "we ought to try on another pair."[46]

Although Dean did not advocate recognizing Beijing, he still came under vicious attacks from the Nationalists' congressional supporters. Herman Welker took the floor of the Senate to accuse Dean of promoting the same excuse about dividing the Communist giants long used by "pro–Red China apologists in the State Department." Welker demanded to know whether Dean spoke "with the blessing of the Secretary of State or the President of the United States," since Assistant Secretary of State Walter Robertson and Admiral Arthur Radford, chairman of the Joint Chiefs of Staff, were known not to support such heresy. The State Department denied that China policy was under review, and Dulles privately assured Knowland that Dean did not favor the recognition of China or its acceptance in the United Nations. Dean, though, never retracted his views; indeed he went on to develop his critique of China policy and the U.S. approach to the Sino-Soviet alliance in an article in *Foreign Affairs*, which appeared at the high point of the Jinmen-Mazu offshore island crisis in April 1955.[47]

Dean, in fact, was a member of a semiofficial study group that was extensively discussing what could be done about dividing China and the Soviet Union. Organized by the Council on Foreign Relations (CFR), an elite group of government officials, business leaders, and academic specialists, and the most important nongovernmental body concerned with foreign policy, the group included such prominent figures as W. Averell Harriman, Dean Rusk, John J. McCloy, John D. Rockefeller III, Chester Bowles, Robert Amory, Jr., of the CIA, Robert Bowie, and General L. L. Lemnitzer. For more than a year, from late 1953 to early 1955, as these men met to examine the state of American-Soviet relations, they could not avoid giving attention to the Sino-Soviet alliance and U.S. China policy.[48]

The study group confronted such questions as how much weight to give to the possibility of a weakening or a rupture of the Chinese-Soviet alliance in the formulation of China policy; whether the United States could influence such a rupture and if so how; and what the U.S. might do to contribute to the overthrow of the Chinese Communist regime. Holding out little hope for Chiang's return to the mainland, the group specifically discussed the respective merits of a "hard" and "soft" policy toward undermining the Sino-Soviet alliance. It doubted that either approach would be very effective, even though the group detected broad areas of potential problems between the two countries. "Separating Chinese from Soviet power" was nevertheless a "desirable good," noted a subgroup on Asia headed by Dean and including Bowles and Rockefeller.[49]

Even as the CFR study group questioned Washington's ability to weaken the ties between Beijing and Moscow, members of the administration were giving attention to how the United States might effectively use trade as a weapon to divide the two Communist states, just as Dean had suggested and conservatives feared. The idea of trying to pry China away from the Soviet Union remained attractive, despite the administration's commitment to a policy of pressure. A hint of this interest appeared in a major State Department study on the Sino-Soviet relationship issued on the eve of the Geneva Conference.[50] The paper focused on the potential sources of differences between the two countries.

The State Department expressed confidence that the Sino-Soviet alliance faced far greater potential problems than did the alliance between the United States and Great Britain. Despite Beijing's "ideological fanaticism," which played a "critical role in the obeisance of Peiping to Moscow," there were a number of problem areas. Competition for power, border frictions, and "doctrinal differences" all might at some point create difficulties. The most likely source of important Sino-Soviet differences, though, lay in "Communist China's need for industrial and technical services," given that modernization was one of the country's most important objectives.

True, Western controls on trade with China helped make its "dependence on the USSR the more complete," and this tended to "maximize Moscow's inadequacies and Peiping's dissatisfaction therewith and temptation to seek alternative sources in the West or Japan." But as trade patterns between China and the Soviet Union became set, and China's economy became dependent on Russian industrial techniques, technology, and equipment, it would be increasingly difficult for Beijing to turn to other sources for its economic needs. In addition the frictions caused by China's dependence on Moscow were eased by other advantages Moscow and Beijing gained from their economic link. The study's implication was that the closed-door strategy of division was having only a qualified success in splitting the two Communist powers.

In a mid-April 1954 NSC meeting Eisenhower himself introduced the idea of using the lure of trade with the West to fracture the Sino-Soviet bloc. Dulles was in Europe, but all the other major figures in the administration were present. During a discussion of Far East policy, Eisenhower asked Admiral Radford whether the JCS had developed "any views as to the efficacy of certain kinds of trade as a means of straining the existing relationship between Communist China and the Soviet Union." Apart from trade, the president said, he "could discern no other effective means of weakening the tie between these two nations." Eisenhower had raised this thought in the NSC a year earlier.[51]

Radford, we may assume, was opposed to the idea. Like the China Lobby he favored finding a way to eliminate Communist China from the face of the earth. Radford believed it was hopeless even to try to split Beijing and Moscow, but he avoided directly answering Eisenhower's question, merely mumbling that splitting China away from Russia was "a very long-range objective." Secretary of Defense Charles E. Wilson was less careful and openly challenged Eisenhower's proposal. He was not adverse to figuring out how to undermine the Sino-Soviet alliance, he said, but the problem was that the United States was "indirectly waging war against Communist China," refusing to recognize the regime, opposing its presence in the United Nations, and supporting Chiang Kai-shek. At that very moment, he noted, Dulles was trying to rally the allies to prevent the military victory of the Communists in Southeast Asia. How could the United States even consider trade with China under such circumstances? The inconsistency of Eisenhower's suggestion with current U.S. China policy appeared as self-evident to Wilson as Wilson's obtuseness probably seemed to Eisenhower.

Eisenhower, who frequently suggested expanded trade as a way to solve a host of international problems, impatiently rebuffed Wilson's criticism. What he had in mind was not trade with the regime, but trade with "the people," he said. "If we opened up trade the whole population of China would benefit and might actually be induced to upset the ruling Communist clique." Moreover, if the United States sold everyday goods the ordinary Chinese wanted but the Soviets could not provide, it would be "good psychological warfare." Allen Dulles interrupted to report that the CIA at that moment was preparing a study on "ways and means of creating and exploiting friction between China and Russia." Eisenhower said that was exactly what he had in mind. Sending the Chinese people "supplies of food and clothing would be a very good means."[52]

Vice-President Nixon now chimed in to support Eisenhower: why couldn't they use trade as a negotiating point with the Chinese? The United States had not recognized the Soviet regime for over fifteen years but still traded with them. Nixon suggested that a "hard-headed study" should be made on what could be done with trade if China changed some of its ways. But Wilson returned to Eisenhower's point about trading with "the Chinese people." How could such a thing be done, considering that Beijing controlled all commerce?

The president, apparently in all seriousness, responded that he "would let the Chinese junks sail over to Japan and fill up with everything they could buy. That's the best way to influence the Chinese people against their Communist government." Not surprisingly, Wilson remained unconvinced by Eisenhower's naïve plan. He pointed out that the Chinese Communists would be all too happy to buy everything they needed for their war machine. Secretary of the Treasury George Humphrey ended the dispute for the moment by asking what seemed to be an obvious question. Was the United States giving up the effort to destroy the Chinese Communist regime, or was it now willing to accept the PRC's existence and focus on trying to separate it from Moscow? In Humphrey's opinion this question had to be answered before more specific actions were considered, including even whether the United States should continue to support the Nationalists. No one replied to Humphrey's blunt query.[53]

The dispute in the NSC over China and trade had to wait until the conclusion of the Geneva Conference, which had acknowledged further Communist success in Asia and elevated the status of China in world affairs. In light of these new realities, the administration began a review of its policies for the Far East. Eisenhower expected the process to be a short one, taking a few weeks at most. But the final result involved almost five months of wrangling, during which the NSC became bitterly divided, the chief of staff of the Army argued for preserving Chinese military power to forestall Soviet expansionism, the usually decisive John Foster Dulles hesitated to make policy, and the chairman of the JCS insinuated that recommendations by the secretary of state would lay the groundwork for the loss of Taiwan, Japan, and the whole of Asia to the Communists. The stage for this drama was the discussion of policy paper NSC 5429, "United States Policy in the Far East."[54]

As first drafted by the NSC Planning Board on August 4, 1954, NSC 5429 confronted four challenges: the offshore islands, general political and economic measures for the Far East, Southeast Asia, and Communist China. The board anticipated that the question of China would be most controversial and presented four alternatives for the NSC to consider. These ranged from a "soft" position of admitting China to the United Nations and recognizing it as the government of the mainland to an extreme hard line of "rolling back" Chinese influence. While the NSC reached agreement on most of the draft paper during its first discussion on August 12, the sections on China pleased no one. The NSC had to extend its deliberations to the following week.[55]

At that meeting the differences on China policy erupted into the open. The spark was a paper Army Chief of Staff Matthew Ridgway circulated to the NSC listing his own objections to NSC 5429 and the position of other JCS members. Ridgway, who had replaced Douglas MacArthur in Korea after Truman sacked the temperamental general, rejected the draft as woefully inadequate, charging that it omitted placing the problem of the Far East in a global perspective. It seemed "axiomatic" that "one principal objective" of U.S. policy "should be to split Communist China from the Soviet Bloc"; none of the four alternatives listed in the position paper directly addressed that goal. If the United States wanted to split China and the Soviet Union, Ridgway argued, it should

bring Red China to a realization that its long-range benefits derive from friendliness with America, not with the USSR, which casts acquisitive eyes on its territory and resources; that these benefits could reasonably be expected *in time*, if Red China would mend its ways, abjure its offensively aggressive actions toward the West, and take steps to remove the stigma of "aggressor" with which it is now branded.

Ridgway audaciously suggested the United States had a certain interest in preserving China's military capability! "I would regard the destruction of [China's military power] as inimical to the long-range interests of the United States," he wrote. "It would result in the creation of a power vacuum into which but one other nation could move, namely Soviet Russia."[56]

Following the reading of Ridgway's paper to the stunned NSC, Dulles added his comments about the China problem. The PRC's situation was currently "very intricate," with its relations with other countries changing daily. For example, the "shifting relations" between China and the Soviet Union were "so delicate as to make them extremely hard to appreciate." Moreover, the allies and the "mood of the rest of the free world toward Communist China" had changed in recent months, a shift that the United States had to consider. In fact the entire problem of China, Dulles admitted, required "a great deal more thought." Dulles hesitated to be explicit and wanted the NSC to postpone a decision, but his comments suggested that he was not averse to considering a moderation of U.S. policy toward China. And then, undoubtedly to the shock of those present, Secretary of State Dulles stated that "there was much value in the comments of General Ridgway."[57]

Admiral Radford, chairman of the JCS, completely rejected Ridgway's and Dulles's views. The Sino-Soviet alliance "was something religious in nature," Radford scoffed, and he doubted the possibility of ever breaking it. "We had been trying to do precisely this ever since 1950, and with very scant success." The admiral feared for the future of the whole of Asia, warning that "if China continued to be Communist and continued to increase its power," Japan and the rest of the Far East would have to capitulate and fall to communism. With or without the support of the European allies, Radford saw no choice but eventual war with China. During discussions about the fighting in Southeast Asia earlier in the year, Radford had wanted the United States to use the opportunity to launch a war, using nuclear weapons, against "the source of the peril" in Asia, China.[58]

Eisenhower immediately interjected to say he was in "complete agreement with everything that Admiral Radford had said." In the president's view "it was hopeless to imagine that we could break China away from the Soviets and from Communism short of some great cataclysm." In any case the United States should not count on such a split, although jealousies would probably spring up when the two dictatorships grew too large. In his enthusiasm for Radford Eisenhower apparently completely forgot his earlier musings about using trade with "the Chinese people" to create problems for the Communist countries. He was now impatient with such talk. Moreover, he was especially short with Ridgway's opinion that destroying the military power of China was not in the interests of the United States. That idea, Eisenhower said later in the discussion, "scared the hell out of him." Dulles did not defend Ridgway, but he wanted to make sure that the NSC did not abandon all thoughts of dividing China and the Soviets. Responding to the president, Dulles said that China and Russia would in the end "split apart because of the pressure of basic historical forces and because the religious decline of Communism would have died down. . . . The Chinese were very proud of their own history, and Chinese did not like Russians. In the end, therefore, they would split apart." The problem, said Dulles, was whether the West could hold out for a split that might take place over the next twenty-five years. "Could we afford to wait that long for a split between these two enemies?"[59] Dulles at least was consistent with what he had put forth in the past.

Finally Vice-President Nixon presented his opinion. He was not sympathetic to Radford's extremism, contrary to his reputation as a Chiang stalwart. Nixon's actual views were more sophisticated. Earlier in the year in Hong Kong, he had told the British colonial governor that the West should be patient with China and impressed the British official with his moderation. On his return from the Far East, Nixon told other administration officials that trying to overthrow the Beijing regime had little chance and that trade with China was inevitable. He also recommended that the United States tell Chiang that he should not try to go back to the mainland but should concentrate instead on constructing Taiwan as a center of overseas Chinese culture.[60] Now, in the NSC meeting, Nixon agreed with Dulles that more thought had to be given to China policy since "China was the key to Asia." Nixon said he personally rejected the "soft" policy of the British and some Americans who advocated recognition, full trade, and the PRC's admission to the United

Nations as the way to make Mao into a Tito. This sort of appeasement would not produce a split but only ensure the Chinese Communists' domination of Asia. But Nixon also rejected the conclusion that the only alternative to "appeasement" was war, as Radford had maintained. Nixon told the NSC there was "an area of action in between war and appeasement" that ought to be explored, "on the basis that in the long run Soviet Russia and Communist China can and must be split apart." In the long run a policy of what he called "tough coexistence" might be the best method of driving a wedge between China and Soviet Russia. Although he did not elaborate, Nixon's message was that the United States should accept the PRC as a more or less permanent fact. That did not require U.S. friendship or conciliation, but neither did it assume war, even as the United States actively contained China.[61]

Eisenhower was not persuaded by either Dulles or Nixon, and directed the NSC to come to a decision. The president endorsed the JCS majority's aggressive policy statement urging the United States to "reduce the power of Communist China in Asia even at the risk of, but without deliberately provoking war." Phrased in another way, this statement seemed to sanction an aggressive policy even if it led to unintentional war. The United States was to "react with immediate, positive, armed force against any belligerent move by Communist China." The statement was a significant escalation from NSC 166/1, the administration's earlier position. Under Eisenhower's leadership the NSC adopted the JCS view as an interim position, labeling the new policy NSC 5429/2. Though the NSC retained the goal of impairing Sino-Soviet relations, no specifics were given on how this was to be accomplished. But because of Dulles's hesitations the NSC agreed that he should present a full exposition of his views at another meeting within a month. Further consideration of policy was to be based on that discussion.[62]

Events, though, delayed the NSC's final decision. Two weeks after the acceptance of NSC 5429/2, a crisis erupted in the Taiwan Strait. The offshore crisis, discussed in the next chapter, forced the United States to back away from the provocative implications of the "rollback" philosophy of NSC 5429/2 and return to a view that was closer to Nixon's "tough coexistence" and Dulles's "policy of pressure."

The final NSC position on NSC 5429, which the president signed in late December 1954, dropped the JCS's "rollback" idea of risking war with China to reduce its power in Asia. While the NSC still committed the United States to an intransigent policy of nonrecognition, it explicitly acknowledged the value of possible negotiations with China and the Soviet Union to resolve "individual issues" or even "a general settlement of major issues." The new position totally infuriated Assistant Secretary of State Robertson, who charged that it contradicted the basic national security policy of the country.[63]

The NSC paper also viewed China as a relatively discrete problem, whatever Beijing's orientation toward the Soviets. The NSC decided that the United States should expose to the people of Asia not only the danger of "world Communism" but also the "menace of Chinese imperialism." At the same time it held out hope for a possible rupture between Beijing and Moscow. The NSC agreed to try to disrupt the Communist alliance by encouraging Sino-Soviet differences and conflicts.[64] But the question, as usual, was how: what could Washington actually do to encourage Communist discord?

An NSC meeting on December 1, 1954, revealed the depth of the divisions among policymakers over how to disrupt the Sino-Soviet alliance, even as China pressed the offshore crisis. Would the United States follow an "open" or "closed" door policy toward Beijing? Eisenhower again raised his idea about detaching China from the Soviet Union. Had anyone in the intelligence community foreseen Tito's break with the Soviet Union? he asked. Such things sometimes happened quite unexpectedly, the president said, and he wanted to make sure the NSC did not rule out such a turn of events in China. Secretary of Commerce Sinclair Weeks turned the discussion to the particular problem of trade with China. He pointed out the inconsistencies in the current U.S. position: the United States maintained a complete embargo on China but traded with the Soviet Union, except for goods of a strategic or military value. Since the Soviets had extensive commercial relations with China, the Chinese presumably could get from them whatever they received from the West. Furthermore the embargo was causing conflicts with the allies. The British and other Europeans were liberalizing their trade restrictions with Communist countries. Many Japanese interested in resuming their commerce with the mainland were also resentful of the U.S. embargo. There was good reason to doubt both the effectiveness and the wisdom of the embargo.[65]

Weeks thought that the NSC tended to look at the Soviet Union and China as a "single unit," and that it was of two, quite different minds about undermining the Sino-Soviet alliance. One group in the NSC "wished to maximize China's dependence on Russia as a means of destroying their close relationship," while the other, which seemed to be in the minority, "desired to minimize China's dependence on Russia to the same end." To force the resolution of this division, Weeks proposed that the NSC examine two sharply contrasting policies toward China. One would recognize "two Chinas," permit Beijing to join the United Nations, and place trade with China on the same basis as the European Soviet bloc. Harold Stassen, now the director of Foreign Operations, spoke in favor of relaxing restrictions, even though a few months earlier he had attacked as fallacious the idea that the West could ever woo China away from the Soviets. Weeks's alternative proposal was to force other countries to stop trade with China completely and further limit commerce with the European Communist countries. Those measures would make China's draining dependency on the Soviets all the more complete. The Defense Department and the JCS supported the hard-line proposal.[66]

Dulles favored neither alternative. He believed the first would lead to disaster and the second would be impossible to implement. Both he and the president agreed that the United States might have to modify its opposition to trade with China, considering the pressures from other countries. The differences between the United States and its allies over China were so great that the United States, according to the CIA, faced isolation in the United Nations and increasing trouble in carrying out its Far Eastern policies. Dulles informed the NSC that the United States had to accept the possibility of revising U.S. trade policy to hold the Western alliance together. Dulles eventually won out; just as he had earlier rejected the two extremes of "appeasement" and "inevitable war" in favor of an adjusted policy of pressure, so he rejected Weeks's extremes on trade policy. The United States would keep the door essentially closed to China but permit some flexibility to respond to the trade policies of other countries. The United States could not alienate its friends in its effort to split its enemies.[67]

A few days before Christmas Day 1954, Dulles and Eisenhower chatted about the future of China and its relationship with the Soviets. Dulles thought that the "long-range prospects" for change in China favorable to the United States would come either from "the traditional tendency of the Chinese to be individualistic" or from "the traditional Chinese dislike of foreigners"; that dislike was bound in the long run to impair relations with Russia. The day before Dulles had told the NSC that China would inevitably take an increasingly independent line from the Soviet Union and the United States should be confident that the future would bring the splintering of the Communist bloc. Eisenhower wondered under what conditions the United States could begin to change its policy toward Beijing.[68]

The challenge for Eisenhower and Dulles was to find a way to maintain the pressure and encourage conditions that would help realize those "long-range prospects." The immediate problem, though, was to end the volatile offshore island crisis. Examining the way the United States handled the crisis reveals how the administration tried to implement its policy of pressure on Beijing, and also the serious limitations and dangers inherent in that policy.

FOUR

To the Nuclear Brink

Victory goes to him who can keep his nerve to the last fifteen
minutes.   —John Foster Dulles, 1956

The Korean War had barely been over a year before the United States confronted the possibility of renewed
hostilities with the People's Republic of China. On September 3,
1954, while Secretary of State Dulles was in Manila making
final arrangements for the establishment of the anticommunist
military pact known as the Southeast Asia Treaty Organization (SEATO), Chinese Communist coastal batteries opened up
on Jinmen, one of the small Nationalist-held islands off the
coast of the mainland. Acting Secretary of Defense Robert Anderson warned President Eisenhower that the intensity of the
shelling seemed a prelude to an all-out assault. Over the next
nine months the United States, in supporting the Nationalists'
stubborn defense of these islands, lurched toward disaster—in
Eisenhower's own recollection the crisis almost caused a "split
between the United States and nearly all its allies" and seemingly carried the country to the "edge of war."[1] In fact the crisis
was even more serious than Eisenhower described. Before tensions finally subsided at the end of April 1955, the United States
had come dangerously close to using nuclear weapons against
the Chinese mainland.

I

In 1954 the United States believed that the legal status of
Jinmen (Quemoy), Mazu (Matsu), Dachen, and several other
clusters of small offshore islands under the control of the Nationalists differed from that of Taiwan and the Penghus (Pesca-

dores). The last two had been colonized by the Japanese after the Sino-Japanese War of 1895, and even though they had reverted to Chinese jurisdiction following World War II, the United States considered their ultimate disposition unsettled. The offshore islands—some thirty in number—just off the central coast of the mainland had remained subject to China, and there was no question that they were legally Chinese territory. As the Nationalists retreated from the mainland to Taiwan in 1949, they retained control of the offshore islands for use as staging areas to harass the mainland and shipping, even though the bits of land possessed questionable value for the defense of Taiwan, a hundred miles away on the opposite side of the Taiwan Strait. The several thousand inhabitants of the small islands were mainly farmers and fishermen.

Eisenhower described many of the offshore islands as practically within "wading distance" of the mainland shore, including two important harbors. The Jinmen group is just two miles from the port of Xiamen (Amoy), and the Mazu group ten miles from the port of Fuzhou. Both lie opposite Taiwan. The third main group, the Dachens, are located some 200 miles north of Taiwan.

The Communists and Nationalists had occasionally skirmished over the islands since 1949, but by late 1954 Chiang, with American help and encouragement, had transformed them into formidable forward positions. Since 1949 Washington had provided $1.6 billion in economic and military aid to the Nationalists. More than 50,000 Nationalist soldiers, many of them first-line regulars, were stationed on Jinmen alone. Apparently Chiang was preparing the islands as stepping-stones for his future invasion of the mainland.[2]

In July 1950 the U.S. military had not believed that the offshore islands warranted the commitment of American forces to their defense. But the standoff in Korea, followed by Communist gains in Southeast Asia, had heightened U.S. concerns about the further erosion of the Western position in Asia. In quick order the United States took several steps to construct a system of military alliances to surround China, notably the conclusion of a mutual defense treaty with the South Korean government in August 1953, the formation of SEATO in 1954, and movement toward a defense treaty with the Republic of

China (ROC). In May Eisenhower and his top advisers, in response to intelligence reports about an increase in Communist forces along the Strait, ordered the American military to make a show of strength in the Taiwan area. Warships from the U.S. Seventh Fleet soon called in at several of the offshore islands, and American aircraft patrolled the skies. High-ranking officials, including the secretary of defense and General Van Fleet, repeatedly visited Taipei on highly publicized trips. In early August Zhou Enlai accused the United States of trying to organize a Northeast Asia treaty organization that would provocatively link the United States, Japan, South Korea, and the ROC in an anti-China bloc.[3]

In the aftermath of the Korean War, China too had launched an offensive, but more diplomatic in nature, to secure its relations with neighboring countries. It improved its ties with Japan, reached an understanding with India about Tibet, and, during the Geneva Conference in 1954, agreed to establish full formal relations with Britain. In August Beijing in grand style hosted a British Labour Party delegation led by former Prime Minister Clement Attlee.[4]

At the same time China's press lashed out at "the mounting threat" from the United States and Taiwan. With resolutions of the conflicts in Korea and Indochina, only the Taiwan area remained unsettled in China's view. While en route from the Geneva Conference at the end of July, Zhou Enlai received a cable from Mao informing him that China had to "raise before the entire country and to the world the call to 'liberate Taiwan,' in order to break up the military and political alliance of the United States and Chiang." "We were wrong not to raise the task of 'liberate Taiwan' right away after the Korean ceasefire," Mao told Zhou. "If we were to continue to drag our heels now, we would be making a serious political mistake." Mao's strategy of division, like that of the United States, also relied on a policy of pressure. Washington observed that Beijing's propaganda about liberating the offshore islands and Taiwan began to escalate.[5]

More ominously, air and naval clashes between Communist and Nationalist forces had by then raised tensions in the Taiwan Strait. Although the rest of the world paid little attention,

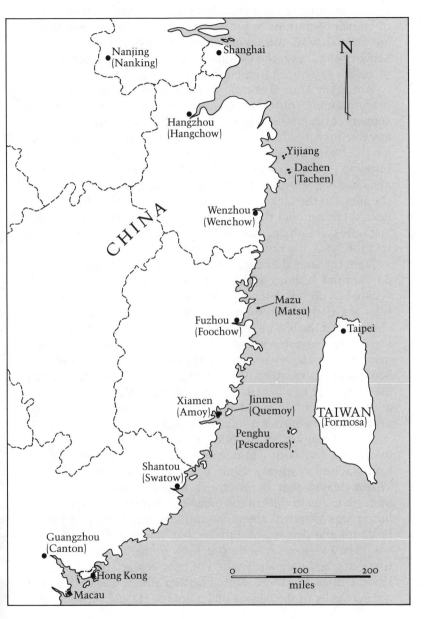

Offshore islands in the Taiwan Strait

U.S. intelligence anticipated that the Communists were about to launch operations to probe American intentions and retaliate against ROC intrusions along the coastal area. Then, on September 3, 1954, the Communists rained some 6,000 rounds of artillery shells on Jinmen in just five hours.[6]

Would the United States, opposed to any further expansion of Communist control of territory and fully committed to the support of the Nationalist regime, which refused to budge from any territory it held, go to war with China over these specks of land? Although U.S. intelligence estimated that a Communist invasion of Jinmen was probably not imminent, the Communists had concentrated significant land, sea, and air strength in the area. On the morning of September 5 three U.S. aircraft carriers, a cruiser, and three destroyer divisions took up position just miles off Jinmen.[7] For the United States, John Foster Dulles told the NSC, the crisis was a "horrible dilemma."[8]

From the start the administration was divided about what to do. Admiral Radford, speaking for the majority of the JCS, advocated an all-out defense of the islands and the use of atomic weapons if the Communists launched a major assault. The chairman of the JCS believed that the United States had to take a stand in the interests of the global battle against communism. "If we fail to resist this aggression," Radford said at a September 12 meeting of the NSC, "we commit the United States further to a negative policy which could result in a progressive loss of free world strength to local aggression until or unless all-out conflict is forced upon us."[9]

But the majority of the NSC, reluctant to face the prospect of another war with China so soon after Korea, backed away from Radford's military solution. Secretary of Defense Charles Wilson feared that involvement would reinject the United States into the middle of the ongoing Chinese civil war. Eisenhower was skeptical about the military importance of the islands for the defense of Taiwan, but believed that their loss would be a serious, even mortal, blow to the morale of the Nationalists, and that war would not be necessary to hold the islands. Dulles, likewise, wanted neither all-out war with China nor surrender of the islands under duress. He and the president opted to try to defuse the immediate situation while continuing to back the Nationalists.[10]

In the following weeks, as Communist and Nationalist forces sparred with each other, the administration publicly condemned the Communist threat and reemphasized its support for the defense of Taiwan and the Penghus. But to keep Beijing guessing about U.S. intentions, Eisenhower and Dulles left vague whether the commitment to the Nationalists extended to the offshore islands under their control. The two also wanted to avoid alienating European and Asian allies, who strongly opposed American involvement in the offshore area. The Taiwan question was the "sorest spot" in Anglo-American differences over China policy, according to the U.S. consul general in Hong Kong.[11] To try to strengthen the American diplomatic position and limit the crisis, Dulles went to work with Western nations on a U.N. ceasefire plan and possible neutralization of the offshore islands. Simultaneously, to remove any doubt about Washington's support of the Nationalists, he concluded and signed in early December a mutual defense treaty with Chiang's regime. The treaty explicitly covered Taiwan and the Penghus and provided for an extension to other Nationalist-held territories on the mutual agreement of the two signatories. In return for this protection and to ensure that it would not be drawn into a precipitous war with China, Washington required Chiang to pledge secretly that he would end offensive actions against the mainland without U.S. approval.[12] An unhappy Admiral Radford charged that these public and private agreements were paving the way for the fall of all Asia to communism.[13]

II

In spite of the administration's efforts, the situation in the Taiwan Strait continued to deteriorate through 1954, and, then, in Eisenhower's description, took a "turn for the worse" at the start of 1955. Both the Communists and Nationalists now predicted imminent widespread hostilities. On January 10 a hundred planes from the mainland raided the Dachens, and on

January 18 Communist forces overwhelmed 1,000 Nationalist guerrillas (and eight American military personnel) on Yijiang Island, just north of the Dachens. The Nationalists counterattacked with air strikes on mainland ports and shipping. The CIA reported that on the morning of January 23 some 20,000 to 30,000 Communist troops embarked from Qingdao for Shanghai, evidently for use against the Dachens in the opinion of the intelligence agency. From Washington's vantage point all-out war for the offshore islands and perhaps Taiwan itself seemed to loom.[14]

Eisenhower concluded that since the Dachens were not reachable from Taiwan's airfields, they were not as defensible militarily as Jinmen and Mazu. Nevertheless, he decided that the United States had to clarify its position. On January 19, in a meeting with Dulles and Radford, the president agreed with their assessment that the remaining offshore islands could not be held without "U.S. interposition." As he wrote in his memoirs, "the time had come to draw the line" over what territories the United States would fight for. Dulles, on Eisenhower's instructions, confidentially informed Nationalist Foreign Minister George K. C. Yeh, then visiting Washington, that the United States would publicly announce its intention to join in the defense of Jinmen if Chiang would withdraw from the Dachens.[15]

On the next day, January 20, the NSC argued heatedly about the path Eisenhower and Dulles had chosen. On behalf of the president, Dulles reviewed U.S. policy: the United States had obscured its public stand to confuse the enemy. This policy, though, had begun to "backfire." The Communists now seemed convinced the United States would not fight for any of the offshore islands. Dulles recommended that, while continuing to seek a ceasefire through the United Nations, the administration should ask Congress to grant the president the explicit power to commit U.S. forces to the defense of Taiwan and related areas not specifically mentioned in the Mutual Defense Treaty. These "related areas" would include Jinmen, and probably Mazu, so long as the Communists professed an intention to attack Taiwan. The United States had to remove any ambiguity about what territories it would defend. Leaving the U.S. position unclear, Dulles judged, would now create "greater risk."[16]

Robert Cutler, the President's national security adviser, Treasury Secretary George Humphrey, and Defense Secretary Charles Wilson all vehemently objected to Dulles's view: the United States was going to be drawn directly into war with China over territory of minimal value. Wilson felt the United States should just hold Taiwan and the Penghus and "let the others go." The president, however, just as vehemently endorsed all of Dulles's recommendations. The Dachens could be given up, he conceded, but unless the United States was prepared "completely to discount Formosa," the NSC had to make up its mind about Jinmen and Mazu, the most important remaining offshore islands. If Chiang lost these, the damage to Nationalist morale might be irreparable. Ever since masses of Chiang's troops had surrendered without a fight in 1949, Washington had doubted the loyalty and determination of his forces. Even a symbolic setback might undermine the entire Nationalist cause. According to Eisenhower, a statement of U.S. resolve would reduce the danger of war with China and correct the current "dangerous drift" in policy. In any case, the president said, it was clear to him that Jinmen and Mazu "were the outposts for the defense of Formosa."[17]

The NSC continued its discussion the following day. Eisenhower remained adamant in his demand that Congress give him broad general authority to defend the islands under Nationalist control. He was "absolutely determined" to avoid at all costs "another Yalu River sanctuary situation in any struggle over Quemoy," he told the NSC. The president wanted no restraints if the United States became involved, and while he wished to avoid being pinned down to a permanent defense of Jinmen and Mazu, he would not abandon them so long as the Communists menaced the islands. Eisenhower said the United States might change its policy in the future after tensions eased, but at present it had to help hold the islands to protect Taiwan. Everyone present should be sure of one thing, he declared: no matter how a congressional resolution was worded, if there was an emergency during this crisis, he would do whatever had to be done to protect the vital interests of the United States, "even if his actions should be interpreted as acts of war." He "would rather be impeached than fail to do his duty."[18]

Three days later Eisenhower sent his special request to Congress, and on January 28, 1955, the Senate, following the House of Representatives, passed what became known as the Formosa Resolution, giving the president a virtual blank check. The president was authorized to employ the armed forces of the United States for the protection of Taiwan and the Penghus and "related positions and territories of that area now in friendly hands." Eisenhower, though, had changed his mind about publicly naming which offshore islands he would defend. None were specified. Eisenhower said that the United States would intervene only if a Communist attack appeared to be preliminary to an assault on Taiwan itself. James Reston of the *New York Times* called the United States line "calculated imprecision."[19] This ambiguity was selective, however: on January 31 Washington directed its ambassador on Taiwan, Karl Rankin, to inform Chiang privately of the U.S. intention to defend Jinmen and Mazu during the present crisis. In exchange for its commitment to Jinmen and Mazu, the United States received Chiang's agreement to withdraw his forces from the Dachens. The islands' 24,000 civilians and soldiers, with the assistance of the U.S. Seventh Fleet, were evacuated a few days later.[20]

Chiang may have agreed to the withdrawal, but he was livid at Washington's actions. His understanding, based on Dulles's talk with Foreign Minister Yeh on January 19, had been that the United States would make a public commitment to defend Jinmen and Mazu. Even though Dulles and Robertson had subsequently informed the Nationalists of the administration's change of mind, Chiang had insisted that Washington live up to its original proposal, or he would not withdraw from the Dachens. Although he felt double-crossed, he finally relented under American pressures. Just before the evacuation of the Dachens, Radford and Dulles's subordinates in the State Department reviewed the confused situation and concluded that Chiang's "misunderstanding" about the U.S. position was legitimate. The officials admitted that even they were unsure of exactly what agreements the administration had reached with the Nationalists about the Dachens.[21]

III

After the fall of the Dachens the Communists continued to build their airfields, artillery emplacements, and roads on the mainland adjacent to Jinmen and Mazu in what the administration viewed as preparations for an eventual assault. During an NSC meeting Admiral Radford decried the weakness of American operational intelligence regarding the Communist buildup and reminded the administration of America's recent nightmare with the surprise entry of Chinese forces into Korea. "We must assume that the Chinese Communists are getting ready just as fast as they can" for an attack, he said.[22]

Dulles also feared that the United States was running out of options to end the crisis without wider hostilities. The U.N. ceasefire plan was getting nowhere—neither the Nationalists nor Communists would go along with the idea. Chiang would not budge from Jinmen and Mazu, and the United States had committed itself to backing the Nationalists. There was nothing else to do, Eisenhower told the NSC in mid-February, but "to watch the situation as it develops on a day-to-day basis." He reminded the NSC of his belief that the surrender of the offshore islands would result in the collapse of Chiang's government. The president coolly joked that the United States was now in the hands of "a fellow who hasn't anything to lose."[23]

Indeed the United States was backing itself into a corner, helped along by Chiang, who was far from being a simple puppet of Washington. With the war-making discretion granted by the Formosa Resolution, Eisenhower staked his own personal reputation and the prestige of the United States on the defense of the tenuous Nationalist cause, now centered on the offshore islands. Their loss to a Communist assault would have been humiliating and devastating to American credibility.[24] The United States would never have allowed the destruction of one-quarter of Chiang's best troops and the loss of Jinmen and Mazu, even without the secret pledge of Chiang.

During a trip to Taiwan and the Far East at the end of February, Dulles concluded that the situation was even more serious than he had thought. Apparently neither the mutual defense treaty with the Nationalist regime nor the Formosa Resolution had discouraged the Communists. He was now convinced that the Communists intended to take Taiwan by force, reversing his previous estimate that their immediate interest was only the offshore islands. After a meeting in Honolulu with Admiral Felix Stump, commander-in-chief of the Pacific, Dulles cabled Washington that he was disturbed by the considerable increase in Communist forces and activity in the area. Moreover, Dulles warned, "they are skilled at camouflage and may be able to conceal timing." The fanaticism and intransigence of the Communists were even greater than he had feared.[25]

On his return to Washington on March 6, Dulles reported to the president that if the Communists crushed the Nationalists on Jinmen and Mazu, the reaction would be catastrophic not only for the ROC but also for the rest of Asia. The two reaffirmed their commitment to defending the two island groups and concluded that this would require drastic measures, including "the use of atomic missiles," by which they evidently meant tactical nuclear weapons. Eisenhower had earlier agreed with Admiral Radford that the United States would be unable to destroy the Communist gun emplacements opposite the offshore islands without the use of nuclear weapons. To prepare public opinion Eisenhower directed Dulles to state in a nationally televised speech on March 8 that the administration considered atomic weapons "interchangeable with the conventional weapons" in the American arsenal.[26]

On March 10 Dulles reported to the NSC what he had discussed with the president, stating that the Communists were determined to take Taiwan and the United States had to realize that a fight with them was thus now a matter of "time not fact." He also expressed concern about the loyalty of Chiang's troops. If the Communists succeeded in landing on Taiwan, the KMT forces might disintegrate. The United States should try to avoid involvement for the next several weeks during sensitive discussions on strengthening Western European unity, but the administration had to start preparing the American people for hostilities involving U.S. forces in the Taiwan area and for the use of nuclear weapons in the defense of the offshore islands. "The need for such use, to make up for deficiency in conventional forces," said Dulles, "outweighs the repercussive effect of such use upon free world nations in Europe and the Far East. United States and world public opinion must be prepared." Dulles predicted that Communist pressure would continue "until the United States decides to 'shoot off a gun' in the area."[27]

Admiral Radford heartily endorsed Dulles's position on the use of nuclear weapons, noting that the JCS had consistently advocated such a view. In fact the JCS had recently ordered the Strategic Air Command to begin, "on an urgent basis," target selection for an "enlarged atomic offensive" against China. The JCS knew Chiang was not averse to the use of atomic weapons against his people on the mainland. As long as "they were warned in advance," Chiang had told Admiral Stump, the Chinese people would accept such attacks "as a war necessity."[28] The other members of the NSC were practically speechless. Dulles made it clear that his conclusions had the support of Eisenhower, who was presiding over the meeting. It was at the president's direction, he noted, that he had included the reference to tactical nuclear weapons in his recent speech. But much more public relations work had to be done if the United States was to use atomic weapons within the "next month or two."

After the meeting Eisenhower and National Security Adviser Robert Cutler reviewed top secret policy papers on nuclear warfare. The papers supported Eisenhower's personal opinion that the United States should regard nuclear weapons in the same way as any other "munition." For some time he had wanted to change public attitudes about the atomic bomb and reduce the widespread squeamishness about its use.[29] The administration's policy authorized the early use of nuclear weapons, since the United States, for budgetary reasons, could not maintain both a conventional and a nuclear deterrent against the Communists. That policy became known as the doctrine of "massive retaliation." As early as January 1954 Dulles had publicly announced that the United States was prepared to use its "massive retaliatory power" to punish aggression "vigorously at places and with means of its own choosing."[30] The United States began test explosions of hydrogen bombs in February.

The public relations effort Dulles suggested at the March 10 meeting began immediately. In public statements over the next several days, the administration deliberately introduced specific comments about employing tactical nuclear weapons if war broke out in the Taiwan Strait. Eisenhower caused a furor when, at a news conference on March 16, he said he saw no reason "why they shouldn't be used just exactly as you would use a bullet or anything else." On March 17 in Chicago Vice-President Nixon echoed the president, stating that "tactical atomic weapons are now conventional and will be used against the targets of any aggressive force." He warned China against making any belligerent moves.[31] These references were meant to deter the Communists as much as to prepare the American people for atomic warfare. At some point during the crisis, the administration developed plans for the possible use of several atomic bombs of ten to fifteen kilotons—about the yield of the bomb that destroyed Hiroshima—to be dropped on coastal air bases. Eisenhower recognized that civilian casualties could number "in the millions" from such attacks.[32]

The Chinese Communists took Eisenhower's threats seriously and began to prepare the population for hostilities, possibly including nuclear weapons, with the United States. Mao reportedly told the Finnish ambassador to China that if the United States destroyed Beijing or Shanghai with atomic weapons, American cities would suffer the same fate, and that the present leaders of the United States were bound to be replaced as a result. Mao did not make clear who—Russia or China—was supposed to bomb the American targets.[33]

IV

In moving toward war with China the Eisenhower administration virtually ignored the Soviet Union's potential responses. From the start of the crisis Washington doubted the credibility of Moscow's support for the Communist Chinese position. When Soviet party leader Nikita Khrushchev made a blustery speech in Beijing on China's National Day, October 1, 1954, in which he condemned American interference in China's affairs and supported the liberation of Taiwan, Eisenhower labeled the performance mere "bluffing." In Moscow Ambassador Charles

Bohlen discerned a distancing from the Taiwan issue, even though Khrushchev had concluded agreements with the Chinese on other matters when he was in Beijing. American observers reported that the agreements favored China and reflected its improved position in the Sino-Soviet relationship.[34] The Soviets surrendered their last special territorial rights and privileges in China and granted further economic assistance. The Far Eastern Bureau of the State Department interpreted the accords as reflecting China's status of an almost-equal "junior partner" and noted that, though the Sino-Soviet alliance was firm, each ally clearly had its own distinct interests. The Soviets were believed to be uneasy about the Chinese campaign in the Taiwan Strait.[35]

The Soviet Union's attention was then mainly focused on its own internal problems. A leadership struggle in the Kremlin had started in late 1954, and by the end of January 1955 CIA director Allen Dulles reported to the NSC that "stresses and strains" in Moscow had become clearly visible. The Kremlin had assembled from abroad its largest group of ambassadors since the death of Stalin and had convened a special session of the Supreme Soviet. The CIA believed there was a dispute over economic issues and the relative importance of the military, a "guns versus butter" conflict.[36] On February 8, 1955, Moscow announced the ouster of Georgi Malenkov and his replacement by Nikolai Bulganin and Nikita Khrushchev. The new top leaders quickly signaled their interest in improving relations with the West. London concluded that the Soviet position on the offshore islands was like its own: neither wanted to see fighting break out, but one was as much at a loss as the other on how to moderate the behavior of its allies.[37]

Eisenhower and Dulles in fact believed that Soviet influence over China was not as great as was commonly held in the United States, and that China was acting largely on its own in the crisis. In executive session with the House Committee on Foreign Affairs, Dulles observed, "As far as surface appearances go, the Soviet line has been less violent than the Chinese Communist line, and when judged only by superficial impressions, one would infer that their disposition is to hold back the Chinese Communists. They have, for instance, avoided any formal, explicit endorsement of [the Chinese] position with reference to the conquest and what they call liberation of Formosa."[38] (The Soviet Union's ambassador to the United Nations, Yakov Malik, was spreading the word there that the Soviets were trying to restrain the Chinese but were having a difficult time, since the Chinese were so proud and sensitive about their recent emergence as a world power.[39]) The leadership struggle in the Kremlin also confirmed for Dulles the correctness of the policy of pressure on the Communists. He suspected that the Soviet Union was overextended and having difficulties meeting the demands of the satellite countries, especially China's. He remarked to Foreign Minister George Yeh on February 10 that the strain on the Soviets "must be very great."[40]

Dulles openly played on the emerging differences between the Soviets and the Chinese. In a major speech to the Foreign Policy Association on February 16, he observed that the struggle in the Kremlin was not merely one for personal power: what seemed to be at issue was whether the Soviet Union was going to sacrifice its own national interests, its security, and the welfare of its people to the expansionist ambitions of "international communism." Dulles spoke favorably of the elements in the leadership that were devoted to the nation's internal concerns, and offered them the prospect of "worthwhile negotiations and practical agreements between the United States and the new Russia." "Then," he said, "there might be reactivated the historic friendship between our countries and our peoples."[41]

Immediately after this overture to Moscow, Dulles turned to denouncing Beijing, whose extreme tactics and ambitions threatened the peace of Asia. The Chinese Communists were "the initiators of violence" in the Taiwan Strait, he said. The United States did not expect them to surrender their claim to Taiwan but, putting on a reasonable face, Dulles asked rhetorically, "might they not renounce their efforts to realize their goals by force?" As a news commentator later observed, Dulles seemed to be "trying to induce Nikita S. Khrushchev or some other high Soviet leaders to become a Tito and cut loose from Peiping."[42] In light of the government's long-standing interest in making Mao an "Asian Tito," Dulles's appeal to the Soviets was a novel ploy.

Eisenhower himself discounted the likelihood of Soviet involvement if hostilities broke out between the United States and China. He told Prime Minister Winston Churchill, NATO General Alfred Gruenther, and the NSC that he did not believe the Soviets would go to war over Taiwan. The Soviet Union would "pour supplies into China" but would not risk provoking a U.S. attack on its own territory. The Soviets might be trying to sap American strength by involving the United States in a land war in Asia, but they were not interested in general conflict. A real shooting war, Eisenhower wrote Gruenther, would create a great dilemma for the Soviet Union.[43]

V

Eisenhower was fully prepared, but reluctant, to use nuclear weapons in the Taiwan Strait crisis. Both he and Dulles feared damaging repercussions in Europe if they were used. The secretary of state told the president on March 11 that, for the moment, direct U.S. participation in the defense of the offshore islands, "particularly involving atomic missiles," should be avoided, but after negotiations about forming a European confederation were "buttoned up," they would have more freedom of action in Asia.[44] Later in the day he and the president met with other officials and decided that they had to do everything possible to improve the Nationalists' defense capability to avoid the need for U.S. intervention. If the United States did enter the fight, Eisenhower indicated, it would do so first with conventional weapons; atomic weapons "should only come at the end."[45] The administration considered the remaining days of March critical as the Nationalists completed their fortifications against the ever-growing Communist forces massing opposite the offshore islands. The United States blustered to put off the Communists and give more time to the Nationalists. In a speech on March 21 Dulles accused Beijing of being "dizzy with success" and an "acute and immediate threat." In the short run China might prove "more dangerous and provocative of war" than the Soviet Union. "The aggressive fanaticism of the Chinese Communist leaders," he added ominously, "presents a certain parallel to that of Hitler. Also, it contrasts to the *past* tactics of Soviet Communism."[46] Dulles's emotional words were clearly calculated: he classed the Chinese Communists with the Nazis but explicitly distinguished Moscow from Beijing.

On March 25 Admiral Robert Carney, chief of staff of the Navy, leaked to the press that the United States had plans for an all-out attack on China. Carney said he himself expected that war might break out by April 15, the start of the Afro-Asian Conference in Bandung, Indonesia. Eisenhower was furious with Carney's disclosure and publicly tried to downplay his remarks without explicitly contradicting them. Privately Eisenhower conceded that Carney might be right about the need for the United States to fight, "because the Red Chinese appear to be completely indifferent as to human losses."[47] U.S. military intelligence estimated that the Communists could assemble sufficient air, naval, and land capabilities in just two to three days to take "any or all" of the offshore islands from the Nationalists, barring U.S. intervention.[48]

As Carney had revealed, the U.S. military planning envisaged extensive nuclear attacks on China. On March 31 General Curtis LeMay, commander of the Strategic Air Command, cabled General Nathan Twining, chief of staff of the Air Force. LeMay was personally familiar with China, having directed the firebombing of Japan from the mainland during World War II. His message read in part:

Plans have been developed and are ready for immed execution by use of B-36 type acft [aircraft] based on Guam to deal with any eventuality involving Communist China. One wg [wing = 30 planes] is in pos at Guam now and two other wgs in the United States are on warning alert for this task. One of these two wgs can move to Guam immed. Guam has capability of supporting sixty B-36 type acft. These will have an immed capability for combat opns [operations]. . . . Target selections have been made, coordinated with other responsible comdrs and asgd [assigned] to B-36 crew.[49]

The following day, according to the Chinese, eighteen U.S. warplanes in four different waves flew over Chinese territory in both the north and the south. The Chinese officially condemned the flights as "military provocations." A week later a plane carrying Chinese officials to the Bandung Conference exploded, killing all aboard. There was little doubt that sabotage was responsible, and the Chinese accused both the Nationalists and the United States.* Eisenhower tried to contain the American public's growing fear of war, while leaving his military options open. Disingenuously, he told a group of senators on March 31 that he did not know, and could not know in advance, if he would intervene militarily in the offshore islands in the event of a Communist attack. His decision, he said, would be based on whether the actual objective was Taiwan, not just the offshore islands.[50]

In private, however, the administration was considering extreme measures to end the crisis. Dulles met with his top advisers in the State Department and his brother Allen, director of the CIA, on March 28 to discuss what to do. They began by debating the possibility of again approaching the United Nations, but the idea got nowhere. Talk then centered on the military options open to the United States. The secretary of state proposed blockading the entire China coast to relieve the pressure on the offshore islands. Next, he raised for discussion the possibility of threatening a "generalized" attack with conventional and nuclear weapons, in response to any Chinese assault on Jinmen and Mazu, that would destroy China's "great POL dumps" (petroleum, oil, and lubricants) and the communication and rail lines "across the length and breadth of China." If the Chinese knew that this would be the American reaction, they might not attack, he argued. Robert Bowie, head of the PPS and one of the more moderate elements toward China in the administration, suggested that the United States announce it would "from time to time" drop nuclear bombs on Jinmen and Mazu if they were captured by the Communists. Dulles thought this impractical: it would be a "considerable waste" of valuable weapons. The United States could not afford to "splurge" its nuclear arsenal, Dulles cautioned. In any case such a plan would only wind up killing "harmless" fishermen. But Dulles and his colleagues could not come up with any more-attractive idea.[51]

New York Times, April 3, 12, 1955, pp. 3, 1, respectively. British authorities in Hong Kong eventually charged an airport worker with the crime. After confessing to planting a bomb on the *Kashmir Princess*, Chow Tse Ming, who had ties with KMT intelligence operatives, fled to Taiwan, which refused to extradite him to Hong Kong. During the course of the investigation, the Hong Kong government arrested over 50 people. The ROC denied having any link to the explosion. Colonial Office to Foreign Office, Jan. 5, 1956, PRO, FO371/120963/FC1381/3.

Several days later Eisenhower decided to try one other maneuver. He thought the United States might seek to persuade Chiang to reduce his forces on the offshore islands—to recognize them as "outposts, not citadels"—and de-emphasize their importance to his government. If Chiang's prestige was less involved with the islands, the United States could gradually reduce its own commitment and concentrate on Taiwan and the Penghus. This might well minimize the impact of the loss of the offshore islands on Nationalist morale. Eisenhower presented these ideas to Dulles in a ten-page, single-spaced memo on April 5 and urged the secretary of state to come up with a specific course of action. The United States, wrote Eisenhower, could no longer "remain inert awaiting the inevitable moment of decision between [the] two unacceptable choices": an unpopular, divisive, and disadvantageous war over the islands or retreat before a Chinese attack that could lead to the disintegration of "all Asian opposition" to communism and the loss of the whole continent.[52]

Over the next several days pressures on the administration to take decisive action increased. General William Chase, chief of the U.S. Military Assistance Advisory Group on Taiwan, and Ambassador Rankin urged Washington to authorize the Nationalists to bomb Communist airfields and to blockade shipping along the China coast. At the same time Admiral Felix Stump backed the Nationalist request for U.S. approval (pursuant to Chiang's secret pledge) to conduct air strikes on mainland targets. American aerial intelligence had just confirmed that the Communists were constructing two new airfields along the Strait; when completed, they might give the Communists air superiority over the offshore islands and bring Taiwan into MiG intercept range.[53] Opposite advice came from within the State Department. Robert Bowie now wanted the United States to announce that it would not defend the offshore islands in order to coerce Chiang into seeing them as "expendable outposts" and perhaps consenting to withdraw from them altogether.[54]

Finally Dulles flew to Augusta, Georgia, on April 17 for a private two-hour meeting with the president. The secretary presented the ideas that he, Deputy Secretary of Defense Robert

Anderson, Admiral Radford, Under Secretary of State Herbert Hoover, Jr., Assistant Secretary of State Robertson, and CIA Director Allen Dulles had developed in response to Eisenhower's April 5 memo. Eisenhower had wanted a way to de-emphasize the offshore islands, to make them into "outposts," but Dulles and his group had concluded that such a path was self-defeating. If the United States was not going to stop onshore Communist preparations for an attack on the islands, they were as good as lost. Even as "outposts" their capture would still be terribly destructive for the Nationalists. It would be better, Dulles argued, for the United States "to encourage a clean break"—get off the islands—and then blockade the China coast along the entire Taiwan Strait, some 500 miles. The position paper Dulles showed Eisenhower read: "Unless and until the Chicoms [Chinese Communists] in good faith renounce their avowed purpose to take Formosa by force, the United States and Chinats [Chinese Nationalists] will, as a measure of self-defense, institute a naval interdiction along the China Coast from and including Swatow in the south to approximately Wenchow in the north." The blockade would aim at stopping the Communists from building up their supplies and facilities for an attack against Taiwan, something they could not easily accomplish overland because of rough terrain. Dulles also proposed stationing nuclear weapons on Taiwan to demonstrate U.S. resolve.[55] His plan thus combined a retreat with a wild counterattack and envisioned the eventual creation of two Chinas effectively separated by the Taiwan Strait.

Eisenhower, after some hesitation, approved Dulles's plan with a few revisions. The United States must not force Chiang into anything he did not want, he insisted; the Nationalists themselves should decide whether they would retain Jinmen and Mazu or give them up. By the end of the discussion, the two men were pleased with themselves, confident that their program "would immeasurably serve to consolidate world opinion" in favor of the United States. After the meeting Dulles spoke to reporters, saying that he and the president discussed questions related to Austria, Vietnam, and the "grave implications" of the offensive buildup of the Chinese Communists in the Taiwan Strait area. The two men, he announced, had concluded that peace "is now in grave jeopardy."[56] Three days later, on April 20, Admiral Radford and Assistant Secretary of State Robertson left for Taipei to present the Dulles-Eisenhower plan to Chiang Kai-shek.

Before meeting with the generalissimo Radford and Robertson conferred with Ambassador Rankin to give him details of the proposal: if the Nationalists withdrew from Jinmen and Mazu, the United States would intercept all seaborne traffic of "a contraband or war-making character" and would "lay mine fields which would force coastwise junk traffic to come out where it also could be intercepted and controlled." Logistically the plan was feasible—the Seventh Fleet and elements of the Fifth Air Force were already in the area, and other naval forces in Okinawa and the Philippines were only twenty-four hours away. Rankin, who usually favored an aggressive policy toward the Chinese Communists and had supported the idea of a Nationalist blockade of the coast, was aghast. This proposal meant war, he told Radford and Robertson. How could the Communists accept a blockade of their coast or the mining of their territorial waters? Radford agreed with Rankin's characterization of the proposal, adding that it would only be a matter of time before Chinese aircraft attacked American ships. He had fully informed Eisenhower of this probable outcome, he said.[57]

While the United States might have extracted itself from the precarious situation in the offshore islands with the evacuation and blockade, it would have doomed itself to a hell on the high seas. The Chinese Communists would never have renounced their claims over Taiwan or their option of using force to bring the island under their suzerainty (Beijing still has not ruled out such a possibility). A naval blockade had military advantages over a static defense of small islands vulnerable to Chinese ground forces, but the United States would have had to maintain a costly act of war indefinitely. China certainly would not have let such an affront go unchallenged.

Fortunately, neither the rest of the world nor the Chinese Communists were ever required to respond to the Dulles-Eisenhower plan. Despite several days of talks Chiang refused to entertain the idea of reducing his forces on the islands, let alone abandoning them to the Communists. Radford and Robertson tried to press Chiang by telling him the United States was withdrawing its secret January 31 pledge to join in the defense of Jinmen and Mazu, though Chiang could still count on U.S. logistical support. Chiang still would not budge. Rankin later surmised that the generalissimo rejected the blockade plan because he distrusted the Americans. After having been betrayed (in his view) by the United States during the evacuation of the Dachens, Chiang could hardly be expected to be receptive to a proposal that depended completely on Washington's reliability.[58]

The initiative that finally ended the crisis came not from Washington but unexpectedly from the Chinese Communists. On April 23, just before Robertson and Radford talked with Chiang, Premier Zhou Enlai dramatically announced at the Bandung Conference that his government wanted no war with the United States. "The Chinese people are friendly to the American people," he said, and China was willing to negotiate with the United States for the reduction of tensions in the Taiwan area. On April 26 Dulles, seizing the chance to extricate the United States from its predicament, indicated that Washington would talk with Beijing about a ceasefire. The shelling soon tapered off, and the area quieted.

VI

Why did Beijing end the crisis? The Chinese may have been concerned that Washington was about to start a general war— it was no secret that Eisenhower's emissaries, with their hard-line reputations, were headed for Taiwan—and hoped to solicit the sympathy of other Asian nations, fearful of a new conflagration in the Far East.[59] It is also possible that the Soviets persuaded the Chinese to end their campaign in the Strait. Washington later heard, and apparently believed, a rumor that Zhou Enlai had secretly visited Moscow in April 1955 (perhaps before the Bandung Conference) and learned that China would not get any support from the Soviet Union in a war over the offshore islands. Khrushchev reportedly told him that he considered the islands a local problem, and the continuation of the crisis inconsistent with the Soviet aim of relaxing tensions with the United States.[60]

Whatever the truth of the matter, it was obvious by early

April 1955 that the Chinese and Soviets were on different tracks. The contrast in their behavior was not lost on the Eisenhower administration. While the Chinese were keeping the pressure on in the Strait, and the United States was signaling its preparation for nuclear war against them, the Soviets were eagerly seeking an improvement of relations with the West. Moscow indicated that it was willing to conclude an Austrian state treaty and end the joint occupation of the country. The news thrilled Washington. For years the United States had considered the Austrian question an explicit test of Soviet intentions. The Austrian chancellor arrived in Moscow on April 11 to receive the Kremlin's treaty proposals, and in a few short days reached agreement with the Soviets on terms described as very favorable to the West.[61] Allen Dulles privately hailed the Soviet move "as the most significant action since the end of World War II." It indicated greater flexibility in Soviet policy, he told the NSC, and perhaps a greater degree of weakness. In any case, Dulles pointed out, "it constituted the first substantial Soviet concession to the West in Europe since the end of the war."[62]

The years between Khrushchev's visit to Beijing in September 1954 and the Soviet 20th Party Congress in February 1956 have been called the golden period of Sino-Soviet relations,[63] but even then the relationship was an uneasy one. Moreover, the Eisenhower administration was sensitive to the signs of discord and minimized the importance of the Soviet alliance with China during the entire offshore crisis. Ignoring formal Communist solidarity and dismissing the Soviet Union's "nuclear umbrella" over China, the United States tried to intimidate Beijing. Eisenhower and Dulles did not once mention the Soviet Union and its possible reaction in their discussion about blockading the China coast. They were reasonably confident that they confronted a relatively independent actor in China. They did not believe that Moscow was the source of the provocation or that it was even seriously interested in supporting its Communist friend. In fact Dulles subtly tried to separate the Soviets and Chinese by dangling the carrot of détente before the eyes of the new Khrushchev leadership while increasing threats against Beijing. The events of April that led to the end of the crisis suggest that Dulles's tactic may actually have had a measure of success. A State Department intelligence assessment of the crisis, conducted several months later, concluded that the Chinese were probably not satisfied with Soviet backing.[64]

In his biography of Eisenhower Stephen Ambrose lauds the president's handling of the crisis as a *"tour de force,"* hailing as the key his "deliberate ambiguity and deception" on the stand he would take if the islands were besieged. Ambrose supports the historian Robert Divine's praise of Eisenhower: "The beauty of Eisenhower's policy is that to this day no one can be sure whether or not he would have responded militarily to an invasion of the offshore islands, and whether he would have used nuclear weapons." Ambrose embellishes this, claiming, "the full truth is that Eisenhower himself did not know."[65] But these conclusions were premature; they are contradicted by the evidence now available. Between January 31 and April 24, 1955, the United States was formally pledged to support the defense of Jinmen and Mazu. Even before January 31 Eisenhower expressed his belief that the islands were essential to the basic morale and viability of the Nationalist government. His distinction between a Communist attack aimed at taking just Jinmen and Mazu and one that was a prelude to an assault on Taiwan may have seemed real in his own mind, but it was hardly realistic.

Eisenhower, it has been suggested, successfully kept his options open throughout the crisis. But in fact his obdurate attachment to Chiang (Chiang's suspicions of American trustworthiness notwithstanding) steadily reduced U.S. flexibility. If the Communists had committed sufficient forces to take Jinmen or Mazu in March or April 1955, Eisenhower could not have stood aside and watched: he was clearly pledged to intervene. And he was confident the Communists understood that he would use whatever military means were necessary to stop them. After all, as he told the NSC on March 31, one ought not underestimate their sanity. As far as the president himself was concerned, there was no question in his mind what he would do in the event of an attack in force. The United States would have gone to war.[66]

One of the reasons the crisis has been misunderstood is Eisenhower's own account of it. In his 1963 memoirs, *Mandate for Change*, he vaguely describes what his response to a Communist attack might have been. This has been interpreted as reflecting Eisenhower's suppleness. But in fact, as we now know, Eisenhower did make secret commitments to the defense of Jinmen and Mazu. Chiang himself long maintained that he received a promise from the United States that after the evacuation of the Dachens, the United States would "jointly defend Quemoy and Matsu."[67]

Eisenhower has also deliberately falsified his account of the Radford-Robertson trip to Taiwan. In his memoirs he focuses attention on the long April 5 memo to Dulles in which he recommended that the United States try to convince Chiang to de-emphasize the offshore islands. Excerpts from the memo in an appendix (subsequently cited by many historians) give the impression that it guided the Radford-Robertson mission, and that Eisenhower sincerely searched for a reasonable exit from the crisis. But Radford and Robertson followed, not the April 5 memo, but the program Eisenhower and Dulles devised on April 17 for the evacuation of the islands and the blockade of the China coast.

After he heard of Chiang's vehement rejection of the U.S. proposal, Eisenhower tried to distance himself from what had been presented in Taiwan. He told Dulles that he "had never expected that the Generalissimo would give up outright on Quemoy and the Matsus," and criticized his emissaries for not understanding the "outpost" theory.[68] From Eisenhower's afterthoughts one thing is clear: either he was operating on profoundly different assumptions about what Radford and Robertson were to accomplish on their important mission or the two men, deliberately or not, failed to carry out the president's critical instructions. Whatever the case, Eisenhower's leadership of his subordinates again appears to have been seriously flawed at a decisive moment in the offshore island crisis.

Eisenhower further claims that his administration never tried to persuade Chiang to withdraw from Jinmen and Mazu. This falsehood helped corroborate statements made by his vice-president, Richard Nixon. During the presidential campaign of

1960, John Kennedy questioned the Eisenhower administration's commitment to Chiang and accused it of trying to get him to quit the islands. Nixon's public reply was that the administration only wanted Chiang to reduce his garrisons.* In fact Eisenhower had authorized an act of war to save Chiang's neck.

Eisenhower worked closely with Secretary of State Dulles throughout the crisis and paid close attention to the details of military deployment, as well as the diplomatic problems with nervous allies. And because he was not a detached chief executive, he must bear direct responsibility for leading the country dangerously close to war. U.S.-China hostilities might have occurred in one of two ways. First, the ambiguity of his public stand on the offshore islands (in the apparent absence of any attempt to send secret messages to Beijing) might very well have allowed the Communists to miscalculate American intentions and thus have invited an attack. The result, given Washington's secret commitments to Chiang *and* the administration's own private determination to retain the islands, would have been armed conflict between the United States and China. Second, war would certainly have come if Chiang had accepted the evacuation-blockade plan. It is inconceivable that the Chinese Communists would have acquiesced in such a violation of their sovereignty by the United States.[69]

Finally, it is worth noting that Washington's brandishing of the nuclear cudgel during the crisis provoked a development that would later haunt the United States: Eisenhower's threats apparently helped convince the Chinese Communists that they needed nuclear weapons of their own. In January 1955, in the midst of the offshore crisis and under American pressure, Mao Zedong and other top PRC leaders decided to launch China's nuclear program.[70] The Eisenhower administration's use of nuclear deterrence to protect territory that even Dulles admitted was never considered "essential" to American interests came at great cost.[71]

---

*When the Nationalists and Communists again clashed over the offshore islands in 1958, John Foster Dulles specifically reminded Nixon that Robertson and Radford had tried to get the Nationalists to give up the islands in 1955. Telephone call, Sept. 25, 1958, Dulles Papers, Eisenhower Library, Telephone Calls, box 9, Memoranda of Telephone Conversations—General 8/1/58–10/31/58 (3).

FIVE

China the Main Enemy?

A man cannot be too careful in the choice of his enemies.
—Oscar Wilde, *The Picture of Dorian Gray*

Before the 1954–55 offshore island crisis, Secretary of State John Foster Dulles believed that a closed-door policy toward China would be the best method of straining the Sino-Soviet alliance. Chinese dependency on Moscow would irritate the hard-pressed Soviets, and inadequate Soviet help for China would frustrate the needy and ambitious Chinese. Ultimately the Chinese would become disenchanted with the paucity of Soviet assistance and its attached strings. On the other hand a policy of trying to entice China away from Moscow with the prospects of trade with the United States or a reduction of tensions would only help the Beijing regime consolidate itself and lighten the Soviet load. The Sino-Soviet tie would remain. Thus Dulles concluded that a policy of pressure, not inducement, would contribute to China's alienation from Moscow and help crack the Communist bloc.

This belief in the policy of pressure reinforced the Eisenhower administration's attachment to Chiang Kai-shek's regime. Aside from the traditional Republican sympathy for the KMT and Washington's general policy of containing communism, the Nationalists played a useful role in the strategy of division. They were one more bothersome worry for Beijing.[1] But the 1954–55 offshore island crisis and ensuing events prompted the administration to modify its views both of the China area and of the Sino-Soviet relationship. Pressures increased on the administration to moderate its inflexible China policy; other developments encouraged it to keep the door tightly closed. By the end of 1957 the administration considered China more dangerous than the Soviet Union, which appeared determined to achieve détente with the West. It seemed more likely that the splintering of the Sino-Soviet alliance would come about not when Beijing disabused itself of Moscow, but when Moscow, prompted by Washington, abandoned its militant Asian partner. As an American journalist had speculated during the 1955 offshore island crisis, Washington might have been trying to make Khrushchev, not Mao, into the new Tito.

I

During the crisis of 1954–55 the Eisenhower administration realized that its commitment to the defense of Jinmen and Mazu and, for that matter, its "one China" policy of dealing exclusively with the Nationalists could not be sustained indefinitely. The administration concluded that Chiang's chance of recapturing the mainland was about as great as that of the Communists ever representing the genuine interests of the Chinese people. The Communist claim of legitimacy possessed little credibility in Washington's eyes, of course, but it was clear that the Beijing government was not going to disappear from the mainland. Dulles was fond of publicly dismissing the Communist government as a "passing phase," but his words more accurately described Chiang's regime, not Mao's.

Two weeks after the start of the offshore island crisis, Eisenhower read a dismal CIA report about Taiwan. The Nationalist government, the report bluntly stated, was an "anomaly." It continued to "exist only because of US support." Moreover, the regime was "superimposed upon a native Taiwanese population" that outnumbered Chiang Kai-shek's mainlanders four to one in a total of about ten million, resented the KMT, and had "no effective voice in the determination of national policies." An autocrat ruled the island through manipulation, turning a blind eye to rampant incompetence, inefficiency, and political factionalism in order to maintain his position. The island's economy was not "viable" and faced declining productivity. And "the attrition of age" was steadily sapping the vigor of the bloated military establishment, which was already incapable of defending Taiwan from an all-out Communist assault on its own.[2]

The report's prognosis was bleak. The CIA observed that "the future fortunes of the Chinese National Government will be determined to a very large extent by US policy, and will depend increasingly upon the scale and character of US aid and support." But while dependency on the United States would rise, the Nationalist government's international position would deteriorate, its preoccupation with military affairs would divert attention away from the development of the island, and the hope of returning to the mainland would become even more distant. As a result "the National Government's task of maintaining its own morale and that of its armed forces and the former mainlanders on Taiwan will become increasingly difficult." The CIA concluded that if trends continued, "a greatly weakened Republic of China will in time probably be reduced either to an aspirant for control of China, largely discarded by the world, or to a modest republic of the island of Taiwan."

The CIA discounted the possibility of Chiang's ever returning to the mainland, except perhaps during an all-out war between the United States and China, a war that the administration wanted to avoid. The CIA indicated that conditions on Taiwan would continue to deteriorate as long as Chiang actively entertained his restorationist fantasy. The administration continued to mouth public support for the KMT's crusade of retaking the mainland, but Eisenhower and Dulles began to think seriously about a "two-China" solution. Official papers did not explicitly approve such a position, but it was what Eisenhower and Dulles were prepared to accept as a future settlement in the area, even as they scrambled for a way out of the immediate confrontation with Beijing. A "modest republic of the island of Taiwan" probably seemed the least distasteful alternative.

Under a two-China solution Washington would accede to the existence of two Chinese governments, one on the mainland and one on Taiwan, or some other formula that separated Taiwan from the mainland, such as "one China, one Taiwan." Ideally a two-China policy would allow the United States to maintain all its ties with the Nationalists, deny Taiwan to the Communists, and free U.S. hands in dealing with Beijing.

Washington could also answer the almost universal criticism beyond its borders that it was purely perverse in not officially acknowledging the existence of the government of the most populous country on earth. As early as January 1955 Eisenhower admitted during a press conference that the recognition of Communist China and Nationalist China as "separate independent nations" was being studied as one possible solution to the offshore island predicament.[3]

The two-China concept did not necessarily contradict the policy of pressure on the Communists. John Foster Dulles himself had actually tried to "create" two Chinas for years. In early January 1950 the then–special ambassador for the State Department drafted a proposal to have the United Nations "neutralize" Taiwan, prevent its fall to the Communists, and create an independent republic. Dulles's effort was consistent with the Truman administration's hope that the Communists could be denied Taiwan. Though Dulles endorsed the Nationalists' harassment of the mainland as a contribution to the Korean War effort, even then he supected that Chiang's exile on Taiwan was permanent, short of a cataclysm on the mainland.[4] (In a conversation with Harold Macmillan, Dulles once confessed that he had always been wary of "émigré" leaders after learning an embarrassing lesson while working for President Woodrow Wilson in Paris after World War I. He had urged Wilson to make a speech recognizing the White Russian leader Admiral Alexander Kolchak, who was leading the fight against the triumphant Bolsheviks, as head of the legitimate government of Russia. The speech was mislaid and not given. Three days later the Bolsheviks had liquidated Kolchak. Dulles said his general theory was that émigré movements could never return to power unless they did so quickly.[5])

In June 1953 Secretary of State Dulles and his advisers began formulating post–Korean War China policy. They devised a preliminary scheme to allow both China and Taiwan into the General Assembly when the U.N. charter was revised in 1955. Dulles quietly pursued the idea with Eisenhower's approval.[6] Later, with the start of the offshore island crisis in 1954, Dulles concluded that the Nationalist harassment of the mainland was no longer in America's interests and contributed to the region's instability. He resumed an active pursuit of a two-China solution, telling the NSC that if the United Nations ended the immediate hostilities in the Strait, he was willing to accept the loss of the offshore islands and the likely independence of Taiwan as an "*ultimate* outcome." In a memo to himself Dulles reasoned that "Quemoy cannot be held indefinitely without a general war with Red China in which the Communists are defeated. The Reds might agree to the independence of Formosa, but never the alienation of the off-shore islands like Quemoy."[7]

Although the U.N. effort failed, in part because both Beijing and Taipei understood that its involvement would jeopardize their claims to complete sovereignty, Dulles made sure that U.S. decisions did not preclude a future two-China policy. As part of the deal for the mutual defense treaty with Taipei, Dulles insisted that the Nationalists end all offensive actions against the mainland that had not received U.S. approval. Besides restraining Chiang's recklessness Dulles hoped that the restriction would further dispel the troublesome fiction that the Chinese civil war still raged. Chiang was pleased with the defense treaty insofar as it guaranteed the protection of his island fortress, but he also correctly sensed that the United States was trying to edge him toward accepting Taiwan as his permanent home.[8] Dulles personally tried to persuade Chiang to stop his incessant harping about using military means to return to the mainland and recommended that the Nationalist leader wait patiently for future troubles on the mainland. More candidly, Dulles told Foreign Minister Yeh and Ambassador Koo that two Chinas existed, "just as there were two Germanies, two Koreas and two Viet-Nams."[9]

A two-China formula was not only expedient for the United States, but also consistent with the interests of the people of Taiwan and their right to self-determination, in Dulles's view. Toward the end of the Strait crisis, Dulles opined to Under Secretary of State Herbert Hoover, Jr., that given a choice the people of Taiwan would vote to become an independent state. In drafting the mutual defense treaty Dulles carefully selected language to avoid a "final commitment" that title to Taiwan and the Penghus would be transferred to the Taipei government. The way was left open for an independent Taiwan, and as

Dulles mentioned to Anthony Eden at the time, for the possibility of allowing "two Chinas" into the United Nations.[10]

Others in the NSC also questioned the wisdom of accepting the Nationalists as the sole government of the Chinese people. In a memo to the entire NSC early in the offshore island conflict, Secretary of Defense Wilson, usually tougher on China than even Dulles, branded U.S. policy toward the Nationalists as "out of date" and leading toward war. He proposed "putting Formosa and the Pescadores under the mandate of the United Nations or setting them up as an independent, autonomous State." As Wilson blurted during an NSC meeting in October 1954, Chiang was incapable of regaining the mainland: the "'Gimo' is out." ("Gimo" was one of several derogatory American nicknames for the generalissimo.)[11]

The president and Dulles knew that U.S. policy toward Beijing and Taipei only temporized. But both men hoped that time would bring about favorable changes. The Strait might be defused in a decade, Dulles told the NSC in March 1955, when the "native Formosans" would have replaced the mainland Chinese in the Nationalist Army. Dulles claimed that the Taiwanese would have less interest in defending the offshore islands and more in just protecting their home island. The threat of an attack from Taiwan on the mainland would also diminish. Under those conditions, said Dulles, the China area might not be so volatile.[12]

Even the desperate Dulles-Eisenhower program to end the offshore crisis by blockading the China coast envisioned an eventual two-China settlement. If the Nationalists had withdrawn from the offshore islands and the Communists had renounced the use of force against Taiwan, as Washington proposed, the Taiwan Strait would have become an effective barrier separating the warring sides. Eisenhower realized the implications of Dulles's plan, even as he approved it. He confessed that while he would reaffirm the U.S. policy of not recognizing China for the moment, the United States might have to accept the two-China concept eventually, perhaps in five years. After the island crisis subsided Eisenhower continued to be interested in the two-China formula. On July 9, 1955, he spoke with Secretary of Defense Wilson about the situation on Taiwan.

The president "thought that opinion on Formosa should be quietly and carefully compiled to learn what the people want, and referred to a recent report that their preference, in order, would be independence, reunion with Japan, joining with Communist China."[13]

The offshore island crisis acted as a catalyst in changing U.S. official policy toward the Republic of China and Taiwan. Before the crisis the policy was to support a large ROC military, not only to defend Taiwan, but also to have available a "mobile anti-Communist army which might be used to assist free world forces in fighting in Korea, Indo-China, or elsewhere on the mainland." Defense expenditures accounted for a whopping 61 percent of the ROC's entire budget for fiscal 1955. The revised policy of 1955, in contrast, did not envision the use of the Nationalist Army beyond Taiwan and the offshore islands. Although the U.S. had poured money and material into the ROC military during the crisis, Washington began to encourage Chiang's government to reduce its military spending and focus on economic construction after tensions in the Strait subsided.[14]

On its face the interest in a two-China policy might seem to indicate a lessening of U.S. hostility toward China, but that was not the case. Dulles favored the two-China concept as part of his overall approach toward China, consistent with aggressive efforts to isolate the Chinese Communists. It would free the United States from being hitched to Chiang's war-wagon, a major source of divisiveness in the Western alliance, while permitting the continuation of a closed-door policy toward the mainland. The problem for Washington, however, was that neither Beijing nor Taipei would accept the two-China formula. For all their differences, the Communists and Nationalists agreed on a fundamental point: there was only one China.

II

In some ways the administration's vilification of the Beijing regime actually escalated after 1955. The offshore crisis seemed to elevate China's threat in Washington's estimation. For Dulles the experience confirmed that the Chinese Communists aimed to drive "U.S. influence away from the entire offshore island chain, from the Aleutians to New Zealand, and [to become] themselves dominant in that part of the world." In May 1955 he warned the NATO foreign ministers that the Chinese Communists were "more belligerent" than the Soviets, controlled a huge population, and possessed a cultural prestige in Asia "not enjoyed by Russia in Europe." He and Eisenhower believed that the 22,000,000 overseas Chinese throughout Asia might be used as a potent fifth column by the Communists. Beijing's unique advantages, in Dulles's eyes, made it a mortal threat to Western interests and perhaps even more dangerous than Moscow.[15] The hope that coercive pressure on the Sino-Soviet alliance might be divisive became less of a reason for the closed-door policy than the emerging conviction that China was America's main, immediate enemy.

Dulles did not have to compare the Soviets and Chinese, but contrasting these two independent, allied enemies helped clarify the nature of their relationship and relative dangers. The inclination of national leaders is to try to distinguish and divide enemies. Thus the Soviets' dramatic expression of interest in détente with the West in the midst of the offshore island crisis in 1955, exemplified by the agreement on an Austrian state treaty and rapprochement with Yugoslavia, highlighted the impression of Chinese belligerence. An intelligence report from the CIA in mid-May 1955 reflected the U.S. sensitivity to Sino-Soviet differences and noted the change in the Soviet attitude toward the West *and* China. According to the CIA, though the Soviets were still bent on expanding their influence in the world, they had recently made some important concessions to the West, apparently wanted to avoid military conflict, and desired "a substantial and prolonged reduction in international tensions." Furthermore, the CIA expected that the Soviets would try to moderate Chinese actions to avoid being drawn into an unwanted clash with the United States. It seemed that the Soviets held a "more cautious view than the Chinese of the risks appropriate to the pursuit of Communist objectives in Asia." The Sino-Soviet relationship was one of "allied powers having common interests and a common ideology, but also separate and potentially conflicting national objectives."[16]

Illustrative of the developing high-level thinking on how the

West might increase tensions in the Sino-Soviet alliance was a secret study conducted by a special panel of foreign affairs experts convened by Nelson Rockefeller, Eisenhower's assistant on Cold War strategy. Called the Quantico Vulnerabilities Panel, and headed by Walt Whitman Rostow, then a professor at the Massachusetts Institute of Technology and later Lyndon Johnson's national security adviser, the group explored "methods of exploiting Communist bloc vulnerabilities" during a week of deliberations at Quantico, Virginia, in early June 1955. Cold War specialists both in and out of the government composed the panel, which included C. D. Jackson, who had returned to work with Henry Luce at Time Inc., Professors Frederick Dunn and Max Millikan from MIT's Center for International Studies, Philip Mosely from Columbia University's Russian Institute, and Hans Speier from the RAND Corporation. Henry Kissinger, a lecturer at Harvard, joined some sessions, as did representatives of the Departments of State and Defense, the CIA, the NSC, and the Operations Control Board.[17] The panelists studied the specific problem of U.S. participation in the upcoming Geneva Conference, the first postwar summit meeting of the United States, the Soviet Union, Great Britain, and France, but also reviewed other issues related to the Cold War, such as the arms race, German reunification, and European security. The panel's conclusions specifically encouraged the effort to "worsen difficulties between the Soviet Union and Red China" by taking steps "to put strains on the Moscow-Peiping alliance." Its report made explicit many of the assumptions that were actually guiding the administration's strategy of division.

In an annex to the report Paul M. A. Linebarger of the Johns Hopkins School for Advanced International Studies elaborated on how Washington might best strain Communist relations. Linebarger was a leading authority on psychological warfare and had helped organize the Army's psychological warfare section. He was also a specialist on Chinese politics, inheriting the interest from his father, a legal adviser and biographer of Sun Yat-sen, leader of the 1911 Revolution that ended Manchu rule. Linebarger argued that there was no foreseeable chance for the United States "to seduce Chinese Communist leaders from their loyalty to world Communism as represented by Moscow." But by playing on Chinese fears (allegedly held by both Communists and Nationalists) of "deals between alien Westerners (e.g. 'white men') at their expense" and the sense of "paranoia" engendered by Communist systems, Washington could seriously undermine Beijing's confidence in the Soviets. For the purpose of "manipulating" Beijing, Linebarger recommended that the U.S. "deal with the USSR concerning Red China but seek to minimize dealing with Red China concerning Red China."[18]

Linebarger suggested that Washington, over the next several years, give the impression that a U.S.-Soviet deal might solve the China problem. At some point Washington should even leak word to the press that it was pursuing a two-China settlement with the Russians. For now, said Linebarger, the practical approach was to erode the Sino-Soviet alliance through the Russians, not the Chinese: the United States "should seek to make Russia, as the principal Communist power, responsible for all the consequences of Communist leadership. This will impose a sustained strain on Sino-Russian relations."[19]

By minimizing U.S. contact with China and depriving the PRC of the status it believed it deserved, Linebarger thought, the Chinese might eventually be prodded "to do something about our 'shaming of them.'" He implied that the Chinese might accuse the Soviets of sharing some responsibility for preventing China from gaining its due respect. The report discounted the possibility, or even the desirability, of trying to lessen tensions between Washington and Beijing. The authors of the Quantico Report assumed that a future polycentric Communist world was of great value to the United States, but the path to that end would be through the U.S. interim emphasis on the bipolar relationship between Washington and Moscow, at least as regarded Beijing. The focus of the U.S. strategy of division was decisively shifting toward Moscow.[20]

"Exhilarating" was the word C. D. Jackson used to describe the Quantico meeting to Dulles. He encouraged the secretary of state to give the report his full attention, telling him that it contained "a development of your own beliefs." Dulles later informed Jackson that he had read the document "with much interest and much agreement." The president also let Jackson know he found it of considerable value.[21]

Nelson Rockefeller advised Eisenhower that he should approach the Soviets at Geneva along the lines suggested by the Quantico panel. The Soviets might be interested in exploring ways that the United States and the USSR could resolve Far Eastern, especially Chinese, issues. The president should encourage the Soviets to restrain the Chinese Communists, just as the United States was trying to do with the Nationalists, and see if agreement might not be reached on a two-China policy. The "underlying reason" for making these overtures, wrote Rockefeller, "is to initiate a series of actions aimed at undermining the trust and confidence of Communist China in the USSR. The ultimate objective is to sever the close tie between the two powers."[22]

On their part the Soviets were making it easy for the United States to moderate its policy toward them. On July 4, 1955, Soviet leaders Khrushchev and Bulganin paid an unannounced and completely unexpected visit to the U.S. embassy in Moscow. They dropped by to join the Independence Day celebration, the first such participation by any Soviet leaders in history.[23]

III

When the Geneva Conference took place in mid-July, Eisenhower did indeed take the opportunity to raise the problem of China during private meetings with Soviet leaders. He urged his old wartime acquaintance, Marshal G. K. Zhukov, to use his "good offices" to bring about the release of a number of Americans imprisoned in China. He also tried to impress on Zhukov that the United States had acted with great restraint during the recent Strait crisis. Several days later Eisenhower again spoke with Zhukov about China. Solicitously, Eisenhower said he knew that the Soviets wanted peace, just as the United States did, and that great progress had been made with many of the "divided countries." A settlement had been achieved in Austria, the fighting had ended in Korea and Indochina, and there was hope for a German settlement. But there was still the problem of a "divided China." The United States asked the Soviet government to "use its influence with the Chinese in order to persuade them that problems should not be settled by fighting," the president told Zhukov, adding, "it was important that the Chinese not do something which all would subsequently regret." Zhukov immediately responded, saying that he "agreed and held similar views." Eisenhower indicated that he was not holding the Soviets responsible for Chinese actions, but his clarification simply underscored his message: if Moscow desired détente with Washington, something should be done about the Chinese.[24]

Soviet and American leaders got along well personally at Geneva, even though they failed to agree on major steps to improve relations. The Soviets were especially eager to have the Americans recognize their new friendliness. Zhukov told Eisenhower that he must have observed "the respect and good feelings" that Khrushchev, Bulganin, and the rest of the Soviet delegation entertained for the president. Zhukov went so far as to say that "this was also an expression of their feeling for the American people, since they looked upon the President as the representative of the people of the United States."[25] While Zhukov's compliment may have just been a momentary departure from the Soviet custom of distinguishing the American people from their imperialist leaders, the Soviets gave other signals that they were radically revising their attitude toward the Cold War, the West, and China.

During the Geneva summit Soviet leaders complained to Prime Minister Macmillan that China was draining Moscow's resources. The Soviets were agitated, too, about the volatile situation in Asia, in particular the offshore islands. War was distant in Europe, but the same could not be said about Asia, the Soviets and British agreed. During a dinner conversation with Khrushchev and Bulganin, Anthony Eden commented that the United States "would be very happy if Quemoy and [the] Matsus were sunk under the sea." This suggestion, the foreign minister noted, "appeared to receive universal approbation except, possibly, we all admitted, from an absent Chou En-lai." "The Master of the House is absent," the Russians observed. The Soviet behavior at Geneva led Macmillan to conclude that Moscow actually feared China as a potential danger.[26]

A few months after Geneva Khrushchev confided to West German Chancellor Konrad Adenauer, a close friend of Dulles, that the millions of Chinese born every year were creating tremendous difficulties for the Soviets. Khrushchev pleaded, "We could solve these problems! But it is very difficult. Therefore I ask you to help us. Help us to cope with Red China!" As an afterthought Khrushchev also asked for help in dealing with the Americans, but Soviet anxiety about China was obvious. Bonn passed the information on to Washington.[27]

Eisenhower and Dulles assessed the Geneva summit as a tremendous victory for the West. Dulles was so encouraged by the new Soviet attitude that he departed from his cautious ways and predicted at an NSC meeting that the two Germanys would be reunified within two years. A resurrected German state had been one of the administration's key objectives in its global strategy against the Soviet empire; reunification would change the entire complexion of European politics.[28] Progress with the Soviets even seemed possible in arms control and in the peaceful uses of nuclear power.

IV

Détente with the Soviets did not have to preclude simultaneous efforts to move forward with the Chinese, but the administration remained uninterested in an accommodation with Beijing. The thaw in Soviet policy only emphasized the glacial movement in U.S.-China relations. The administration's attitude toward the Sino-American bilateral talks, which began in the summer of 1955 in Geneva (and were later moved to Warsaw), revealed that the basic U.S. position had not changed, contrary to the suspicions of conservatives and the Nationalists.

The decision to meet with the Chinese was a response to Zhou Enlai's appeal at the Bandung Conference for direct contact between Beijing and Washington, and to tremendous domestic and foreign pressures on the administration. After months of preparation and stalling the United States agreed to discussions concerning the return of civilians held in each other's country. China wanted to discuss a number of other issues, including trade and a meeting of foreign ministers, but

Dulles wanted to use the talks mainly as a way to deflect European criticism of U.S. China policy and to complicate a Chinese renewal of hostilities in the offshore island area.[29]

Dulles's own guidelines laid out two specific and limited U.S. objectives in the talks: "to settle repatriation of U.S. civilians and other practical problems" and "to maintain a 'talking' relationship which would make it less likely that the PRC would attack in the Formosa area." Uninterested in seeking an overall improvement of relations with Beijing, the secretary of state set rigid restrictions on the U.S. representative: the U.S. "must not recognize Chicoms as legal government," "must not give Chicoms a propaganda advantage," and "must not create conditions prejudicial to U.S. objectives of sustaining the noncommunist governments of the Western Pacific." Dulles hoped that if the talks forestalled a Communist attack on the islands, the United States could use the time to build up world opinion to force the Chinese into accepting the status quo in the Strait. He wanted to attain, as he told Eisenhower, a situation similar to that existing in "Germany, Korea, Vietnam, and indeed Ireland" with regard to the nonuse of force to unify divided regions. Dulles told the president that "we were not anxious to push [the bilateral talks] to a conclusion, except as to getting out our civilians. . . . We needed time by which to stabilize the situation." The U.S. representative to the talks, U. Alexis Johnson, recalled that Dulles was content to have the talks drag on. When Johnson received his instructions before leaving for Geneva, he asked Dulles how long he envisioned the talks continuing. "I will be happy if you are sitting there three months from now," was Dulles's sardonic reply. Johnson took the comment to mean that Dulles favored the talks but was in no hurry for results.[30]

After the United States and the PRC quickly concluded an agreement on the repatriation of citizens, the Chinese wanted to discuss other concrete matters. Washington, though, insisted that Beijing first accept what amounted to a two-China solution. The United States demanded that China renounce the use of force in the Taiwan area, except for defensive purposes, and accept the presence of the United States in the area as legal and legitimate. Washington argued that collective-security agreements with the Nationalist government sanctioned the U.S. position. Beijing refused to accept such reasoning, seeing Taiwan as strictly an internal concern of the Chinese people. The Chinese representative repeatedly offered to declare that China would settle disputes with the United States peacefully and proclaim its desire to see Taiwan liberated without force through direct negotiations between Beijing and "the authorities on Taiwan." But Washington repeatedly rejected these offers, which finally provoked the Chinese ambassador, Wang Bingnan, to accuse it of advocating a two-China policy. Johnson was stunned, for he was unfamiliar with the reference. As a career diplomat detached from policy formulation, he did not know that Wang in fact had accurately characterized the Eisenhower-Dulles position. The talks sputtered along until late 1957, when the United States virtually suspended them. Only after China initiated the 1958 Jinmen crisis were they renewed, but the two sides never resolved the Taiwan issue during the entire sixteen-year history of the bilateral talks. Having served as a channel of communication, the talks finally ended with Henry Kissinger's secret 1971 visit to Beijing.[31]

V

In early 1956 the administration witnessed a startling turning point in the Communist world. At the Twentieth Party Congress of the Communist Party of the Soviet Union (CPSU) in February, Khrushchev presented his not so "secret speech" denouncing Joseph Stalin. Transcripts of the tirade, which quickly found their way into the hands of the U.S. government, delighted the administration. Although Khrushchev spoke mainly of Stalin's domestic policies, his report seemed to confirm that the Soviet Union was serious about charting a course away from the entire legacy of the former Soviet leader, whom the United States had blamed as the source of the Cold War. Indeed, in other speeches to the congress, Khrushchev outlined bold new directions for Soviet policies. In foreign affairs he accepted the possibility of different roads to socialism, thus tacitly conceding that Tito had been right all along in his dispute with Moscow, and pledged the Soviet Union to "peaceful competition" with the capitalist countries. Khrushchev stated that war and violence in the world could be avoided through the improvement of relations among the world's "great powers," especially the United States and the Soviet Union. It seemed that the new Soviet line, which Washington had encouraged over the previous several years, was willing to subordinate or even sacrifice support for anti-imperialist struggles to the effort to achieve accord with the United States. On February 28 Dulles proclaimed that the CPSU Congress likely signaled "a permanent shift of direction" for the Soviet Union.[32]

Khrushchev's performance threw the Communist world into turmoil, as other Communist Parties evaluated the radical change in line of the world's leading socialist state. The CCP officially saluted the CPSU for rejecting the Stalin cult but also openly disputed some of Moscow's pronouncements for the first time. The Chinese Communists rejected the thesis of a peaceful transition to socialism and maintained that Stalin, for all his grievous errors, was still "a great Marxist-Leninist." The real issue for the Chinese was not the evaluation of Stalin as such, but Khrushchev's implicit denigration of many of the Soviet Union's socialist policies under Stalin's rule. In their view Khrushchev's sensational condemnation diverted attention from the CPSU's quiet replacement of revolutionary Marxism-Leninism with revisionism. The Soviet leaders at the Twentieth Congress had abandoned not only the "sword of Stalin" but the "sword of Lenin" as well, Mao told his CCP colleagues. The Chinese Party, for its part, would "stick to studying Marxism-Leninism and learning from the October Revolution."[33]

Khrushchev's speech also caught the United States off guard. Allen Dulles confessed to the NSC that Khrushchev's motive for attacking Stalin was "a puzzling problem." There were a number of possible explanations, Dulles offered, including a Soviet effort to try to gain respectability abroad by breaking with the past. Perhaps Khrushchev was just drunk, he suggested. In any case, Allen Dulles, John Foster Dulles, and Eisenhower all agreed, the events in the Kremlin presented "a great opportunity" for the United States. The Soviets would have many problems deciding which policies and officials, both in the Soviet Union and in the satellite countries, to throw out and which to retain. Allen Dulles concluded, with undoubted glee, that Khrushchev was "guilty of a most serious mistake."[34]

Throughout the spring of 1956 Eisenhower and Dulles both warily praised in public what they called the Soviets' "new look." At an April 3 press conference Dulles lauded the de-Stalinization campaign as "highly significant" and encouraging for the hopes for peace. Several months later he stated that the forces transforming the Soviet Union were "irresistible" and indicated that "we can really hopefully look forward to a transformation of the international scene." Eisenhower told the American Society of Newspaper Editors on April 21 that though the Soviets had not surrendered their aim of conquering the world, they had "very markedly" changed their policies. They were moderating their "policy of violence and hostility" and turning toward economic and political means to achieve their ends. In the past, Eisenhower claimed, the Soviets depended entirely on force; now "they have gone into an entirely different attitude."[35]

Allen Dulles linked the change in Soviet foreign policy to domestic developments in the Soviet Union. The Soviets were losing some of their "ideological, revolutionary fervor," he stated in a speech in April. "We are convinced," he said, "that the society in the Soviet Union is becoming highly stratified and that various classes in a so-called 'classless' society are growing up."[36]

Eisenhower wanted to give the Soviets every possible chance to prove the sincerity of their professed interest in détente with the United States. In response to Soviet protests to U.S. overflights, Eisenhower instructed CIA chief Allen Dulles and JCS members Arthur Radford and Nathan Twining to be "wise and careful in what we do." The United States should "give the Soviets every chance to move in peaceful directions and to put our relations on a better basis—and to see how far they will go." Later in the year Eisenhower suspended the overflights. Even the Soviets' intervention in Eastern Europe in the fall of 1956 and saber-rattling during the Suez crisis did not completely dampen the new U.S.-Soviet relationship.* Trade and cultural exchanges between the two countries continued to mount.[37]

The Eisenhower administration's sanguine attitude about the Soviets contrasted sharply with its continuing nastiness toward China. China's adherence to revolutionary Marxism, in contrast to Khrushchev's "new look," was repugnant to U.S. policymakers. Dulles openly blasted the Chinese Communists for not dissociating themselves from Stalin: China's leaders, according to Dulles, were "the most dedicated imitators of Stalin" and had even sought to outdo Stalin in brutality. In private he told Secretary of the Treasury Humphrey and Secretary of Defense Wilson in mid-April "that from a political standpoint, I judged that the Soviet Union was now sufficiently committed to policies of non-violence so that I doubted that we would see from their side any repetition of the attack on South Korea." But as far as Communist China was concerned, he felt "that the risk was greater than from Soviet Russia and that we could not assume that fighting might not break out in any one of the three danger spots—Taiwan, Vietnam or Korea." Dulles suggested that military planning should take account of some of "the political changes resulting from the Soviet 'new look.'"[38]

As for the ROC, the United States nudged the ruling KMT along a path consistent with a two-China policy, while maintaining its military capability. By 1957 the Nationalist government was devoting more attention to improved living conditions and long-term economic development. Eisenhower made absolutely clear to Chiang Kai-shek that the United States opposed ROC proposals to use military force to try to unseat the Communists on the mainland. At the same time the United States bankrolled the ROC and helped it maintain a formidable military force for the defense of the territory under its control. American economic aid allocated to the ROC totaled

---

*Even as the uprisings in Poland and Hungary were occurring that fall, Dulles still publicly spoke encouragingly of the changes in Soviet foreign policy. On October 27, just four days before the Soviets began pouring troops into Hungary, he stated that the Soviets were less of a danger to the West than the Chinese Communists, who were still an aggressive threat. Speech at the Dallas Council on World Affairs, Oct. 27, *Department of State Bulletin*, Nov. 5, 1956, p. 696.

$683,000,000 from 1951 to 1957; military assistance totaled $1.47 billion from 1950 to 1957, representing 63 percent of the total ROC military budget; 530,000 military personnel in a total of 590,000 were supported in part by U.S. funds.[39]

The Pentagon strengthened the ROC's military capability in mid-1957 by installing Matador "tactical" missiles capable of carrying nuclear warheads on Taiwan. Never before had nuclear weapons been stationed on land so close to the mainland. Wang Bingnan denounced the move as a "hostile act" and "provocation." Meanwhile Dulles had begun to issue some of his most abusive statements ever about China. In June 1957 he dismissed the Beijing regime as a "passing and not a perpetual phase," an insult that Chinese officials still vividly recall. (Dulles knew that China would not soon pass from the scene—the CIA had only recently predicted that it might be the world's third-most-powerful economy in ten years.) The United States would not alter its policies of nonrecognition and nonintercourse with China. While "basic power rivalries" existed between China and the Soviet Union, Dulles declared, the United States was not about to help Beijing "wax strong" so that it might break with Moscow. No one had advocated tolerating or assisting any partner of the Axis as a way to defeat the Fascist alliance during World War II, and the United States would not adopt a different stance toward the Sino-Soviet bloc. The United States and China, Dulles told the Council on Foreign Relations, were in a "virtual state of war."[40]

U.S. animosity toward Beijing thus remained bitter despite substantial evidence in preceding years of Chinese interest in reducing Sino-American tensions. Zhou Enlai had ended the 1955 offshore island crisis and announced that China would adhere to the "five principles of peaceful coexistence" (respect for sovereignty and territorial integrity, noninterference in the internal affairs of other countries, nonaggression, equality and mutual benefit, and peaceful coexistence). Soon after the U.S.-China bilateral talks began in 1955, China had agreed to release a number of American prisoners and pledged its peaceful intentions in international relations and the Taiwan area. In August 1956 Zhou had offered to grant visas to fifteen American newsmen who had asked to visit China, but the State Department upheld its long-standing travel ban. A year later China suggested an exchange of visits by American and Chinese newsmen. Again Washington rejected the overture.

According to many China specialists, these conciliatory gestures represented a genuine Chinese interest in improved U.S.-China relations during what is now known as the Bandung phase in Chinese foreign policy, the period from mid-1955 to the end of 1957. Thereafter, they generally agree, Beijing reversed its attitude, ending a chance to set the relationship on a new basis until the early 1970's.[41] Two of the most common explanations of the administration's behavior are Dulles's rigid anticommunism and right-wing domestic political pressures.[42]

But blaming Dulles for refusing to seek an understanding with China because of excessive moralism and ideological inflexibility is not persuasive. Dulles sought an improvement of relations with other Communist countries, including the Soviet Union. He also was sensitive to the advantages of dividing the Eastern European nations from Moscow, and was convinced that friendly ties with Yugoslavia paid handsomely in encouraging aspirations for independence among the other satellite countries and helped increase the strains on Moscow. In East Europe Dulles generally favored a policy of enticement to split the Communist bloc. Dulles even got along well personally with Tito, and according to his aide, Herman Phleger, would have been happy to have "the form of Tito socialism in Eastern Europe."[43] In any case it now seems clear that Eisenhower, not Dulles, was in command of major foreign policy decisions—and his rhetoric was hardly characterized by a rectitude or legalism like Dulles's.[44]

Domestic political pressures undoubtedly complicated any movement toward a revision of China policy. American public opinion consistently supported the Nationalists—the platforms of the Democratic and Republican parties in the 1956 presidential election were virtually identical in their support of the ROC. But partisan political considerations, especially by 1957, do not fully explain the continuing antagonism toward the PRC. Eisenhower and Dulles explored the possibilities of a two-China formula despite its unpopularity with the Republican Right. Anything less than complete support for Chiang was anathema to Senator William Knowland and his cohorts. And though the administration often tried to anticipate the conservatives' response to its decisions, Eisenhower and Dulles apparently never felt constrained from doing more on the China question. After the offshore island crisis the British ambassador to the United States told his government that Eisenhower, because of his popularity, would be able to pursue a less rigid policy toward China "with an unusual degree of freedom." Some years later, in 1965, Allen Dulles admonished those who believed that "pressure groups" had adversely influenced the Eisenhower administration's China policy. Dulles wrote Robert Blum, an Asian specialist heading a special Council on Foreign Relations project on China, that his brother, Dean Acheson, Dean Rusk, and others involved with China policy "were not influenced by the China Lobby and the like." By the late 1950's the main force of the China Lobby was spent.[45]

A case can even be made that influential Democrats would have backed the administration if it had responded to China's overtures. Walter George, chairman of the Senate Foreign Relations Committee, publicly called on Dulles to meet with Zhou Enlai at the start of the bilateral talks in Geneva. Dulles confided to the president that he felt pressured by George's grandstand play and the press attention it received, but had rejected the recommendation.[46] Such other leading Democrats as Chester Bowles, Senators J. William Fulbright and John F. Kennedy, and the party's 1956 presidential candidate, Adlai Stevenson, all favored a change in China policy and efforts to begin a serious dialogue with Beijing. Dean Acheson suggested to Senate Majority Leader Lyndon Johnson in 1957 that the Eisenhower administration was politically vulnerable on the China question, pointing out that the press was thoroughly incensed over the ban against newsmen traveling to China.[47]

Criticism of the administration's China policy was not just partisan, though. Calls for a change sometimes came from unlikely quarters. Thomas K. Finletter, Truman's tough secretary of the Air Force during the Korean War, attacked the Eisenhower policy as counterproductive. It was simply forcing the Chinese into the arms of the Russians, he said. A British official at the conference where Finletter made his remarks was surprised to find so many of the academics and businessmen there accepting the inevitability of U.S. recognition of China. The automobile magnate Henry Ford II received wide support for his call in January 1957 for possible trade and even aid to China. By its intransigent position the United States was playing into the hands of the Soviets, Ford maintained: the United States ought to offer an alternative to dependency on the Kremlin.[48]

One organized expression of sentiment favoring a revision of U.S. China policy was a conference convened by the American Assembly, a nonpartisan group that sponsored discussions on major topics of the day. (The assembly had been started in 1950 by Eisenhower himself, as president of Columbia University.) In late 1956 the assembly brought together 60 participants, mainly prominent corporate executives, Asia specialists, and former government officials, to discuss the situation in Asia and U.S. policy. As the leader of the China discussion, A. Doak Barnett, rapidly becoming one of the most influential China-watchers outside of government, called for an end to the trade embargo, the negotiation of China's acceptance into the United Nations, the Nationalists' withdrawal from the offshore islands, and the transformation of the Chiang government into a "stable, local regime ruling Taiwan and the Pescadores" with no aspirations to the mainland. Though the assembly did not adopt all of Barnett's view, it did call on the administration to increase trade, permit journalists to travel in China, and pursue negotiations with China to resolve disputes.[49]

In 1955, just before the Big Four Geneva Conference, the administration learned from public opinion polls that 70 percent of the Americans surveyed approved of bilateral talks with China and that two out of three favored a summit conference that would include China. Such findings indicated that the public was likely to be receptive to initiatives on the China problem, if the administration had wanted to introduce some movement.[50] Why then did the Eisenhower administration choose not to seize the opportunity to introduce a new approach when there was some openness on the Chinese side? The pressure of conservatives and the continuing rancor from the Korean War certainly were problems. But there were also major developments in international politics that figured prominently in the decision to continue the closed-door policy. The increased U.S. commitment to the anticommunist fight in Southeast Asia in 1957 and the growing evidence of a major transformation in Soviet life also help to explain America's continued intransigence toward Beijing.

VI

U.S. entanglement in Indochina had mounted steadily after the end of World War II, and by early 1954 Washington was funding more than 75 percent of France's costs in its war against the Communist Viet Minh. When the French faced defeat at Dienbienphu, U.S. concern turned to alarm. In April 1954 Eisenhower introduced to the American public the image of noncommunist nations falling like so many dominos. He warned that if the Communists seized Southeast Asia, the damage would be catastrophic for American interests. Behind this horrible prospect, allegedly, was China.[51]

To repulse the Chinese hordes from sweeping over Vietnam and the rest of Indochina, the Eisenhower administration planned nuclear strikes against China in the spring and early summer of 1954. Although the Chinese invasions never occurred, and the Geneva Conference temporarily ended the fighting, the Eisenhower administration remained convinced that Beijing coveted Southeast Asia, and that the local Communists were their obedient instruments. After the French government abolished its military High Command in South Vietnam in April 1956, the United States assumed full responsibility for training the South Vietnamese Army. The NSC's Planning Board began an extensive review of U.S. policy toward the region, culminating in NSC 5612/1, "U.S. Policy in Mainland Southeast Asia." The NSC quickly approved the paper. That document, with its affirmation of the decision to pursue "nation building" in South Vietnam, was a turning point in U.S. involvement in Southeast Asia and reinforced the hard-line policy toward China.[52]

According to NSC 5612/1, "international communism" (that is, Soviet-directed communism) was emphasizing nonmilitary methods to advance its interests in the world. China, however, was another story. The PRC still threatened aggression in Southeast Asia, whose loss would have "far-reaching consequences seriously adverse to U.S. security interests." In the first formal commitment of the United States to the defense of South Vietnam, the NSC decided that, given the PRC threat, the United States must militarily support the regime of Ngo Dinh Diem. In order to build up the region's strength and spirit to resist the Chinese threat, the United States also committed itself to pushing the South's economic, political, and social development, unleashing a river of aid that by the end of the decade amounted to two billion dollars, one of the largest U.S. programs in the world.[53]

The administration concluded that the United States had to embody anti-China resistance as a model for weaker nations and avoid any impression that it was softening its stand against the Chinese Communists. Dulles believed that the ripple from even a small hint that Washington might reconcile itself to Beijing's existence would cause a catastrophic deluge. In mid-1957 he argued, in his own tortured version of the domino thesis, that if it seemed that the United States was going to accept the Chinese Communists, "all these countries in Asia, these little countries which are isolated, an island or peninsula, . . . they say, 'Well, if that's inevitable, I guess we better succumb to it,' and the first thing we know, we will have lost the major defense line which we depend upon to keep the Pacific Ocean a friendly body of water." America would then face a hostile Asia, including Japan. Dulles, with awkward imagery, warned that the Asian nations were "little outposts with vast land masses of Communist China beating against them," and their determination to hold out was dependent on the United States.[54] Some years later Allen Dulles recalled that the concern with Southeast Asia largely explained his brother's opposition to the recognition of China. That move, according to Allen Dulles, would have subverted the anticommunist nations and pushed them into the hands of Beijing.[55]

The CIA endorsed John Foster Dulles's contention. At the end of 1957 it warned that China's influence in Asia was increasing, and that "any modification of U.S. policy which appeared to Asians as a significant softening of U.S. constancy and firmness in opposing Communist China and in helping Asian countries to achieve their aspirations would enhance Peiping's prospects." Eisenhower agreed. With Southeast Asia in mind, he wrote Henry Wallace in 1957 that "the purpose of creating divisive rather than unifying influences between China and the Soviets is obviously a correct one. The problem is to discover ways of doing this without weakening our own ties with numerous Allies—particularly in the Far East." Just a few weeks earlier Eisenhower, with great ceremony and publicity, had officially welcomed Ngo Dinh Diem on a state visit, listened as he addressed a joint session of Congress, and pledged to provide increased aid to South Vietnam.[56]

Ironically, it had been the need to contain China that had largely spurred the U.S. interest in Southeast Asia in the first place. But by the late 1950's the tail was wagging the dog, in a manner of speaking. The commitment to Southeast Asia itself helped block a reduction of tensions between the United States and China that might have led to a stabilization of the entire continent. The Vietnamese Communists were not willing tools of Beijing, but as the Geneva Conference in 1954 had shown, they were responsive to influences from their Communist allies.[57]

The new importance of Indochina to the administration was a part of its developing concern about communist and anti-Western activity in the Third World. In 1956–57 the contention between the United States and Soviet Union was shifting from direct confrontation to rivalry over the fate of the developing countries in the Middle East, Africa, and Asia. Dulles, according to the recollection of several of his contemporaries in the administration, was the first man at senior levels to understand the importance of the shift. The U.S. struggle for influence over the developing countries, however, was complicated by China. Unlike Europe, where the Soviet Union was Washington's principal worry, the Third World was susceptible to China's anti-imperialist appeal. China was a colored, non-Western country with a history of colonial exploitation. Dulles pointed out to his old friends in the Council on Foreign Relations in 1957 that the many "new nations" that had emerged since World War II harbored mistrust and fear of the West, and "also of the white man and his power." The development of "good relations with these countries is fraught with very great difficulties."[58] Under the circumstances the United States could ill afford to give the Chinese contagion a chance to spread in the Third World.

The changes taking place within the Soviet Union itself in the mid-1950's also bolstered the U.S. conviction that it had to maintain pressure on China. On several occasions in 1957 Dulles proclaimed his faith in the inevitable passing of revolutionary communism, if only the West could fend off the pressure to relax its policies. The proof of this, he argued, was Khrushchev's own disavowal of Stalin and the liberalization occurring in the Soviet Union. Western policies contributed to the favorable turn of events, Dulles claimed, and détente with the Soviet Union would encourage the continuation of that positive trend. But China was at an earlier stage of development; overtures would only inspire its arrogance and frustrate the desired change. A policy of pressure had worked on the Soviet Union and it eventually would work on China as well.[59]

Furthermore, Dulles felt that the Soviet Union's interest in advancing its own relations with the West was impairing Sino-Soviet relations. He believed (incorrectly) that the Soviets were not helping China develop nuclear weapons and might even conclude a disarmament treaty with the United States with provisions obstructing China's nuclear road. He defended the much-maligned trade embargo on China by pointing out that the Soviets were contributing to the effectiveness of the restrictions. Critics had argued that the disparity in trade restrictions with Communist countries was nonsensical, since the Chinese could get what they wanted through the Soviet Union, but Dulles stated that "the Soviet Union itself [was] not too anxious to have the Communist Chinese develop an independent war potential" and was therefore not making available all that China wanted.[60] Though the subject had not been discussed explicitly, it appeared that the United States and the Soviet Union, despite other differences, were beginning to find common ground in retarding China's development. In the face of great pressures from Japan and Britain, the administration stubbornly resisted revision of the embargo policy.[61] Moreover, Moscow's palpable uneasiness with the Chinese seemed to vindicate the administration's policy of pressure. Why should the United States take the heat off now? Dulles could take satisfaction in seeing that the Chinese albatross was chafing Khrushchev's neck.

Some historians have faulted the Eisenhower administration for not recognizing and exploiting early Sino-Soviet differences.[62] But that criticism is based on several now-invalid assumptions. One is that the administration's noisy public diatribes against the danger of a monolithic "international communism" were all there was to U.S. policy. The administration's internal considerations were in fact not so simplistic. Top administration officials paid considerable attention to distinctions among the Communist states. A second assumption is that the U.S. hard line toward China was symptomatic of a blindness to the possibilities—that a lenient policy would have encouraged a more independent China. But the administration's closed-door strategy to divide the Communist giants simply differed from the liberals' "open door" alternative in its tactics—it was a difference over the means of creating a division, not the end. Furthermore, by the late 1950's the administration tended to see that the division would come from U.S.-Soviet cooperation. China had now become America's number one immediate enemy.

Finally, there is an assumption that China was "wooable" from the Soviet Union. Now, it is true that the Chinese Communists sought improved relations with Washington, insofar as such progress would undermine U.S. ties with the Nationalists and reduce tensions in Asia. But that does not mean they would have embraced the United States over the Soviets. The Chinese criticized the Soviets for being too eager to reach accord with the West. In the pantheon of enemies and friends, Mao Zedong was convinced that the main enemy of the people of the world was U.S. imperialism. And he was in no hurry to normalize relations with the United States. As he frankly told his Party associates in 1957, "I still think it preferable to put off the establishment of diplomatic relations with the United States for some years. This will be more to our advantage." Mao believed that if diplomatic relations were postponed, China could consolidate its revolution and the United States would further isolate itself in the world. He was certain that the U.S. would eventually change its nonrecognition policy and guessed that this would take at least until the late 1960's. As it turned out, his prediction was not far off the mark.[63]

VII

There is one factor that has not been given sufficient attention in understanding U.S. policy toward Beijing and Moscow in the 1950's. Prejudice against Asians permeated the entire top levels of the administration. Exclamations of racial fear, mistrust, and disdain often intruded into the discussions of policymakers. Eisenhower, for example, was convinced that the Chinese valued life less than Westerners did, including the Soviets. In a cabinet discussion about a food crisis in China, he observed that the Chinese held "peculiar attitudes" toward human life and would consider the starvation of 50,000,000 of its people a "gain." In his memoirs he openly invokes the specter of the Yellow Peril: he and Dulles had kept a sharp eye on the Chinese because they were a "smart people, . . . tremendous in number, and their leaders seem absolutely indifferent to the prospect of losing millions of people." In contrast, "among Western statesmen, human life is weighed carefully—to understate our attitude." To Eisenhower the difference between the West and the East was obvious and intrinsic.[64]

The ease with which leading members of the administration frequently considered the massive use of nuclear weapons against the mainland, including civilian targets, disputes the consistency of the Western humanism claimed by Eisenhower. One of these top officials was the president's own national security adviser, Dillon Anderson, whom Eisenhower later recommended as a possible running mate for Richard Nixon in 1960. When asked during an interview in 1969 whether the administration seriously considered using nuclear weapons against China during the 1955 offshore island crisis, Anderson crudely offered:

That was our policy, to use them wherever appropriate, and if atomic weapons had been required to carry out our commitments to [Chiang] or trying to land American forces on the Chinese mainland with 700 million Chinamen, it would have not been the latter. Good God, they can breed them faster in the zone of the interior than you can kill them in the combat zone.[65]

Eisenhower's and Dillon's sentiments were not unusually vicious but typical of many in their generation. The first half of the twentieth century witnessed the heyday of anti-Asian racism in the United States. Eisenhower's administration was staffed by men who had grown to maturity during years when Asians tended to be identified as both inferior and insidious.[66] The beliefs of a number of Eisenhower's men were also shaped by their personal military or diplomatic experiences in the area. Admiral Radford, General Curtis LeMay, Under Secretary of State Walter Bedell Smith, disarmament adviser Harold Stassen, Assistant Secretary of State Walter Robertson, Assistant Secretary of State Livingston Merchant, and Eisenhower himself had all lived in China or some other Asian country at one time. The families of John Foster and Allen Dulles, C. D. Jackson, and Under Secretary of State Herbert Hoover, Jr., were proud of their long, close ties with China. These contacts, however superficial, boosted their notions that they possessed an expertise about Asians, and Chinese in particular.

Eisenhower, according to the historian Robert Divine, supposedly felt uncomfortable in dealing with Asia, since his experience had mainly been in Europe. But whatever inadequacy he may have felt, he was not timorous in judging the nature of "Orientals." Eisenhower's attitudes themselves were a mixture of paternalism and dread. He once tried to indulge Krishna Menon of India by observing that during four and a half years of life in the Far East, he came to be very fond of the Chinese. "I liked them tremendously," said the president, trying to convince Menon that U.S. hostility toward Beijing was not racially motivated. Eisenhower cited the long record of American friendliness toward the Chinese people, who had received the benefits of unselfishly built hospitals, roads, and schools. Eisenhower wanted Menon to appreciate the American reaction to the CCP's ingratitude.[67] Washington's costly embroilment in Chinese politics in the 1930's and 1940's, only to result in the bitter disappointment of the Communist victory in 1949, reinforced American frustration with the Chinese.

Eisenhower's prejudice was not limited to the Communists. He feared the overseas Chinese in other parts of Asia as a potential fifth column in their host countries. Eisenhower also often expressed impatience with Chiang Kai-shek, frequently the butt of banter in the NSC. The president was especially nasty one day during the 1955 offshore crisis when he cautioned the NSC to be vigilant for any tricks from Chiang. "We are always wrong when we believe that Orientals think logically as we do," Eisenhower instructed, according to the notes of that meeting. The president recalled a fable about a mule that walks into a brick wall, saying that saving face was all-important to Orientals. They "would rather lose everything than lose face." The president ended his lesson on the psychology of Asians with the admonition that "he had learned that the only way to deal with Orientals was on an empirical day-to-day basis."[68] The notes of the meeting do not make clear what fable Eisenhower was referring to, but the story does show that Eisenhower's anti-Asian racism was at least indiscriminate: he mistrusted communist and anticommunist Asians alike.

Dulles, whom his relatives credit as having a fondness for traditional China, likewise was wary of the East. Apparently oblivious to the likelihood that his words would be offensive, Dulles once informed Wellington Koo that "the Oriental mind . . . was always more devious" than that of the Occidental. Unfortunately, the Nationalist ambassador's notes do not record his response.[69] With such racial attitudes, the reasons for the administration's unresponsiveness to Chinese overtures take on an added dimension. Signs of flexibility on China's part could easily be dismissed as Asian trickery. On the other hand Chinese hostility seemed to confirm Asian fanaticism. Typical in this respect were Radford's views. At one point during the 1955 offshore crisis, Radford told the NSC that even though U.S. photo reconnaissance had revealed no Communist preparations for an immediate assault, "we must assume that the

Chinese Communists are getting ready just as fast as they can." Without indisputable evidence to the contrary, one had to think the worst of the Chinese Communists.[70]

Specialists like those who gathered at the June 1955 Quantico meeting called by Nelson Rockefeller provided academic sanction to the administration's racial predispositions. Paul Linebarger, the expert on Asian political behavior, explained Chinese Communist politics in the light of his interpretation of Chinese tradition. According to him, mendacity had characterized Chinese diplomacy from imperial times to the present. Even the Russians, he wrote in his annex to the Quantico Report, realized that "sheer outright symbolic lying was a daily requisite to getting along in Communist China." Linebarger drew an erudite, but standard, image of the Yellow Peril. The Chinese were fixated with "honor" and "face." The Chinese were irrational: they did not take atomic weapons seriously but considered them "firecrackers." And the Chinese were duplicitous and presumptuous: they craved power and international status.[71] Linebarger expressed the prevailing conviction that China was a peculiarly formidable and menacing enemy: the dreaded Yellow Peril had converged with the detested Red Peril.

Racial thinking also distinguished the administration's thinking about the relative threats of the Soviets and the Chinese. Eisenhower points out in his memoirs that "no matter what differences in culture and tradition, values or language, the Russian leaders were human beings, and they wanted to remain alive." But the president had no such generous words for the Chinese, referring to them as "hysterical," "irrational," and "fanatical." As Dulles once pointed out in comparing the Chinese with the Russians, the Russians were "calculating" in their actions, whereas "emotion played a large part in [China's] conduct."[72] In the administration's view, however terrible the power and ambition of the Soviets, they at least were a comprehensible, European adversary.

It is difficult to judge the extent to which these prejudices influenced policymaking in the Eisenhower era. Historians, and the memoirs of policymakers themselves, usually emphasize that frank calculations of national interests determine foreign policy. But as shown above, the denigrating assumptions about the nature of Chinese were pervasive and comfortably held. The mixed, inflamed images of the Red and Yellow Perils colored the perceptions of events and conditions. Prejudiced remarks often punctuated high-level deliberations. If nothing else the racist images reinforced the rationales for the U.S. closed-door policy toward China in the 1950's. To the administration nothing could have been worse: Mao and his comrades were communist *and* Chinese.

SIX

Toward a U.S.-Soviet Community of Interest

The weak fear the strong; the strong fear the resolute; the resolute fear the desperate. —Chinese aphorism

American policy toward the Sino-Soviet relationship was a widely debated issue in elite circles outside the administration in the mid-1950's. But few except the most die-hard anticommunists saw the relationship as monolithic. Most accepted it as an alliance of partners, not as one of overlord and vassal. And though most also agreed that a fracturing of the Communist alliance would benefit the United States, no one was hopeful that an actual split was possible in the foreseeable future.

The lingering assumption that an eventual division between the two powers would come when China became dissatisfied with the Soviet Union contributed to this pessimistic appraisal, since Beijing was showing no signs of disenchantment with Leninism. Its adherence to communist doctrine, in fact, seemed to be growing. Those who assumed that the Chinese would initiate a Sino-Soviet division, however, were being left behind by the thinking of John Foster Dulles and others in the administration who suspected that Washington might be able to induce Moscow to distance itself from Beijing. By late 1958 influential voices even began speaking of a Washington-Moscow "community of interest" against the Chinese Communists.

I

The most important nongovernmental group to devote attention to the question of China and the Sino-Soviet alliance was the Council on Foreign Relations. The notes of its study groups, meetings, and lectures, held in a congenial and clubby atmosphere, often reveal the sentiment of America's foreign policy elite at more candid moments than in wider public settings.

From October 1955 to March 1956 the CFR sponsored a special study group on Sino-Soviet relations and U.S. policy. Arthur Dean, the CFR director who had sparked a controversy in 1954 by suggesting that an effort to reach accommodation with Beijing might create problems between China and the Soviet Union, led the discussions.[1] Dean's group included a number of leading Asia and foreign affairs specialists, and unusually close ties with Washington made it semiofficial. Joining the academics were Dean Rusk, then head of the Rockefeller Foundation; Robert Amory, Jr., of the CIA; George H. Greene, Jr., of the NSC; Walter P. McConaughy, director of the Office of Chinese Affairs of the State Department; and several ranking Army officers. Henry Kissinger was not officially part of the group but joined at least one session.[2]

At the study group's first meeting in late October 1955, Dean emphasized that their objective was not academic, but "to determine the best U.S. policy toward the Chinese Communist government and the Sino-Soviet relationship." He hoped that they could clarify what was happening in China and the nature of its relationship with the Soviet Union, and identify "constructive, alternative solutions" for Washington. The group then discussed a paper entitled "The Sino-Soviet Alliance in the Struggle with the West," by Howard L. Boorman, a China-watcher from Columbia University who had been with the American consulate in Beiping in 1949 and later monitored Communist China from Hong Kong for the State Department.[3]

Boorman described the history of the relations between the two Communist movements and the dynamics of the alliance, especially in Asia. He devoted his attention to the Chinese side of the equation, but not just because China was his specialty. All of the study group's discussion papers focused on Beijing rather than Moscow. That apparently reflected an inclination to see China as the more active, or perhaps less understood, partner in shaping the alliance. While the Soviet Union benefited from the relationship in seemingly obvious ways, it was

China that had voluntarily allied itself with the Kremlin, and the motivations of the Chinese Communists were not as clear.

In some ways Boorman's assessment of China resembled George Kennan's conclusions about the Soviet Union in 1947. Like Kennan Boorman identified the sources of Communist behavior in feudal traditions and psychohistorical experience. Marxism-Leninism gave modern form and impetus to deep imperial impulses, creating a Chinese foreign policy that was "a new and potent brew," according to Boorman. Beijing was "heir" to "the psychological tradition of Chinese dominance and superiority in Asia." Also like Kennan, Boorman counseled the need for Western perseverance in combating communism. Boorman gloomily ended his essay with a warning from a nineteenth-century missionary that it was "in his staying qualities that the Chinese excels the world."

But where Kennan's Soviet Union shrewdly calculated its response to "counter-force," Boorman saw an irrationality in Chinese behavior. Unlike Russia China still smarted from the humiliation of the West's triumph in Asia and had never adjusted to its humbled position in the modern world. China's prideful ambitions still reigned fierce and, for that reason, it found the alliance with the Soviet Union immensely advantageous. The Soviets provided not only political, economic, and military support, but also international prestige. The Soviet Union also accrued substantial benefits from the alliance. The alliance was the key element in its Far Eastern strategy, and Chinese manpower and "machinations" challenged the West and diverted its resources from Europe and other areas of Soviet interest. The Soviets were all too happy to pay the economic price for such an ally. Thus in Boorman's evaluation the Sino-Soviet alliance was "not only expedient but necessary" for both partners.

The study group found little to disagree with in Boorman's report and concluded that the impact of the Sino-Soviet alliance on world politics was ominous and monumental. As one participant ventured, the historian E. H. Carr should retitle his well-known book "The *Sino*-Soviet Impact on the Western World."[4] (The CFR generally did not attribute comments in its records.)

The first session set the tone for those that followed. Whether discussing ideology, economics, or common border areas, the group identified no differences potentially mortal to the Sino-Soviet alliance. Whatever economic and ideological conflicts existed, they paled in light of broader power objectives. When it came time to summarize their findings and implications for U.S. policy, the members of the CFR study group decided that the convergence of Chinese and Soviet interests greatly exceeded any immediate divergences. None of the participants was confident that the alliance would weaken even in the long run. One went so far as to say that the Soviet Union had more of a chance of separating Britain and the United States than the West had of dividing China and Russia. The study group concluded that "in the present or foreseeable future there appears to be no means of creating major friction between Communist China and Russia," and offered no suggestions for an improvement in U.S. policy toward the alliance. *The Moscow-Peking Axis*, the ominous title of the book containing the revised discussion papers, well expressed the participants' estimation of the challenge. The problem remained, as Arthur Dean conceded, whether the best way to strain relations between China and the Soviet Union was to "push them together," or "pull them apart." That issue, which Chester Bowles and John Foster Dulles had privately debated in 1952, continued to vex policymakers.[5]

Soon after the conclusion of the CFR's study, the Rockefeller family, through the Rockefeller Brothers Fund, initiated a massive project that also devoted considerable attention to the Sino-Soviet alliance. The Rockefellers brought together a variety of leaders from many walks of life to study the problems that were expected to confront America over the next decade. From mid-1956 to 1960 the more than 100 participants met in panels to discuss foreign, military, economic, social, educational, and political issues, and develop recommendations for improving national policy. The effort was nonpartisan, with liberals like Chester Bowles and Theodore Hesburgh, president of the University of Notre Dame, sitting alongside conservatives like *Time* publisher Henry Luce and the retail tycoon Justin Dart. Business leaders included John D. Rockefeller III; Laurance, Nelson, and David Rockefeller; Charles H. Percy, president of Bell and Howell Company; and David Sarnoff

Vice-President Richard Nixon and Chiang Kai-shek, Taiwan, July 7, 1956. Nixon carried a message from President Eisenhower of "continuing support." Photo courtesy Bettmann Newsphotos, Inc./United Press International.

Eisenhower meeting with (l. to r.) Dr. V. K. Wellington Koo, ROC ambassador to the United States; Dr. George K. C. Yeh, ROC minister for foreign affairs; and Walter Robertson, assistant secretary of state. Photo courtesy Dwight D. Eisenhower Library; National Park Service.

Mao welcoming Khrushchev to Beijing, September 30, 1959. This would be the last Sino-Soviet summit for thirty years. Photo courtesy New China News Agency.

President Eisenhower on a state visit to Taiwan, with Generalissimo and Mme Chiang Kai-shek, June 1960. Photo courtesy Dwight D. Eisenhower Library.

Eisenhower and Khrushchev, Camp David, Maryland, September 25, 1959. Photo courtesy Dwight D. Eisenhower Library; U.S. Navy.

The send-off of the Chinese delegation to the Sino-Soviet party talks in Moscow; Beijing airport, July 5, 1963; (l. to r.) Zhu De (with cane), Liu Shaoqi, Zhou Enlai, Deng Xiaoping, Peng Zhen, and Chen Boda (with sunglasses). Photo courtesy New China News Agency.

Soviet party leader Mikhail Suslov greeting Deng Xiaoping at the Moscow airport, July 5, 1963, on the arrival of the Chinese delegation to the Sino-Soviet talks. On the left is Peng Zhen. Photo courtesy New China News Agency.

Khrushchev with W. Averell Harriman (left), head of the U.S. delegation, and Lord Hailsham (Quentin Hogg; right), head of the British delegation, to the tripartite talks on a limited nuclear test ban treaty, Moscow, July 1963. Khrushchev joked, "I'm surrounded by imperialists." Reproduced by permission from *Life*, July 26, 1963, p. 26.

President Kennedy delivering the commencement address at American University, Washington, D.C., June 10, 1963. In this address, Kennedy urged U.S.-Soviet cooperation in reducing world tensions. Photo courtesy John F. Kennedy Library.

President Kennedy signing the instrument ratifying the Limited Test Ban Treaty, October 7, 1963, before Senate and administration leaders (l. to r.): Adrian Fisher, deputy director, Arms Control and Disarmament Agency; Senator John O. Pastore; Ambassador-at-Large W. Averell Harriman; Senator George Smathers; Senator J. William Fulbright; Secretary of State Dean Rusk; Senator George D. Aiken; Senator Hubert Humphrey; Senator Everett Dirksen; Senator Thomas Kuchel; Senator John Tower; Senator Leverett Saltonstall; Senator Henry M. Jackson; Vice-President Lyndon Johnson. Photo courtesy John F. Kennedy Library.

Chen Yi (second from left) and Zhou Enlai (second from right) greeting Soviet Premier Alexei Kosygin (center) and a Soviet delegation to North Vietnam on a stopover at Beijing airport, February 6, 1965. With Kosygin were Yuri Andropov (far left) and Vasily Kuznetsov (far right). Photo courtesy New China News Agency.

Mao Zedong meeting with President Nixon and National Security Adviser Henry Kissinger, in Mao's study, Beijing, February 21, 1972. Photo courtesy New China News Agency.

President Johnson meeting with Premier Kosygin at Glassboro, N.J., June 1969.
Photo courtesy Lyndon Baines Johnson Library.

Mao greeting George Bush, then-chief of the U.S. Liaison Office in Beijing, during the visit of President and Mrs. Gerald Ford to Beijing, December 2, 1975. Mao died nine months later. Photo courtesy New China News Agency.

of RCA. There were plenty of former and future government and military luminaries, among them former Assistant Secretary of State Adolf Berle; General Lucius D. Clay; the economist Arthur Burns; John W. Gardner, president of the Carnegie Corporation; Gordon Dean, former chairman of the Atomic Energy Commission; James R. Killian, president of MIT and later Eisenhower's special assistant on science and technology; Dean Rusk; the physicist Edward Teller; Robert B. Anderson, soon to become Eisenhower's treasury secretary; and Roswell L. Gilpatric, former under secretary of the Air Force. Henry Kissinger served as director through most of the project.[6]

Dean Rusk chaired the subpanel on foreign policy. His subject proved to be the most difficult, and U.S. policy toward China and the Sino-Soviet alliance the biggest quandary. The China question arose in almost every session, but the discussion during the third meeting (January 1957) especially reflected the divisiveness and difficulty of the issue.

The Japan scholar Robert Scalapino, of the University of California, Berkeley, started the discussion by observing that though China was clearly a long-range enemy, the United States should moderate its hard line to try to weaken the Communist bloc. Howard Boorman took a contrary position, similar to the one he had put forward in the CFR study group: China was a dangerous adversary, and the Sino-Soviet alliance, "a powerful threat to the Free World," was growing stronger, not weaker. In his opinion "the effect of U.S. policy on the Chinese Communists' actions would be minor."[7]

Boorman's assessment was challenged in turn by John W. Nason, president of the Foreign Policy Association, and Joseph E. Johnson, president of the Carnegie Endowment for International Peace, who asked him whether there was a split in the Sino-Soviet alliance. Boorman assured them there was not. Max Millikan of MIT argued that though the Chinese might be discontented with the Soviets, they had no alternative but to continue their alliance with them. He wondered whether the United States could offer a choice to the Chinese. Boorman agreed that "a real conflict" between China and the Soviet Union might eventually occur but believed the PRC would depend on the alliance for the next five years or so.[8]

The debate over the prospects of the Sino-Soviet challenge

went unresolved. Dean Rusk, unwilling to end the day's discussion on an ambiguous note, turned to what seemed to him the crucial immediate question: the U.N. seat. The United States, he remarked, had to realize that it was "in a losing position on this matter." The world was shifting its views toward China, and it was only a matter of time before the PRC would be seated in the international body. The future secretary of state stressed that the United States must take the initiative in working out a plan of negotiations with the Chinese over this and other issues.[9]

Saville R. Davis, managing editor of the *Christian Science Monitor*, went further, to argue that Washington should try to negotiate with China over a broad range of issues, including not only U.N. membership but also the reunification of both Korea and Vietnam, the renunciation of force against Taiwan, the jurisdiction of the offshore islands, and diplomatic recognition, while vigorously containing China's expansionist tendencies. He believed that substantive talks with the Chinese might encourage their independence from Moscow. Although several participants, including Rusk, urged that great care was necessary to do what Davis suggested, no one directly opposed his views. The panelists, however, still did not reach any decision on China policy. Several months later they admitted: "The most serious lack of any purposeful decision by the subpanel, either in its papers or deliberations, is in the area of U.S.-China relationships. Do we work for a *pax pacifica* via long-range efforts to accommodate with China, or settle down to a long struggle at every level with her, or can we attempt to stay on [the] side lines?"[10]

In May 1957, when Rusk reported on the work of his group to the so-called Overall Panel in charge of the entire project, he said that his panelists recognized the great difficulty of the China problem, but believed Washington should consider altering its policies toward the PRC, especially on the U.N. question. The United States had to begin to talk about its long-range policy toward China, according to Rusk. "When you add up such evidence as we have [about its economic development] you better not underestimate what is going on in Red China. I don't think that we ought to stand by and wait for Red China to collapse." John Cowles, the influential head of the publishing empire bearing his name, endorsed Rusk's views but was inclined to be less "cautious," as he put it, in his proposals. Cowles wanted the United States to adopt an affirmative attitude toward China, criticizing current policy as "a dead-end street, a blind alley in which we are going to eventually be defeated if we continue." Later, in discussing the Soviet Union, Cowles elaborated on his comments about China. Saying he spoke for himself, James Killian, and Edward Teller (a strange threesome), Cowles argued, "You can't consider our relations with Russia without referring also to our relations with China and the effect our changed relations with China may have on our relations with Russia." The United States had to place China policy in that context, for any consideration of bringing pressure on the Soviet Union "would not be complete without considering the possibility of the West encouraging an increasing independence in policies and attitudes on the part of China toward Russia." Cowles added, "And of course to do that requires a much greater flexibility in our program toward Red China. We think that there is [a] possibility if we change our attitude towards Red China, that Red China is apt to, or [may], become more independent toward Russia, maybe over a period of time, [which would] tend to have a more profound effect upon our relations with Russia."[11] Cowles's comments indicate that opinion on the China issue was not strictly split along partisan lines; even conservatives like Teller had their reasons for wanting to introduce some flexibility into China policy.

While the other panels completed their final reports by the end of 1958, Rusk's group did not publish its findings until December 1959. August Heckscher, director of the Twentieth Century Fund, was responsible for writing the report. Early outlines and drafts of the paper accurately reflected the discussion favoring a modification of U.S. China policy (even perhaps ending nonrecognition) and the active pursuit of measures to erode the Communist alliance. But successive drafts became increasingly pedestrian, perhaps because the 1958 offshore island crisis made talk of reaching out to Beijing inopportune.[12] When the report finally appeared, all fresh ideas had been eliminated. Despite years of work and the intention of taking a new look at the nation's purposes, the analysis contained only stale Cold War rhetoric and perspectives. The published report stated that the Communists were waging "one co-ordinated conflict" against the West. China and the Soviet Union might not always see eye to eye, but their alliance seemed "structurally and ideologically sound." And though Washington should watch for strains between the two Communist giants, "policies specifically designed to drive a wedge between Moscow and Peiping" would not produce any "effective results." As for China itself, it was a "fanatical" enemy of the United States, expansionist and intransigent. Because of China's attitude, "the alternatives of policy are, for the short run, lacking in creative possibilities." Neither recognition by the United States nor admission to the United Nations would end the Chinese danger. Consequently, Washington had to maintain a tenacious containment policy, strengthen the "free world," and build a powerful military defense, especially an "atomic capability."[13] Again public reiterations of Cold War generalities obscured the diversity of views that America's foreign policy elite expressed in more private settings.

II

While American specialists and politicians speculated about what the United States should or even could do about the Sino-Soviet alliance, deteriorating relations between the two Communist powers were steadily changing the nature of the debate. In 1958 tensions previously restrained by a desire to present a united front began to influence their major policy decisions. Most specialists in Soviet and Chinese affairs believe that year marked a turning point in the deterioration of Sino-Soviet relations and saw the first overt appearance of triangular politics in the foreign policy considerations of Moscow and Beijing. Many also charge that the United States was obtuse in not seeing the obvious signs of discord and failed to seize opportunities provided by the emerging rift.[14]

But in fact the Eisenhower administration's perception and attitude toward the Sino-Soviet alliance did shift in 1958. In the wake of the newest Jinmen crisis, many top administration figures became convinced that America's adversaries were having serious differences that Washington might systematically manipulate.

Beijing's principal reason for initiating the 1958 Jinmen crisis, as can be surmised from the evidence that is now available, was to try to shatter the stalemate in U.S.-China relations and end the combined U.S.-ROC military threat from the offshore islands. Since April 1955, when Beijing ended the first offshore crisis, the PRC had pursued a path of negotiation and moderation to try to improve U.S.-China relations. After some initial progress in the bilateral talks, China's leaders apparently concluded that the United States was using the meetings to buy time and pursue a two-China policy to separate Taiwan from the mainland. At the end of 1957 Washington postponed the talks indefinitely. Concurrently, the administration continued its opposition to the seating of Beijing in the United Nations, its trade and travel embargo, and its vehement anti-China rhetoric. The United States was well aware of Beijing's unhappiness about the situation.[15]

China also watched as U.S. economic assistance and military aid, including the publicized installation of the Matador missiles in 1957, steadily strengthened the ROC position on Taiwan. Chiang increased his troops on the offshore islands to 100,000, almost one-third of his ground forces. The disruption of Communist shipping and guerrilla operations actually mounted in the years after the 1955 crisis. Because of the Nationalists' harassment of shipping, "a negligible amount of foreign shipping transits the Taiwan Straits," a U.S. military estimate concluded only a year later.[16] Beijing probably hoped that a dramatic political-military operation might significantly weaken Taipei and pressure Washington to alter its intransigent position.

But there were other factors in Beijing's decision to strike and initiate a new offshore island crisis. The Soviet launching of Sputnik I in October 1957 prompted Mao to declare in November that the strength of the "East Wind," the world's revolutionary forces, now exceeded that of the "West Wind," the forces of imperialism. Mao apparently concluded that the danger of U.S. nuclear blackmail had decreased significantly. China also enjoyed an increase in stature in the socialist camp as a result of Zhou Enlai's mediating efforts following the uprisings in Hungary and Poland in 1956 and 1957. By the spring of 1958 a confident CCP leadership confirmed a leftward direction by deciding to launch the Great Leap Forward, Mao's experiment in trying to transform China into an industrialized socialist nation by mobilizing its hundreds of millions of people in mass construction projects.

The offshore island crisis of 1958 began in the midst of international tensions caused by the intervention of U.S. forces in Lebanon in mid-July. With world attention focused on the Middle East, Chinese Communist batteries opened fire on Jinmen and Mazu on August 23 (Taiwan time) in an apparent effort to stop supplies from reaching the fortified Nationalist garrisons. Some 50,000 shells fell on the islands on that first day alone, and the pounding continued over the following weeks. The Communist attack alarmed but did not completely surprise the administration. There had been some advance warning that the Communists were about to launch a new campaign against Jinmen: they had openly augmented their artillery and anti-aircraft strength, started a new "liberate Taiwan" propaganda campaign, and conducted a series of flights over the offshore islands.[17]

American officials on Taiwan believed that the Communists intended to attack the offshore islands after weakening them through a combination of blockade and bombardment.[18] But the CIA concluded that the Communists did not have sufficient forces mobilized for an actual assault on the islands and were simply hoping to starve the Nationalist troops into surrender. Nevertheless Eisenhower felt that the stakes in the offshore islands were in some ways greater than in the 1955 crisis. Even though he still believed that the islands served little purpose, he judged that the loss of so many of Chiang's forces would be as catastrophic for the morale of all the rest of anticommunist Asia as it would be for the Nationalists. The president ordered U.S. military forces in Asia to stand on "readiness alert" for war operations and display a massive show of force. Two aircraft carrier groups immediately sailed to join the Seventh Fleet stationed in the Taiwan area. Within days the United States had assembled off the China coast the most powerful armada the world had ever seen: six carriers, with a complement of 96 planes capable of delivering nuclear weapons, three heavy cruisers, forty destroyers, a submarine division, and twenty other support craft. The United States also expedited the shipment of artillery, planes, and special weaponry, such as the deadly Sidewinder air-to-air missile, to the Nationalists. Even so, the U.S. ambassador to the ROC reported that Chiang Kai-shek was "obsessed" with the possible strangulation of the off-shore islands and "pleaded" for further help to break the Communists' interdiction of supplies to his troops.[19] It seemed that Washington was simply picking up where it had left off from the first crisis.*

On August 27 Eisenhower publicly announced that the off-shore islands were more important to the defense of Taiwan than they had been in 1955. London and Tokyo immediately expressed their opposition to expanded hostilities and to possible U.S. intervention. Dulles's letter to Prime Minister Harold Macmillan defending the American stand, with its exaggerated appraisal of the offshore islands' importance, undoubtedly heightened rather than diminished British concern. In it he said (with Eisenhower's approval) that the fall of the offshore islands would destabilize Taiwan, which would then

be exposed to subversive and military action which would probably bring about a government that would eventually advocate union with Communist China; that if this occurred it would seriously jeopardize the anti-Communist barrier, including Japan, the Republic of Korea, the Republic of China, the Republic of the Philippines, Thailand, and Vietnam; that other governments in Southeast Asia such as those of

---

*Comments made in 1972 by Arleigh A. Burke, who was chief of naval operations during the crisis, reveal the emotional and intangible considerations that affected U.S. decisionmaking. The offshore islands "'don't mean anything,'" Burke recalls telling Eisenhower in 1958. "'It's a purely symbolic thing; they don't mean anything except, who's daddy? Who runs that part of the world, the Red Chinese or the Nationalist Chinese? But physically it doesn't make any difference.' I said, 'It's just like the virtue of a man's wife. The wife's the same. But you don't let anybody else attack her. You just don't do it.'" During the crisis "daddy" more appropriately described the United States than the Nationalists, a fact that Burke almost seems to admit unwittingly. Burke oral history, Nov. 12, 1972, pp. 44–45.

Indonesia, Malaya, Cambodia, Laos and Burma would gradually come fully under Communist influence; that Japan with its great industrial potential would probably fall within the Sino-Soviet orbit, and Australia and New Zealand would become stategically isolated.

Dulles concluded by suggesting that if the United States intervened, it might have to use atomic weapons. "I hope no more than small air bursts without fallout," he said consolingly.[20]

Eisenhower kept U.S. public commitments to the offshore area vague, in his words, to "keep the Communists guessing," as he had tried to do in 1955. He also did not want to provide Chiang with a blank check to draw on U.S. forces. He once again told the NSC that "Orientals can be very devious," and if the United States put itself "on the line with a full commitment, [the Nationalists] would then call the tune."[21]

For the next six weeks, until October 6, when the Communists lifted the siege, the world feared imminent war. For most Americans the confrontation sickeningly recalled the 1954–55 crisis. It appeared that the United States was again pinned to defending some barren bits of land with no discernible military value on the doorstep of the fanatical Chinese Communists, on behalf of an irascible, unpredictable dictator who counted on World War III to restore him to his former glory. Midway through the crisis Eisenhower privately admitted that two-thirds of world opinion opposed his support of Chiang in the offshore islands. If ever there was to be a war in the wrong place and at the wrong time, this seemed to be it, Senator Theodore Green, chairman of the Senate Foreign Relations Committee, wrote Eisenhower.[22]

Despite the outward similarities to the 1954–55 episode, the 1958 crisis was not simply a reprise. Most importantly, there had been a profound change in the U.S.–Soviet Union–China interrelationship over the years: Beijing saw Washington and Moscow moving toward a superpower détente that had threatening implications for China and the international Communist movement. In his memoirs Wang Bingnan, the Chinese ambassador to the Sino-U.S. talks in Warsaw, recalls the Chinese sensitivity to the emerging triangular political configuration. Wang asserts that Beijing had a twofold purpose in initiating the 1958 crisis: to "punish the reckless activity" of Chiang

Kai-shek and the "bluster" of the United States, and to counter indirectly what he calls Khrushchev's appeasement policy of the United States.[23] Soviet writers also charge that Mao launched the crisis to sabotage the emerging détente. In any case serious differences over grand strategy and the sharing of advanced weaponry were beginning to plague Sino-Soviet relations. Upset at what they believed was Chinese recklessness, the Soviets stalled on their deliveries of technical aid and material for China's fledgling strategic weapons program.[24] In this context the crisis became almost as much a test of the Soviet Union's fidelity to China as it was of the administration's commitment to the Nationalists.[25]

During the early days of the crisis, opinion in the Eisenhower administration was sharply divided over the state of Sino-Soviet relations. Eisenhower recalled the questions confronting his advisers in this way: "Why, we wondered, were [the Communists] choosing this moment to stir up trouble in the Far East? Was Khrushchev still trying to hold Mao back, as some believed, or was he urging him on?" For his part Eisenhower was certain that Khrushchev was behind the troubles. The Soviet leader had visited China in early August, and it was inconceivable to Eisenhower that Mao and Khrushchev could not have discussed the operation.[26]

Eisenhower's intelligence experts, contending that all was not well between the two countries, were of a different mind. The CIA believed that Khrushchev had traveled to Beijing precisely because of problems in the alliance. China was pressing the Soviets to adopt a tougher line against the West and also seemed upset at them for recently proposing that India, not China, be included in a five-power summit conference on the Middle East. After his visit Khrushchev dropped his proposal for the summit conference. As the intelligence expert William P. Bundy recalls it, "I and others in the CIA at the time concluded that there must by then be really significant differences emerging [between the Soviet Union and China], and that these were accentuated by the very lukewarm Soviet attitude during the offshore islands crisis." Bundy also recalls that as a result of these developments, "the sense of serious differences between China and Russia became fairly acute *no later than the summer of 1958* [before the Strait crisis]."[27] The CIA, it now appears, had a good handle on the situation, for all of Eisenhower's suspicions. According to Soviet sources, Mao never fully informed Khrushchev of his plans for the offshore island area.[28]

In spite of, or perhaps because of, Eisenhower's misassessment the course of action the United States adopted could not have aggravated tensions more between the two Communist powers. The United States mobilized for all-out war with China and repeatedly charged the Soviets with collusion in instigating the troubles. Yet while Eisenhower and Khrushchev publicly blustered at one another, Washington quietly continued to pursue détente with Moscow. Again the United States threatened China with the stick, while offering the carrot to Moscow. The eventual outcome of the crisis, which pleased Washington, seemed to endorse the wisdom of the two tactics. By the end of 1958 leading figures in the Eisenhower administration sensed that the Soviets had finally recognized that they shared some common interests with the United States in restraining the Chinese.

On August 29, a week after the shelling of Jinmen began, Eisenhower and his advisers agreed that the United States would escort Nationalist supply ships trying to make their way to the islands, although the vessels were to stay in international waters.[29] On the same day the U.S. air force deployed a fighter squadron from Okinawa to Taiwan and sent units of the mobile Composite Air Strike Force from the States. The CASF was a specialized attack group recently developed for use in local wars and possessed atomic capability. With supplements from the Air Force and Marines, the Pacific command soon had well over 200 "atomic aircraft" available for use in the Taiwan area. No secret was made of these shifts of forces from the United States to Asia. The "influx of aircraft, personnel, supplies, and equipment into Pacific bases" was so great it created "confusion" for local commanders. If all this activity was not obvious enough to the Communists, Eisenhower instructed the Defense Department to leak a "few revealing words" to the press about the moves. The president was sure that "these would not escape the notice of the Communists."[30]

Eisenhower refused, however, to authorize the possible use of tactical atomic weapons against the mainland and specifically reserved judgment to see how events developed. His view had changed considerably since the 1955 crisis, when he tried to prepare the world for atomic war by comparing an atomic bomb to a bullet. Even in 1956 he still maintained that military planning should assume the use of tactical atomic weapons in small wars, since that was no more likely to trigger a big war than the use of twenty-ton "block busters."[31] But in 1958 Eisenhower was more apprehensive of the backlash from world opinion if the weapons were used and of the increased might of the Soviet nuclear arsenal.

Neither Dulles nor General Nathan Twining, now chairman of the JCS, was pleased with Eisenhower's directive. The JCS's view was that "the best hope of quickly and decisively stopping Communist attacks against the off-shore islands, Taiwan and the Penghus is an immediate counter-attack with atomic weapons." Dulles was supportive, telling Twining that "there was no use of having a lot of stuff and never be[ing] able to use it."[32] In response to Eisenhower's directive the JCS hurriedly formulated new contingency plans involving only conventional weapons. Responding with atomic weapons was not to be contemplated even for a Communist assault on Taiwan itself.[33]

The injunction against nuclear weapons caused "much anxiety" for Admiral Harry D. Felt, the newly appointed commander-in-chief of the U.S. Pacific forces, according to an Air Force historian. Felt and his staff worried that a conventional defense might not be able to withstand the numerically superior Communist forces. Aircraft and military supplies in the area were woefully inadequate to support a sustained conventional battle. Consequently, Felt urgently requested, in addition to more warplanes, an infusion of conventional bombs, ammunition, fuel, and support equipment. By the end of the crisis, 5,554 tons of emergency materiel had been airlifted to Asia for Felt. The backlog was so great that the military could not handle it all and had to hire commercial airliners to carry large portions of the supplies.[34]

Ironically, Eisenhower's injunction against the use of nuclear weapons may have actually encouraged local commanders to assemble what appeared to be a more threatening force than if they had had the nuclear option. The Communists of course did not know of Eisenhower's decision. From their perspective it must have seemed as though Washington was preparing in earnest for wide-scale nuclear and conventional war. Mao later admitted that the ferocity of the American response surprised him.[35]

Still, Jinmen continued to be heavily shelled through August and into September, effectively isolating the island. Then, on September 4, the administration drew the string tighter, issuing a blunt warning to the Communists. In a press conference at Newport, Rhode Island, Dulles made an unambiguous commitment to the defense of Jinmen, cautioning Beijing that Washington would regard the use of force to seize territory as "an issue far transcending the offshore islands and even the security of Taiwan. [It] would forecast a widespread use of force in the Far East which would endanger vital free world positions and the security of the United States." According to Dulles, the mainland itself would be a target in efforts to protect U.S. interests. But there was a way out: Dulles offered the hope of negotiation to settle the conflict and urged the Communists to meet the United States at the bargaining table.[36]

The American show of force and Chinese pugnacity apparently worried Moscow. On September 5, the day after Dulles's tough talk, Foreign Minister Andrei Gromyko, accompanied by M. S. Kapitsa, one of the Soviet government's China specialists, secretly arrived in Beijing to discuss the matter with the top leaders. Years later Kapitsa claimed that Gromyko was appalled by what he found on his visit. Not only was Mao supposedly unconcerned about the danger of a nuclear conflict; he even presented a plan to use nuclear weapons against American forces. In his memoirs Gromyko claims that Mao expected an attack on the mainland at this point, and proposed to have his forces retreat, drawing U.S. ground troops into China's heartland, where the Soviet Union would then destroy them "with all its means," that is, nuclear weapons. Gromyko says he flatly turned down the suggestion. Gromyko's account is difficult to believe—it seems doubtful that Mao really expected the United States to land troops on the mainland. That serious disputes existed between the two over the crisis, however, now seems undeniable.[37]

Whatever transpired in Beijing, Gromyko apparently had some effect on the Chinese, for on September 6 Zhou Enlai called for a resumption of the suspended talks with Washington at Warsaw. Eisenhower and his top advisers discussed Zhou's statement at length the same day. The president wanted to issue "a concrete and definite acceptance" of the offer to negotiate. Talks began about a week later, but they plowed no new ground—China demanded U.S. recognition of Beijing's sovereignty over Taiwan, while the United States maintained that the crisis was an international issue, not a domestic one for the Chinese, and that the status of Taiwan was still undetermined. Jacob Beam, the American representative at the bilateral talks, argued that legitimate treaty obligations with an ally sanctioned the American presence in the area.[38]

To the Soviets, who were railing against the insanity of nuclear war, Mao's alleged insouciance was horrifying. Chinese actions in the Taiwan Strait were jeopardizing the Soviet Union's effort to achieve its premier foreign policy objective: a major arms control agreement with Washington. In the summer of 1958 American and Soviet scientists and experts had met in Geneva to discuss the problems of a monitoring system for the detection of secret nuclear blasts. Resolving the technical difficulties for such a system might pave the way for ending atomic testing altogether, something that both the United States and the Soviet Union said they wished to achieve. The amiable and businesslike attitude of the discussions indicated the serious intent on both sides. Dulles told Eisenhower on August 12 that the United States should begin to formulate a new policy toward testing since it seemed likely that the Geneva meeting was going to reach an agreement.[39] The final communiqué, issued when the talks successfully concluded on August 21, optimistically announced that the scientists had found it technically feasible to set up "a workable and effective control system for the detections of violations and a possible agreement on the world-wide cessation of nuclear weapons tests."[40] The breakthrough was hailed throughout the world.

It was at about this time that Khrushchev suddenly visited

China. In the course of his stay, from July 31 to August 3, Soviet and Chinese leaders undoubtedly discussed the touchy subject of arms control, an issue oddly overlooked by the CIA in its analysis of the visit. A universal test ban would have damaged, if not ended completely, China's prospects for acquiring the nuclear capability it was after. The documents from the Geneva conference specifically called for a "worldwide" control system that would include Chinese territory. While the Chinese and Soviets already differed over the importance of nuclear weapons and arms control (Mao argued that the bomb, like imperialism, was a "paper tiger" and should not be held in awe), the Chinese press increased its implicit criticisms of the Soviets following Khrushchev's visit. Beijing commentators in mid-August attacked "those" who believed "that peace can be achieved only by currying favor and compromising with the aggressors."[41]

On August 21 Eisenhower dramatically issued a public invitation to the Soviets to meet with the United States and other nuclear nations to negotiate a ban on all atomic weapons testing and the creation of an international control system. He asked for the meeting to take place in late October in New York.[42] On the very next day Beijing initiated the Strait crisis. The timing could hardly have been fortuitous. The problem the Soviets now faced was how to continue to make progress with the United States on arms control while trying to mollify their Asian ally. Though it seems that Beijing was not fooled, Moscow's juggling act confused Washington for a while.

On August 29 Khrushchev publicly accepted Eisenhower's invitation; at that point the Soviets were still circumspect in their press coverage of the developments in the offshore islands. But only a week later, on September 7, Khrushchev sent a blustery letter to Eisenhower attacking the U.S. position in the conflict. It is important to note the chronology here: the letter was sent only after Gromyko made his secret trip to Beijing and both the Americans and Chinese had expressed their interest in negotiations. Khrushchev called on Eisenhower to seek "common language" with him to forestall the slide toward war.[43]

Dulles found Khrushchev's letter "tough" and so extreme

as to be "counterproductive." It did not occur to him that Khrushchev might have been deliberately strident in order to placate the Chinese. Dulles therefore suggested that a comprehensive response be given to Khrushchev's allegations, and several days later Eisenhower sent an angry reply to Moscow. In it he refuted the Soviet accusations and said he could find no "common language" in Khrushchev's letter that might help lift the danger. The president concluded by recommending that Khrushchev persuade the Chinese Communists to negotiate in good faith and practice conciliation. The president still believed that the Soviets fully supported the Chinese Communists.[44]

But even as Khrushchev and Eisenhower vented their anger at each other over the Strait crisis, Washington methodically engaged Moscow in the preparations for the test ban negotiations. Just a few days after receiving Khrushchev's vitriolic message of September 7, the administration sent a cordial communication to Moscow confirming the date, place, and subject of the test ban meeting, and announcing the chairman of the U.S. delegation. A week later, on September 15, the Soviets accepted a U.S. proposal to convene a special technical conference on ways to prevent surprise attacks. The Soviets even suggested broadening the meeting to include other Western and Eastern Bloc countries, with a start date of November 10. Clearly the Soviets were signaling that, despite the hot talk over Asia, they were not going to sacrifice their developing dialogue with Washington. Throughout the entire crisis the Soviets made no military moves even remotely related to the Strait crisis.[45]

As Chinese artillery shells rained on the offshore islands, official American delegations busily concluded major cultural exchanges with the Soviets in Moscow. Soon Soviet audiences were enjoying such Hollywood movies as *Oklahoma, Roman Holiday,* and *The Old Man and the Sea.* On September 10 the United States and the Soviets signed an unprecedented agreement for an exchange of national exhibitions, which resulted, among other things, in Vice-President Nixon's famous trip to Moscow to open the U.S. exhibition in Gorki Park.[46]

On October 1 the Soviets sent another letter to Washington concerning the test ban conference and suggested that, because of the importance of the subject and the need to reach a rapid agreement, the Soviet foreign minister and U.S. secretary of state should hold a direct meeting at the summit. Washington did not reject the idea but deferred a decision. The actual talks began in Geneva on October 31, just as Eisenhower had originally proposed.[47]

III

Even if Washington had succeeded in figuring out what the Chinese and Soviet Communists were up to, it still had Chiang Kai-shek to contend with. The administration feared that the Nationalists were trying to drag the United States into a wider conflict, just as Moscow evidently felt Beijing was trying to do. The United States had to restrain Chiang from escalating his attacks against the mainland and concluded that the Nationalists, exaggerating the difficulties facing them in the Strait, were being deliberately inept in their attempts to resupply the offshore islands.[48] As in the 1955 crisis the administration tried to defuse the situation by neutralizing or demilitarizing the islands. Eisenhower again decided that the problem was to get the Nationalists to reduce their garrisons on the islands and de-emphasize their value to the Nationalist cause. Chiang, though, seemed to be such a problem that Secretary of Defense Neil McElroy was prompted to wonder whether, if "we cannot persuade Chiang to get off the islands without losing control in Formosa, [there might be] someone else who could step into the position." Eisenhower on this occasion did not seem receptive to the idea of a coup or some other machination to replace the aging friend of the United States; but on the other hand he did not rule out a future change of mind.[49]

Unlike the 1954–55 episode the 1958 crisis peaked quickly. By mid-September the U.S. military had solved the resupply problem. In a highly publicized move the United States helped land on Jinmen three eight-inch howitzers capable of firing tactical nuclear shells, and on September 19 the Nationalists successfully completed their largest supply operation since the shelling began. Thereafter the situation continued to improve for the United States. Although the bombardment continued, the danger of losing the islands had passed.[50]

Yet Washington was still puzzled about the Chinese and Soviet relationship in the crisis. Were the two Communist powers working in concert, despite hints to the contrary? According to the Intelligence Division of the State Department, the
Soviets were making the "strongest expressions of support for
Communist China on the Taiwan question since the Peiping
regime was founded in 1949." The report stated that the Chinese Communists were now probably even more confident of
Moscow's support.[51] In public Washington still accused both
Moscow and Beijing of perpetuating the crisis. In a televised
speech on September 11, Eisenhower again taxed the Soviets
with inspiring the Jinmen conflict and charged that "the Chinese Communists and the Soviet Union appear[ed] to be working hand in hand" in an effort to seize the western Pacific area
through armed conquest. And in his reply to a letter from Senator Green at the end of September, Eisenhower described the
conflict as against a united Communist alliance: "The Chinese
and Soviet Communist leaders assert . . . that if they can take
Quemoy and Matsu by armed assault that will open the way for
them to take Formosa and the Pescadores and, as they put it,
'expel' the United States from the West Pacific and cause its
Fleet to leave international waters and 'go home.' I cannot dismiss these boastings as mere bluff." Eisenhower condemned
what he characterized as "Sino-Soviet armed aggression."[52]
Washington let Moscow know it was responsible for the consequences of Beijing's actions.

But Dulles suspected that all might not be well between
Beijing and Moscow. At an off-the-record meeting with the
press on September 17, he said that if there was war with China,
the Soviets would come to its aid. The Soviets, he explained,
were already providing much of China's military equipment.
But when asked if there were not differences between the Chinese and the Soviets, Dulles's reply was curiously tentative: he
said that Mao and Khrushchev had probably talked about the
offshore islands at their recent meeting in Beijing, but admitted:

I can't even guess intelligently as to what took place at that meeting.
Whether the Russians egged the Chinese on, whether Khrushchev began to boast about how powerful they were and how we always gave in
when they threatened and Mao said if that's the case I might as well
pick up something as long as you will make the threat to back us up,

or whether the Chinese pressed the Soviet and the Soviet reluctantly gave in—I just can't guess. . . . You have got three broad lines of possible approach and it is anybody's guess which is the right one.[53]

Dulles seemed genuinely perplexed by Soviet actions. He pointed out that, on the one hand, the Soviets were "trying to create in the world and in their own country the impression that they now have a military power in terms of missiles and the like which enables them to dominate the world and which has so frightened the world and which has so frightened other nations that they do not dare to stand up to them." But on the other hand it was clear that Moscow and Washington were making progress in arms control talks. He could only say that "there are many inconsistencies in Soviet policy and they do the most inconsistent things. . . . I can't explain the vagaries and the apparent inconsistencies of Soviet policy." That Soviet behavior might be inexplicable was an uncharacteristic admission for the experienced secretary of state.

Another long, intemperate letter Khrushchev sent to Eisenhower on September 19 could only have contributed further to Dulles's disorientation. Khrushchev's tirade seemed to confirm that the Chinese and Soviets were closely collaborating. The president refused even to accept the message and returned it to Moscow. As in his letter of September 6, Khrushchev warned Washington not to attack China and seemed to endorse China's territorial claims. But he also encouraged Washington to take a "reasonable, realistic attitude" in the discussions with China. Khrushchev's tone was hostile, but Kenneth Young, who was involved in the Warsaw talks with China, later observed that, with the real crisis over, Khrushchev was in a position to "talk forcefully with little risk."[54]

Soon both the United States and Soviet Union began to soften their support for their allies. First, the United States took a step away from Chiang. On September 30 Dulles harshly criticized the Nationalists for concentrating their forces on the offshore islands. He declared that the United States had no legal commitment to defend Jinmen and Mazu or to assist Chiang in returning to the mainland. Chiang was taken aback at Dulles's abrupt statements, which were clearly meant to pressure him to reduce or evacuate his forces from the offshore islands. Several days later, on October 5, the Soviet news agency Tass released comments by Khrushchev in which he carefully dissociated the Soviet Union from the Strait crisis: the conflict was purely an internal matter of the Chinese people; the Soviets were not involved, and they would respond only if the United States actually attacked China. This too seemed to be a new, more limited position.[55]

Then, as suddenly as it had started, the crisis ended. On October 6, in a broadcast to Taiwan, Chinese Defense Minister Peng Dehuai declared that the siege of the offshore islands would end if the United States ceased convoying Nationalist ships. Peng called for reconciliation with the Nationalists and warned that the Americans would abandon the Nationalists one day, referring to Dulles's pronouncements of September 30. The problem of the Strait and Taiwan should be negotiated just between "you and us" without U.S. interference.

The United States claimed victory in foiling the Communist effort to starve out the offshore islands, even though China had never attempted an all-out interdiction of shipping.[56] For all practical purposes, however, the Communists unilaterally stopped the hostilities. Beijing later oddly claimed that its purpose by the end of the crisis was to *prevent* the United States from forcing Chiang to vacate the offshore islands. The effort to create two Chinas, an outcome that Beijing knew Washington favored, would have been helped if Chiang's forces retreated back across the Strait. A hundred miles of water would make an effective barrier.

The United States, in fact, worked to attain that goal as the immediate offshore island pressures passed. The administration scrambled to devise ways to have Chiang rethink his attachment to the unimportant bits of land. In late September Dulles asked John J. McCloy, chairman of the Council on Foreign Relations, to "go along with Secretary [of Defense] McElroy on his trip to Formosa and try to talk Chiang into giving up the Islands." Dulles may have had in mind a plan similar to his 1955 scheme, which had the United States blockading the South China coast. McCloy was convinced that he wanted to go substantially farther than the administration in reducing the commitment to the offshore islands and hesitated. Dulles told him that there would be no problem with the administration, only with Chiang. Still McCloy turned him down.[57] Dulles was not deterred. Something had to be done, since the United States could not afford to be placed in such a position again. The 1955 offshore island crisis had been bad enough, he told aides, but the 1958 episode "had strained our relations with Congress and foreign governments almost to the breaking point."[58]

Eisenhower was of like mind and insisted on finding a way to shake Chiang loose from the offshore territory. After hearing of McCloy's refusal to cooperate, he directed General Twining to have the Pentagon think about "what could be done with Chiang to get him out of the offshore islands." A week later Eisenhower sent Dulles a memo proposing that if Washington provided a strong amphibious capability to Chiang, thereby improving his chances for a successful return to the mainland in the event of future disorders, he might "simultaneously remove all or nearly all his garrisons from the offshore islands." He thought Chiang might accept the plan, since it appeared to sustain the Nationalist hope of returning to the mainland one day. Eisenhower had General Twining work with Dulles on this "package deal."[59]

Although Eisenhower was not hopeful and was becoming impatient with Chiang (he blurted out to Under Secretary of State Christian Herter that he was "just about ready to tell Chiang Kai-shek where he [Chiang] got off"), he sent Dulles out to Taiwan anyway in mid-October to present the administration's ideas. After three days of strenuous talks Dulles, to his great surprise, succeeded in convincing Chiang to reduce his forces on the offshore islands and pledge to de-emphasize military means to retake the mainland. Chiang said he would stress a "non-force," political approach to "liberate" the Chinese people. Eisenhower and Dulles were pleased with Chiang's apparent change of attitude.[60] They thought they had bought more time to realize the long-term changes necessary for a two-China arrangement.

With the heat of the immediate crisis past, the administration was also encouraged in its review of the behavior of the Soviets in the past weeks. During an October 12 talk with Senator Green of the Senate Foreign Relations Committee,

Dulles was asked about the Russian attitude during the crisis. He carefully replied that one could only speculate on the subject, since the United States had no hard information to go on. Dulles's comments were rather mild considering his and the president's recent official denunciations of Sino-Soviet collusion.[61] Soon afterward, though, Allen Dulles gave an intriguing reassessment of the Chinese-Soviet relationship.

IV

On the evening of October 28 the Council on Foreign Relations hosted an exclusive "dinner-meeting" for Allen Dulles, one of its directors. Dulles began a lengthy talk by expressing his delight in sharing some highlights of the CIA's "current thinking on [the] Sino-Soviet problem." Washington's long-term views of Soviet political strategy had changed little during the previous six months, according to Dulles, but the Taiwan Strait crisis had prompted the CIA to alter some of its evaluations; the manner in which the recent crisis had developed "has led us at least to re-examine some of our accepted concepts as to Sino-Soviet relations and the relative viewpoints of Chinese and Soviet leaders."[62]

The West's military strength still exceeded that of the Soviets, but the day was soon approaching when both the United States and the Soviet Union could destroy each other in surprise attacks. Thus Moscow was now "as concerned as we are to avoid devastating nuclear war," and Dulles was now convinced that the Soviets wanted to advance their ends "by essentially non-military means." As for Khrushchev, he struck him as a man in a hurry, eager to "insure his place in history." A "shrewd politician," of a "pragmatic, flexible temperament," he was promising an improved material life for the Soviet citizen. His de-Stalinization campaign was bringing positive changes to Soviet society, including improved relationships between the government and people, a system of legality, and an end to state terror.[63] The picture Dulles drew of the Soviet Union was that of a formidable and dangerous adversary of the United States, but also of a country that he respected.

But all was not well in the Communist world, according to

Dulles. A number of serious problems accompanied the changes in the Soviet Union. One of the greatest of these problems, "fraught with long term implications for Soviet leaders, [was the] growing strength, prestige, [and] assertiveness of Communist China." Dulles conceded that Sino-Soviet relations was a subject about which the CIA had little information, but there were some things that could be said with confidence: the Chinese had grown in stature within the Sino-Soviet bloc, and strong bonds of ideology, common hostility to the United States, and mutual dependence continued to tie the two powers together. "However," in the language of Dulles's outline,

> many little indications convince me Moscow nervous about future relationship (our Ambassador Moscow shares this view). Interesting that so far as we know Soviets have not given Chinese nuclear weapons, for which we suspect Peiping has long since asked. Also interesting no evidence of new long term capital credits to Peiping. Mikoyan told [Adlai] Stevenson Peiping in effect on cash and carry basis. . . .
>
> Not sure Moscow and Peiping always in full accord on foreign policy tactics, perhaps even in Taiwan Strait. Chinese may be more brash than Soviets, less concerned over nuclear devastation. . . .
>
> These things difficult to judge, but incline to see Soviets the more cautious partner, not anxious to see Chicom strength grow too rapidly, but yielding (where essential to maintain amity) to importunities of ally. Perhaps not too different from our own relations with some of our more volatile allies.[64]

The United States would be closely watching Soviet and Eastern European reaction to the recently established communes in China, a "peculiarly Chinese deviation from Leninist norms" and "the worst political slavery the world has ever seen," according to the CIA chief. Dulles's take-home message was that Washington was "paying considerable attention to Communist China these days, as Moscow no doubt doing too. One thing we can say for certain, Peiping will play an increasingly large role in overall Bloc policy, with results no one can foresee."[65]

In the question-and-answer session that followed, Dulles was asked if the masses in China were "happy and contented." "They have driven the interfering foreigner out and have become somewhat of an influence in world affairs," he responded. "The average Chinaman is very impressed by his country's new importance and independence." Another questioner wanted more information on the Sino-Soviet link and its potential problems. Dulles replied: "The Soviet Union feels the necessity of good relations with the Chinese. They are not very happy about the present situation. China is demanding a great deal from Russia. . . . The Russians hope to always maintain a veto over Chinese actions. However, the Russians are not absolutely sure that they hold this veto. It must be remembered that each country is extremely essential to the other."[66]

Though Allen Dulles tried to be judicious in his evaluation of Sino-Soviet relations—after all, the political and military policy implications of a major rift between the Soviet Union and China were staggering—his remarks still convey his sense that an epic transformation was in the making. But what the United States might do to widen the division was still unclear. In the recollection of William Bundy, Allen Dulles was sensitive to Sino-Soviet discord but did not think that Washington could bring about an actual split.[67] Still, curiosity about the Sino-Soviet relationship and the feeling that something was seriously wrong between the two powers grew within the administration in the following months.

On November 5, 1958, Eisenhower met with William C. Foster, General Otto P. Weyland, and Dr. George B. Kistiakowsky, who were on their way to the conference with the Soviets on preventing surprise attacks, and with Gordon Gray, his national security adviser. Eisenhower instructed his delegates to watch for an occasion when the Russians might become "freely talkative" and reveal their real thoughts about the Chinese. Eisenhower "wondered if the Soviets were not really becoming concerned about Communist China as a possible threat to them in the future." Foster said he would keep the president's question in mind, adding that it had occurred to him that such an exchange of views might have been one of the things the Soviets wanted to accomplish in the discussions. If the Soviets were not yet worried about the Chinese, Foster said, "they certainly should be."[68]

It is not clear whether the delegates ever had a chance to loosen the tongues of their Soviet counterparts, but soon after the end of the conference Gray wrote a forceful memo on the need to update China policy. He pointed out that the United States was doing "virtually nothing" to exploit Sino-Soviet differences, even though basic national security policy called for such efforts. He pressed his associates to take up this "very important policy." Gray mentioned that Llewellyn Thompson, the U.S. ambassador to the Soviet Union, concurred and was convinced that "new opportunities" were developing.[69] As one of the participants in a new CFR study group on China observed in the early spring of 1959: "Not so long ago people spoke lightly of a U.S.-U.S.S.R. community of interest vis-à-vis China." But, he added perceptively, "now the idea is spoken of somewhat more seriously." John Foster Dulles's former assistant Robert Bowie, now out of government, quickly emphasized that this was "something that should be considered."[70] Washington would not disappoint Bowie.

SEVEN

Bolsheviks, Mensheviks, and Imperialists

[The Sino-Soviet split was] largely our accomplishment.
—CIA, 1963

At this point in the account it is useful to review the history of Sino-Soviet relations during the 1950's, the
sources of Moscow's and Beijing's troubles with each other, and
the influence of U.S. policy on that relationship. Without access to Chinese and Soviet archival sources, an assessment can
only be partial and suggestive, based largely on what Beijing
and Moscow have themselves made public.

China and the Soviet Union had persuasive and seemingly
obvious reasons to unite in the late 1940's: they shared a powerful ideology that presumed the unity of Communists of different lands; they had a common, threatening adversary, the
United States; and, in constructing socialism, they faced requirements that encouraged close economic cooperation. Soviet assistance to China was of undeniable importance during
the next decade. China constructed its great industrial centers
in Manchuria with substantial amounts of Soviet material and
technical help. The respected Soviet historian Roy Medvedev
claims that more than "250 major industrial enterprises, work-
shops and sites" in China were constructed with Soviet help
and equipped with the best Soviet machinery. From 1950 to
1960 more than 8,500 Chinese technical specialists and 1,500
specialists in science and other fields studied in the Soviet
Union, as did 11,000 Chinese students and graduates.[1] Even
allowing for some exaggeration, these figures speak to the substantial benefits China gained from its Soviet connection.

China's national security, too, was boosted by the alliance

with the Soviets. The Chinese believed that the Friendship Treaty of 1950 served as a deterrent to hostile forces during the Korean War, the Indochina conflict, and the offshore island crises. The Chinese gained access to Soviet advanced weaponry, including nuclear technology. The Soviets provided critical assistance in the early stages of China's nuclear weapons program, a centerpiece of Beijing's national security strategy.[2] Moscow promoted China as one of the world's important powers.

Yet the Chinese also often found the Soviets penurious and self-serving. Moscow required Beijing to repay all the assistance rendered during the Korean War; China's aid to North Korea, by contrast, was given gratis. Many Chinese who had direct contact with the Soviets recall their arrogance. If Nikita Khrushchev is at all representative, it is not surprising that Russians and Chinese had troubles getting along. In his memoirs Khrushchev recalls that from the time of his first trip to China in 1954, he disdained Chinese and Asian ways and suspected his Chinese comrades of duplicity. "Conflict with China is inevitable," he warned his aides in 1954. Khrushchev made little effort in his memoirs to contain his chauvinist contempt for the Chinese.[3]

Soviet military assistance, too, in the Chinese view, often came with strings attached. From 1955 to 1957 Khrushchev tried unsuccessfully to get the Chinese to enter into a closer military relationship with the Soviets and form a Warsaw-like pact. In their explanation of the causes of the split, the Chinese denounce other Khrushchev moves in that direction in July 1958, when he unsuccessfully tried to pressure them to install a long-range radio station in China to facilitate communications with the Soviet submarine fleet operating in the Pacific and to form a joint Sino-Soviet Pacific Fleet. The Chinese interpreted these proposals as efforts to gain greater leverage over them. (The radio station, the CCP leaders believed at the time, would enable the Soviets to "control our intelligence information and secret communications."[4])

By early 1958, largely because of this growing estrangement, the CCP leaders decided to adopt a more self-reliant path, and soon afterward Mao broke with the Soviet model of socialist development by launching the Great Leap Forward and forming the people's communes. China then initiated a crisis with the United States over the offshore islands, angering Moscow.[5] The Sino-Soviet rift had begun.

On their part the Soviets gained important advantages from their China connection. Most important was the immense enhancement of the prestige of the Soviet Union and the socialist system among the peoples of Asia and the Third World. As Dean Rusk observed in 1950, the loss of China to the Communists had marked "a shift in the balance of power in favor of Soviet Russia."[6] Moscow also reaped considerable economic benefits from its exploitation of Chinese mineral resources through joint-stock companies, and from advantageous trade and currency arrangements. Yet by the late 1950's the relationship's perceived liabilities for both the Soviets and the Chinese began to call into question the value of the alliance itself.

Sino-Soviet animus grew as a result of developing contradictions between each country's basic conception of its national security. Ancient tensions and rivalries, personality conflicts, contrasting models of socialist construction, and competition for the leadership of the international Communist movement all had their role in the split, but they were aggravations rather than causes. Through the 1950's Chinese and Soviet leaders became aware that their convictions of what was essential for the continued development, well-being, and progress of their respective societies clashed in some fundamental ways. That helps to explain the depth of the antagonism as well as the intensity of the feelings.

More specifically, the Chinese and Soviet leaders developed very different ideas of how their societies would survive and advance in a world in which capitalism remained a powerful force, led by a hostile, even mortal enemy, the United States. After the death of Stalin the Soviets began to conceptualize a different "grand strategy" to realize prosperity and their most general goals in the world. (High-level American officials might use the term "basic national security" to mean roughly the same thing.) Aside from the central design of strengthening the country militarily, politically, and economically, the new strategy abandoned Stalin's assumption of the inevitability of war between the Western capitalist bloc, led by the United States, and the socialist countries, led by the Soviet Union. The Soviet leaders now believed that coexistence and peaceful competition between the two social systems was appropriate for the contemporary era. The increased strength of the Soviet Union, the decline of capitalism, and the advent of nuclear weapons that could destroy much of humanity made this new strategy both possible and necessary. The great danger to world socialism and the Soviet Union, in Moscow's eyes, was nuclear war between the superpowers, launched by imperialism.[7] It therefore became the responsibility of the Soviet Union to diminish the threat by continuing to increase and consolidate its power in its spheres of influence, on the one hand, and by recasting its relationship with the United States to contain antagonisms and reduce the possibility of war, on the other. Seeking understandings with Washington and controlling what the United States might consider provocations (without jeopardizing essential Soviet interests, such as control of the Eastern European countries) pushed toward the top of the Kremlin's foreign policy agenda.

The doctrinal turnaround was more than the Chinese Communists could stomach. Not far removed from their own revolutionary experience, Mao and his comrades more closely identified China's interests with those of others conducting revolutionary struggle against imperialism, particularly in the Third World, than with those of the Soviet Union. Though they did not rule out diplomacy, the PRC leaders believed that the pursuit of the anti-imperialist struggle would better serve China's interests (and world socialism) than the search for an accord with the United States. Moreover, the CCP's enemy lingered on Taiwan, backed by the United States; accommodation with Washington would require substantive progress toward reuniting Taiwan with the mainland. In Beijing's view the principal danger in the world came less from nuclear war than from discouraging struggle that would further isolate and weaken the imperialists.

The Chinese and Soviets originally forged their alliance largely because of their concern about the United States. But as their thinking on how to deal with that enemy diverged, their alliance not only floundered but finally fell apart when each came to perceive the other as a major, if not principal, obstacle toward improving its position vis-à-vis their main adversary.

What, then, was the role, if any, of the United States in this development? "Substantial" would have to be the answer, given the previous assessment of the evolution of Chinese and Soviet outlooks. Washington's "selective accommodation," in the words of the Sino-Soviet specialist Donald Zagoria (or put another way, discriminate hostility), certainly exacerbated frictions between Beijing and Moscow.[8] Washington's generally positive response to improved relations with Moscow helped sustain Khrushchev's assumptions about the possibility of superpower accord. Meanwhile, its continued hard line toward China, despite Beijing's efforts from 1955 to 1957 to moderate the hostility in the bilateral relationship, confirmed in the PRC leaders' minds the futility, and even danger, of Moscow's approach. By the conclusion of the offshore island crisis of 1958, the antagonism between the two countries was barely disguised, with the Chinese suspecting that the Soviets wanted to restrain them and appease the United States, and the Soviets persuaded that the Chinese were unpredictable allies who threatened to disrupt peaceful coexistence with the United States, the emerging cornerstone of their own national security strategy. For the time being, though, the two managed to obscure the depth of their differences from the United States.

From this one might conclude that the closed-door policy toward China, as articulated by John Foster Dulles and others, achieved the goal of driving a wedge between Moscow and Beijing. Hard-nosed, geopolitical objectives did sustain Dulles's intransigent China policy, it must be said, not blind moralism or mere emotional animosity toward the Chinese Communists. As Dulles confided to Roger Makins of the British Foreign Office in February 1955, his long-term aim for Asia was to attain a degree of independence between China and Russia and achieve some balance of power. With that development, Dulles suggested, the United States could be less involved in Asia than it then had to be because of Japan's inability to play a larger role in the area.[9] But to credit the closed-door policy with breaking the Sino-Soviet alliance would be to overstate the case and suggest that Dulles was more prescient than he was.

The U.S. hard line toward China was sustained by a number

of considerations over and above the long-term aspiration of dividing Beijing and Moscow. Domestic popular animosities toward the Chinese Communists, the continuing attachment to Chiang Kai-shek, racial prejudice, and the heightened commitment to the fight against communism in Southeast Asia were all contributing factors. For a variety of reasons, therefore, China had become America's number one Communist villain by the late 1950's. Moreover, U.S. efforts at détente with the Soviet Union perhaps had as much to do with the split as the hard line toward China did, if not more. The closed-door policy was based on the premise that forced dependence on the Soviets would lead to Chinese disillusionment, a break, and China's reconciliation with the West. In that scenario China was to be the active agent in the division. But as it turned out, U.S.-Soviet efforts at rapprochement seemed to be much of the cause of the erosion of the Sino-Soviet alliance. The Soviets were at least as much to blame for precipitating the crisis in Sino-Soviet relations as the Chinese. Finally, the assumption that the closed door would eventually result in China's return to the West was incorrect. Chinese enmity toward the West increased, not decreased, with the Sino-Soviet rift, obstructing reconciliation for more than a decade.

One can only speculate what might have happened if Washington had simultaneously tried to extend its accommodationist efforts to Beijing. If China had been responsive—from 1955 to 1957 it had sent clear signals of its interest in a rapprochement with the United States—perhaps Beijing would not have adopted the radical international and domestic line that it did in the late 1950's and 1960's. And while the United States might not have forced a full Sino-Soviet "split," it could conceivably have helped realize at an earlier date some form of the balanced triangular relationship that emerged between the United States, China, and the Soviet Union in the late 1980's.

I

Following the 1958 offshore island crisis, the whiff of Sino-Soviet discord whetted the appetites of Eisenhower officials, and they eagerly followed the growing evidence of the Communist powers' estrangement. In December 1958 Khrushchev openly disparaged China's communes to Senator Hubert Humphrey: the Soviet Union had tried that arrangement but rejected it, he said. Eisenhower read regular reports on the growing discord between Mao and Khrushchev.[10] During the U.S. visit of the Soviet leader Anastas Mikoyan in January 1959, American officials everywhere quizzed him about his country's relations with China. Even over dinner Vice-President Nixon annoyed Mikoyan with questions about divergences in Sino-Soviet policies. Mikoyan properly refuted allegations of Sino-Soviet problems, but his uneasiness was obvious. By the summer of 1959 Eisenhower agreed with Norman Cousins, editor of the *Saturday Review*, that Communist ideological differences were deepening, and that the United States should do everything possible to strengthen the Soviet leaders in resisting Chinese demands for a return to the goal of world revolution.[11]

Nikita Khrushchev's historic visit to the United States, the first ever by a top Soviet leader, and his meetings with Eisenhower at the presidential retreat at Camp David on September 26 and 27, 1959, catalyzed the Eisenhower administration's interest in the possibilities of playing triangular politics. Issues concerning Europe, it is assumed, dominated their talks, and some observers have chastised Eisenhower for being unprepared to discuss the China problem. By neglecting to engage the Soviet Party chairman in such an exchange, Eisenhower, according to Adam Ulam, allowed a moment to pass "which might have changed the course of history." Eisenhower's own misleading description of the Camp David talks in his memoirs has encouraged that conclusion. Eisenhower implies that he refused to discuss China with Khrushchev because U.S.-Soviet differences were too great to overcome.[12] In truth Eisenhower was well prepared to discuss China at length with the Soviet leader. His aides had prepared him to needle Khrushchev about Communist differences and the Soviets' contradictory attitudes toward the relaxation of East-West tensions, especially on disarmament.[13]

Before Khrushchev's arrival Henry A. Wallace, Roosevelt's former progressive vice-president turned Eisenhower loyalist, counseled the president on what he might expect from the Soviet leader. Wallace thought that Khrushchev "really wanted to talk China" because he feared the Chinese. Wallace reminded

Eisenhower that "the great bond between the US and Russia is that we are both 'Have Nations' and that both of us are threatened by the tensions which so rapidly are presented by the 'Have Not' nations." Expressing the idea of a "community of interest" in his own way, Wallace concluded that "in the long run Russia is far more threatened by the 'Have Not' nations than the US because of the unique capacities of China." Eisenhower sent Wallace a cordial reply, saying he suspected that Khrushchev might want to discuss not only the economic potential of the Chinese, "but also their very evident desire to be one of the 'nuclear' nations."[14]

The Camp David talks went surprisingly well, and Khrushchev himself finally raised the question of China during one of the last meetings. After the two leaders amicably discussed their mutual interest in avoiding nuclear war and achieving disarmament, Khrushchev suggested an exchange of views about China. Since he would soon be visiting Beijing, he said, he wished the president to describe what "the future course" of Washington's China policy might be.

Eisenhower responded with a rendition of the traditional closed-door policy, indicating that it was up to the Chinese to change their attitude if there was to be any movement in relations. Khrushchev said that he would talk with China's leaders about the problem of American detainees in China, a sore point in U.S.-China relations, but that he strongly disagreed with Washington's stubbornness on the Taiwan question. That was something for the Chinese to decide themselves, he maintained, and the United States, in the interests of general peace, should stop supporting Chiang. How would the United States feel if a "mutinous general," supported by the Soviet Union, detached some islands from the United States? Eisenhower angrily rejected the analogy. The United States had proper commitments to Chiang. In any case, Eisenhower said, U.S. and Soviet views were so divergent there was no point in discussing the problem in detail. The United States held that China was a divided country, like Germany, Korea, and Vietnam, and sought "peaceful settlements" in all these cases. After further exchange proved futile, Khrushchev concluded by saying that "he did not insist on a military solution in China"; there could be a peaceful settlement if only Washington stopped its military support of Taipei. The two men agreed that the China problem would persist for a long time.[15]

The sharp exchange so upset Secretary of State Christian Herter, who had taken over after John Foster Dulles's death in 1959, that he immediately wrote an impassioned memorandum to the president. "All day I have been haunted by the statements made by Mr. Khrushchev with regard to Taiwan," Herter wrote. "They are so completely contrary to the spirit of the things for which you, and ostensibly he, are working." Herter wanted to give the "spirit of Camp David" one last chance to envelop the China problem. He attached a draft letter for the president to consider sending personally to the Soviet leader.[16]

In his four-page draft Herter played on the apparent contradiction between Khrushchev's professed desire for the relaxation of world tensions and his support for the Chinese Communists' campaign against Taiwan. The issue was not a "domestic question" as Khrushchev argued, wrote Herter. Rather, "the importance of the China question" was related "to our common interest in the peace of the world." Herter linked the German issue, one of Moscow's principal worries, with China, lecturing Khrushchev:

The world in which we live is in a sense an indivisible one. . . . On the one hand you spoke of the need for a peaceful solution of the German question. On the other hand you said the People's Republic could legitimately use force in China. We, of course, disagree with you. However, if one should apply your precept with regard to China to the German question, one would come inevitably to the proposition that the Federal Republic of Germany was entitled to deal with East Germany, that is the Democratic People's Republic, as a rebel. . . . In my view both are international matters and it is on this basis that I have been willing to discuss the Germany question with you seriously in the hope of reaching a peaceful conclusion in the interests of our two countries and mankind as a whole. I think that the question of the two Chinas can in time be resolved in the same way.

If the hint of promise as well as threat on the German question was not clear enough, Herter continued to the matter of arms control:

You have stressed to me that the central question of our times is disarmament and I have agreed with you both privately and publicly. I cannot think of any way in which to destroy our common objective, disarmament, more effectively than to insist that the China question is a domestic question within the sole competence of the People's Republic of China.

Herter ended on a dark note: failing a "renunciation of the use of force" in the China area, the United States and the Soviet Union "may indeed be faced with precisely the kind of situation which it is your intention and mine to avoid." Herter urged the president to send the letter through special channels to reach Khrushchev before his scheduled trip to China.

It is unclear whether the letter was ever actually sent. Certainly, Eisenhower's advisers were not confident about how Khrushchev might respond. His erratic behavior, in fact, had kept Washington off balance. Just before his trip to the United States, Khrushchev feinted from the left. He belligerently boasted to Averell Harriman that the Soviets had given the Chinese missiles capable of hitting Taiwan and the U.S. Seventh Fleet from positions in China's hinterland. If the Chinese decided to take Taiwan, he blustered, the Soviet Union would support them "even if this meant war." Harriman was so appalled that he told Washington he considered Khrushchev an even "more dangerous man than Stalin."[17] As it turns out, Khrushchev's boast about giving the Chinese missiles was totally false, but it contributed to the inability of U.S. intelligence to gauge accurately the sensitive state of Sino-Soviet relations. Just before Khrushchev traveled to Beijing, the CIA warned that it would be a "grave imprudence" to assume major discord within the "Moscow-Peking axis." China's tenth anniversary celebration would be "a most impressive demonstration of Communist solidarity and dynamic purpose." Moscow was not trying to restrain Mao, the CIA estimated. He and Khrushchev would stand side by side as "comrades in arms."[18] This time the intelligence agency was seriously mistaken.

During his brief visit to Beijing for the anniversary celebration, Khrushchev and his hosts quarreled incessantly. According to Chinese sources, at the formal national day banquet Khrushchev attacked Beijing's policy toward Taiwan as "incendiary." He charged that China was "craving for war like a cock for a fight" and warned his hosts not to test the resolve of capitalism. During a seven-hour talk with Mao, Khrushchev blamed

China for the "Soviet troubles" caused by the Chinese shelling of the offshore islands in 1958. Worse still, from the Chinese point of view, he proposed what amounted to a two-China approach to settle the Taiwan matter. The following day at Zhongnanhai, headquarters of the CCP Central Committee, Foreign Minister Chen Yi rebutted Khrushchev's charges point by point. The outraged Soviet leader cut short his visit and returned to Moscow in a huff.[19]

The Eisenhower administration had no specific knowledge of the altercation in Beijing, but it was immensely encouraged by what it sensed from Khrushchev's public statements. Herter informed the cabinet that Khrushchev apparently "did all he could to soft-pedal" the U.S. position while in China. What Washington did not know at the time was that even before Camp David the Soviets had taken a major step in reducing their support for Beijing. On the eve of Khrushchev's journey to the United States, Moscow abruptly suspended its commitment to help China develop nuclear weapons. Sino-Soviet relations rapidly degenerated thereafter.[20] Soon after the Camp David meeting, Eisenhower told Japanese Prime Minister Nobusuke Kishi that the summit had made him more hopeful about future relations with the Soviets. Khrushchev might even fear that a strong Red China would challenge the Soviet Union, he speculated.[21]

II

Khrushchev's behavior in the United States and in the aftermath of his trip appeared to confirm for Beijing that Moscow had abandoned its revolutionary principles. Beijing prepared to go public with its criticisms to pressure Moscow and influence the international Communist movement. In April 1960 the CCP used the occasion of the ninetieth anniversary of Lenin's birth to issue a series of essays that attacked "modern revisionism" and affirmed the validity of orthodox Leninism for the contemporary socialist revolution. The CCP styled itself the defender of Lenin's teachings on the nature of imperialism, the impossibility of a "peaceful transition" to socialism, the bourgeois state, and the danger of opportunism within the

Marxist movement. Although neither the CPSU nor Khrushchev was mentioned by name, there was no mistaking to whom the epithets "Titoists" and "modern revisionists" referred. The CCP charged that infatuation with reaching accommodation with the United States, and the rationale supporting such a deviation, sabotaged the international Communist movement, especially the national liberation struggle in the Third World.[22]

The frequent reference to Lenin's fight with Eduard Bernstein and the Second International in the early twentieth century indicated that Beijing considered the controversy with Moscow of the highest importance. According to Beijing, the choice facing the international proletariat was again between revolution or capitulation to the class enemy. The CCP had raised many of its differences with the CPSU following Khrushchev's de-Stalinization speech in 1956. But the public and comprehensive nature of its 1960 ideological broadside raised the dispute to a new level of hostility. Camp David brought to a head a whole series of disputes that had festered between the two Communist powers in the 1950's: the formation of the people's communes in China's countryside and the 1958 Great Leap Forward had provoked Moscow's scorn; Mao's reliance on ideological inspiration to propel socialist construction had challenged Soviet bureaucratic wisdom; and Moscow's pursuit of détente with the United States, to the detriment of the revolutionary struggles in other lands, and Khrushchev's oft-expressed fear of war with imperialism had appeared irresolute and self-serving to Beijing. In China's view Soviet advances in science and military strength were accompanied not by a stiffening of political purpose, but by efforts to seek a condominium of global interests with the United States. Although the Soviet launching of the world's first space satellite fueled Cold War fears in the West, the Chinese later liked to say that "when Sputnik went up in the heavens, the red flag came down on earth."[23]

Chinese anger at Khrushchev placed the Soviet Union in an awkward position. Beijing made it clear that progress with the United States would come only at the expense of further estranging the Chinese. For the next several years Moscow would attempt to walk a tightrope between seeking rapprochement with the United States and placating the Chinese. Intent on pursuing détente but distracted from the Left by Chinese militancy, by the fear of isolation from the upsurge of revolutionary activity in the Third World, and by the hope of maintaining some semblance of Communist fraternity, the Kremlin's policy became erratic and confounding for Washington. Khrushchev's volatile personality only exacerbated the tensions inherent in the Soviets' contradictory purposes.

Illustrative of Khrushchev's dilemma was the U-2 incident that scuttled the Paris summit conference of 1960. Two weeks after Beijing's publication of "Long Live Leninism!" with its suggestion that Moscow was appeasing imperialism, the Soviets shot down a U.S. high-altitude spy plane on an overflight of Soviet territory and captured its pilot, Francis Gary Powers. The incident was a profound embarrassment for Khrushchev, who had staked his reputation on achieving peaceful coexistence with the United States. He had praised Eisenhower as a man of "wise statesmanship, . . . courage and will power" and was about to meet the president again. Although Khrushchev dramatically released news about the downing of the U-2, he provided ample opportunity for Washington to absolve Eisenhower of direct personal involvement. When the president unexpectedly accepted responsibility for the flight, Khrushchev had no choice but to rant before the world's press. Denouncing Eisenhower by name, the theatrical Soviet leader stormed out of Paris. A frost settled on the emerging Soviet-American détente. George Kennan concluded that the episode had the unfortunate effect of increasing the influence of the Chinese within the Communist bloc.[24]

Even though it was an American plane that violated Soviet airspace, Khrushchev's public counterattack over the next two months was not primarily against the imperialists in Washington but against the "ultra-leftists" in Beijing. In June he assailed the CCP at a Rumanian Communist Party Congress in Bucharest. Addressing leading representatives of the major Communist parties, including the CCP, Khrushchev disparaged the Chinese views as dogmatic and provocative, and succeeded in forcing most of those present to fall dutifully in line behind him. The CCP leaders, unlike Tito in 1948, who had only re-

buffed the Soviet Union's authority over Yugoslavian matters, challenged the very legitimacy of the Soviet Union as the
leader of the entire socialist camp and self-proclaimed bulwark of peace and progress in the world. To create even further problems for Mao and his colleagues, Khrushchev in July
suddenly ordered the withdrawal of all Soviet technicians and
advisers from China and ended hundreds of agreements and
contracts. The specialists—almost 1,400 in number—took
blueprints and factory plans as they departed, leaving construction projects half-completed and plants inoperable. Coin-
ciding with several years of agricultural disasters, Khrushchev's
pressure tactics brought the Chinese economy to the verge of
calamity. China entered what is called the "three hard years,"
when millions approached starvation. Still, the CCP leaders
refused to buckle, and the acrimony between the two countries continued to escalate. It would be twenty-five years before there would again be any significant Sino-Soviet economic
cooperation.[25]

In the West the rupturing Communist alliance attracted the
keen attention of specialists and political observers. The popular press, as well as prestigious journals like *Foreign Affairs*,
Asian Survey, *China Quarterly*, and the U.S.-government-
sponsored *Problems of Communism*, published a steady stream
of articles on the state of Sino-Soviet affairs.[26] The Communists, in conducting so much of their dispute along ideological
lines within their own media, spawned a whole generation
of "content analysts" in the West. Specialists pored over the
latest Communist print and broadcast materials, and exhaus-
tively chronicled the doctrinal divergence between the Communist giants. But Western researchers had a more difficult
time determining which factors other than ideology explained
the animosity, not least because of the secretiveness of intra-
communist affairs. Researchers speculated about personality
conflicts between Mao and Khrushchev, ancient geopolitical
confrontations, racial animosities, rivalry for leadership of the
Communist movement, national ambitions, and stages of revolutionary development. Though some commentators on the
political right dismissed the rift as Communist-fabricated or
exaggerated,[27] most specialists recognized that the dispute was

genuine. But because ideological disagreement over interpretations of Marxism-Leninism seemed a slippery basis on which to explain such a momentous development in world history, and with the usual American skepticism toward accepting ideology as motivation, most specialists were circumspect in their predictions about the future course of Sino-Soviet relations and in their recommendations for American policy.[28]

III

While Eisenhower's policy of discriminate hostility played a major role in helping produce the Sino-Soviet rift, the full exploitation of that rift was to be the task of his successor, John F. Kennedy. In fact the Eisenhower administration's actions in the China area had occasioned one of the rare tiffs over foreign policy between Kennedy and his opponent, Richard Nixon, during the 1960 presidential campaign. Nixon predictably defended the Eisenhower record, including the defense of Jinmen and Mazu in the offshore island crisis of 1958. During the famous televised debates between the candidates, Kennedy questioned the value of the small islands to the defense of Taiwan, but neither man pressed the issue.

During his career in the Senate, Kennedy had occasionally expressed discomfort with certain Republican foreign policies, but he never took the floor to offer a substantive critique or alternative for the country in world affairs. In his October 1957 article in *Foreign Affairs*, "A Democrat Looks at Foreign Policy," he argued that U.S. policy had become unresponsive to the world's changing power relations. Bipolarity, which had characterized global politics, was retreating before a new configuration in which other major centers of power, such as Communist China and Europe, were emerging. Charging that U.S. policy had been excessively militaristic and rigid toward China, Kennedy called for a policy reassessment, although he affirmed that the reasons for nonrecognition were still "compelling." But even this critique was short on specifics.[29]

The president-elect surrounded himself with foreign policy advisers who did have a variety of opinions about how the United States should respond to the growing strength and diversity of Communist and revolutionary forces in the world. The new administration faced a whole host of challenges in this department: the Cuban revolution of 1959; the upsurge of African liberation; an insurgency in Southeast Asia; deteriorating Soviet control over Eastern Europe, highlighted by Communist Albania's decision to ally with China against Moscow; and the continuing East-West confrontation over Berlin. But surprisingly enough, when it came to the Sino-Soviet rift, Kennedy's advisers held many common opinions.

Still, they were inconsistent at times. Chester Bowles, a spokesman for American liberalism, seemed of two minds about China policy, for example. Respecting Bowles's diplomatic experience in Asia and concern about the Third World, Kennedy made him under secretary of state and a personal adviser on foreign affairs. Since his tenure as ambassador to India during the Truman years, Bowles had taken a special interest in China policy. In the 1950's he had strongly disagreed with John Foster Dulles's closed-door approach to pressuring the Sino-Soviet alliance, but over the years he had become increasingly alarmed over the growing might of Chinese communism. China policy urgently needed revision, in Bowles's opinion.

He and his former aide, James C. Thomson, Jr., a China scholar who became a special assistant on Far Eastern affairs in the State Department and later joined the NSC staff, were bitterly critical of the Republicans' record on China. In Bowles's view Eisenhower had conducted a patronizing, arrogant policy toward Beijing and had failed to appreciate the possibilities for exploiting the differences between Beijing and Moscow. The Sino-Soviet relationship was not "rigid, monolithic, unchangeable," he declared in a *Foreign Affairs* article in April 1960. Bowles urged the United States to adopt a two-China policy, contending that this would at once protect the Nationalists on Taiwan and permit flexibility in dealings with the mainland, including some trade.[30] But several months later, in a rough draft for a Kennedy campaign speech, Bowles shifted gears, to emphasize how badly the Republicans had underestimated the "inherently imperialistic and expansionist" nature of any Chinese regime. Undercutting his own recommendations for a change in policy, Bowles likened China to Nazi Germany and

Japan. China's impulse was to enlarge its "living space" for its teeming population and for sources of fuel and food; Mao, in Bowles's view, was in many ways the new Hitler. A Democratic administration, Bowles suggested, would recognize the potential differences between the Soviet Union and China but would not "indulge in wishful thinking which could lead us to underestimate the bonds that now hold China and Russia together."[31]

Yet not long after, Bowles seemed ready to indulge in some of that "wishful thinking." "As a practical matter," he told Kennedy in October, "the only force that can effectively contain and restrain China during the next decade is the Soviet Union, which largely controls her oil and which is advantageously postured in a military sense." Despite Khrushchev's recent belligerency during the 1958–59 Berlin crisis, Bowles believed that the Soviets wanted to moderate Chinese behavior. By July 1961 Bowles was urging Kennedy to explore ways to involve the Russians in the long-term containment of Communist China.[32]

Adlai Stevenson, leader of the Democrats for a decade and now ambassador to the United Nations, was also on record as urging the adoption of a two-China policy. And like Bowles Stevenson believed that the Kremlin's effort to control Mao was in American interests. In late 1959 he published his view that "in the long run, the degree to which Russia is willing and able to moderate China's imperialistic designs will be a major factor in world peace." Dean Rusk, whom Kennedy hired away from the presidency of the Rockefeller Foundation to become secretary of state, had the reputation of opposing any revision of the policy of active containment and isolation of Beijing. Many observers believed Rusk's tough attitude toward China had changed little since his days as assistant secretary of state for Far Eastern Affairs just before and during the Korean War. But he too had come to favor the two-China solution and was well aware of the Sino-Soviet split.[33]

These leading Democrats all favored unhooking the United States from Chiang Kai-shek, stranded on Taiwan. It was not that any favored jettisoning the Nationalists in order to improve relations with Beijing, only that they saw the lack of formal contact with Beijing, other than through the ritualized Warsaw talks, as constrictive of American options and self-defeating. At the same time the Kennedy men concluded that, in the Sino-Soviet dispute, the Chinese represented the greater menace to American interests. Even though China did not pose a direct military threat to the United States and was the weaker of the two Communist powers, Beijing seemed to imperil the whole of Southeast Asia, an area that the United States highly valued. More broadly, the CCP's encouragement of uncompromising hostility toward American imperialism and its support for revolutionary struggle had international implications, especially for elements within the Soviet Union unconvinced of the value of Khrushchev's peaceful coexistence effort.

George Kennan, even more than Bowles and Stevenson, was certain that the United States had a substantial stake in helping the Soviets oppose Beijing. Kennedy brought Kennan out of the relative tranquility of academia to advise him on Soviet-American relations and to become ambassador for the critical post of Yugoslavia. "Nothing is more important to us, in this coming period," Kennan had written to the candidate Kennedy, "than to assure a divergence of outlook and policy as between the Russians and the Chinese. The best way to do this is to offer opportunities to the Russians, in the way of a relationship with the West, which provide them with an alternative to an exclusive intimacy with, and dependence on, the Chinese." Kennan's advice made explicit what had been quietly discussed and pursued during the closing months of the Eisenhower administration. Kennan was no less keen on exploiting fissures in the Communist world than he had been in 1948 and 1949, but he now talked of Soviet "dependency" on the Chinese (not the other way around) and the possibility of winning Moscow away from Beijing. In little more than a decade, the shifting political positions of China, the Soviet Union, and the United States prompted Kennan to reverse his tactics toward the Communist giants completely.[34]

Kennedy ordered an intensive study of the "Sino-Soviet dispute" as soon as he entered office, and he himself continued to follow the emerging split closely.[35] In contrast to Kennan's confident opinion about what should be done about Sino-Soviet relations, staff researchers drew only cautious and limited conclusions from their extensive research. The depth, permanence, and future prospects of the Communist division defied comfortable prediction. Would the split heal after Khrushchev or Mao left the scene? Should the United States depend on the split, clearly a volatile development, to make major policy decisions? Could it exploit the rift without jeopardizing other interests? Could it do anything to exacerbate the differences between the Communists? What exactly would constitute a "split"? These were some of the vexing questions that American specialists now faced.[36]

Adding to the complexity of the issue was the way in which the long-awaited Sino-Soviet division was unfolding. For years many Americans assumed that if a split came, China and the United States would be the ones to find common ground against Russian expansionism. It now appeared, however, that Moscow and Washington shared interests in opposing Beijing. Moreover, the implications of a genuine Sino-Soviet split were awesome. Since policy toward the United States appeared to be one of the principal issues in the dispute, Washington might have to rethink its entire military-strategic posture, its attitude toward revolutionary and Communist movements throughout the world, and in general its conduct of the Cold War. Indeed, the world situation appeared surprisingly fluid to many in the administration. Even the Cuban revolutionary Che Guevara reportedly sought "some kind of accommodation with us," Carl Kaysen of the PPS reported to Arthur Schlesinger, one of Kennedy's top aides. There is a "real possibility that if we are willing to make the gamble, we can buy another Yugoslavia," Kaysen mused.[37]

For the time being, at least, the fledgling administration decided to adopt a circumscribed attitude in public toward the troubles in the Communist world and make no overt efforts to exploit the rifts. The very importance of a Sino-Soviet split militated against hasty conclusions.[38] At one of Rusk's first press conferences in 1961, he cautioned that, even though there was evidence of Sino-Soviet tensions, the two Communist powers still shared a "certain doctrinal framework"; the United States could not base policy on the tensions between them.[39]

Apparently statements like these were not just for public consumption. According to James Thomson's recollection, it was only after a high-level State Department meeting with Dean Rusk on January 2, 1962, that "all the powers of State" seemed "to focus for the first time on the reality of a permanent Sino-Soviet split. . . . The impact on the minds around the table that morning was dramatic and you could hear the ice of 12 years begin to snap and crackle as an intellectual thaw set in. . . . One after another State's operators and planners toyed with the new world possibilities that non-monolithic communism might offer to US policies."[40] The matter at hand was a 77-page research paper entitled "The Sino-Soviet Conflict and U.S. Policy," produced apparently by the PPS. Its basic finding was that, thanks to the Sino-Soviet conflict, "monolithic unity and control no longer exist in the communist camp. . . . There is no single line of command, no prime source of authority, no common program of action, no ideological uniformity." The conflict, which was now completely out in the open, had implications far beyond the bilateral relationship of Beijing and Moscow. The entire Communist world was experiencing "fractionalization." The researchers believed that much more than ideology was involved. There were conflicts over supremacy in the Communist movement and foreign policy, as well as Chinese dissatisfaction with Soviet assistance and Russian chauvinism. Though couched in universalist Marxist-Leninist terms, the dispute was at base a clash of "national interests" over what was best for each power. At work was Lenin's "Law of Uneven Development" in reverse, as the PPS saw it. The conflict, with no reconciliation expected, was deemed immensely beneficial for American interests in the long run. The United States would no longer face a united threat, Communist prestige would be severely tarnished, and the United States could increasingly deal "with Russia as Russia and China as China," using traditional "power politics" methods. The PPS, however, was less optimistic in its evaluation of the short-run advantages of the split. Both the Soviet Union and China continued to oppose the United States, and in some areas, such as

Southeast Asia, the United States faced an explosive situation because of Chinese militancy.[41]

The difficulty in determining the immediate policy implications for the United States was evident in the January 2 meeting, according to James Thomson's notes of the discussion. Walt Rostow, the new head of the PPS, began by saying that the Moscow-Beijing split was an unprecedented and historic development, but quickly added that "no one knows what to do about it." There was insufficient intelligence about what was actually going on. Rusk proposed that the State Department initiate more studies on Sino-Soviet relations both within and outside the government. Rostow and others pointed out that some regional conflicts might actually be aggravated by the Communist competition.

Charles Bohlen, the senior Soviet specialist in Washington, observed that the essence of the rift was simply that "the Russians have become the Mensheviks, while the Chinese are Bolsheviks." Rusk was not so sure, pointing out that Mao's regime combined "old-fashioned Chinese imperialism as well as left-wing Communist deviationism." He agreed that the United States might favor "right-wing deviationists," such as Tito, but not leftists like the Chinese. A wide-ranging speculative discussion of particular issues, including China's development of a nuclear capability, ensued. Rusk finally concluded the meeting with a call for further study of the conflict and investigation of the stability of the Chinese Communist government. Rusk himself was careful in drawing overall conclusions for the future direction of U.S. policy.[42]

According to Roger Hilsman, then director of the State Department's Bureau of Intelligence and Research and later assistant secretary of state for Far Eastern Affairs during the Kennedy years, the United States approached the problem of the Sino-Soviet split "gingerly."[43] China was still an emotional and highly partisan issue in the country, and many aspects of the split were puzzling. Zbigniew Brzezinski, a Columbia University political scientist and later national security adviser when Jimmy Carter normalized relations with China in 1979, recommended continuing to ostracize Beijing so as to place further strains on Moscow. Richard Nixon, on the other hand, thought that the United States "could no more encourage a split between Red China and Russia than fly without wings."[44]

IV

The growing dispute between the Soviet Union and China also absorbed the attention of Taipei, which had as much difficulty as Washington deciding what to think about the Communist rift. Like the officials in the Kennedy administration, Chiang Kai-shek's government saw both possibilities and dangers in the situation.

By the time Kennedy took office, Taiwan had attained one of the highest standards of living in Asia, and the morale of the population was good. Its military had become a credible deterrent to military threats from the mainland. The Taipei government continued to hold China's seat in the United Nations and maintained more extensive diplomatic relations than Beijing, all of course with the strong backing of the United States.[45] But for all this, the situation on Taiwan remained anomalous. A one-man dictatorship that was a continuing embarrassment to the professed democratic ideals of Washington claimed to preside over the "genuine" China, a fiction that was gradually losing credibility in the world. Each year saw a few more countries extend diplomatic recognition to Beijing. Chiang Kai-shek kept the country in a constant state of war-readiness and devoted some 13 percent of the gross national product to the military, one of the highest proportions in the noncommunist world. His armed forces numbered close to 700,000, out of a total population of just 11,000,000.[46] The aging Chiang Kai-shek understood that he might never set foot on the mainland again.

In the Sino-Soviet rift and the deteriorating economic condition on the mainland Chiang saw what would perhaps be his last opportunity to launch his promised offensive. Early in 1962 he announced, "There is no doubt that we can annihilate the Communists, reunify our country and restore freedom to the people on the mainland in the nearest future." He openly talked about an invasion of the mainland. Chiang believed that if several Nationalist divisions succeeded in gaining a toehold there, the Chinese people would rally in revolt and overthrow the Communists.[47] Chiang also believed that if he did not strike soon, the United States, in its desire to exploit the Sino-Soviet split, would move openly toward a two-China policy, leaving him stranded on Taiwan.[48] Chiang's statements disturbed many State Department officials, who saw little sign of the possibility of revolt on the mainland despite the serious food shortages and the sudden flood of refugees streaming into Hong Kong.[49] According to Roger Hilsman, however, there were "plenty of people" within the administration who agreed that the time might be right to see if the Beijing regime could be toppled. Many top U.S. military leaders and the CIA were also sympathetic to Chiang's assessment.[50]

The renewed tensions in the China area ignited a policy debate within the United States that had many familiar overtones. On one side were those who believed that China's severe economic problems might make it receptive to new overtures from the United States. Supreme Court Justice William O. Douglas, Senator Hubert H. Humphrey, and others suggested that easing trade restrictions or offering famine relief might reduce Beijing's hostility and help split China and the Soviet Union. Within the administration Averell Harriman and Chester Bowles also wanted to pursue the food program. Harriman even toyed with the idea that the United States ought to "open the door" to Chinese technical and medical students. On the other side of the debate were those who argued that relaxing the hard line toward China would make it easier for the Communists to survive their crisis and that, if anything, pressures should be increased. Arguing as he had in 1949, Foy Kohler, now assistant secretary of state for European Affairs and soon-to-be U.S. ambassador to the Soviet Union, opposed any change in policy to try to entice China toward the West. The Soviet Union, he argued, might even welcome American help in alleviating China's food crisis because that would remove "an important source of friction" in Sino-Soviet relations.[51]

Chiang did not wait for a consensus in Washington. In the early summer of 1962 he ordered immediate extensive efforts to place Nationalist agents on the mainland and pressed the United States for its backing. The CIA's top man in Taiwan flew back to Washington to argue Chiang's case for an ex-

panded Bay of Pigs–type operation on the mainland. Harry D.
Felt, commander-in-chief of the Pacific, also favored Chiang's
plans. When the PRC responded to Chiang's actions by increasing its military forces opposite Taiwan by half a million men in
June, the administration was prompted to clarify its position.[52]
After Kennedy met with his advisers on June 20, the United
States communicated to the Nationalists, the Chinese Communists, and the Soviets that it would neither encourage nor
support a Nationalist attack on the mainland. At the same
time it reaffirmed its support of the Nationalists and their defense of the territories under their control, including the offshore islands. Following Kennedy's public enunciation of the
administration's stand, military tensions slowly subsided in
the Taiwan Strait, ending the third offshore island crisis.[53]

Although Washington's declared opposition to the use of
force in the Taiwan Strait area defused the immediate situation, Chiang was still set on his mission. He pestered Washington for more military aid, and though the Kennedy administration turned down his requests for material that could be used
for a major assault on the mainland, it did supply planes and
equipment useful for airdrops of commando teams and amphibious operations.[54] As 1962 wore on, Chiang dispatched
scores of twelve-man guerrilla teams to the mainland. All to no
avail: they failed to foment any rebellion and wound up being
killed or captured by the Communists.[55]

Chiang still tried to convince Washington that the escalating Sino-Soviet dispute made the time right for action. In a last
futile letter to Kennedy in September 1963, he argued that the
two Communist powers were engaged in a mortal battle for
power and the control of the Communist bloc. In his view
Khrushchev and Mao could "no longer tolerate each other's
existence." Khrushchev wanted to overthrow Mao and would
not come to his side if the Nationalists "counterattacked."
Chiang wanted "to airdrop trained guerrillas [of] 100–300 men
at a time, and to launch commando raids [of] 300–500 men at a
time, more than 10 sorties each." These forces would touch off
"an anti-tyranny revolutionary movement on the mainland."
American forces would not even be needed. Timing was critical, according to Chiang, since the emergence of a new pro-

Soviet leader on the mainland or a Mao triumph would be catastrophic. "An enemy, once freed," Chiang warned with an old Chinese adage, "will become a cause of trouble for generations."[56]

Chiang's new preoccupation with the possibilities offered by the Sino-Soviet split completely reversed his many previous years of trying to discredit and frustrate any interest in it. While visiting Taiwan in 1960, Eisenhower heard Chiang rail against the theory that Communist China and the Soviet Union might split, or that the Soviet Union saw Communist China as a "threat." Such an idea, according to Chiang, was a Soviet trick to make the West believe that Moscow was sincerely interested in détente and to get Beijing into the United Nations. If Mao actually opposed the Kremlin, Chiang maintained, he would be overthrown.[57] A Sino-Soviet split had been anathema to the generalissimo, who understood that Washington would reduce its aid to him if Beijing distanced itself from Moscow. Even as late as spring 1961 he insisted that there was "no possibility of a split" between China and the Soviet Union. He told President Kennedy that the CCP was the "offspring of the Russian Communist Party" and "totally dependent upon the Soviet Union for material support."[58]

But Chiang's time was running out and he knew it. His plans became more and more desperate. After Beijing exploded its first nuclear device in October 1964, Chiang wanted Washington to "give him [the] wherewithal to take out [Beijing's] nukes." American officials were certain that what Chiang still wanted was to provoke an all-out war between China and the United States in order to regain his lost power. In the ungracious description of the U.S. ambassador to Taiwan, the "Gimo and Madame eat—sleep—love—dream 'counterattack.'"[59]

Though Washington continued to value Chiang's retention of Taiwan and his potent military force, the Nationalists figured only peripherally in its considerations about the implications of the Sino-Soviet split. It would be John F. Kennedy's effort to find a way to cooperate with the Soviet Union in preventing China's acquisition of a nuclear capability that most dramatically revealed the new triangular strategic thinking.

EIGHT

JFK, China, and the Bomb

When elephants fight, the grass suffers. When elephants
make love, the grass also suffers.   —Asian proverb

William F. Buckley, Jr.,'s *National Review*
launched into 1965 with a startling proposal: the United States
should "destroy—destroy literally, physically—the present
Chinese nuclear capability" to guarantee that the PRC could
not develop a nuclear arsenal for years. The magazine's editorial, "Should We Bomb Red China's Bomb?" advocated an
American air strike against atomic installations in China to
protect Asia and the United States. Such a "mission," according to "an unimpeachable, fully qualified source within our
military command structure," would be entirely feasible from
a "military-technological standpoint."[1]

The conservative journal contended that national security
interests required such radical action. China had exploded its
first nuclear device several months before, in October 1964,
and was expected to begin stockpiling weapons. Although the
Chinese had no intercontinental missiles, *National Review*
warned that China already had planes that could drop atomic
bombs on all of Asia, and that "even today a ship can carry a
Chinese bomb into the harbors of New Orleans, San Francisco,
New York or London." With such a frightening prospect before
the nation, the United States could not sit passively "like a
man who merely watches and waits while the guillotine is constructed to chop his head off." The magazine's editors, mod-
estly conceding the possibility that they had not addressed
"every relevant doubt and question that may legitimately be
raised" about their plan, were sincerely convinced "that this
proposal deserves serious discussion by serious men."

Buckley probably assumed that only the political right wing had sufficient anticommunist mettle to advance so audacious a proposal. In this instance, however, his presumption was mistaken. Unknown to Buckley, President John F. Kennedy and his closest advisers, in their quest for a nuclear test ban, had not only seriously discussed but actively pursued the possibility of some kind of joint military action *with the Soviets* at least a year and a half earlier.

I

From the start of Kennedy's administration, government researchers and officials devoted close attention to weapons development in China and concluded that the PRC would soon join the nuclear club. In January 1961 the commander-in-chief of the U.S. forces in the Pacific advised Washington that China might explode an atomic device by the end of 1962 and have a small arsenal of nuclear weapons by 1965. Such a prospect chilled the president who, according to the recollection of Walt Rostow, believed that "the biggest event of the 1960s may well be the Chinese explosion of a nuclear weapon." Rostow himself at the time feared that some of China's leaders believed that a nuclear world war "would be good" for China. Under Secretary of State Chester Bowles shared Kennedy's concern, and in the fall of 1961 he publicly warned that Communist China was "far more dangerous, in many ways, than even the Committee of One Million would have us think." The conservative Committee of One Million, a leading American support group for Chiang Kai-shek, had vigorously championed the Nationalist cause for years.[2]

The Kennedy administration was also certain that the prospect of a China armed with nuclear weapons weighed heavily on the Soviets, whose own ideological and political differences with the Chinese were continuing to grow. On February 11, 1961, soon after taking office, President Kennedy, Vice-President Lyndon B. Johnson, Secretary of State Dean Rusk, Ambassadors Averell Harriman and Llewellyn Thompson, former ambassadors Charles Bohlen and George Kennan, and Special Assistant for National Security Affairs McGeorge Bundy met in the White House to review the "thinking of the Soviet leader-

ship." Kennedy already knew that Harriman was deeply interested in having the United States exploit Sino-Soviet tensions;
he had sent the president-elect reports of his conversations
with Soviet leaders about their differences with Beijing. Kennan, as well, wanted to take advantage of Sino-Soviet discord.
"The main target of our diplomacy," he wrote then-Senator
Kennedy in August 1960, "should be to heighten the divisive
tendencies within the Soviet bloc. The best means to do this
lies in the improvement in our relations with Moscow." This
trend of thought ran throughout the entire post-election White
House meeting. In discussing Soviet attitudes on foreign affairs, the officials speculated that Khrushchev might be eager
for some diplomatic success with the West, perhaps on arms
control. "Soviet interest in this area appears real." They also
concluded that, after the United States, Germany and China
represented "the great long-run worries of the Soviet Union."
"These are the countries whose relation to the atomic problem
seems an important one to the Soviet Union, and indeed effective restraint of the Chinese Communists is a continuing task
of the Soviet government." The discussion ended after talk
about the merits of an early meeting between Kennedy and
Khrushchev. A summit was soon scheduled for June at Vienna.
The acute interest in the Sino-Soviet division that the administration exhibited in private contrasted sharply with its
circumspect attitude in public. Washington wanted to avoid
making any comment that might possibly be used to help heal
the rift.[3]

During the preparations for the Vienna summit, Kennedy's
advisers recommended that the president exploit Sino-Soviet
tensions and seek a common understanding with Khrushchev
about China, including the need to prevent it from becoming a
nuclear power. By emphasizing the Chinese threat to both
Washington and Moscow, it was suggested, Kennedy might accomplish two related objectives: gaining Soviet agreement to
restrain Chinese aggressiveness, and encouraging a condominium of interests in a "stable viable world order" dominated by
the two superpowers. Kennedy's advisers suggested that the
president inform Khrushchev that "so long as Peiping adheres
to a doctrine of 'unremitting struggle' against the United States

and our allies, we will have no recourse but to maintain our systems of individual and collective security arrangements." Thus, if the Soviet Union "sincerely desires peace throughout the world, it should urge Communist China to renounce the use of force in the conduct of its foreign relations." The president should stress that "it is neither in the interests of the USSR nor of the United States to allow Communist China to pursue policies which risk touching off a general war." He should take the initiative in calling for a halt to nuclear proliferation and tell Khrushchev that, alarmed though the United States was about China's strident denunciations of the West, Washington wanted to learn what the Soviet attitude was toward the burgeoning nuclear danger. "Does the USSR really believe that the chances of avoiding a nuclear war will not be lessened after [Communist China] becomes a nuclear power? Can the USSR safely conclude that its espousal of the policies of a militant, expansionist [China] is fully consistent with Soviet national interests?" Kennedy's advisers were curious about Khrushchev's possible answers to these questions, but they were already convinced that the Soviet Union's fear of a nuclear China helped explain its interest in arms control. The aim of the questioning was to elicit the Soviet leader's thoughts on what actually could be done about Beijing's nuclear development. Background papers for the Vienna meeting speculated that the Soviet Union might want to use a nuclear nonproliferation treaty to frustrate the Chinese atomic program.[4]

But Khrushchev's behavior at Vienna disappointed and disturbed Kennedy. The atmosphere was grim throughout the meetings. The two men sparred over practically every issue, including China, with Khrushchev unwavering in his support for China's recovery of both its U.N. seat and Taiwan. The Soviet leader did not lunge for the "China bait" when Kennedy invoked the specter of an expanded nuclear community. At one point in the meetings, Kennedy cited a Chinese proverb about a long journey beginning with a single step and urged the Soviets to take that step toward an arms agreement with the United States. But Khrushchev rebuffed the president. Kennedy seemed to know the Chinese well, he quipped, but so did he. Kennedy, needling Khrushchev in turn, retorted that the

Soviets might get to know the Chinese "even better." Khrushchev ended the verbal duel by saying that he was already well familiar with them.[5]

Kennedy discovered at Vienna that, however sensitive the Soviets were about China's growing power, they were not ready to reject their former partner and enter into a marriage of convenience with the United States. Khrushchev evidently did not want to lend further credence to the Chinese charge that he was conciliating imperialism. As some of Kennedy's advisers had observed, Moscow's behavior was ambivalent: Khrushchev wanted to pursue détente with the United States but could not appear overeager for fear of validating Chinese accusations that he was "soft" on the United States. Sections of the international Communist movement were already leaning toward Beijing in the internecine dispute. "Chip" Bohlen, Kennedy's close adviser on the Soviet Union, had warned before the Vienna meeting that Khrushchev might act more "Bolshevik" to avoid being outflanked by the Chinese from the left.[6]

Kennedy, however, was undeterred by the lack of substantive progress in U.S.-Soviet relations at Vienna, and even after the erection of the Berlin Wall in August 1961, the most graphic symbol of the Cold War confrontation, he continued to seek a modus vivendi with Khrushchev to prevent the spread of nuclear weapons. The president's concern about Beijing in particular mounted. He gloomily told the *New York Times* columnist Arthur Krock in October 1961 that the "domino theory" had lost its validity: China was bound to develop an atomic bomb, and when it did, all of Southeast Asia would fall to the Chinese Communists. The administration already suspected Chinese involvement in the Communist insurgency in Laos. In January 1962 Kennedy directed the NSC to confront and resolve the "special unsolved problem" of a China with nuclear weapons and its effect "on our dispositions in Southeast Asia."[7]

But he did not wait for the NSC's "resolution." Unresigned to watching Beijing assemble its nuclear capability unrestrained, Kennedy decided to devote more of his own attention to achieving a nuclear test ban treaty with the Soviet Union. This was a significant change in attitude for him. Kennedy had not been serious about a test ban during the first year and a half of his administration; his interest in disarmament, according to his aide Theodore Sorensen, had been limited mainly to its "propaganda" effect on world public opinion.[8] But during the late summer of 1962, months before the Cuban missile crisis, Kennedy's growing consternation about China's atomic program stimulated a real search for a test ban, which he hoped might somehow prevent the Chinese from developing their atomic weapons. How the administration thought the negotiation of a test ban treaty could achieve such an end became clearer in the ensuing months.

II

A ban on the testing of nuclear weapons tests was not a new idea. During the last few years of the Eisenhower administration, Washington had sought understandings with Moscow about ending nuclear testing, and in mid-1958 the United States, the Soviet Union, and the United Kingdom, the only three nuclear powers at the time, even agreed to a moratorium on all testing. But the U-2 incident in May 1960 scuttled prospects for a formal agreement, and negotiations at a trilateral Geneva Conference on the Discontinuance of Nuclear Weapons Tests bogged down in recriminations. Conflicts over technical issues, such as methods of verification against clandestine testing, obscured the larger issues and underlying political suspicions. The discussions conducted with the Soviets after Kennedy assumed office also made little headway. Neither side found compelling reasons, including the threat of China, to override the perceived disadvantages of a formal treaty forbidding testing. The trilateral meetings in Geneva collapsed altogether in January 1962.[9]

Nevertheless, in mid-1962 Kennedy ordered a review of the Western position on nuclear testing and the drafting of new treaty proposals. Three factors have been cited as explanations of Kennedy's heightened interest in negotiations: the pressure of adverse world opinion following the resumption of Soviet atmospheric testing in 1961 (followed by the United States in 1962); a changing American strategic doctrine that de-emphasized nuclear weaponry; and technological break-throughs that greatly improved the ability of the United States to detect distant underground nuclear explosions. But excerpts from the private journal of Glenn Seaborg, head of the Atomic Energy Commission under Kennedy, provide some new insights. His notes of a series of meetings Kennedy held with his top arms control and national security advisers at the end of July and early August 1962 reveal that the administration was profoundly dismayed about the imminent acquisition of nuclear weapons by China and other countries. Assistant Secretary of Defense Paul Nitze, in a meeting with the president and his top advisers on July 30, 1962, presented a report commissioned by Kennedy on the potential spread of nuclear weapons without a comprehensive test ban treaty. Nitze said that a "test ban would be a necessary, but not a sufficient, condition for inhibiting this proliferation, and that to prevent it would require collaboration by the U.S. and USSR." Soon after, Washington presented two major new draft test ban treaties to the Soviets at the recently formed Eighteen Nation Disarmament Committee in Geneva.[10]

The first of the treaties, presented by U.S. Ambassador Arthur Dean on August 27, called for a comprehensive ban. The outlook for this proposal was not bright. The administration expected the Soviets to reject the provisions requiring the installation of monitoring stations and inspections to detect violations. The Soviets argued that a verification system was unnecessary and would be used for espionage purposes. Dean said he knew, even before he presented the treaty, that the Soviets would reject any plan requiring on-site inspections. But the second, backup treaty seemed more promising. It proposed a partial ban that sidestepped the sticky problem of underground explosions by outlawing testing only in the atmosphere, in outer space, and under water. But this too was turned down by the Soviets. What is noteworthy about this draft, however, is that it was virtually identical to the Limited Test Ban Treaty the Soviets agreed to less than a year later. Moscow's change of mind would be inseparable from its own widening rupture with Beijing.[11]

Even though the Soviets rejected both draft treaties, saying they gave unfair advantages to the United States, Kennedy remained convinced that a test ban agreement might help end nuclear proliferation. He thought that if the (now) four existing nuclear powers—France had exploded its first atomic device in February 1960—could all agree on a test ban, they could pressure other countries to follow suit and sign. The result would be the end of nuclear proliferation, since (the thinking went) no additional country could develop a bomb without testing. The nuclear powers would also conveniently retain their monopoly.

The Cuban missile crisis in October 1962 seemed to drive home to both Kennedy and Khrushchev the importance of arms control and of reducing tensions. Following the showdown the two leaders drew closer to each other, while Sino-Soviet relations continued to deteriorate. China accused Khrushchev both of recklessness in installing the missiles in the first place and of surrender in subsequently withdrawing them when confronted by the United States. Then, in November, Moscow adopted a neutral attitude toward China's border fight with India, which was strongly backed by the United States. The Chinese took umbrage at Moscow's lack of support. By January 1963 the CIA reported that Sino-Soviet relations had reached a "new crisis." Ideological and national differences had become so fundamental that, "for most practical purposes, a 'split' has already occurred. . . . The USSR and China are now two separate powers whose interests conflict on almost every major issue." According to the CIA, this development would "obviously have many important advantages for the West," although a separate "Asian Communist Bloc" under Beijing could have grave implications for the United States in the Far East.[12]

The CIA made an additional observation that must have caught the eye of anyone on the American side who was contemplating a possible military clash with China. CIA analysts believed that the Sino-Soviet breach would continue to widen and that, though the "public military alliance between the two countries probably would not be openly repudiated," this was "not really a key question." "Already, neither side can consider treaty obligations as an important element in future calculations; each recognizes that, in crises which raise the possibility of nuclear war, for example in the Taiwan Strait, neither can expect its 'ally' to expose itself to major military risks unless the 'ally' itself feels its vital interests to be threatened." The CIA concluded that in all matters "short of survival," "China and the USSR will increasingly view each other as hostile rivals and competing powers."[13]

III

Another problem complicated the effort to get the Soviets to agree to a test ban. France's entry into the nuclear club and its adamant refusal to limit its program were balking Kennedy's initiative, for it appeared that only if he could bring the French into a test ban would the Soviets be willing to exert pressure on the Chinese. In any case the Soviet Union seemed unlikely to accede to a test ban unless Great Britain and France, regardless of their avowed independence from the United States, did so as well.

In early January 1963 Kennedy tried to send a message to French President Charles de Gaulle through Minister of Culture André Malraux, then visiting the United States to present the Louvre's *Mona Lisa* for exhibition. Hoping to convince Paris to join in arms talks, Kennedy drew a terrifying picture of a world imperiled by a China armed with atomic weapons. Over dinner in the White House with Malraux, as William R. Tyler, assistant secretary of state for European Affairs, recalls, Kennedy stressed that a nuclear China would be the "great menace in the future to humanity, the free world, and freedom on earth." Revealing his own alarm and racial bias, Kennedy claimed that the Chinese "would be perfectly prepared to sacrifice hundreds of millions of their own lives" to carry out their "aggressive and militant policies." De Gaulle and other European leaders had to realize that the differences within the Western alliance paled in the face of such a threat. According to Tyler, Kennedy believed that the Chinese attached a "lower value" to human life.[14]

William C. Foster, head of the Arms Control and Disarmament Agency (ACDA) under Kennedy, also recalls that the president was certain the United States had to do "something about ostracizing or containing China. He felt that somehow there must be a way in which the rest of the world [could] prevent China from becoming a [nuclear threat]." That the prevention of China from acquiring the bomb was looming in Kennedy's thoughts about a test ban is revealed in remarks he made to his closest advisers. At an NSC meeting on January 22, 1963, he emphasized that the test ban treaty was important for one reason—"Chicom," as the Chinese Communists were called in the jargon of the day. The declassified notes of Roger Hilsman, director of the State Department's Intelligence Bureau, indicate that Kennedy observed, "If the Soviets want this and if it can help in keeping the Chinese Communists from getting a full nuclear capacity, then it is worth it. Can't foresee what the world would be like with this. Chinese Communists are a grave danger. Ban is good if it does prevent them from becoming a nuclear power. Can't afford to let them do this. Important if it has potential effect on Chicoms."[15]

Two weeks later, on February 8, Kennedy reiterated this theme to his top officials on arms control—Lyndon Johnson, Dean Rusk, Robert S. McNamara, McGeorge Bundy, Glenn Seaborg, and William Foster. Kennedy asserted that "the principal reason" for seeking a treaty was its possible effect in preventing the spread of nuclear weapons to other countries, "particularly China." If it were not for that possible gain, the treaty would not be worth all the trouble of fighting with Congress and the political disruption. To press his point Kennedy said that if the Chinese could be denied the bomb, he would even accept some cheating by the Soviets on a comprehensive test ban.[16]

But how would a test ban stop the Chinese from developing a nuclear capacity if Beijing refused to sign a treaty? Glenn Seaborg recalls that he was never clear on this point, and conservative members of Congress, who were closely monitoring the test ban negotiations, also had serious doubts. William Foster confronted the problem in May 1963 during his testimony before the Senate Preparedness Investigating Subcommittee (popularly known as the Stennis Committee, after its chairman, John Stennis), which questioned the value of a test ban. Foster argued that a treaty would slow the arms race, help maintain U.S. military superiority by stopping the Soviets from improving their nuclear weaponry, reduce nuclear fallout, and end nuclear proliferation. Foster admitted, though, that the administration had "no illusions that China would sign a test ban treaty in the near future. Its leaders [had] made it clear that they have no such intentions." He then posed the obvious question: why did the administration think that a treaty would have any effect on China? Foster suggested that a test ban would give added force to the Soviet Union's own efforts to frustrate the Chinese nuclear program. If there was a treaty, the Chinese could not point to U.S. or Soviet testing to justify their own program. The Soviet Union and other countries trading with China might also exert more economic and political pressures on Beijing. And in any event there was the not insignificant consideration that "the treaty would have a divisive effect on Sino-Soviet relations." The senators remained unconvinced by Foster's testimony; his vague argument for a test ban seemed to rely largely on trusting the Soviets to turn on their erstwhile ally. For many in the Senate who were unsure about the nature and depth of the Sino-Soviet division, Foster's thinking must have appeared wishful at best. If the Soviets were so interested in stopping China's nuclear program, they wondered, why were they stalling on the test ban negotiations? [17]

In fact progress toward a test ban was slow during the spring of 1963. Kennedy had no success with de Gaulle, and the American press focused on the Soviet-U.S. differences over verification procedures. But the real block to an agreement was the Soviet Union's fixation on its worsening conflict with Beijing. The Soviets hesitated to make an accommodation with the West until they had resolved what to do about their eastern flank.

The Chinese, in increasingly shrill terms, charged Khrushchev with abandoning communism in exchange for improved relations with U.S. imperialism. Throughout the first months of 1963 the CCP openly polemicized against many of the major Communist parties of the world that were aligned with the CPSU, including those in France, Italy, and the United States. To undercut the Chinese Khrushchev temporarily hardened his position toward Washington and tried to rally as much of the international Communist movement as possible against the CCP. The CCP, according to the CIA, had succeeded in winning major portions of the international Communist movement to its position. Although the CCP was still in the "distinct minority," it had "gathered increasing strength in the movement. Each new attempt by Khrushchev to force the Chinese into isolation has alienated more Communist leaders and more of the rank and file." The CIA concluded that "Khrushchev and his colleagues [appeared] more concerned with the problems in the Communist world than with any other single issue."[18]

Ambassador Foy Kohler, describing the chill in U.S.-Soviet relations in a long telegram from Moscow in March 1963, predicted that there would be no progress on the test ban, on Germany, or on any other outstanding matters until the Soviet leadership "decides how to deal with Chicoms and starts to do so." In fact open hostilities between Moscow and Beijing already seemed a distinct possibility. The president learned of extensive troop movements along the Soviet-Chinese border and military clashes between the two sides.[19]

As late as May 22 President Kennedy still publicly admitted that he had seen no interest on the part of the Soviets in a test ban treaty. Their position had remained unchanged for five months, he lamented, and the prospects were not bright. He was afraid the nuclear "genie," in his words, might soon escape from the bottle. Secretary of State Rusk expressed similar pessimism in a press conference the following week.[20]

Then suddenly, to Washington's astonishment, it appeared that the volatile Khrushchev had made up his mind to shift direction. On June 7 he accepted a proposal that Kennedy and Harold Macmillan had made in a secret message to him in April for a high-level tripartite conference on a test ban treaty. Kennedy quickly followed up, revealing the Khrushchev communication in a speech at American University on June 10 and re-emphasizing the urgent need for U.S.-Soviet cooperation in reducing tensions in the world. The Soviets glowingly responded to Kennedy's conciliatory address, disseminating it in its entirety through the Soviet media. American intelligence experts wondered if Khrushchev's volte-face was aimed at using the test ban negotiations as a lever or even as an implied threat against the Chinese.[21]

In contrast to Kennedy's well-received gesture toward the Soviets, the CCP on June 14, just four days after the American University speech, delivered a major letter to the Central Committee of the CPSU, detailing the comprehensive and fundamental differences dividing the two parties. The tone and content of the letter virtually foreclosed any possibility that a high-level bilateral Party meeting scheduled to begin on July 5 would be able to close the rift. A study conducted by the American embassy in Moscow after the Limited Test Ban Treaty had been signed in August concluded that "it was the outbreak of virtually undeclared war between Moscow and Peiping [in the] spring which explained Soviet acceptance of a partial test ban agreement which it could have had at any time during the past year."[22]

The Sino-Soviet split was in fact a mixed blessing for Kennedy. He of course welcomed the splintering of the Communist world; ever since the Chinese revolution of 1949, Washington had longed for such a development. But now, even if the Soviets themselves would agree to a treaty, it was highly unlikely that they could pressure the Chinese to sign, as Foster had tried to convince Congress they would. The two countries were simply too distant from each other. Kennedy himself mentioned to German Chancellor Konrad Adenauer in late June that Khrushchev had a real problem with the Chinese and no way to bring them into a test ban.[23] Those of an ironic mind in the Kennedy administration must have asked, Where was the "Sino-Soviet bloc" now that the United States "needed" it?

The president gave few public hints of how he would resolve his quandary, but at a press conference in Bonn, West Germany, on June 24, he dropped a vague threat. In response to a questioner who wanted to know how the proposed test ban treaty would prevent China or others from gaining the bomb, Kennedy pointed out that one of the provisions might be that signatories would "use all the influence that they had in their possession to persuade others not to grasp the nuclear nettle." Kennedy quickly added, "quite obviously" countries seeking the bomb "may not accept this persuasion and then, as I say, they will get the false security which goes with nuclear diffusion."[24] Was Kennedy implying that a nation's acquisition of nuclear power heightened, not lessened, the threat to its well-being and invited possible retaliation from other powers?

The president selected the veteran diplomat and Soviet expert Averell Harriman as the U.S. representative to the tripartite Moscow meeting. Harriman had closely followed the Sino-Soviet split for years and was convinced that it was genuine and profound. He confided to the Danish ambassador on July 1 that "Khrushchev's main preoccupation" was with the Chinese. "There has never been close confidence between Moscow and Peiping," he said. In preparing for the Moscow meeting, Kennedy and his people were buoyed by Khrushchev's surprise announcement on July 2 that he was ready to accept a limited test ban treaty, provided a nonaggression pact between NATO and the Warsaw Pact nations was signed at the same time. Still, the administration remained outwardly cautious, for there was always the possibility that the Soviets might sacrifice an East-West accord for a resolution of the Sino-Soviet dispute.[25]

As the date for the Moscow conference approached, the administration busily formulated the U.S. position. Invariably, the recommendations called for Harriman to approach the Soviets to see if they would cooperate in taking action against the Chinese nuclear program. Using phrases such as "removing the potential capability" or "action to deny the Chicoms a nuclear capability," Kennedy's advisers made clear they were willing to go to almost any length to stop China's nuclear development. Although Harriman doubted whether Khrushchev would want to talk with him about China, Kennedy, according to Arthur Schlesinger's later cryptic description, told Harriman just before he left for Moscow that he "could go as far as he wished in exploring the possibility of a Soviet-American understanding with regard to China." What Schlesinger only dared to hint at, declassified documents begin to reveal.[26]

On July 14 Soviet Deputy Foreign Minister Valerian Zorin warmly welcomed Harriman and his delegation in Moscow. The British team, headed by Lord Hailsham (Quentin Hogg), received an equally hospitable reception. On the same day a CPSU letter blasting the Chinese Communists got first-page treatment in Pravda. The open Sino-Soviet acrimony boosted U.S. hopes for a successful outcome of the talks, according to American newspaper reports. Harriman publicly declared that he would be prepared to discuss any matter that Khrushchev might raise. The next day Khrushchev himself opened the negotiations. In a mood described by the press as "relaxed and jovial," he bantered with the U.S. and British delegations for three and a half hours about the test ban and related matters, including China. Meanwhile, across town, the Chinese-Soviet Party showdown remained under a cloud. Deng Xiaoping, the general secretary of the CCP and leader of the Chinese delegation, was getting nowhere in resolving the differences with the Soviets, and the Soviet press had virtually ignored the bilateral conference from the day it began, in early July. Beijing's *People's Daily* charged that Kennedy's strategy was one of "wooing the Soviet Union, opposing China, and poisoning Sino-Soviet relations." Moscow, according to Beijing, was falling into Washington's trap.[27]

Kennedy personally controlled the monitoring of the discussions in Moscow and took unusual precautions to ensure complete secrecy in the communications between Washington and Harriman. In contrast to the customary wide circulation of cable traffic during a negotiation, all messages from Moscow were sent on a hand-delivered, "for-your-eyes-only" basis. Just six top officials outside the White House—Rusk, Under Secretary of State George Ball, McNamara, John McCone of the CIA, Thompson, and Foster—were permitted to read them. All messages from Washington to the American delegation were cleared through the president. Kennedy followed the negotiations with "a devouring interest," according to Assistant Secretary of State Benjamin Read, who was responsible for communications during the talks.[28]

The opening session in Moscow greatly encouraged Harriman, and he immediately reported the good news to the president. Kennedy, revealing his preoccupation with the Chinese, responded to Harriman the same evening. On July 15 Kennedy gave Read a provocative directive for Harriman, which the president had personally drafted in longhand. It discloses that Kennedy was determined to use the test ban talks to find a way to stop China's development of nuclear weapons. His cable to Harriman reads in part:

I remain convinced that Chinese problem is more serious than Khrushchev comments in first meeting suggest, and believe you should press question in private meeting with him. I agree that large stockpiles are characteristic of US and USSR only, but consider that relatively small forces in hands of people like CHICOMS could be very dangerous to us all. Further believe even limited test ban can and should be means to limit diffusion. *You should try to elicit Khrushchev's view of means of limiting or preventing Chinese nuclear development and his willingness either to take Soviet action or to accept US action aimed in this direction.*[29]

Kennedy did not spell out exactly what kind of Soviet or American "action" he had in mind, but it is clear that he was suggesting more than political methods. He knew that the Soviets had little chance of persuading China to abandon its quest for the bomb. As he had dejectedly confessed to Adenauer in Germany in late June, the Soviets had no way of bringing China into a test ban.[30]

Might the Soviets have been able to coerce the Chinese into abandoning their quest where persuasion failed? That, too, was unlikely, since Moscow had little remaining leverage to use against Beijing. Moscow, top administration officials were almost certain, had ended its assistance to China's atomic program as early as 1960 or 1961. By 1963 China's nuclear industry was wholly independent. And whatever economic and political weapons the Soviets might have had, they had largely been expended in their futile counterattack against the Chinese ideological offensive. The Soviet attempt at economic coercion had failed to bring Beijing into line in 1960, trade between China and the Soviet bloc had fallen precipitously, and the recent effort to isolate Beijing in the international Communist movement had not intimidated the Chinese Communists. If anything Beijing had become more antagonistic to the Soviets.[31]

The United States possessed even fewer means of influencing China. There were no trade or normal diplomatic relations at all between the two countries. And in any case China's economy was autarkic—even world economic sanctions against Beijing would hardly have been decisive. Having invested so much material and political capital in the nuclear program, the Chinese leaders were unlikely to have surrendered to external pressures. Unless there was a total prohibition of nuclear weapons in the world, Beijing had announced, it would reject a test ban treaty and continue to develop its own capability in order to break the atomic monopoly. With the Chinese on the verge of exploding an atomic device, Kennedy must have understood that only force, military "action," would have had any possible chance in actually "preventing" China from becoming the world's fifth nuclear power.

The option of taking military action to stop the proliferation of nuclear weapons had in fact been discussed at the top levels of the administration for months before the Moscow meeting. In February 1963 Secretary of Defense McNamara drafted a memorandum for Kennedy on the prospects and implications of the "diffusion of nuclear weapons." He concluded that the spread of nuclear weapons was "clearly not in the interest of the US." Though he thought that a test ban would help slow proliferation, a more important factor would be "the pressures the US, the USSR and others are willing to employ in restraining others from testing." He also saw "a potential importance" in "the cooperation that may develop between the US and USSR, as a result. . . . In some cases, we, and others, would probably have to employ stronger incentives and sanctions than has seriously been considered so far. However, a comprehensive test ban would make it more likely that stronger steps could be taken and would be effective." McNamara cited the "sharing of weapons information" with countries like France and Israel as an example of "positive incentives," and suggested the use of "penalties (economic or military)" against uncooperative states.[32]

More explicit were the "top secret" briefing books prepared just before the July Moscow meeting. Although much is still classified, including a section labeled "Military and Other Sanctions Against Communist China,"[33] one paper discussed at length possible Soviet responses to a U.S. proposal "to take radical steps, in cooperation with the USSR, to prevent the further proliferation of nuclear capabilities." The paper reviewed the principal factors that would influence Soviet acceptance of a "joint program" with the United States, including the national security of the Soviet Union, the concept of U.S.-Soviet partnership in global affairs, and the impact on the Communist world. If the Soviets accepted the U.S. proposal, the author noted, they would understand that "they would be obliged to see it through to the very end," which might require "Soviet, or possibly joint US-USSR, use of military force" against China. The ramifications of using "military force against a Communist nation" on the position of the Soviet Union as "leader of the Communist world" would "assume significant, perhaps overriding, weight in determining whether or not to accept the US proposal." The author did not speculate on what the Soviet decision might be.[34]

The kind of military force the administration may have been contemplating is not made explicit in the documents that have been declassified so far. But one possible option would have been an air strike on China's nuclear weapons facilities, which were located deep in the western part of the country. According to a former high-level official in the administration, a joint U.S.-Soviet preemptive nuclear attack was actually discussed. One idea was to have both a Soviet and an American bomber fly over the facilities at Lop Nor, with each dropping a bomb, only one of which would be armed. The official, who did not wish to have his identity revealed, maintains that this plan did not get to the planning stage. Some ten years later, however, Joseph Alsop reported that the Kremlin had been well aware of Kennedy's interest in collaborating in an attack to destroy China's nuclear program. Alsop did not say how the Soviets got their information.[35]

In Moscow the test ban talks proceeded swiftly. General agreement on a limited treaty was reached within the first two days, although Foreign Minister Andrei Gromyko continued to press for a nonaggression pact. (Gromyko represented the Soviet side because Khrushchev was busy with the visiting Hungarian premier, János Kádár.) By July 18 Secretary of State Rusk was able to instruct the U.S. ambassador to West Germany to inform the Bonn government that a three-environment test ban was "likely to be agreed upon," and that no commitment to a "nonaggression arrangement" would be made without consultation. On July 20 the United States, the Soviet Union, and Great Britain announced that they had tentatively concluded an agreement on a limited test ban treaty, exempting underground testing. It was not linked to any other agreement. That same day Beijing's *People's Daily* condemned the Moscow talks and published a statement by Mao Zedong exhorting the people of the world to defy nuclear blackmail. The Chinese denounced the test ban treaty as a fraud aimed at maintaining U.S. nuclear superiority and preventing them from acquiring their own nuclear capability. Deng Xiaoping's delegation left Moscow the same evening, ending the obviously unsuccessful Party summit. In a rare move the entire top leadership of the CCP came out to give Deng a hero's welcome at the Beijing airport. In a slap back at China, the CPSU accused Beijing of wanting to "build Communism on corpses."[36]

Since Gromyko handled the negotiations for the Soviets, Harriman did not have a chance to talk with Khrushchev for several days. But Washington did not give up hope that something could be done with the Russians about the Chinese. Harriman believed that the Soviets wanted the treaty "to obtain leverage on Peking" but doubted that they would entertain more radical solutions. On July 23 he cabled Washington that, though it had become "crystal clear" that the Soviets wished to isolate China in the world, Khrushchev wanted the "pressure to appear to come on Chicoms from other countries, particularly the underdeveloped," rather than from Moscow. Another Harriman message later in the day reiterated that Khrushchev and Gromyko had "clearly shown that their way of getting nondissemination is through adherence of maximum number of states to test ban treaty, thus isolating and bringing pressure on Chicoms."[37]

But Kennedy was still not satisfied. That night he again pressed Harriman to raise the China issue with Khrushchev. The president, the directive read, "still hopes very much you will find an opportunity for private discussion with Khrushchev on China." When Harriman finally succeeded in cornering Khrushchev long enough to bring up the subject of China's acquisition of nuclear weapons, he asked the Soviet leader what he would do if Chinese missiles were targeted at his country.

Khrushchev did not respond. It is not clear whether Harriman actually presented Kennedy's thought about joint action against China, but Khrushchev was clearly not ready to take the step with Washington.[38]

Kennedy must have been sorely disappointed at the failure to gain Khrushchev's cooperation in stopping China's nuclear development, and he could not resist taking some public swipes at the Chinese. In his televised speech announcing the test ban treaty, he referred to China several times and even used a quote from one of Khrushchev's own diatribes against Beijing to the effect that the Chinese Communists "would envy the dead" in the event of a nuclear war. In one last deliberate affront Kennedy concluded his speech with a Chinese proverb: "A journey of a thousand miles must begin with a single step," he said solemnly, referring to the goal of world peace.*

William Buckley's *National Review* condemned the Moscow treaty as a "diplomatic Pearl Harbor for America."[39] But the magazine had it wrong: the treaty could have been the avenue for a surprise attack on China.

IV

Would Washington now accept the inevitability of seeing China acquire the bomb, even though one of Kennedy's principal reasons in seeking the test ban had been to frustrate China's nuclear program? Apparently not. As Dean Rusk had informed the U.S. ambassador in West Germany just after agree-

---

* *New York Times*, July 22, 1963, p. 2. Just hours before the president was to go before the nation, a draft of his speech was sent to Harriman for his opinion. The draft contained several references to China that were omitted in the final version. One of the most revealing was, "I do not, of course, expect the Communist Chinese to sign this treaty. They have already denounced it as a Capitalist plot. But if the response to this treaty can serve to increase their isolation from the world community—if it can encourage other nations to apply sanctions against their nuclear development—then the outlook is not altogether gloomy." On the whole the draft was pervaded by a bitterness about the Chinese not found in the final version. It was also more restrained about the value of the treaty and included comments about how the "communist split" had played a major role in bringing about the U.S.-Soviet agreement. Rusk to Harriman (cable), July 26, 1963, Freedom of Information Act release in author's possession.

ment had been reached, wide acceptance of the treaty would place "powerful pressures on Peiping not to go down the nuclear path." But if China persisted, Rusk stated, "other action might have to be taken to prevent this."[40]

Khrushchev's own attitude remained a principal consideration in deciding what might be done. In Moscow he had not been receptive to the suggestion of taking action against China, but he could always change his mind. Administration officials believed this was a real possibility, depending on the course of the Sino-Soviet split. As Rusk testified on August 28 in executive session during the Senate Foreign Relations Committee's review of the treaty, the Sino-Soviet split was "getting wider and deeper."[41] The test ban treaty and subsequent amicable U.S.-Soviet relations could so aggravate the division in the Communist world that a variety of advantageous possibilities might develop for Washington. This prospect appeared sufficiently plausible and attractive that it helped win the military's endorsement of the negotiated treaty.

In June, during preparations for Harriman's trip to Moscow, top military personnel who testified before executive sessions of the Stennis Committee questioned the wisdom of a test ban treaty. Air Force Chief of Staff Curtis LeMay doubted whether a treaty would stop the spread of nuclear weapons, particularly to China. Directly responding to a question about common U.S.-Soviet interests in opposing China, the general discounted the possibility of reaching agreements and argued that the Soviet Union might actually provide China with nuclear weapons at some point. As late as two days before Harriman was to leave for Moscow, the chairman of the JCS, General Maxwell D. Taylor, questioned even a limited test ban treaty at a White House meeting with the president. The JCS wanted further study to determine whether an atmospheric test ban was in American interests. Kennedy had rebuffed Taylor.[42]

But now, during the August Senate hearings to ratify the treaty, the JCS rallied behind the Moscow agreement, endorsing it as in the national interest. Following the Moscow meeting Kennedy, Rusk, and others had met repeatedly with JCS members to report on the Moscow events and current Soviet attitudes. The administration, in addition to using promises of new weapons procurements to calm the military, managed to convince them of the political desirability of the treaty. General Taylor admitted that, though the treaty contained certain military disadvantages, it also had "major political achievements" having "important and favorable military implications." He vaguely listed restraining nuclear proliferation and reducing causes of world tension as positive aspects. But General LeMay, with his characteristic bluntness, better clarified before the Stennis Committee what these "political advantages" were. He said he had spoken with Rusk and Harriman "at great length," and the biggest advantage they pointed to was "if we could really divide the Chinese and Russians." Although he was less optimistic of this development than they, LeMay agreed that a Sino-Soviet split would be truly significant if it occurred, and he was clearly more persuaded of the possibility than before the Moscow meeting. General Earle G. Wheeler, Army chief of staff, and Admiral David L. McDonald, chief of Naval Operations, expressed similar points of view. Wheeler observed that it was "always a sound military principle to divide your enemies if you can, or to contribute to any division that there may be between them." If the United States could do this, "it would be a solid military advantage." He added that, while the Soviets would not like to see the CCP replaced, Khrushchev "would enjoy seeing the Chinese Communists get a bloody nose." What kind of punch Wheeler envisioned he kept to himself.[43]

The Limited Test Ban Treaty sparked an explosion, exactly as the administration wanted: it split the Sino-Soviet rift wide open. Through the rest of 1963 and into 1964, the Soviet and Chinese parties exchanged the most strident polemics ever seen in the history of the international Communist movement. American officials closely watched the unfolding battle and nervously monitored the development of China's nuclear program. Yet Washington, worried that a U.S. strike against China might still reunite the two Communist giants, still hesitated to take unilateral action against Beijing. It continued to pursue its strategy of playing for the Soviets' favor and waiting for Khrushchev to change his mind about taking possible joint action against China.

On September 15, 1964, on the eve of China's first atomic test (which U.S. intelligence accurately predicted to within days of the explosion[44]), President Lyndon B. Johnson and the same advisers who had counseled Kennedy again discussed the problem of China's nuclear weapons. The confident and concrete tenor of the conclusions indicate the subject was a familiar one. Military leaders had been urging that overt or covert action be taken to impede China's nuclear development. National Security Adviser McGeorge Bundy recorded the decisions:

We discussed the question of Chinese nuclear weapons today, first in a lunch at the State Department given by Secretary Rusk for McNamara, McCone and myself, and later at a meeting with the President. . . .

At the luncheon we developed the following position:

(1) We are not in favor of unprovoked unilateral U.S. military action against Chinese nuclear installations at this time. We would prefer to have a Chinese test take place than to initiate such action now. If for other reasons we should find ourselves in military hostilities at any level with the Chinese Communists, we would expect to give very close attention to the possibility of an appropriate military action against Chinese nuclear facilities.

(2) We believe that there are many possibilities for joint action with the Soviet Government if that Government is interested. Such possibilities include a warning to the Chinese against tests, a possible undertaking to give up underground testing and to hold the Chinese accountable if they test in any way, and even a possible agreement to cooperate in preventive military action. We therefore agreed that it would be most desirable for the Secretary of State to explore this matter very privately with Ambassador Dobrynin as soon as possible. . . .

[Several sanitized sentences from the memorandum follow.]

These preliminary decisions were reported to the President in the Cabinet Room, and he indicated his approval. The Secretary of State now intends to consult promptly with the Soviet Ambassador.[45]

Again it seems that the U.S. overture came to naught. The Chinese detonated their first atomic device on October 16, 1964. At almost the exact same time the CPSU replaced Nikita Khrushchev as Party leader for what were officially called "health reasons." The actual circumstances are still not completely known, but Roger Hilsman, director of the State Department's Bureau of Intelligence and Research, concluded that Khrushchev's poor handling of the dispute with China was a major reason for his ouster.[46]

Was Kennedy's extreme alarm about China justified? Others in his administration did not share his dread. A number of officials in the White House and State Department wanted the United States to adopt a less, not more, hostile stance toward China. Roger Hilsman commented in public in 1962 that, as "dramatic" as the prospect of China's exploding a nuclear device might seem, "it will not change the balance of power in Asia, much less throughout the world." He pointed out that the Chinese had actually been rather cautious in the Taiwan Strait. In late July 1963, after the Limited Test Ban Treaty had been concluded, a CIA report on China's anticipated response to the agreement observed that, "over the past few years, in spite of [the Chinese Communists'] warlike oratory, they have followed a generally cautious policy." Observing that the Chinese had thus far shown "marked respect for US power," the authors "[did] not expect them to change this basic attitude." The CIA discounted the possibility of increased Chinese aggressiveness. General Maxwell Taylor stated during the Senate ratification hearings that he had seen no evidence showing that the Chinese believed they would gain from a nuclear war. He also observed that there was "a pretty hardheaded group of Chinese in Peking" who would not do something reckless. The military generally downplayed the significance of China's acquisition of nuclear weapons.[47]

The administration had even received overtures from Beijing not long after Kennedy had taken office in 1961. Wang Bingnan, who was meeting with American representatives at the ongoing bilateral talks, made "friendly gestures" at Geneva and Warsaw. In 1962 Kennedy received reports indicating that the Chinese believed the United States was not necessarily wedded to a policy of hostility toward China. Even immediately after the conclusion of the Moscow treaty, Beijing continued to try to impress on the American representative at the Sino-U.S. talks in Warsaw, John Cabot, that it was interested in improving relations with Washington. Cabot reported that he believed China wanted to conclude an arms control agreement, despite its vitriolic public condemnation of the Limited Test Ban Treaty. Roger Hilsman's interpretation of Cabot's message was that China hoped to refute Khrushchev's allegation that Beijing wanted to provoke war between the West and the Communist bloc. But the United States discounted those tentative approaches and pursued its policy of siding with the Soviets and inciting China.[48]

Kennedy's boosters tout his foreign policy as a "strategy of peace," a phrase from the title of his 1960 campaign book. They also tout the Limited Test Ban Treaty as a breakthrough in the struggle for world stability and as ending the threat of war. But behind the rhetoric Kennedy and his associates sought to aggravate tensions between the Soviet Union and China to the point that the Soviets would join with the United States, possibly even in a military action against the PRC, an attack that would certainly have thrown Asia into greater turmoil than any other single act since the Korean War.

The Kennedy administration could have tried to improve relations simultaneously with both the Chinese and the Soviets, but there is no evidence that it (or the Johnson administration after it) seriously considered that possibility. Instead, Kennedy's policies sharpened the Sino-Soviet split, which eventually produced armed clashes between the two states, increased the pressures on the Soviets by a provoked Chinese leadership, and began to construct a limited U.S.-Soviet stewardship over the world. Administration officials clearly understood these would be some of the results of the Limited Test Ban Treaty. About the time the treaty was concluded, the CIA boasted that the disintegration of the Sino-Soviet alliance had been "largely our accomplishment," as McGeorge Bundy reported to Kennedy.[49] And though it might be argued that Kennedy's policies toward China, the Soviet Union, and the bomb were sophisticated and in the imperial interests of the United States, to claim they were fully consistent with the interests of international peace is doubtful. Indeed the Kennedy administration came dangerously close to answering in the affirmative the question posed by the *National Review*: "Should we bomb Red China's bomb?"

NINE

Full Circle?

We have no eternal allies, we have no perpetual enemies. Our interests are eternal and perpetual. —Lord Palmerston, 1848

One of the great tragic consequences of the Sino-Soviet split, which the United States itself had encouraged, was the role it played in the Johnson administration's fateful decision in 1964–65 to escalate the American intervention in the Vietnamese revolution. Lyndon Johnson had inherited the problem of Vietnam from John Kennedy, who had made the initial limited military commitment to support the Saigon regime against the Hanoi-backed insurgency. But it is Johnson who will go down in history as the American president responsible for plunging the United States irrevocably into the Vietnam debacle.

It was not so much that the officials of the Johnson administration believed that the divided Communist world made the Vietnamese revolutionaries vulnerable, although this was a consideration. Rather, Vietnam appeared to American leaders as the test for whether Moscow's seemingly more benign "Menshevism" or Beijing's "Bolshevism" would triumph in the international Communist movement. Vietnamese Communist success, it was believed, would dramatically encourage the radical national liberation doctrine espoused by China. "Imagine a dissident Bolshevism loose in Asia," Walter Judd had warned in 1949, when he disputed the alleged benefits of Chinese Titoism. Free of the "onus of Russian influence," an independent Communist China would try to transform the world revolution into one of *"haves versus have-nots* on international lines."[1] In the early 1960's it appeared that the specter

Judd had conjured had finally materialized to haunt Southeast
Asia. The United States could not ignore the challenge. Many
of the themes that had appeared in Washington's handling of
Sino-Soviet affairs over the years surfaced again in the discussions about the war in Vietnam, but with some unexpected and
far-reaching changes in opinion.

I

China and Vietnam were inextricably linked in Lyndon
Johnson's mind. "I am not going to lose Vietnam," he told
Henry Cabot Lodge soon after taking office in late 1963 on the
assassination of John Kennedy, "I am not going to be the President who saw Southeast Asia go the way China went."[2] The
Democrats had never fully recovered from the conservatives'
inquisition into "the loss of China" during the 1950's and the
charge that they were "soft" on communism. The Vietnam
scenario seemed ominously familiar: a violent Asian revolutionary movement supported by a powerful Communist
neighbor threatened to overthrow a corrupt, but pro-American,
government. Only this time Johnson was determined not to
abandon South Vietnam, as the Republicans had accused Truman of doing with the Chinese Nationalists in 1949.

Aside from the pressures of domestic politics, however, the
U.S. policy of militarily opposing the expansion of communism in Southeast Asia was a long-standing one. To have not
intervened in Vietnam to prevent Saigon's fall would have been
to break with history. Dean Acheson's China White Paper of
1949 had stated that the United States would not countenance
the expansion of Chinese Communist influence into Southeast
Asia. Throughout the 1950's the United States strengthened
South Vietnam as part of the containment of China. In the
early 1960's Washington simply assumed that Beijing stood immediately behind the leaders of North Vietnam, who in turn
were the principal force behind the National Liberation Front
(NLF), or Viet Cong, of South Vietnam. The Communist leaders of Vietnam and China had close personal ties—Ho Chi
Minh, the patriarch of Vietnam's revolution, had himself lived
in China. Other North Vietnamese Communists were veterans

of Mao's legendary Yanan base area in the 1930's. Opposing Vietnamese communism was inseparable from the decision to enter the Korean War, the formation of SEATO, the involvement in the offshore island crises of 1954–55 and 1958, and the continued support for the Nationalists on Taiwan.[3]

This is not to say that American views of Asia and communism had not changed over the years. In fact there were indications that at least some in the top circles of government were beginning to see the world in a different way. A major CIA report in mid-1964 acknowledged many of the profound developments that were reshaping world politics. In the CIA's view the problems facing the Communist world were "spectacular." Schism, economic malaise, the end of doctrinal authority, all plagued the socialist bloc. The CIA even perceptively predicted that "the national and doctrinal antagonisms [in the Communist world] may occasionally lead to armed conflict; the Communist world may come to be as diverse and undisciplined as the non-Communist world." The CIA observed that the monopolization of power was ending not only for the Soviets, but for the Americans as well. "World power is proliferating, divergencies are emerging, and diversity has been encouraged."[4]

The CIA tried to understand what the implications of these new conditions were for the United States. Overall the intelligence agency was hopeful that the erosion of bipolarity would help promote a further improvement in U.S.-Soviet relations and reduce the danger of nuclear holocaust. It was less sanguine about whether the great powers would respond wisely to the challenges from the Third World. The circumstances there were "so disorderly that many situations are likely to develop from which the great powers will have difficulty remaining aloof or which they will have difficulty controlling if they do get involved." Presciently, the CIA went on to warn against what would, in fact, become the fate of the United States in faraway Indochina in the coming years: "once outside powers do become involved [in conflicts in the Third World], whether by accident or design, crises can develop which will engage their prestige to a degree incommensurate with the intrinsic or strategic value of the area itself."[5]

While the CIA report tried to appreciate the growing national diversity in both the Communist and the capitalist worlds and the need for flexible policy, its insights were not always shared by the top levels of the Johnson administration. There the dominant assumption remained that the Chinese Communists were the vanguard of the most aggressive wing of world communism and had to be stopped. Johnson himself was convinced that if the NLF was not defeated, the world would soon face the prospect of 200,000,000 Chinese soldiers swarming down the trails into Vietnam. He was sure that Beijing wanted nothing less than a Red Asia, by force of arms if necessary. As General Wheeler of the JCS remarked during a meeting with Johnson's principal advisers on Vietnam in September 1964, if the Communists won in South Vietnam, "country after country on the periphery would give way and look toward Communist China as the rising power of the area." The United States would then lose all of Southeast Asia. Dean Rusk firmly agreed with Wheeler.[6]

One of Johnson's closest foreign policy advisers was Walt Rostow, who had come to Washington from MIT to work in the Kennedy administration as McGeorge Bundy's assistant for national security affairs. Rostow soon took over the post of chairman of the PPS, and, after Bundy himself left the Johnson administration in 1966, became Johnson's national security adviser. For twenty years in or close to government and as counselor to powerful men like Henry Luce of Time, Inc., Rostow had well prepared himself to be one of the country's leading strategists. Although his early specialty had been European economic history, Rostow became known as an Asian expert and contributing architect to the Johnson administration's Vietnam policy. The evolution of his thinking about Communist China tells us much about the policy assumptions behind America's disastrous Asia policy in the 1960's.

As Rostow tells his story, his study of China began as a twist of fate. The purge of Asian experts from government in the early 1950's created a need for informed opinion about the Communist giant, and he was promoted to do the job.[7] In 1954 the energetic and prolific Rostow produced an important book, *Prospects for Communist China*, which endorsed the Eisenhower administration's policy of pressure on Beijing. Rostow also supported the Dulles closed-door approach to fostering the Sino-Soviet frictions. Throughout the rest of his government career, Rostow harbored deeply hostile assumptions about China's intentions.

Rostow was fascinated by the Sino-Soviet alliance and thought continuously about what might be done to erode it. "So long as Mao is alive, we would doubt that Communist China will openly dissociate itself from Moscow," he wrote Allen Dulles in 1953. Nevertheless, he was certain that the United States could find ways to weaken the Communist alliance. Rostow suggested to the CIA chief that a "private" center for displaced Chinese students and intellectuals be established in the United States to support their research and study. "Such a center might furnish a captive audience," Rostow told Dulles, "a microcosm of Chinese mentality, for a variety of purposes." In 1954 Rostow proposed that the United States spread rumors that the Soviet Union was taking over the Chinese government, encroaching on Chinese territory in the northwest and northeast, and creating food shortages by taking China's supplies to pay the salaries of Russian advisers.[8]

During the offshore island crisis of 1955, Rostow endorsed taking a hard line against Beijing. In a private letter to C. D. Jackson, Eisenhower's close friend and adviser, he urged "drawing a line on Peking and indicating that the U.S. is prepared to back its play." Total war with China, such as having to send troops to Beijing, was unlikely, he said, but some "limited military operations" might be necessary if the Chinese did not heed the American ultimatum. Facetiously calling himself a "war-monger," Rostow conceded, however, that the United States could not ignore other pressing matters. "We can't drop everything and just have fun plastering the bastards, much as we'd like to."[9]

Rostow's tough stance toward the PRC was bolstered by his conviction that, despite China's self-assured rhetoric, it was an economic disaster. Throughout the mid-1950's he predicted imminent mass starvation in the country and urged the United States to take bold steps to exploit the situation. Persuaded by

Rostow's analysis, Henry Luce formulated a bizarre plan aimed at peacefully overthrowing communism on the mainland. Luce proposed that the United States assemble:

1. An economic agency, armed with resources of $20 billion, which would direct China's economic development over the next decade;
2. A political agency, with a membership divided three ways among the PRC (one-half), the ROC (one-quarter), and other Chinese selected by the United Nations who were associated with neither the mainland nor Taiwan, which would reorganize the government based on Sun Yat-sen's teachings; and
3. An international agency, which would explore how China could be "received into the family of nations as a reliably peace-loving nation."[10]

Rostow's prediction of the "greatest human disaster" imaginable failed to materialize, dashing Luce's pipe dream. But Rostow did not surrender his conviction that China would suffer serious economic difficulties. He suggested to President Kennedy, early in the administration, that China's food needs might force its leaders to moderate its aggressive policies and adopt a less hostile orientation toward the West. At the same time Rostow feared that at least some of the leaders, driven by the desire for national aggrandizement, actually believed a third world war, a nuclear war, "would be good for communism—at least Chinese Communism."[11]

As head of the PPS in 1962, Rostow had an opportunity to elaborate his ideas about U.S. policy toward the Communist bloc, and China specifically. In a 284-page paper called "Basic National Security Policy," he expounded his analysis of the "diffusion of power" in the world and drew a generally optimistic picture of the possibilities of interaction with Moscow. In his view there had been a "certain mellowing" in Soviet domestic and foreign policy since Stalin's death that had made it a more responsible power. He wrote encouragingly of the Soviets' "sporadic movements" toward détente with the United States and West. China, however, was a different case. Rostow saw little chance that its belligerence toward the West would soon diminish; thus he advocated a policy that differed little from the policy of containment and isolation pursued by the Eisenhower administration. Circumstances continued to require the United States to retain a "capability for directly harassing Communist China," he wrote. And like Eisenhower and John Foster Dulles, he urged the United States to work for two Chinas as part of a long-range solution in the Far East.[12]

Rostow heartily welcomed the Sino-Soviet split as "definitely in the U.S. interest." It would likely lead to increased Soviet accommodation with the West and national diversity in the Communist world, he believed. And though he saw that there was little Washington could do to further the Communist division at the moment, the United States should avoid measures that might help heal it, such as embarrassing the Soviets by openly siding with them. All the same it was important that the United States respond positively to Soviet efforts to explore negotiation and peaceful settlement with the West, and make clear that "the contrary Chinese view, if put to the test, [was] likely to entail swift disaster." Therefore, Rostow, whose views remained remarkably consistent throughout his tenure in the Kennedy and Johnson administrations (and even afterward), concluded that it was "critically important that South Viet-Nam maintain its independence and that the present North Viet-Nam offensive be frustrated."[13]

II

The assumption that China was the underlying threat in Vietnam was reinforced by the Soviets themselves. Moscow's vilification of Beijing almost surpassed that of the United States. By 1964 the public statements had gone far beyond the earlier criticisms of factionalism and adventurism to become crude abuse, including charges that the CCP leaders were drug dealers (the Chinese supposedly cultivated poppies to help finance the Great Leap Forward), expansionists, and even racists. A leading Soviet official in April 1964 accused Beijing of trying to pit the yellow and black races "against the whites," a tack that was "no different from Nazism."[14] The Soviet caricature of the Chinese as warlike and fanatic resonated with American beliefs.

What appeared to be at stake in Vietnam was not only the continued existence of the South Vietnamese regime, but whether actual experience would confirm the validity of China's revolutionary line. "We have tried to make it clear over and over again," Dean Rusk told the Senate Foreign Relations Committee investigating the Vietnam War in early 1966, "that although Hanoi is the prime actor in this situation, . . . it is the policy of Peking that has greatly stimulated Hanoi. . . . If the bellicose doctrines of the Asian Communists should reap a substantial reward, the outlook for peace in the world would be grim indeed." Rusk stated, "the doctrines and the policies espoused by Peking today constitute perhaps the most important single problem of peace." To back that contention, he mentioned that a "foreign minister on the other side of the [iron] curtain" had concurred with his assessment of the sanguinary Chinese.[15] Might Rusk have been referring to Andrei Gromyko himself?

In 1963–64 it did seem as though the North Vietnamese were leaning toward the Chinese in the Sino-Soviet split. North Vietnam joined with China in refusing to sign the 1963 Limited Test Ban Treaty, criticized revisionism, and supported "people's war" against imperialism. But the Hanoi-Moscow-Beijing relationship was more complex. Relations between Hanoi and Moscow had always been cordial, and Hanoi had skillfully played Beijing and Moscow against each other over the years by first leaning toward one side and then the other. Because neither Beijing nor Moscow wanted to appear laggard in its support of the Vietnamese revolution, Hanoi could maintain its independence and extract as much material aid and support as possible from both sides.[16] If the Communist world had really been monolithic, Hanoi might have had a more difficult time hewing to its own revolutionary strategy. The Sino-Soviet split, strangely enough, worked to Ho Chi Minh's advantage.

But if what Washington and Moscow said about China had all been true—that its violent doctrine and aggressiveness isolated it from the world family of nations—Beijing would not have been so troublesome. The problem was that Beijing was not a complete pariah in the world community. Its actual influence and position in the international system steadily improved in the early 1960's, to the consternation of both superpowers.

In January 1964 France infuriated Washington by breaking relations with the ROC on Taiwan and recognizing the PRC. Trade between China and Japan, Canada, Australia, Rumania, and Britain increased, despite the objections of the United States. Even more spectacular was the success of Beijing's diplomatic offensive in Africa. Premier Zhou Enlai and Foreign Minister Chen Yi conducted a dramatic tour through Africa in January 1964 to confirm friendly ties with Tunisia, Ghana, Mali, Guinea, Ethiopia, and Somalia. Soon afterward fourteen African nations recognized Beijing, leaving only fifteen to continue their relations with Taipei. In Asia Beijing formed close links with Burma, Pakistan, and Indonesia. China's explosion of its first atomic device in October 1964 further elevated its stature in the eyes of many in the developing nations. President Johnson tried to downplay the explosion—"its military significance should not be overestimated," he told the world— but soon after the test an aide to National Security Adviser McGeorge Bundy dejectedly reported that the admission of China to the United Nations was a "virtual certainty" in the foreseeable future.[17]

As Eisenhower had done to a degree, and then Kennedy, Johnson wanted to promote Moscow's conciliatory trend while isolating the more militant Chinese. During his 1964 presidential campaign he stressed that the diversity of the Communist world offered new possibilities for world peace. In contrast Barry Goldwater, his Republican opponent, assumed the existence of "a single monolithic, omnipotent, hydra-headed Communist horror," according to McGeorge Bundy. As Bundy reminded Johnson before a press conference a month after his landslide election victory over the conservative Republican:

—our policy toward the Soviets is as you described it. . . . Firm on essentials, but always friendly and always seeking ways toward peace
—you mean it about bridges to Eastern Europe and you are increasingly impressed by the fact that business and commercial leaders want peaceful trade in this part of the world
—Communist China is quite a different problem, and both her nu-

clear explosion and her aggressive attitudes toward her neighbors make her a major problem for all peaceful people. This is not the time to give her increased prestige or to reward her belligerence—at the UN or elsewhere.[18]

Beyond playing a major role in the administration's decision to commit the United States to the defense of South Vietnam, the Sino-Soviet split influenced thinking on how the war should be conducted. Harlan Cleveland's comments to George Ball in late 1964 are typical of the thinking of many top officials. Cleveland, who had been responsible for the economic aid program for China in 1948 and 1949 and was now an assistant secretary of state, argued that the American involvement in Vietnam was exacerbating, not healing, the conflict between the Soviet Union and China. Cleveland claimed that American military punishment, combined with efforts toward negotiation, would place great pressures on Hanoi to stop its support of the revolution in South Vietnam. "One of the advantages in this double-headed approach," he argued, "is that it may help drive the wedge more deeply between the CHICOMS and the USSR. As military escalation increases, so will the Soviet Union's concern about the dangers of war in Asia. And as long as we are at the same time offering an opportunity for a negotiated settlement based on stabilizing the *status quo* [an independent South Vietnam], Russian interests should coincide even more closely with our own in wanting to see an end of the affair." Cleveland's thinking mirrored the hard-soft policy toward the Sino-Soviet alliance that Washington had followed since the early 1950's.[19]

But a very different way of thinking about the Sino-Soviet split was beginning to be expressed. Although a distinct minority, some influential Americans suggested that Beijing's independence and hostility toward Moscow might provide a basis for rapprochement. The American consul general in Hong Kong, Washington's principal China-watching post, suggested that the estrangement from Moscow should prompt Chinese leaders to reconsider their relations with the United States. In "strictly balance-of-power terms," he observed, one should not have hostile relations with both "the principal land power along one's borders and the principal sea-air power off one's coast." Although the consul general saw no indication that the Chinese were changing their attitude toward the United States, his report anticipated an alternative approach Washington might one day pursue to exploit the Communist division.[20]

More surprising proposals came from people on opposite poles of the political spectrum. Retired General James Van Fleet, Korean War Army commander, one-time backer of Joseph McCarthy, and outspoken conservative, publicly called for Washington's recognition of the Beijing regime. In his view the Moscow-Beijing rift provided the opportunity for the United States to take steps toward establishing diplomatic relations with the Chinese. "They are our future friends" and natural ally against the Soviet Union, Van Fleet declared in early 1964. The Russians are "our very bad enemy," and though Washington had diplomatic relations with the Soviet Union and none with China, it "should be just the reverse." These ideas, coming from a man who during the 1950's had urged Washington to overthrow communism on the mainland by force of arms, startled the public. Within the U.S. government, Edwin O. Reischauer, the liberal ambassador to Japan, was voicing ideas compatible with Van Fleet's. In Reischauer's view the Soviet Union, not China, was the bigger enemy of the United States. Reischauer continued to agitate for a radical change in China policy over the ensuing years.[21]

III

As Americans thought about the implications of the Sino-Soviet split for the United States, the U.S. military commitment rapidly escalated in Vietnam. American ground forces increased from approximately 17,000 at the beginning of 1964 to almost 185,000 by the end of 1965 (in January 1969 the number of troops in Vietnam peaked at 542,400). The systematic bombing of North Vietnam began in February 1965, even as Soviet Foreign Minister Andrei Gromyko was visiting Hanoi. The escalation provoked strongly conflicting opinions in American society about the wisdom of the administration's Vietnam policies, including their effect on the Sino-Soviet split. In March 1965, when Congress conducted its first hearings devoted specifically to the Communist rift, experts sharply divided over their evaluation of the war's consequences for Moscow-Beijing relations.

The Subcommittee on the Far East and the Pacific of the House Committee on Foreign Affairs listened to eight days of testimony from leading specialists on communism and from top administration officials. Though the specialists concentrated on explaining the history and nature of the Sino-Soviet split, they frequently commented on how the Vietnam War was affecting the Communist world. George Kennan, again out of government service at Princeton's Institute for Advanced Study, was deeply upset by the American involvement in Vietnam. It was "a classic example of the sort of situation we ought to avoid." Vietnam was not "vital" to U.S. interests and diminished the chances of reaching an understanding with the Soviet Union over such crucial problems as Germany and arms control. According to Kennan, Moscow faced a juncture in its foreign policy. Soviet relations with the West could deteriorate, requiring Moscow to reconcile with Beijing and adopt a militant international line, or the Soviet Union could continue to seek an improvement in relations with the United States, which would strengthen the hands of both Washington and Moscow in dealing with Mao's China, a country that disgusted Kennan.* The United States "will find it easier to deal with

*In private Kennan further revealed why he favored the Soviets over the Chinese. About the same time as he was preparing his presentation for the subcommittee, he wrote in a letter to Roger Hagan (Dec. 11, 1964; Kennan Papers, Princeton, box 31, Outgoing Letters): "There has always been, despite strong ideological disagreement and antagonism, an important under current of real desire on both sides [the United States and the Soviet Union] for a many-sided and mutually-fruitful relationship. Russia is, after all, in spiritual and cultural character largely a western country." The same could not be said of China, which was marked by a "basic xenophobia and national arrogance." In early 1966 Kennan frequently expressed his distaste for Chinese communism with its regimentation and emotionalism (see, for example, Kennan to David Horowitz, Jan. 17, 1966, ibid.). In "Comments on Starobin's *Paris to Peking*," he wrote that Chinese "forms of thought control and manipulation of mass psychology" were "as degrading and sickening as anything described in Orwell's *1984*" (draft of unsent letter, March 1956, ibid., box 26). Aside from reacting to the more extreme features of Chinese communism, Kennan seemed to harbor an emotional antipathy toward the Chinese. "Only a psychiatrist could explain how people who owed so much, in point of their own education, to American

the Chinese in the long run," Kennan argued, "if the Russians remain in a reasonably close and intimate relationship with the West." Which road Moscow chose, he said, depended on the actions of the United States.[22]

Kennan also resurrected a perspective that he had advanced fifteen years earlier, though in a revised form that recognized the new turbulence in the Communist world. When China was in revolution in 1949, he had urged the United States to avoid actions, such as overt military intervention, that would drive the Chinese closer to the Soviets. If China was left alone, he said, the nationalist tendencies inherent in the revolution would mature and inevitably clash with Soviet imperialism. Now, in the mid-1960's, Kennan similarly recommended that Washington adopt an aloof attitude toward the revolutionary upheavals in what he called "these remote countries scattered across the southern hemisphere." Without an American military presence to serve as a unifying element, Sino-Soviet rivalry would flourish and, he predicted, "the local regimes, whether nominally Communist or otherwise, are almost bound to begin to act independently in many ways—to develop, in other words, Titoist tendencies." But other than voicing lugubrious misgivings about the original U.S. military commitment to Vietnam, Kennan had no concrete recommendations for changing policy. When pressed, he grudgingly concurred with administration policy, admitting that the United States could not now "afford simply to get out and to turn [Vietnam] over to the Chinese Communists."

Donald Zagoria of Columbia University, perhaps the leading specialist on the Sino-Soviet conflict (he published the first comprehensive study on it in 1962), sharply differed with Kennan during the hearings. The United States had actually been "a silent, if largely unwitting, participant in the Sino-Soviet dispute," Zagoria told the House subcommittee. Employing a geometric reference that would become increasingly popular in the years ahead, he described the "Russian-Ameri-

---

generosity, could turn so violently against the country that once endeavored to befriend them." One wonders to what extent cultural prejudices influenced the development of his critique of U.S. Far East policy.

can-Chinese relationship" as a "triangle," and argued that a "change in the relationship of any two of the powers unavoidably affects the third." According to Zagoria, Washington's past practice of what he later called "selective accommodation"[23]— détente with Moscow, ostracism of Beijing—had helped stimulate Sino-Soviet discord. The conduct of the United States in the Vietnam War could have a similar result. "The most significant consequence of the American bombing of North Vietnam," Zagoria observed, was "the widening of the Sino-Soviet split. Instead of bringing the two Communist giants closer together . . . the limited escalation of the war has so far produced precisely the opposite effect." Zagoria pointed out that the bombing was creating an agonizing dilemma for Moscow. If the Soviet Union confronted the United States and ended détente, Beijing's militant line would seemingly be vindicated. On the other hand, if the Soviet Union continued to acquiesce in U.S. attacks on North Vietnam, the Chinese would cry "capitulationism" to discredit the Soviets in the Communist movement. Thus a negotiated settlement was the "only way out" for Moscow.

Zagoria suggested that the Soviet predicament could be exploited by adopting a "subtle and flexible" policy. The administration should take advantage of Moscow's and Washington's "common interest" by trying to end the war "on terms acceptable to both sides and thereby help substitute Soviet for Chinese influence in Hanoi." The limited U.S. escalation of the war, therefore, actually helped "the Russians to impress on Hanoi the desirability of early negotiations." Unlike Kennan Zagoria saw almost no chance that the Soviets would revert to a militant line just to please the Chinese; they were committed to pursuing détente with the West for the more profound reason of avoiding thermonuclear war and a costly arms race. But just as Kennan had neglected any consideration of the independent interests of the Vietnamese Communists, so also Zagoria mistakenly concluded that "the Chinese are the only ones who have something to gain" by the continuation of the war, whereas "the Russians and the Americans both have much to lose."[24] Once again, like the State Department in 1949, the specialists in 1965 overestimated the ability of outside major powers to affect the course of a determined local revolutionary struggle.

Administration officials who came before the subcommittee were careful in what they had to say about the sensitive subject of official policy toward the Sino-Soviet split. As in the past American officials hesitated to divulge their strategic thinking publicly—Dean Rusk could hardly say he wanted Moscow to dominate Hanoi. Because of this need for caution, American officials often seemed oblivious to the implications of the Sino-Soviet rift. But it was evident that their thinking was closer to Zagoria's than to Kennan's. When questioned, Deputy Assistant Secretary of State for Far Eastern Affairs Marshall Green revealed that the feeling in the State Department was that a policy of firmness, as in Vietnam, had "produced a continuation of the rift rather than a bringing together" of Moscow and Beijing. The ever-cautious secretary of state, Dean Rusk, minimized the possibility of cooperating with the Soviets against the Chinese over Vietnam. American leaders had had little discussion with top Soviet officials about the Chinese, he reported. But he also admitted that he was "quite convinced" "that the Russians as Russians are concerned about the prospect of living next to a billion Chinese armed with nuclear weapons." American military might had forced the Soviets to move toward peaceful coexistence, Rusk said, a doctrine that he thought might be beneficial for Russian national interests but would not "produce a militant and convincing communism . . . that is going to transform the rest of the world into Communists." Rusk was certain the United States had to force China to move in the same direction as the one the Russians had taken.[25]

Contrary to Kennan's expressed apprehensions, Sino-Soviet relations continued to deteriorate as the United States escalated its intervention in Vietnam. Both Moscow and Beijing used the war in their polemical attacks against each other. The Soviets charged that the Chinese refusal to agree to "united action" with Moscow to support Vietnam sabotaged the struggle against imperialism. The Chinese were supposedly even guilty of obstructing Soviet deliveries of aid to North Vietnam. On their part the Chinese accused the Soviets of collaborating with the United States against the Vietnamese and other revolutions. "United action is impossible with those who transpose enemies and friends," the *People's Daily* declared. The Soviet Union "regarded U.S. imperialism . . . as its closest friend, and the Marxist-Leninists of the world . . . as its principal enemy." Exaggerated as that view was, the Soviets were worried enough about the escalating war by early 1965 to inform Western governments of their wish to settle the conflict through negotiations in which Moscow would have a major role.[26] By mid-1965 the administration was convinced that the Soviets' commitment to a long-term improvement of relations with the West did take precedence over their support for Hanoi. The State Department estimated that the Sino-Soviet split would continue, and that the Communist world would splinter still further. As Dean Rusk told the NSC in July 1965, he saw "no real reason for a basic difference between the U.S. and the U.S.S.R. on Vietnam. . . . At the other end of the spectrum was Peking which was adamant against negotiations."[27]

The CIA went even farther in its analysis, suggesting in effect that it was in the U.S. interest for the Soviets to increase their influence over North Vietnam. According to the CIA, Moscow did "not wish the kind of Communist victory [in Vietnam] which would magnify the prestige and power of China." Later in the year, in considering a pause in Operation Rolling Thunder, the code name for the bombing of North Vietnam, administration officials hoped, among other things, that the break in the air attack might strengthen Moscow's ability to persuade Hanoi to agree to peace negotiations.[28]

But the hope that Moscow could bring Hanoi to the negotiating table and end the fighting in South Vietnam was tenuous and ultimately misplaced. The Vietnamese Communists were far more independent of both Moscow and Beijing than Washington suspected. And Hanoi understood that it had little to gain from negotiating with the shell of a government in Saigon. The military junta of Nguyen Cao Ky and Nguyen Van Thieu, which took over in mid-1965, remained largely a creation of Washington. Johnson's own physical embrace of the diminutive Marshal Ky at a highly publicized Honolulu conference in February 1966 symbolized America's domination of the Saigon regime. But it was also clear that American armed forces, which were bearing an increasingly heavy load of the fighting, could not remain in South Vietnam indefinitely. Time was clearly on Hanoi's side.[29]

Though the expansion of Rolling Thunder did in fact push Hanoi toward Moscow for greater assistance, the North Vietnamese did not, as expected, move closer to the bargaining table. By mid-1965 Soviet supplies of more sophisticated types of military aid were flowing into North Vietnam, and Chinese influence began to wane.[30] The United States, though, was no closer to ending the conflict. As one historian of the international history of the Vietnam War puts it: "Perhaps the most serious failing of both the Kennedy and the Johnson administrations was their assumption that China was the principal 'enemy' in Asia, whilst the Soviet Union was potentially a 'friend.'"[31] The miscalculation that Moscow would help end the conflict contributed to Washington's determination to "tough out" the war. By early 1966 the United States had committed all its prestige and credibility to preventing an NLF victory in South Vietnam. Remaining in Vietnam now largely became a matter of avoiding humiliation. The decision for full-scale intervention into the Vietnam quagmire had been made.[32]

IV

The September 1965 publication of Chinese Defense Minister Lin Biao's essay *Long Live the Victory of People's War!* provoked the rhetorical high point of American hostility toward China. Lin announced that just as the CCP had built its strength in the countryside to encircle and eventually conquer China's metropolitan centers, so the revolutionary upheavals of Asia, Africa, and Latin America (the "rural areas") would eventually destroy North American and European imperialism (the "cities"). Neither military might, including the atomic bomb, nor revisionist opposition could stop the tide of revolution.[33] Dean Rusk repeatedly compared Lin's essay to Hitler's *Mein Kampf* as an admission of China's expansionist ambitions.*

*Cohen, *Dean Rusk*, pp. 285–86. Dean Rusk was tough toward Beijing, at least in part, because of his belief that China's revolutionary line possessed the force of logic. In a candid moment before a 1965 congressional hearing on the Sino-Soviet split, Rusk revealed, "If I were a Communist, I would be a Peiping

Lin's ideas were not all that new in fact—the CCP had been saying much the same thing since Mao had proclaimed in 1957 that the "East Wind" was prevailing over the "West Wind" now that the conditions for revolutionary struggle were favorable. Moreover, a close reading of Lin's essay shows that his message was just the opposite of Rusk's interpretation. Behind the bombastic language Lin was actually maintaining that the Vietnamese and other revolutionaries could rely on their own efforts and resources to attain victory, as the Chinese Communists had done. They should not expect supportive intervention from outside. In other words China would not directly involve itself in Vietnam. But the image Lin invoked of an intractable, hostile China leading "one, two, many Vietnams" against the United States could not have more agitated men like Rusk and Rostow, who had assumed the worst from Beijing for so long during their careers. Within the administration Rusk, McNamara, and others expressed growing fears of an American clash with China. Would Chinese and American forces, they wondered, soon be fighting each other again as they had in Korea just a little more than a decade past?[34]

The term for "crisis" in the Chinese language is a combination of two words that separately mean "danger" and "opportunity." In contrast to the largely negative connotation of the English word, the Chinese term can mean something that is both threatening and potentially advantageous. The looming prospect of war between the United States and China over Vietnam proved to be a crisis in the Chinese sense—both meanings were applicable—and sparked American and Chinese leaders alike to re-examine their beliefs and policies.[35]

In late 1965, according to an internal State Department history written in the closing days of the Johnson administration, foreign policy officials began to debate "the interrelated questions as to whether Communist China would intervene in Viet-Nam; what US actions would cause Communist China to intervene; whether or not to create a buffer zone in North Viet-

Communist. I rather believe from the point of view of communism, Peiping probably has the right line . . . in terms of how you [would] best be a Communist under world conditions." Declassified security deletion included in letter from Helen C. Mattas to author, March 9, 1988.

Nam near the Chinese border to avoid accidental US air intrusions into Chinese territory; and how large this zone should be."[36] The review led to a high-level decision to back away from a confrontation with China and cautiously probe for a new relationship with Beijing.

Pressures from lower levels in the foreign policy establishment for a change in China policy had been mounting for several years. James Thomson and Roger Hilsman were especially active in trying to inject new thinking about China into the policy process. They were heartened when Rusk permitted Hilsman to deliver a speech in December 1964 that introduced a modicum of rhetorical moderation into U.S. public policy toward China. In San Francisco, where John Foster Dulles six years earlier had said that Communist China was just a "passing phase," Hilsman stated that the United States was not implacably hostile to the Beijing regime and held out hope for improved relations in the future. An American "open door" for China would be waiting, he said, for the day when its leaders changed their ways.[37]

But Thomson and Hilsman were far from alone in pressing for a change in China policy. Along with Ambassador Reischauer in Japan, many U.S. mission chiefs in the Far East questioned the wisdom of a rigid nonrecognition policy. At a meeting in early 1966, Edward Rice, the U.S. consul general in Hong Kong and America's chief China-watcher in the Far East, urged Washington to consider such steps as removing the embargo on foods and medicines and adopting a "live and let live relationship." Senators Edward Kennedy and Mike Mansfield openly criticized existing China policy and advocated a more flexible approach. Even Dwight Eisenhower's famous cardiologist, Paul Dudley White, sought administration approval in 1965 to visit China to try to break the deadlock in relations.[38]

Moreover, there was widespread international disapproval of Washington's policy. The United States was out of step "with very large circles [of people] in western Europe and very considerable circles in Japan," Assistant Secretary of State for Far Eastern Affairs William P. Bundy conceded. Frustrations about the lack of progress ran high. Among others, Alfred Jenkins, a former member of the U.S. delegation to the Warsaw talks who followed developments in China for the White House, blamed Dean Rusk for being overcautious and blocking progress. "On the one issue of China, his style scares me," Jenkins privately wrote Rostow.[39]

There were signs of some movement at the top, however. William Bundy signaled the slowly emerging new approach in a speech on February 12, 1966. He began by identifying China as "without doubt the most serious and perplexing problem that confronts our foreign policy today." But after the usual diatribe against Chinese expansionist ambitions, he carefully modified the prevailing image of an irrational and irresponsible Beijing: China's leaders "have not wished to seek a confrontation of military power with us, and in any situation that would be likely to lead to wider conflict they are tactically cautious." Mao was not, he corrected, "another Hitler." The United States would continue to oppose Chinese pressures and honor its commitments in Asia, but it also hoped that it could, "over time, open the possibility of increased contacts with Communist China." The obstacle to travel, cultural exchanges, and limited trade, Bundy stated, had been Beijing, not Washington. Bundy's speech, which was not fixated on China's aggressiveness, suggested that the rigidity in U.S. China policy was changing.[40]

At the same time President Johnson stopped referring to China as the instigator of the Vietnam War. Even though the number of Chinese support personnel (engineers, workers, technicians) in North Vietnam increased to 40,000 during the first part of 1966, the United States largely ignored the development in public and began to pin the blame for the conflict solely on Hanoi. Starting with Bundy's speech, U.S. officials also began referring to China's capital as Peking (Beijing, or "northern capital"), the name the Communists adopted in 1949, switching from "Peiping" (Beiping, or "northern peace"), the Nationalists' term. Apparently in response to these gestures Beijing in spring 1966 communicated to Washington that its forces would not become involved in Vietnam if the United States refrained from invading China or North Vietnam and from bombing the North's Red River dikes. President Johnson and other administration officials, in turn, signaled their acceptance of the conditions.[41]

In July 1966 Johnson offered the most conciliatory gesture toward China by an American president in fifteen years. In a major address on "The Essentials for Peace in Asia," he called for "reconciliation between nations that now call themselves enemies" in Asia and reiterated his interest in advancing bilateral contacts. "Cooperation, not hostility" between nations was "really the way of the future in the 20th century." "That day," Johnson concluded, "is not yet here. It may be long in coming, but I tell you it is clearly on its way, because it must come." Soon the administration relaxed its ban on travel to China, and after September 1966 American officials at the bilateral talks in Warsaw ended any mention of Chinese Communist designs on Asia. At the same time the State Department authorized select diplomatic personnel discreetly to establish "informal social contacts with the Chinese Communists" to learn more about individual officials and improve the American standing with them; and the Department of Defense decided to endorse the idea of moving toward a two-China policy in the United Nations. The administration's new line on China became known as "containment without isolation." By the end of the year the Soviets, wildly exaggerating the shift in U.S. policy, were condemning what they called U.S.-China collusion against North Vietnam.[42]

V

In part the administration's new attitude reflected mounting public attention to the China question. When J. William Fulbright's Senate Foreign Relations Committee conducted hearings on U.S. China policy in March 1966, they attracted widespread interest in the country. An impressive array of academia's leading China scholars and foreign policy specialists, including A. Doak Barnett, Benjamin Schwartz, John K. Fairbank, Robert Scalapino, and Hans Morgenthau, presented the most complete discussion of China policy ever given to the American people. With the exception of a few conservatives like George Taylor of the University of Washington and former congressman Walter Judd, the speakers repeatedly encouraged the administration to soften its approach to the PRC, although almost all the speakers also supported the administration on

Vietnam. A parade of witnesses urged the United States to adopt a "one China, one Taiwan" policy, permit Beijing to enter the United Nations, develop further communications and contact with the mainland, and generally pursue a less antagonistic policy toward the PRC. In the midst of the hearings, 200 Asian specialists, in a *New York Times* advertisement, called for the United States to discuss the establishment of formal relations with Beijing.[43]

In 1966, also, the Council on Foreign Relations completed a massive study on U.S. China policy. The three-year-long project produced eight volumes on China and U.S.-China relations by prominent Asian specialists. Though each book formally represented only the opinion of its author, there was a consensus on the need to introduce more flexibility into China policy and begin serious consideration of the recognition question. Funded by the Ford Foundation, chaired by former CIA Director Allen Dulles, and directed by Robert Blum, president of the Asia Foundation, the CFR's effort indicated that a substantial section of the foreign policy elite had come to favor a major change in China policy.[44]

The administration's slight policy shift, however, was not simply an expedient to fend off public pressures, although Washington did hope to put the blame for the lack of progress in Sino-American relations squarely on Beijing's back in order to deflect domestic and international criticism. The administration was quietly seeking alternatives. Beginning in the fall of 1965, a special joint State-Defense study group labored for nine months to produce a 700-page top secret paper on long-term U.S. China policy. A major conclusion of the still-classified study was that the United States should seek to "induce present or future Communist leaders to reappraise US intentions" and "arouse Peking's interest in developing a more constructive relationship with us." At about the same time Dean Rusk explained to the president that by offering Beijing the option of improved relations, Washington might be able "to preclude the possibility that the only place they [the emerging Chinese Communist leaders] can move for improving their international position is through reconciliation with the USSR."[45] Rusk's comment had far-reaching implications. Since the last years of the Eisenhower administration, American officials had hoped that the Soviet Union could control China's militancy. They had favored the Soviet Union in the Sino-Soviet split and assumed that China was implacably hostile to the United States. But Rusk's observation, with its suggestion that the United States had an interest in maintaining Beijing's future independence from the Soviet Union, suggested that Washington could adopt a more sophisticated approach to manipulating Sino-Soviet differences.

Nevertheless, in 1966–67 Moscow and Washington were still seemingly trying to arrange some sort of *Pax Superpowerica* over the world. Andrei Gromyko told President Johnson and Dean Rusk in late November 1966 of the Soviets' growing concern about China's military threat. The Soviets, it appeared, were eager to settle outstanding issues, including a nuclear nonproliferation treaty, to improve relations with the West. According to an American official, the Gromyko talks were the "most direct, honest, objective and non-ideological in several years." On December 6 Soviet Premier A. N. Kosygin told the press that he would like to develop the "community of interests" that existed between the United States and the Soviet Union, if only the war in Vietnam could be ended. Secretly U.S. officials continued to discuss among themselves whether to cooperate with the Soviets to strike against China's nuclear facilities.[46] Chinese Foreign Minister Chen Yi on December 10 condemned the Soviet Union for plotting "world domination with the United States" and threatening a joint Soviet-American attack on China. The following summer a Soviet official confidentially informed U.S. contacts that if the situation in China did not improve for the Soviet Union, Moscow would have to take direct action against Beijing. "Times have changed," remarked the official, "and if and when the time comes to do something about China, the Soviet Union would expect the United States to help."[47]

VI

The times were indeed changing, but they would not develop in the direction anticipated by the Soviet official. Each of the three powers—China, the Soviet Union, and the United States—was moving in ways that would inevitably require a new realignment of relations and an end to the limited Moscow-Washington entente against Beijing.

In China the Great Proletarian Cultural Revolution, which broke out in May 1966, was an outgrowth of Mao's effort to extirpate Soviet-style revisionism from the world Communist movement. Mao's campaign had been foreshadowed by Beijing's publication in July 1964 of the ninth and last installment in a series of commentaries setting out the Chinese case against Moscow. In terms of Marxist-Leninist theory, "On Khrushchev's Phoney Communism and Its Historical Lessons for the World" was the most important of all the documents produced by the Sino-Soviet split. This remarkable essay, rumored to have been crafted by Mao himself, enumerated all the Soviet Union's alleged failings, to construct a devastating critique. The Soviet Union's great nation chauvinism in international affairs, its unsavory record in many spheres of domestic life, its violation of basic Marxist-Leninist tenets, and its quest for accommodation with U.S. imperialism were neither accidents nor quirks, but manifestations of a trend toward a return to capitalism. The logic of that theory led inexorably to the conclusion that the Soviet Union was no longer a socialist country, and that its anti-China hostility was the result of a new imperialism. Borrowing from Lenin's characterization of the socialists in the Second International, who supported their bourgeois governments during World War I, the Chinese accused the Soviet Union of "social imperialism," that is, "socialism" in words, imperialism in deeds. For Beijing the Soviet Union had passed beyond the pale to become an enemy.

Mao's aim in the Cultural Revolution—to re-revolutionize society and especially the younger generation—was to prevent the development of a Khrushchev-style revisionism in China itself. But even with this almost exclusively internal focus, the upheaval profoundly affected China's foreign policy. In an immediate sense the Cultural Revolution destroyed any possibility of the PRC's being able to respond positively to the tentative overtures from the United States. Some veteran Chinese diplomats were purged, and others forced to exhibit the same fanatical zeal as the anti-revisionists at home, with predictably devastating effects on China's international standing, which Zhou Enlai had so skillfully cultivated in the 1960's. Moreover, the Cultural Revolution raised Chinese hostility toward the Soviet Union to new heights. Chinese and Russians physically clashed in the streets of both capital cities. For days in late January 1967, tens of thousands of demonstrators in Beijing surrounded the Soviet embassy and plastered it with posters reading "Shoot Brezhnev" and "Fry Kosygin." By March 1967 U.S. intelligence officials concluded that the Kremlin believed that Beijing regarded "Moscow and not the West as its major enemy."[48] Ambassadorial relations between the two capitals were severed for the next three years.

Beyond the disruption of China's diplomacy, the Cultural Revolution affected China's strategic orientation. Enemies are never of equal magnitude and proximity, and by September 1968, a month after the Soviet invasion of Czechoslovakia, China openly listed the Soviet Union ahead of the United States as a threat. Six months later Chinese and Soviet troops clashed in bloody fighting around Zhenbao Island in the Ussuri River. Scores were killed or wounded. The former fraternal allies began to mass immense military forces on opposite sides of their long common border. China's contradictions with the United States, which began its retreat from Vietnam in 1968, receded in importance.[49]

Ironically, the Cultural Revolution actually helped complete China's development of a fully nonaligned foreign policy. Up to the eve of the Cultural Revolution, powerful forces in the country still hoped for a reconciliation with the Soviet Union, perhaps in "united action" to support Vietnam against the United States. But the upheaval irrevocably discredited any thought of rapprochement with Moscow.[50] With China strategically isolated and vulnerable, its leaders were forced to re-think the PRC's foreign policy in the broadest terms. Faced with the potential might of both the United States and the Soviet Union, Mao and Zhou Enlai resorted to one of the CCP's great skills, honed through years of revolutionary practice: exploiting the contradictions among one's adversaries. Mao's 1970 invitation to the conservative Richard Nixon to visit

China was a paradoxical by-product of the ultra-revolutionary effort to purify the CCP's ranks. Nixon would travel to China in early 1972.

For the Soviet Union the Sino-Soviet split was a devastating blow. Moscow lost its status as the world's undisputed fount of revolution. For almost fifty years after the Bolshevik Revolution, Soviet leaders calculated their foreign policy with the confidence that other Communists supported the Soviet Union's interests as essential, if not paramount, to world progress. The postwar Asian revolutions, the Cuban Revolution, the ferment among the Eastern European nations, and Khrushchev's own anti-Stalin campaign all indicated that the Communist world was tending to become polycentric. But it was not until the split with China that Moscow's hold over other Communist parties was permanently damaged and in some cases broken. Moreover, the Soviet Union had suffered substantial setbacks in international affairs under Khrushchev, the retreat during the 1962 Cuban missile crisis being the most obvious.

In an attempt to recoup, Leonid Brezhnev, Khrushchev's successor, methodically rebuilt Soviet power in the world in the mid-1960's by taking advantage of China's isolation and the U.S. predicament in Vietnam. Within the Communist world Moscow briefly, but unsuccessfully, tried to mend Sino-Soviet fences, steadily improved its ties with Hanoi (by September 1966 Western diplomats in Moscow reported that North Vietnam had moved "into the Soviet political sphere" and away from China[51]), and consolidated its relations with Castro and the rest of the Communist movement sympathetic to the Soviet line. Meanwhile, it hardened its formal position toward the United States and the West, while continuing to seek understandings on concrete issues, and stepped up its political and military presence in South Asia, the Mediterranean, and the Middle East, especially after the 1967 Israeli-Arab war. The Soviet Union's outright invasion and occupation of Czechoslovakia in 1968 prevented a further fracturing of the Eastern European bloc. The so-called Brezhnev doctrine, articulated after the attack, rationalized the Soviet Union's authority to intervene in the affairs of any other socialist country in the name of "proletarian internationalism." The idea was not new, but its blunt expression indicated Moscow's mounting assertiveness.[52]

A nuclear China, the cause of much consternation in the United States, was even more disturbing to Moscow. The emergence of an Asian enemy along the Soviet Union's southern border rekindled ancient, emotional fears of the Yellow Peril. In October 1966, only two years after China's first nuclear test and soon after the outbreak of the Cultural Revolution, the Chinese successfully exploded their fourth nuclear device. This time, though, it was carried some 400 miles on a missile. The Soviet Union now had to plan for possible nuclear attacks from both the East and the West, adding impetus to its military buildup. The Soviets communicated their own interest in the possibility of destroying China's nuclear facilities. "How would you feel," a Soviet leader rhetorically asked Lyndon Johnson at the Glassboro, New Jersey, summit meeting in June 1967, "if there were a billion Chinese in Canada who had nuclear weapons and every day they denounced the Canadian-U.S. border as an illegitimate product of imperialist history?"[53] But Glassboro failed to produce any substantive agreements, and U.S.-Soviet relations remained strained.

The Vietnam War, which the administration could not win but dared not lose, debilitated the United States and isolated it in the world. Although Washington never publicly relinquished its aim of preventing a Communist victory in Vietnam, most policymakers realized after the North's Tet offensive of 1968 that, short of an all-out effort, and perhaps not even then, the war could not be won on the battlefield. The United States began its long, slow retreat from Southeast Asia.

In the later assessment of Henry Kissinger, the Vietnam War forced a reluctant United States to begin to recognize the limits of its power.[54] This difficult realization required foreign policy leaders to reappraise America's position in the world community, just as China's leaders were doing for their own country. Yet the wide disparity of views on U.S.-Sino relations in the late 1960's indicates that a transition in U.S. global thinking was still occurring. A new consensus had yet to be forged.

Senate Majority Leader Mike Mansfield, who had long been interested in Asian affairs, represented one end of the spectrum of opinion in Washington. Mansfield believed that the road to a Vietnam settlement ran "by way of Peking rather than Moscow." He feared that an escalation of the war would drive the Soviet Union and China back together. In April 1967 he recommended that the president make a "clearly conciliatory approach to China," such as sending Mansfield himself to Beijing. As ambassador to Japan, Edwin O. Reischauer was especially worried about the deterioration of the U.S. position in Asia. He saw the current U.S. China policy as the major irritant in Washington's relations with Japan, still restrained by the United States from re-establishing ties, including trade, with the mainland. In February 1968 Reischauer (by now a Harvard professor again) joined a delegation from the newly formed National Committee on United States–China Relations that met with President Johnson to discuss the possibility of taking further initiatives in China policy. The group proposed inducing Chiang to quit the offshore islands, an expansion of the talks in Warsaw, a reduction of trade restrictions, and support for the seating of Beijing in the United Nations while protecting Taipei's presence.[55]

Opposition to significant changes in China policy was still fierce, however. Rusk adamantly resisted the idea of Mansfield going to Beijing. According to Rostow, Rusk felt that "the Soviet Union would be upset and suspicious" of such a move. And Rostow himself was hostile to the proposals of Reischauer and his fellow delegates, since China had been unresponsive to Washington's overtures. "It takes two to play some games," Rostow told Johnson, and Beijing was not interested in playing at present. China policy remained stymied.[56]

Other leading specialists argued against seeking an understanding with Beijing on strategic grounds. George Kennan found the Cultural Revolution totally repugnant and seemed uninterested in, if not hostile to, the idea of seeking an improvement in relations with the PRC. He found China "ugly and menacing," and Mao and other leaders "divorced from reality" and Hitler-like in their embrace of war. Kennan maintained that achieving détente with the Soviet Union was "essential" for the United States and even anticipated, as a future possibility, an alliance with the Soviet Union against China. Chester Bowles, once again the American ambassador to India, was similarly inclined. Most likely influenced by New Delhi's animosity toward Beijing, Bowles no longer endorsed a moderate and flexible policy toward China, as he had in the 1950's. Indeed, he now seemed to fear Chinese military expansionism in Asia even more than the administration did. Like Kennan Bowles maintained that attention to U.S.-Soviet affairs was far more important than trying to advance U.S.-Sino relations.[57] The two men's intransigent stance toward Beijing in the late 1960's sharply contrasted with their previous interest in accommodation with China as the way to erode the Sino-Soviet alliance.

Some prominent Republicans were also revising their views about China at this stage, but their conclusions were novel departures from both the traditional Republican viewpoint and the view held by many prominent Democrats. Skeptical of the Democrats' lopsided attention to détente with Moscow, these Republicans wondered if a tilt toward Beijing might not open new possibilities for the United States to improve its international position.

Several reasons might account for so remarkable a shift in opinion. The Republicans had historically been more sensitive to developments in Asia and China than the Democrats, and the war in Vietnam as well as China's rising power obviously called for a major readjustment in U.S. policy. Moreover, the Democrats, through two administrations dominated by Atlanticists, had made the construction of a relationship favorable to the Soviets against Beijing a cornerstone of their foreign policy. The Republicans were not burdened with that immediate legacy. Being out of office for eight years also made the Republicans more receptive to new strategies. The growing challenge of the Soviet Union, the intensity of Sino-Soviet animosity, and the weakened international position of the United States all called for a new way of handling China and the Sino-Soviet conflict. There was a need to reassess friends and enemies once again.

One of the Republicans who had some new thoughts about

China was Dwight Eisenhower himself. During discussions with his former personal aide, Andrew Goodpaster, whom Lyndon Johnson sent periodically to brief the former president about the course of the war in Vietnam, Eisenhower frequently expressed interest in the latest developments in China and hinted that the United States had a stake in sustaining China's anti-Sovietism. In the spring of 1967, during the height of the Cultural Revolution, Eisenhower asked Goodpaster whether any of the "anti-Mao factions" had ties with Moscow. If they did, he suggested, perhaps the United States should "not be too anxious to see Mao defeated."[58]

Nelson Rockefeller, a contender in the 1968 presidential campaign, also perceived new possibilities in triangular politics. Rockefeller stated in a July 1968 speech that he "would begin a dialogue with Communist China. In a subtle triangle of relations between Washington, Peking, and Moscow, we improve the possibilities of accommodations with each as we increase our options toward both." Henry Kissinger, Rockefeller's foreign policy adviser, later claimed responsibility for the candidate's new geopolitical approach but admitted that he had not appreciated the significance of the Sino-Soviet split in the early 1960's.[59]

The most radical and portentous shift in attitude toward China, though, was Richard Nixon's. Nixon had made his reputation in the late 1940's as a red-baiter and a loyal supporter of Chiang Kai-shek; and during his stint as vice-president he had played the public role of conservative hatchet man for Eisenhower (though as we have seen, within the administration he had expressed more sophisticated opinions about China and its relationship with the Soviet Union, proposing a policy of "tough coexistence" that would avoid both appeasement and war with China). During the rupture of Sino-Soviet relations in the early 1960's, Nixon had joined conservatives in openly rebuking Kennedy and other leaders for the eagerness with which they welcomed the Communist division. As late as April 1963, when Kennedy was pursuing a nuclear test ban treaty with the Soviets, Nixon maintained that the United States could not "take too much comfort" in the Sino-Soviet dispute and discounted its potential advantage for the United

States. He still called for "victory" over communism and for a "free China." Nixon branded coexistence "another word for creeping surrender."[60]

Years later Nixon recalled that it was not until 1966 that he finally acknowledged the existence of the Sino-Soviet split. He does not say in his memoirs what prompted him to change his mind, but his thinking about how to exploit the split appears to have been greatly influenced by his encounters with European leaders in 1967. During a visit to the Continent in March, he heard officials repeatedly attack the assumption that the Soviet Union was interested in reconciliation with the West. Konrad Adenauer of Germany went so far as to suggest that, to counterbalance the growing Soviet threat, the United States should lean toward China.[61] The following month, while traveling through Asia, Nixon discussed some of his new ideas about China with Chester Bowles in India. An incredulous Bowles confidentially reported his conversation to Secretary of State Dean Rusk:

The one somewhat offbeat concept which seemed to be on [Nixon's] mind involved our relationships with the Soviet Union and China. In his opinion we should "stop falling all over ourselves" to improve our relationships with Russia since this would "make better relationships with China impossible."

On several occasions he almost suggested that good relations with China were more important than good relations with the Soviet Union. I disagreed with him strongly on this point, pointing out that the door to Moscow was ajar while the door to Peking was locked and bolted.[62]

On his return from his Far East tour, Nixon wrote his noted essay "Asia After Viet Nam" for *Foreign Affairs*. In it he emphasized that the United States could not "afford to leave China forever outside the family of nations" and recommended "a policy of firm restraint, of no reward, of a creative counterpressure designed to persuade Peking that its interests can be serviced only by accepting the basic rules of international civility." As far as these words went, Nixon did not go much beyond the Johnson administration's position. But he did drop a hint that distanced him from a view frequently linked to the Johnson administration: he explicitly rejected the idea of an alliance with the Soviet Union against China, charging that it carried a racist connotation. Moreover, Nixon used none of the vituperative language George Kennan employed in referring to the Chinese Communists. How strange that Richard Nixon should now appear in retrospect to have been more prescient and hardheaded in his thinking about China policy and the Sino-Soviet split than the detached "realist" George Kennan![63]

Epilogue

We are the number one nation and we are going to stay the
number one nation.   —President Lyndon B. Johnson, 1968

The U.S. is no longer in the position of complete preeminence or predominance. —President Richard M. Nixon, 1971

Now those squint-eyed bastards will get a lesson they'll never forget," fumed Yakov Malik, Soviet ambassador to the United Nations, on learning of an armed clash between Chinese and Soviet troops on the Sino-Soviet border
along the Ussuri River in March 1969. Border tensions had
been mounting over the preceding months. "Who do they think
they are! We'll kill those yellow sons of bitches!" Malik's en-
raged words, so like those uttered by American officials in their
own moments of fury against the Chinese Communists, were
recalled by Arkady N. Shevchenko, one of the most important
Soviet diplomats to defect to the West and Malik's close
associate.

According to Shevchenko, top Soviet officials in Moscow,
after the March and subsequent border incidents, deliberated
whether to conduct a nuclear strike against China to "once and
for all get rid of the Chinese threat." The specter of millions of
Chinese invading the Soviet Union terrified men like Marshal
Andrei Grechko, the minister of defense, who reportedly advocated a massive attack with weapons that would produce a
high level of radioactive fallout and kill millions of Chinese.
Other proposals called for limited operations to destroy Beijing's nuclear facilities. But disagreements over the wisdom
and consequence of undertaking military actions against China
stymied the Politburo for months.[1]

A report from Anatoly Dobrynin, Soviet ambassador to the
United States, finally broke the deadlock. Dobrynin learned

through discreet inquiries that the U.S. government was not sympathetic to the idea of a Soviet attack on China. The news sobered the Soviet leaders, and they dropped any thoughts of a preemptive strike. (Some Soviets must then have regretted Khrushchev's decision not to cooperate with John Kennedy when *he* had been interested in taking action against China's nuclear program in 1963.) Instead the Soviet Union adopted General Secretary Leonid Brezhnev's course of constructing fortifications and concentrating troops armed with nuclear weapons along the entire length of the border in an attempt to intimidate Beijing. Sino-Soviet relations froze in what aptly came to be called "the coldest war." Just as the perception of an unfavorable balance of power in Asia would contribute to America's disastrous Southeast Asia policy in the 1960's, the Soviet Union's concern about a developing alignment of China and the United States would contribute to its ill-fated decisions to intervene in Afghanistan and to support the Vietnamese invasion of Kampuchea in the late 1970's.[2]

Having to reconcile themselves to a standoff with the Chinese was bitter enough for the Soviets, but perhaps even more disturbing was Washington's coolness to their proposal about a preemptive strike. In light of past discussions about China's nuclear threat, a subject that American leaders had alarmingly and repeatedly raised with them, Washington's new stance implied a degree of Sino-American mutual interest. In a geopolitical triangular configuration of power, the Soviets faced the prospect of sliding toward the disadvantageous position of "one versus two." To try to avoid that development, the Soviets worked to improve their relations with the West, including détente with the United States. At the same time the Soviet military continued to prepare for the costly possibility of having to fight a two-front war.

China's leaders, even before the clashes with the Soviets in the vulnerable northeast and northwest border areas, had begun to rethink their strategic posture. The ramifications of the August 1968 Soviet invasion of Czechoslovakia and the so-called Brezhnev doctrine, with its justification of intervention in neighboring socialist states, overshadowed the continuing U.S. war in Vietnam. Beijing condemned the Soviet invasion with a vengeance that exceeded even Western protests: Brezh-nev was the new czar, perhaps even the new Hitler. In November Chinese emissaries in Warsaw notified the United States that Beijing wanted to resume the bilateral talks that had been suspended for a year. President-elect Richard Nixon responded positively. The PRC was signaling that it wanted improved relations with the United States.

For all the anarchy and ideological fanaticism of the Cultural Revolution, China's top leaders thought of the world and China's place in it in some pragmatic ways. How similar the unruly world must have appeared to them to the turmoil in ancient China described in one of Mao Zedong's favorite books, *Romance of the Three Kingdoms.* Three competing states vied for power and survival in this classic novel based on events following the disintegration of China's great Han dynasty in the second century A.D. Mao could surely have sympathized with Liu Bei, righteous and legitimate heir to the Han throne, when Liu and his advisers debated whether they should oppose Cao Cao, their stronger, traditional adversary, or their onetime ally, the ambitious and treacherous Sun Chuan. In a decision that is still the source of argument in China, Liu Bei chose to oppose Sun Chuan. How easy it would have been for Chinese leaders to substitute themselves, the Americans, and the Soviets for those historical characters![3]

Still, advances in Sino-American relations came slowly. Despite China's vulnerable position Beijing moved warily. Washington was the more active partner in the proceedings. From 1969 to 1971 each side probed the other's intentions through secret communications, third-party channels, and awkward meetings of mid-level officials. Neither side knew how far the relationship should, or could, go. Each had to contend with domestic political differences and a twenty-year legacy of suspicion and animosity. In China the ultra-leftist faction around Party vice chairman Lin Biao complicated the process. Mao Zedong placed his public imprimatur on improving Sino-American relations when he had the American author Edgar Snow stand next to him on the reviewing platform during China's national day celebration on October 1, 1970. Mao told Snow that Richard Nixon was welcome to visit China if he wanted. The message, which was immediately conveyed to the highest levels in Washington, startled and excited the president. But the struggle to confirm China's new strategic orientation ended only in September 1971, with the death of Lin Biao, once Mao's chosen successor, in a fiery plane crash following his abortive military coup attempt. Lin had apparently been trying to escape to the Soviet Union. His death came just two months after Henry Kissinger's secret journey to Beijing to meet Mao and Zhou Enlai. Lin had almost certainly opposed pursuing the opening with Washington.[4]

Even before he assumed the presidency, Richard Nixon was fascinated with the possibilities of constructing a new policy toward China. His *Foreign Affairs* article exhibited a sophistication about world affairs that had not been apparent in his previous public statements. Nixon understood that the United States sooner or later had to come to terms with China. One of his first official directives in 1969 put Kissinger's NSC staff to work on a comprehensive review of China policy and the development of alternative approaches. Several months later, as Sino-Soviet frictions escalated, Nixon ordered an NSC study on Sino-Soviet differences and the implications for American policy of a military clash between the two Communist powers. By mid-1969 Nixon and Kissinger arrived at the "revolutionary thesis" that American interests would not be served if the Soviet Union militarily "smashed" China, in Kissinger's words. It was in the strategic interests of the United States, Nixon now understood, to see that Communist China, till now one of America's bitterest and oldest enemies, survived. In a November 1969 speech on Guam, Nixon declared that the United States "shall provide a shield if a nuclear power threatens the freedom of a nation allied with us or of a nation whose survival we consider vital to our security." The president did not explicitly refer to the Soviet Union and China, but his meaning was evident. The United States was signaling that it would not accept the destruction of China and the notion of a new balance of power in Asia based on Sino-American rapprochement.[5]

Although Nixon and Kissinger did not articulate it publicly or privately at the time in so many words, they were moving the United States toward the advantageous position in triangular politics that would find it enjoying better relations with both its adversaries than they had with each other.[6] As Nixon and Kissinger saw it, improved relations with China strengthened Washington's hand in dealing with the Soviet Union. This increased "leverage" over Moscow helped produce the Strategic Arms Limitation Talks treaties and the limited détente with the Soviets in the early 1970's. But more than tactics were involved: Sino-American rapprochement was part of a Nixon-Kissinger effort to construct a new strategic alignment of forces in the world. The Nixon-Kissinger vision, or "grand design," was of a multipolar world in which the dynamics of the U.S.-USSR-PRC triangle would play a dominant role. Abandoned was the assumption that the world was bipolar; rather, a careful and fluid calibration of big power and local interests was necessary to reconstruct the international position of the United States. The hope was that the Soviet Union, and a China engaged with the United States, would acquiesce to an American presence in Asia as a stabilizing force even after the United States had exited Vietnam. The United States would acknowledge the Soviet Union's great-power status and legitimate interests in its spheres, and was prepared to accept it as a responsible participant in world affairs. At the same time the United States would protect its areas of traditional vital interest. Kissinger's study of the history and theory of the balance-of-power international systems that stabilized nineteenth-century Europe provided the intellectual framework for this "grand design."[7]

Nixon's political acumen helped realize his strategic objectives. He encouraged Democratic Senator Mike Mansfield's continuing efforts to make contact with Chinese leaders. He also tried to mollify such former friends as the China Lobby stalwart Walter Judd. In that endeavor Nixon was only partially successful. Nixon never succeeded in winning Judd's support, but the president's conservative political credentials preempted accusations of his being "soft" on communism. Nixon's 1967 article in *Foreign Affairs*, with its moderate line toward China, had upset Judd, but the announcement that Nixon was going to Beijing positively infuriated him. He personally wrote Nixon to protest the "sharp reversal" in China policy. To counteract the Nixon trip, Judd formed the Committee for a Free China, but the usual anti–Chinese Communist shock troops did not jump to rally to the former missionary's call, as in days of old. Even a loyal warrior like Admiral Radford was at best luke-warm about the new group. In fact the onetime proponent of an attack on mainland China was excited by the Nixon demarche. "No one was more surprised than I was when Mr. Nixon announced his visit to Red China last spring," he wrote Judd just before the president left for Beijing. "I do not know what will come of Mr. Nixon's visit to Red China, but I am certain Chou Enlai and he will have a straightforward and probably valuable discussion." He was hoping, Radford concluded, that "[Nixon would] have some success in his basic objective—a more peaceful world."[8]

After listening to Henry Kissinger's report on the triumphant Nixon visit to China in February 1972, the then-governor of California and future president Ronald Reagan quipped that the trip had been a great television "pilot" and should be made into a series.[9] The journey certainly had been a great show, but it was much more than good politics in an election year. Its historic significance was that it confirmed nothing less than the emergence of a dramatically new postwar international system.

In late 1975, three years after the Nixon trip to China, and with future U.S. president George Bush living in Beijing as chief of the U.S. Liaison Office, a House subcommittee conducted hearings on the topic of the "United States–Soviet Union–China: The Great Power Triangle." The first witness was John Paton Davies, the former foreign service officer who had worked with Dean Acheson in 1949 and 1950 to find a way to prevent revolutionary China from falling into the Soviet camp. That hope, of course, had gone a-glimmering. Now, twenty-five years later, he reprimanded past administrations for having wrongly regarded China and the Soviet Union in the 1950's and 1960's as "a bloc, a monolith." In all the excitement created by the rapid development of U.S.-China relations after Nixon's trip, it was easy to dismiss past policymakers as imperceptive and negligent in failing to exploit contradictions between Beijing and Moscow. Speakers before the House subcommittee suggested that an earlier, less hostile relationship with China might have been possible had Washington's impassioned anticommunism not obscured the (now seemingly obvious) differences between Moscow and Beijing. To some Nixon's courting of Mao apparently brought full circle the 1949 interest in creating an Asian Tito. But the similarity was only superficial.[10]

In fact American leaders had been well aware of and at times acutely interested in the differences between China and the Soviet Union since 1949. Leading policymakers, from the Truman through the Johnson administrations, never assumed that the Communist world was monolithic. Rather, they believed that the Sino-Soviet relationship was one of allied powers, each having distinct and ultimately conflicting interests. Ideological opposition to communism played much less of a role in determining how the United States conducted the Cold War than the public record indicates. Though policymakers often railed against "international communism" to win public support for policies, strategic decisions themselves were shrewdly determined on the basis of what were believed to be hardheaded security considerations. Calculation, not histrionics or legalism, characterized U.S. strategy toward China and the Sino-Soviet alliance.

Before the Korean War the main objective of U.S. policy was to prevent China from becoming an "adjunct to Soviet military-political power." On that there was widespread agreement within the Truman administration, but none at all on how it was to be achieved. Some officials believed the United States might be able to entice China away from the Soviets with offers of assistance. Others proposed that a tough policy of denying American largess would be most effective in hastening Chinese disenchantment with the Soviets. Both views vastly overestimated the importance of the United States to China, underestimated Chinese animosity toward the United States, and discounted Beijing's commitment to, and ability to maintain, an independent foreign policy. Events in early 1950 and the Korean War itself ended most thoughts that a lenient American policy toward China could drive a wedge between Beijing and Moscow.

During the 1950's the apparent rigidity of Eisenhower and Dulles in foreign policy masked what at times was a deft handling of the Chinese and Soviets. The administration remained deeply divided about, but seriously interested in, Sino-Soviet relations. In contrast to the Truman administration, which had pinned what hopes it had of dividing the Chinese and Soviets on the Chinese, the Eisenhower policy was to respond positively to Moscow's initiatives while isolating Beijing. The administration was aware of the divisive effects this policy of discriminate hostility was having on the Sino-Soviet alliance. Toward the end of the 1950's Washington began to consider Beijing America's most dangerous immediate enemy, even as Washington understood that the Soviet Union was clearly the more powerful of its two Communist adversaries. (The strategic triangle was never composed of equals.) And though it would be wrong to suggest that the United States produced the accelerating estrangement between Beijing and Moscow, the United States was far more deliberate and conscious in its efforts to manipulate the Communist powers than most observers, including those in China and the Soviet Union even today, have realized or dared to admit.

President John F. Kennedy did not simply tilt toward the Soviet Union in the Sino-Soviet dispute but sought an active entente with it, despite U.S.-Soviet rivalry in other areas. Though he failed in his effort to stop China's nuclear development, the understandings he reached with the Soviets helped to transform the dispute into an irrevocable split. By the end of the decade China and the Soviet Union had become two of the bitterest enemies in the world. Their relations had completely and seemingly finally disintegrated in a way that no American leader could ever have imagined in even his wildest dreams.

The split, however, was not an unalloyed blessing for Washington. U.S. selective accommodation of the Soviet Union and pressure on Beijing helped push China's leaders toward militant revolutionism. Washington took seriously the inflamed rhetoric coming out of Beijing. The U.S. intervention in Vietnam was deemed necessary, in part, to defeat China's revolutionary line. In all this there was an element of self-fulfilling prophecy. Once the United States helped fashion the Chinese bogeyman, it had to be fought and defeated. Midway through the war, though, when it became clear that China was not the cause of the insurgency in Southeast Asia, the United States quietly dropped its anti-China rationale for why it was fighting. But it was too late—it would take years for the United States to extricate itself from Vietnam.

We will probably never know to what extent American hostility affected China's domestic policies. Washington's closed-door policy could only have confirmed the thinking of the most extreme elements within the Chinese Communist leadership. American behavior validated assumptions about the malevolent nature of imperialism and the duplicity of a perceived Soviet revisionism conciliating with the United States. Would the Cultural Revolution itself have occurred if China had been engaged with the Western world? One can only speculate.

This is not to say that China's radical communism and anti-imperialism were simply reactions to outside pressures and not genuine. They were real enough, but much of the virulence of China's anti-Americanism in the 1960's was a by-product of the dispute with the Soviets. Beijing wanted to distance itself from Moscow and from what it believed was a Soviet effort to construct a reactionary stewardship with Washington over the rest of the world. In actual practice Beijing had been reasonably cautious in its foreign policy: it never invaded and occupied another country, as the Soviets had done; its direct involvement with Communists in other countries never approached the level of that of the Soviets; and its military posture remained defensive. The irony of the 1960's is that while the United States was absorbed in fighting China through its supposed proxy Vietnam, the Soviet Union emerged as a genuine military challenge to both China and the United States.[11]

Near the end of his life Dean Acheson included in a letter to his old friend Anthony Eden the admonition that "one of the first requirements in a state's foreign policy [is] to be able to distinguish your friends from your enemies."[12] It was a simple lesson not easily followed. It was also one that did not lend itself to candid public discourse. Letting your adversaries and your supposed friends know what you actually think of them is unwise. But away from public scrutiny American policymakers had consistently tried to distinguish between China and the Soviet Union. Their policies may have been unwise, wrong, or even disastrous—these would be criticisms of judgment. But

American policymakers had never been guilty of indifference to trying to calculate who the friends and enemies of the United States were in the Cold War.

As the United States, China, and the Soviet Union enter the last decade of this century, they are at peace and are seeking to construct non-threatening mutual relations. The threat of war among them has never been more remote. Local areas of conflict and tension in which the three have had active interests—Afghanistan and Kampuchea—are also moving toward resolution. And yet vexing issues loom on the horizon: Beijing is becoming impatient with the continued separation of Taiwan from the mainland (the KMT continues to call its domain the Republic of China); Moscow and Beijing have normalized state and party relations, to the undoubted discomfort of Washington; and Moscow and Washington are themselves seeking a new era of détente, to the concern of Beijing. All three capitals face imposing domestic and foreign economic and political challenges. One can only hope that those who hold power in each will come to realize that their real enemies are not their fellow powerholders, but the common threats of war and nuclear annihilation; of economic malaise and decline; and of environmental destruction. And that their friends are cooperation, the recognition of mutual interdependence, and a world of peace.[13]

Reference Material

Notes

For complete authors' names, titles, and publication data on the works cited in short form in the Notes, see the Sources, pp. 357–75. John Foster Dulles's Papers are cited as "Dulles Papers" and identified by collection (DDE for the papers in the Eisenhower Library; Princeton for those in the Mudd Library); Allen Dulles's full name is used for his collected papers. Similarly, "Johnson Papers" means the papers of Lyndon B. Johnson, and U. Alexis Johnson's name is used in full. Most of the Acheson papers cited are from the Truman Library collection; "Yale" is used for those in the Yale Library. The two Livingston Merchant oral histories are distinguished by "HST" (Truman Library) and "Princeton" (Mudd Library). The spelling Mao Tsetung, the most common form in my period, is adopted throughout in the citations of his works; I use the Pinyin form, Mao Zedong, in my own voice. The following abbreviations are used:

ACDA	Arms Control and Disarmament Agency
CF	Country Files of NSF
CFR	Council on Foreign Relations
DSB	*Department of State Bulletin*
FO	Foreign Office, UK
FRUS	*Foreign Relations of the United States*
JCS	Joint Chiefs of Staff
NA	National Archives
NSC	National Security Council
NSF	National Security Files
NYT	*New York Times*
OSANSA	Office of the Special Assistant for National Security Affairs
OCA	Office of Chinese Affairs, SD
OSD	Office of the Secretary of Defense
POF	President's Office Files

PPS   Policy Planning Staff, SD
PRO   Public Record Office, UK
PSF   Presidential Security Files of NSF
Quantico Report
           "Report of the Quantico Vulnerabilities Panel," June 10,
           1955, Eisenhower Papers, WHCF, Confidential File, Sub-
           jects, box 63, Russia (6)
RG   Record Group, NA
SD   State Department
SSP   Special Studies Project, Rockefeller Archives Center,
           Rockefeller University
VPSF   Vice-Presidential Security Files
WHCF   White House Central Files
WHSF   White House Security Files

BOOK EPIGRAPHS: Acheson to Anthony Eden, May 1971, Acheson
Papers, Yale, box 9, folder 119; Mao Tsetung, "Analysis of the Classes
in Chinese Society" (March 1927), in *Selected Works*, 1: 13.

Introduction

1. F. Dulles, *American Policy*, p. 136. For other interpretations of
the Cold War and China policy, see Dallek, *American Style*, pp. 162–
222; Fairbank, *United States and China*, pp. 452–57; and Ulam, *Rivals*, pp. 212–13.

2. For other recent views on U.S. policy toward China, see the fine
essay by John L. Gaddis, "Dividing Adversaries: The United States
and International Communism, 1945–1958," in Gaddis, *Long Peace*,
pp. 147–94; and Mayers, *Cracking the Monolith*.

Chapter One

EPIGRAPH: Benjamin Franklin to William Strahan, July 5, 1775.

1. "Japan Notes" [early 1950?], Judd Papers, box 140, Acheson (emphasis in the original).

2. On the origin of the Cold War in Asia, see Gallicchio, *Cold
War*; Gardner, *Approaching Vietnam*, pp. 21–62; and Levine, *Anvil*,
pp. 15–51.

3. Cabot to Butterworth, Feb. 6, 1948, *FRUS* 1948, 8: 467–69.

4. Lees, "American Decision"; Blum, "Surprised by Tito"; diary
entry, June 29, 1948, Cabot Papers, 18, no. 00368.

5. Brands, "Redefining the Cold War"; CFR, Kennan, "Longterm
Questions of U.S. Foreign Policy," Feb. 16, 1949, Meetings, vol. 14.

6. NSC-18, "The Attitude of This Government Toward Events in

Yugoslavia," July 6, 1948, *FRUS* 1948, 4: 1079–1081; Lees, "American Decision," pp. 414–19; SD, "Economic Relations Between the United States and Yugoslavia," "Yugoslavia," Feb. 14, Sept. 1, 1949, *FRUS* 1949, 5: 866, 941–44; Brands, "Redefining the Cold War."

7. Miscamble, "Encouraging Chinese Titoism?," pp. 8–9. Several years later, after Yugoslavia and the U.S. had established stable relations, Tito himself confided to American officials that the West's "smartest move" in 1948–49 had been not to court him but to wait "until he came to the West." NA, Marcy to SD, June 21, 1957, RG 59, 1955–59, 611.95/6-2157.

8. Smith to Marshall, July 1, Stuart to Marshall, July 10, 1948, *FRUS* 1948, 7: 333–34, 346–47; Melby to Davies, July 13, 1948, Melby Papers, box 3, China File 1948 (G-P). For other reports, see Stuart to Marshall, July 15, July 27, Nov. 21, Dec. 6, and Clubb to Butterworth, Nov. 16, 1948, *FRUS* 1948, 7: 360, 377–78, 593–97, 631–32, 576–78.

9. Davies, *Dragon*, pp. 363–64, 371; Schaller, *U.S. Crusade*, pp. 181–94; Levine, *Anvil*, pp. 33–43. Also see Shewmaker, *Americans and Chinese Communists*.

10. NA, Sprouse to Battle, May 22, Battle to Acheson, May 23, 1951, RG 59, 793.00/5-2251.

11. *China White Paper*, 1: 92–100; Tsou, *America's Failure*, pp. 176–92, 344; Schaller, *U.S. Crusade*, pp. 288–89.

12. *China White Paper*, p. 187; Tsou, *America's Failure*, pp. 356–57, 369–71.

13. Lilienthal, *Journals*, pp. 525–26.

14. *China White Paper*, pp. 279–80.

15. Marshall memo, meeting with Mme Chiang Kai-shek, Dec. 27, 1948, *FRUS* 1948, 8: 302–4; Lilienthal, *Journals*, p. 525.

16. PPS 39, "U.S. Policy Toward China," Sept. 7, 1948, *FRUS* 1948, 8: 146–55.

17. PPS 39, PPS 39/1, Nov. 23, 1948, ibid., pp. 146–55, 208–11. PPS 39/1 was an elaboration of the essential views in PPS 39.

18. NA, "U.S. Interests in China," May 8, 1950 [?], RG 59, OCA 1948–56, box 26, Trade Policy Toward China 1950.

19. McLean, "American Nationalism." The Pentagon favored greater emphasis on supporting military opposition to the Chinese Communists short of direct U.S. intervention, but also accepted the central proposition of preventing China from becoming "an adjunct of Soviet politico-military power." NSC, "Draft Report on U.S. Policy Toward China," Nov. 2, Butterworth to Lovett, Nov. 3, 1948, *FRUS* 1948, 8: 185–87, 187–89; NSC 34/1, "U.S. Policy Toward China,"

Jan. 11, 1949, *FRUS* 1949, 9: 474–75. Also see Blum, *Drawing the Line*, pp. 30–37; and Mayers, *Cracking the Monolith*, pp. 33–49.

20. *NYT*, Feb. 14, 1949, p. 10, Feb. 18, 1949, p. 8. Also see Nancy B. Tucker, *Patterns*.

21. NSC 34/2, "U.S. Policy Toward China," Feb. 28, 1949, *FRUS* 1949, 9: 491–95.

22. The point about using "clandestine channels" was deleted from the version published in the *FRUS* volume, obscuring Acheson's intrigue. For a full statement of the conclusions of NSC 37/2, see "Policies of the Government, China," Truman Papers, PSF, box 195, NSC Reports 1949, pp. 13–14. On the "two-handed policies," see Schurmann, *Logic*, p. 173. The Truman administration generally was becoming more interested in covert activities at this time. See Isaacson and Thomas, *Wise Men*, p. 448.

23. NSC 41, "U.S. Policy Regarding Trade with China," Feb. 28, 1949, *FRUS* 1949, 9: 826–34; Blum, *Drawing the Line*, pp. 32–33; Schaller, *American Occupation*, pp. 186–88; Yasuhara, "Japan"; Sprouse memo, meeting of Butterworth and others, Feb. 10, 1949, *FRUS* 1949, 9: 823–26.

24. JCS to Forrestal, NSC, 37/3, "The Strategic Importance of Formosa," Feb. 11, 1949, Nov. 24, 1948, *FRUS* 1949, 9: 261–62, 284–86; NA, Lovett to Truman, Jan. 14, 1949, RG 59, PPS 1947–53, Country and Area Files, box 13, China 1949.

25. NA, Lovett to Truman, Jan. 14, 1949, RG 59, PPS 1947–53, Country and Area Files, box 13, China 1949. This version of the document has an appended note saying that Truman and Acheson had "bought the idea" of encouraging Formosan autonomy on Jan. 13. The version published in *FRUS* 1949, 9: 265–67, does not include the appended note.

26. Summaries of NSC's 33rd and 35th meetings, Feb. 3, March 3, 1949, Truman Papers, PSF, box 220, NSC Meetings 1949; Acheson statement at the NSC's 35th meeting, March 3, 1949, *FRUS* 1949, 9: 294–96.

27. Blum, *Drawing the Line*, pp. 34–37.

28. Cleveland to Lapham, Jan. 7, 1949, *FRUS* 1949, 9: 610–13.

29. U.S. Senate Committee on Foreign Relations, *Economic Assistance*, pp. 30–35. James Reston reported (*NYT*, April 24, 1949, sec. iv, p. 3) that top State Dept. officials confidentially discouraged the notion of the possibility of Titoism among China's top leaders. Reston's source was possibly Acheson himself. On Acheson's relationship with Reston, see Isaacson and Thomas, *Wise Men*, pp. 409, 412.

30. NA, "U.S. Policy in the Far East and Asia," Oct. 25, 1949, RG 59, 890.00/11-1849, p. 13. On the controversy among historians, see,

for example, Thomas G. Paterson, "If Europe, Why Not China?"; and Cohen, "Acheson."

31. CIA, "Prospects for Soviet Control of a Communist China," April 15, 1949, Truman Papers, PSF, box 256, Central Intelligence Reports.

32. Kohler to Acheson, Jan. 12, Jan. 28, April 19, 1949, *FRUS 1949*, 8: 38–39, 5: 559–61, 8: 249–51.

33. SD Summary of telegrams, Jan. 31, 1949, Truman Papers, Naval Aides, box 21, SD Briefs, 1/49–4/49; Stuart to Acheson, Jan. 15, Jan. 27, March 22, June 15, 1949, *FRUS 1949*, 8: 51, 88–89, 192–94, 385.

34. Cabot to Butterworth, Dec. 30, 1948, Cabot to Stuart, April 20, Cabot to Acheson, April 27, 1949, *FRUS 1948*, 7: 707–18, 1949, 8: 256–57, 9: 1251–1252; diary entry, June 14, 1949, Cabot Papers, 18, nos. 00649, 00619 (emphasis in original).

35. On Cabot's views, see Cabot to Stuart, Jan. 20, March 23, Cabot to Acheson, May 31, 1949, *FRUS 1949*, 8: 61–64, 195–97, 355–57. Ye Duyi, a leading member of the Democratic League, told Cabot in early 1949 that there was "a real chance of Mao becoming another Tito." Cabot to Sec. State, Jan. 3, ibid., pp. 3–4. The Democratic League was a party of primarily intellectuals who were anti-Chiang, allied with the Communists, and supportive of Western democracy. Interviews with Chinese researchers, 1985.

36. Clubb to Butterworth, Nov. 16, 1948, Clubb to Acheson, April 30, June 2, 1949, *FRUS 1948*, 7: 576–78; 1949, 9: 974–76, 8: 362–64. For a Chinese historian's view of the different American attitudes toward Titoism in China, see Wang Jisi, "1947–1950 nian."

37. Blum, *Drawing the Line*, pp. 19–20; Acheson to Morgenthau, Jan. 16, 1957, Acheson Papers, Yale, box 23, folder 289.

38. Radio broadcast, "What Should We Do About China," July 3, 1949, Hornbeck Papers, box 481, Writings—China and U.S. Policy—1920–60, pp. 6–8.

39. Comments on China Policy, 1948 [1949?], Judd Papers, box 96, China 1950–60 (italics his).

40. Ibid. Judd called for Acheson's resignation in 1950, but by the late 1950's the two men had become good friends.

41. At the end of May Nixon also endorsed the views of Jack Beall, a right-wing radio commentator. In one of his broadcasts Beall accused Acheson of "appeasement" of the Communists in Asia and called for the return of active U.S. opposition to the Communists in China. Nixon also read Beall's diatribe into the *Congressional Record*: 81st Cong., 1st sess. (1949), vol. 95, part 14, pp. A2871 (Dallin), A3342–43 (Beall).

42. Mao Tsetung, "Revolutionary Forces of the World Unite, Fight

Against Imperialist Aggression!," Nov. 1948, in *Selected Works*, 4: 283–86.

43. Mao Tsetung, "Report to the Second Plenary Session of the Seventh Central Committee of the Communist Party of China," March 5, 1949, and "On the Outrages by British Warships—Statement by the Spokesman of the General Headquarters of the Chinese People's Liberation Army," April 30, 1949, in *Selected Works*, 4: 361–75, 401–3; interviews with Chinese officials, Nov. 1985.

44. See Borden, *Pacific Alliance*; and Schaller, *American Occupation*.

45. See Mao Tsetung, "Talk with the American Correspondent Anna Louise Strong," Aug. 1946, in *Selected Works*, 4: 97–102; Mao, "Revolutionary Forces" (as cited in note 42, above).

46. On Soviet advice, see Sulzberger, *Long Row of Candles*, p. 435; and Tucker, *Patterns*, p. 29. On Stalin's views, see Shulman, *Stalin's Foreign Policy*, pp. 105–7; Ulam, *Expansion*, p. 492; and Levine, *Anvil*, pp. 15–33.

47. Ulam, *Expansion*, p. 489; Martin, *Divided Counsel*, pp. 14–15; Gittings, *World and China*, p. 151; Wu Xiuquan, "Sino-Soviet Relations," p. 17; interviews with Chinese researchers, 1985; Wu Xiuquan, *Zai waijiaobu banian de jingli*, pp. 5–10. See also Shi Zhe, "I Accompanied Chairman Mao," *Far Eastern Affairs* (Moscow), 1989, no. 2, pp. 125–33.

48. Wu Xiuquan, "Sino-Soviet Relations," p. 17; interviews with Chinese researchers, 1985; Mao Tsetung, "On the Ten Major Relationships," April 25, 1956, and "On the People's Democratic Dictatorship," June 30, 1949, in *Selected Works*, 5: 304, 4: 415.

49. Acheson statement at NSC's 35th meeting, March 3, 1949, Cabot to Acheson, March 22, Clubb to Acheson, March 26, March 31, April 1, Clark to Acheson, April 1, Stuart to Acheson, April 1, Acheson to Stuart, April 4, 1949, *FRUS* 1949, 9: 294–96, 8: 190, 202, 216–17, 218, 220–21, 229, 225.

50. He Di, "Evolution of the CCP's Policy," p. 31. U.S. complicity, if not direct involvement, in the sinking of the *Chungking* was likely. American naval vessels were in the vicinity of the sinking, and the U.S. maintained a major naval facility at Qingdao in North China, which was not evacuated until May 24, 1949. See Omar Bradley testimony, Jan. 26, 1950, U.S., Senate Committee on Foreign Relations, *Reviews*, p. 240. The U.S. and Nationalist naval forces had coordinated their activities for some time. Even after the American denial of involvement in the attack, the Communists continued to hold the U.S. responsible. Mao Zedong, in his famous commentaries on the China White Paper, charged the U.S. Air Force with bombing and

sinking the *Chungking*. See "Farewell, Leighton Stuart!," Aug. 18, 1949, in *Selected Works*, 4: 434. As late as 1984 Chinese researchers were still accusing the U.S. of the deed. See Li Changjiu, *Zhong-mei*, p. 156.

51. Acheson to Stuart, Feb. 14, Acheson to Krentz, March 2, 1949, *FRUS* 1949, 9: 287–88, 293–94; Merchant oral history, HST, May 27, 1975, pp. 28–33. The U.S. military also apparently was involved. John Cabot's diary entry for Feb. 18, 1949, notes that a "Colonel Meyers" had left for a "*very* confidential mission" to Taiwan. Cabot observed that the NSC wanted "discreetly to encourage [a] Taiwan independence movement." Cabot Papers, 18, no. 00491.

52. Diary entry, March 16, 1949, Cabot Papers, 18, no. 00504; Edgar to Acheson, March 26, 1949, note 46, *FRUS* 1949, 9: 304–5, 328.

53. Acheson to Edgar, April 15, Edgar to Acheson, May 4, Merchant to Butterworth, May 24, Butterworth to Rusk (and attachment), June 9, 1949, *FRUS* 1949, 9: 315–16, 324–26, 337–41, 346–450. In a memo dated June 2, 1949, Merchant, Butterworth, Kennan, Davies, and Krentz called for exploring the possibility of having a third country bring the Taiwan issue to the U.N. See NA, OCA, box 16, Taiwan 4/49–12/49. A few weeks later Kennan recommended that the U.S. simply seize the island and set up a pro-American regime. Kennan memo, July 6, 1949, with annex of June 23, 1949, *FRUS* 1949, 9: 356–64. On U.S. efforts to pursue a "two-China policy," see Grasso, *Truman's Two-China Policy*.

54. Martin, *Divided Counsel*, pp. 54–63; Schurmann, *Logic*, p. 228; memo, meeting with Truman, June 22, 1949, Koo Papers, box 130, notes of conversations 1949, p. 3.

55. Mao Tsetung, "Report to the Second Plenary Session," as cited in note 43, above.

56. NA, "U.S. Interests in China," May 8, [1950,] RG 59, OCA 1948–56, box 26, Trade Policy Toward China 1950.

57. Smyth to Acheson, March 10, Clubb to Acheson, April 30, Acheson to Clubb, March 12, Acheson to Souers, April 14, Acheson to certain diplomatic and consular officers in China, April 1, 1949, *FRUS* 1949, 9: 910–11, 976–77, 911–12, 842–44, 926–27.

58. The British official also reported that Ward was known "as a man of violent temper, as rabidly anti-Communist, and as having a strong antipathy to the Chinese." He was also idiosyncratic—he was said to take "three urns containing ashes of cremated pet cats" wherever he went. Hutchinson to FO, Dec. 6, 1949, PRO, FO371/75952/FO18393; Urquhart to FO, July 30, 1949, PRO, FO371/75765/F11315; Tucker, *Patterns*, pp. 50–51.

59. Michael H. Hunt, "Mao Tse-tung and the Issue of Accommoda-

tion with the United States, 1949–1950," in Borg and Heinrichs, *Uncertain Years*, pp. 203–4; Acheson, *Present at the Creation*, pp. 444, 450; Acheson memo, meeting with Oliver Franks, Dec. 8, 1949, *FRUS 1949*, 9: 219–20.

60. Clubb to Acheson, June 1, June 2, June 24, 1949, *FRUS 1949*, 9: 357–60, 363–64, 397–98. Also see Steven M. Goldstein, "Chinese Communist Policy Toward the United States: Opportunities and Constraints, 1944–1950," in Borg and Heinrichs, *Uncertain Years*, pp. 274–75. In my 1985 interviews with two Chinese officials who were close to Zhou Enlai, they vehemently rejected the authenticity of the "Chou demarche": Huang Hua called the episode "nonsense," and former ambassador to the U.S. Zhang Wenjin said none of the supposed message was true. But Clubb and other U.S. scholars continue to believe in the authenticity of Zhou's approach. See Clubb to Newman, Nov. 27, 1980, *Diplomatic History*, Spring 1981, p. 167; and Tucker, *Patterns*, p. 233 n. 30. It is difficult to accept Zhou's demarche as real, if only because it would have been completely out of Zhou's character to have divulged top internal Party information about major rifts. Only someone desperate, on the verge of defecting from the Party, would have taken such an extreme step. In 1949 the top CCP leadership was reasonably united on major policy questions and had no reason to split on the eve of victory.

61. Stuart to Acheson, May 11, May 14, June 8, June 30, Acheson to Stuart, July 1, 1949, *FRUS 1949*, 8: 741–42, 745–47, 752–53, 766–67, 769; interview with Huang Hua, 1985.

62. Kohler to Acheson, June 27, Stuart to Acheson, July 6, 1949, *FRUS 1949*, 8: 399–400, 405–7.

63. See Donald S. Zagoria, "Choices in the Postwar World (2): Containment and China," in Gati, *Caging the Bear*, pp. 109–27; Cohen, "Acheson," p. 36; and Shaw, "John Leighton Stuart." During our talk in Nov. 1985, when Sino-American relations were perhaps at their best since 1949, Huang Hua downplayed the potential significance of the Stuart affair, emphasizing the deep Chinese resentment at U.S. involvement in the civil war. Former ambassador to the U.S. Zhang Wenjin also recalled that the CCP did not believe it was realistic to expect an early normalization of relations with the U.S.

64. Webb memo, meeting with Truman, June 16, 1949, RG 59, PPS 1947–53, Country and Area Files, box 13, China 1949.

65. Newman, "Self-Inflicted Wound"; *China White Paper*, Van Slyke Intro. (unnum.).

66. *China White Paper*, pp. xvi–xvii.

67. See Tsou, *America's Failure*, pp. 507–10; Patrick J. Hurley, "A

Few Comments About One Thousand Pages of White Paper," Aug. 7, 1949, Judd Papers, box 150, China White Paper 1949; Nixon, *Memoirs*, p. 110.

68. Newman, "Self-Inflicted Wound," pp. 146, 151–53; Cohen, "Acheson," pp. 21, 25; Acheson testimony, Oct. 12, 1949, U.S., Senate Committee on Foreign Relations, *Reviews*, p. 97; NA, "Outline of Far Eastern and Asian Policy for Review with the President," Nov. 11, 1949, RG 59, 890.00/11-1849, p. 1. The assertion that "communism is a tool of Russian imperialism" appears constantly in other internal SD documents in fall 1949. See, for example, NA, Case, Fosdick, and Jessup to Acheson, "Tentative Findings on U.S. Policy in the Far East," Sept. 2, 1949, RG 59, 890.00/11-1849.67.

69. Mao Tsetung, "Why It Is Necessary to Discuss the White Paper," Aug. 28, 1949, *Selected Works*, 4: 442.

70. *China White Paper*, Van Slyke Intro. (unnum.); Mao Tsetung, "The Bankruptcy of the Idealist Conception of History," Sept. 16, 1949, *Selected Works*, 4: 451–58.

71. Press conference, Aug. 11, 1949, U.S., *Public Papers: Truman*, p. 421.

72. *NYT*, Aug. 7, 1949, sec. IV, p. 8.

73. NSC-58/2, "U.S. Policy Toward the Soviet Satellite States in Eastern Europe," Dec. 8, 1949, *FRUS 1949*, 5: 42–54.

74. CIA, "Relative US Security Interest in the European-Mediterranean Area and the Far East," July 14, 1949, Truman Papers, PSF, box 249, Central Intelligence Memos 1949. Reports from China sustained the belief that Titoism was a long-term objective. See Stuart, "Notes on a Future American China Policy," July 14, Clark to Acheson, July 27, and Jones to Acheson, Sept. 3, 1949, *FRUS 1949*, 8: 430–35, 459–61, 519–21.

75. Cohen, "Acheson," pp. 27–28, 37–38; NA, SD, Div. of Far East Research, "Problems of Domestic and Foreign Policy Confronting the Chinese Communists," July 28, 1949, RG 330, OSD, CD 14-1-36, pp. 50–56; Davies memo, Aug. 24, 1949, *FRUS 1949*, 9: 536–40; diary entry, Aug. 25, 1949, Cabot Papers, 18, no. 00597.

76. Acheson to Douglas, July 20, 1949, *FRUS 1949*, 9: 50–51; memo, meeting with Dulles, Aug. 30, 1949, Koo Papers, box 130, notes of conversations 1949.

77. Hillenkoetter memo, CIA report, Nov. 21, 1949, Truman Papers, PSF, box 249, Central Intelligence Memos 1949.

78. Acheson testimony, Jan. 10, 1950, U.S. Senate Committee on Foreign Relations, *Reviews*, p. 138.

79. Interviews with Chinese researchers, 1985; *People's Daily*,

Aug. 13, 1957; *Xinhua*, no. 12, 1957, p. 153; interview with Huang Hua, 1985.

Chapter Two

EPIGRAPH: Paraphrase of Harold Macmillan in Nixon, "American Foreign Policy: The Bush Agenda," *Foreign Affairs*, 68.1: 208.

1. Kirk to Acheson, Nov. 9, 1949, *FRUS* 1949, 5: 672–74.

2. Bevin memo, "Recent Developments in the Civil War in China," and "Annex," Dec. 9, 1948, PRO, C.P. (48) 299, pp. 1–4, 12, CAB 129/31.

3. Stuart to Acheson, May 4, 1949, *FRUS* 1949, 9: 15–16; Acheson testimony, April 21, 1949, U.S., Senate Committee on Foreign Relations, *North Atlantic Treaty*, p. 213.

4. Minutes of 12th Meeting of Washington Exploratory Talks on Security, Feb. 9, 1949, *FRUS* 1949, 4: 73; Acheson, *Present at the Creation*, p. 404.

5. Acheson to certain diplomatic and consular officers, May 6, Acheson to Stuart, May 13, Douglas to Acheson, May 19, 1949, *FRUS* 1949, 9: 17, 21–23, 25–26; *NYT*, May 18, 19, 1949, pp. 10, 1, respectively.

6. Acheson to Stuart, April 22, NSC 41, "U.S. Policy Regarding Trade with China," Feb. 28, NSC 41/1, "U.S. Policy Regarding Trade with China," Nov. 7, Acheson to Douglas, July 20, 25, 1949, *FRUS* 1949, 8: 682–83, 9: 826–34, 889–96, 50–52, 53.

7. Martin, *Divided Counsel*, pp. 57–63; McConaughy to Acheson, Sept. 11, 1949, *FRUS* 1949, 8: 1291–1293.

8. McConaughy to Acheson, Sept. 11, 1949, *FRUS* 1949, 8: 1292; Wolf, "To Secure a Convenience," p. 308.

9. Bevin to prime minister, July 29, 1949, PRO, Bevin Papers, FO800/462/FE49/15; Commercial Relations and Exports Dept., Board of Trade, letter attached to Cox to Scarlett, Nov. 18, 1949, PRO, FO371/75825/F18316.

10. Porter, *Britain*, pp. 31–32; Bevin memo and annex, Dec. 9, 1948, PRO, C.P. (48) 299, p. 12, CAB 129/31.

11. Urquhart to FO, Aug. 3, 1949, PRO, FO371/75765/F.

12. Bevin memo, "China," Aug. 23, 1949, PRO, C.P. (49) 180, pp. 1–3, CAB 129/35. Also see FO memo, "China," attached to Douglas to Acheson, Aug. 17, 1949, *FRUS* 1949, 9: 56–61.

13. Douglas to Acheson, Aug. 26, 1949, *FRUS* 1949, 9: 68–69.

14. NA, Yost memo, "Discussion of Far Eastern Affairs in Preparation for Conversations with Mr. Bevin, Sept. 13, 1949," Sept. 16, 1949, RG 59, OCA 1945–50, box 14; Acheson memo, meeting with Bevin and others, Sept. 12, Jones to Acheson, Sept. 3, 1949, *FRUS* 1949, 9:

81–85, Jones to Acheson, Sept. 3, 1949, *FRUS* 1949, 9: 81–85, 8: 519–21.

15. Acheson memo, meeting with Bevin and others, Sept. 12, *FRUS* 1949, 9: 83. At their second meeting, on Sept. 17, Acheson and Bevin again argued over the recognition issue. Acheson presented seven reasons why the U.S. would not recognize the Chinese Communists, including that they were "bitterly hostile to the United States and were a faithful tool of the Soviet Union." Acheson memo, meeting with Bevin and others, Sept. 17, 1949, ibid., pp. 88–91; NA, "U.S. Policy of Non-Recognition of Chinese Communist Regime," Sept. 26, 1951, RG 59, 611.93/9-1851, pp. 5–6. Also see Acheson, *Present at the Creation*, pp. 429–30. Bevin later wrote Acheson a private note about the Washington discussions. Perhaps referring to the conflict over China policy, he said, "I am afraid that the results of our second series of talks on the [7th?] Floor [of State] were not so encouraging. A stubborn and relentless attitude was displayed in no uncertain manner. At the same time I think our approach was the correct one." Bevin to Acheson, Oct. 11, 1949, Acheson Papers, Yale, box 3, Folder 34.

16. Conclusions of cabinet meeting, Oct. 27, Bevin memo, C.M. (49) 62, p. 58, CAB 128/16, "Recognition of the Chinese Communist Government," Oct. 24, 1949, PRO, C.P. (49) 214, pp. 1–3, CAB 129/37; memo, meeting with Truman, Oct. 17, 1949, Acheson Papers, HST, memos of conversations 1949, box 64, 10/49–11/49; NA, Webb memo, meeting with Truman, Oct. 3, 1949, RG 59, PPS 1947–53, Country and Area Files, box 13, China 1949.

17. Minutes of NSC's 47th meeting, Oct. 20, 1949, Truman Papers, PSF, box 206, NSC Meetings 1949. British opinion generally was strongly for recognition of the PRC. Even Winston Churchill, the old leader of the Conservatives, supported diplomatic relations simply because the Chinese Communists were in control of the mainland. He told the House of Commons, "One may say that when relations are most difficult, that is the time when diplomacy is most needed." See Porter, *Britain*, pp. 28–29.

18. Bacon to Acheson, Nov. 8, 1949, *FRUS* 1949, 9: 181–82.

19. Sprouse memo, meeting of Butterworth and others, Nov. 1, Acheson memo, meeting with Franks, Dec. 8, 1949, ibid., pp. 149–51, 219–20; NA, Sprouse memo, meeting of Merchant and others, Dec. 6, 1949, RG 59, OCA 1945–50, box 14.

20. Conclusions of cabinet meeting, Dec. 15, Bevin memo, "Recognition of the Chinese Communist Government," Dec. 12, 1949, PRO, C.M. (49) 72, pp. 132–33, CAB 128/16; C.P. (49) 248, pp. 1–6, CAB 129/37; Bevin to Acheson, Dec. 16, 1949, *FRUS* 1949, 9: 225–26.

21. *NYT*, Dec. 31, 1949, Jan. 6, 7, 1950 (p. 1 all 3 dates); Mayers, *Cracking the Monolith*, p. 56.

22. Knowland to Lawrence, Oct. 11, 1949, Knowland Papers, box 274, Correspondence—Special Oakland Tribune; Cohen, "Acheson," 49; Tucker, *Patterns*, p. 191.

23. Franks to FO, Dec. 8, 1949, PRO, FO371/75826/F18481; NA, Ogburn minutes, meeting of secretary and consultants, Oct. 26, 1949, RG 59, 890.00/11-1749, p. 8.

24. Jessup, *Birth of Nations*, pp. 26–29; NA, Jessup to Wilds, Aug. 31, 1949, RG 59, 890.00/11-1849.

25. NA, papers from consultants, RG 59, 890.00/11-1849. Also see Yost, *History and Memory*.

26. NA, Yost to Jessup, "U.S. Policy Toward Chinese Communists," Aug. 15, 1949, RG 59, 890.00/11-1849.

27. NA, Yost to Jessup, "Policy Toward the Chinese Communists," Aug. 29, 1949, RG 59, 890.00/11-1849.

28. Tucker, *Patterns*, pp. 126–33; L.A. Chamber of Commerce, World Trade Committee, "Report to Board of Directors," Nov. 18, 1949, pp. 1–5, Knowland Papers, box 273, Special Correspondence Lj-Ma; "Address of Roger D. Lapham Before the Commonwealth Club of California, San Francisco," Sept. 8, 1949, appendix to oral history, "An Interview on Shipping, Labor . . . ," pp. 461, 253–55; transcript of Lapham address, Dec. 28, 1949, RG 59, 793.00/1-450.

29. U.S., Dept. of State, *Transcript of Round Table Discussion*.

30. NA, Yost to Jessup, "U.S. Attitudes Toward Chinese Communists," Sept. 6, 1949, RG 59, 890.00/11-1849. Also see NA, Yost to Jessup, "Policy Toward the Chinese Communists—Concrete Measures," Sept. 1, and "Proposition on China," Sept. 12, 1949, ibid.

31. NA, Fosdick to Jessup, Aug. 29, 1949, RG 59, OCA 1945–50, box 14; NA, Fosdick to Jessup, Oct. 25, 1949, RG 59, 890.00/11-1849. Yost characterized the "benign" viewpoint as one of letting the Communists "stew in their own juice." That attitude, Yost believed, tended to rely "too complacently on the impediment of traditional and material forces to totalitarian-directed social change." NA, Yost to Jessup, "U.S. Attitudes Toward Chinese Communists," Sept. 6, 1949, RG 59, 890.00/11-1849.

32. NA, Jessup, "Proposition on China Culled from Various Discussions," Sept. 10, 1949, RG 59, 890.00/11-1849. While generally agreeing with Jessup, Yost pointed out conflicts in the proposition. NA, Yost to Jessup, "Proposition on China," Sept. 12, 1949, ibid.

33. See NA, Wilds to Jessup, Oct. 25, 1949, and attachment, "U.S. Policy in the Far East and Asia," draft IV; and Case, Fosdick, and

Jessup to Acheson, "Tentative Findings on U.S. Policy in the Far East," Sept. 2, 1949, both in RG 59, 890.00/11-1849. For more on the work of the consultants, see Blum, *Drawing the Line*, pp. 153–59.

34. Acheson testimony, Oct. 12, 1949, U.S., Senate Committee on Foreign Relations, *Reviews*, pp. 96–99; "Supplemental Notes on Executive Session Senate Foreign Relations Committee, Oct. 12, 1949," n.d., Truman Papers, PSF, box 161, China Lobby; Leary and Stueck, "Chennault Plan"; record of discussion of Acheson, Schuman, and Bevin, Nov. 11, 1949, PRO, FO371/75820/F16978.

35. Jessup testimony, Oct. 12, 1949, U.S., Senate Committee on Foreign Relations, *Reviews*, p. 99.

36. NA, Ogburn minutes, meeting of secretary and consultants, Oct. 26, 1949, RG 59, 890.00/11-1749, pp. 1–8.

37. Ibid., p. 8.

38. Blum, *Drawing the Line*, pp. 154–59; Leary and Stueck, "Chennault Plan"; NA, Ogburn minutes, meeting of secretary and consultants, Oct. 26, 1949, RG 59, 890.00/11-1749, pp. 8–13.

39. NA, Ogburn minutes, meeting of secretary and consultants, Oct. 26, 1949, pp. 8–13; ibid., Oct. 27, 1949, p. 5; Blum, *Drawing the Line*, pp. 156–59. The two Ogburn memos, both bearing the title "Decisions Reached by Consensus at the Meeting with the Secretary and the Consultants on the Far East," are identical, except for two crucial sections on China. One paragraph in a version found in the files of the OCA reads: "With regard to Communist China, we should endeavor to see that as great a strain as possible is placed upon the relations between Peiping and Moscow and to see that life for Communist China within the framework of Soviet domination is as unpleasant as possible." The same section of a version in the SD's decimal file and printed in *FRUS* reads: "With regard to Communist China, we anticipate the possibility that great strains will develop between Peiping and Moscow. These strains would not only work to our advantage but would contribute to the desired end of permitting China to develop its own life independently rather than as a Russian satellite."

The other discrepancy also indicated a difference between a more "active" and an "aloof" position. The OCA version reads: "US recognition of the Chinese Communists is not to be regarded as a major instrument for showing our interest in the Chinese people or for winning concessions from the Communist regime. Our attitude on this question should not be an eager one." To these two sentences, the decimal file version added the phrase, "but should be realistic." See NA, Ogburn, "Decisions Reached by Consensus at the Meeting with the Secretary and the Consultants on the Far East," Nov. 2, 1949, RG 59, OCA 1945–50, box 14, and *FRUS* 1949, 9: 160–62.

On Nov. 8, 1949, a week after the conference ended, a frustrated John Cabot, back from Shanghai, recorded in his diary that a meeting of a State Dept. China working group concluded "with about three more opinions than there were people present." On Nov. 12, he wrote: "In my mind we continue to fall between two stools on China policy—on one hand we can't crack down effectively on commies, let alone overthrow them, on other, in refu[sal] to recognize facts, and lay ourselves open to reprisals by commies." Cabot Papers, 18, nos. 00584, 00586.

40. Webb memo, meeting with Truman, Oct. 1, 1949, *FRUS* 1949, 9: 1141; transcript of press conference, Oct. 19, 1949, U.S., *Public Papers: Truman*, 1949, p. 520; Acheson to Truman, Nov. 21, 1949, Truman Papers, PSF, box 173, China 1949; NA, Webb memo, Nov. 14, 1949, RG 59, OCA 1945–50, box 14.

41. Memo, meeting with Truman, Nov. 17, 1949, Acheson Papers, HST, box 64, memos of conversations, 10/49–11/49 (also see Acheson, *Present at the Creation*, p. 450); NA, Perkins to Acheson, Nov. 17, 1949, RG 59, OCA 1945–50, box 14.

42. NSC 48, "The Position of the U.S. with Respect to Asia," Oct. 25, 1949, Truman Papers, PSF, box 207, NSC Meeting no. 50; Bishop to Rusk, Oct. 21, 1949, and attached "Study on the Problems Involved in Military Aid to China," *FRUS* 1949, 9: 561–68; Schaller, *American Occupation*, pp. 201–8; Blum, *Drawing the Line*, pp. 168–70.

43. Schaller, *American Occupation*, pp. 207–8; Tsou, *America's Failure*, p. 529; NSC 37/9, "Possible U.S. Military Action Toward Taiwan Not Involving Major Military Forces," Dec. 27, 1949, with attached JCS memo, Dec. 23, 1949, *FRUS* 1949, 9: 460–61.

44. Acheson memo, meeting with Bradley and others, Dec. 29, 1949, *FRUS* 1949, 9: 463–67; summary of NSC's 50th meeting, Dec. 29, 1949, Truman Papers, PSF, box 220, NSC Meetings 1949; memo, meeting with Truman, Dec. 20, 1949, Acheson Papers, HST, box 64, memos of conversations, 12/49.

45. Handwritten note, phone conversation with Truman, Dec. 30, 1949, Judd Papers, box 136, Truman.

46. *NYT,* Dec. 31, 1949, p. 1; Tsou, *America's Failure,* p. 530; Blum, *Drawing the Line,* p. 179; Porter, *Britain,* p. 68; *People's Daily* editorial, Jan. 5, 1950, cited in NA, Clubb to SD, Jan. 9, 1950, RG 59, 793.00/1-950; Acheson, *Present at the Creation,* pp. 458–59.

47. Acheson, draft statement of Jan. 5, Truman statement on Formosa, Jan. 5, 1950, Truman Papers, PSF, box 173, Foreign Affairs File (China 1945–52), China 1950–52. On the afternoon of Jan. 4 Acheson sent Truman a draft statement disclaiming interest in military involvement on Taiwan, for release the next day. After seeing the president,

Acheson hurried to Capitol Hill, where he convinced Rep. John Kee, chairman of the House Foreign Affairs Committee, that the U.S. must not invite Russian charges of imperialism by taking "overt military action to protect Formosa." Acheson argued that the Chinese Communists did not have the ships and equipment necessary to engineer a successful assault on the island. If Taiwan fell to them, it would be through internal disintegration, he said. Meanwhile, Truman met with Clark Clifford and other members of his personal staff to discuss Acheson's proposal. His advisers were unanimous in opposing the release of the statement. Truman was persuaded, and asked Adm. Sidney Souers, executive secretary of the NSC, to solicit the opinions of Secretary of Defense Louis Johnson and General Bradley. But after speaking with Acheson again, the president reversed himself and decided to present the statement at his press conference on the morning of Jan. 5. The short four paragraphs of the draft reviewed the history of the status of Taiwan and acknowledged it as Chinese territory. It stated that the U.S. "had no desire to obtain special rights or privileges or to establish military bases on Formosa or to detach Formosa from China," did not intend to become involved in the Chinese civil war, and would not provide military aid or advice to the Nationalists, although it would continue economic assistance.

Shortly before the press conference, however, either Bradley or Johnson got Truman to revise the statement by dropping the phrase "to detach Formosa from China." Bradley did not want to rule out the possibility of seizing Taiwan in case the Communists decided to "march south" and there was war. Acheson reluctantly agreed to this change, but did not know about another last-minute alteration: Secretary Johnson had Truman add the qualifier "at this time" to the key sentence, so that the final version read: "The United States had no desire to obtain special rights or privileges or to establish military bases on Formosa *at this time*." Truman read the revised statement at the press conference without informing Acheson or the press secretary, who had to recall the original and replace it with the corrected version. According to the president's close adviser George Elsey, who recorded the incident, "Johnson is angry that the statement was issued; Acheson is angry at the insertion 'at this time.' Clifford . . . knew nothing of the President's change of heart and was annoyed at Acheson's pressure tactics. Everyone seems upset!"

After the statement was released on the afternoon of Jan. 5, Acheson tried to deflect attention away from the discrepancies in the two versions, but rumors persisted about differences between Acheson and Johnson. Moreover, Acheson had no success in persuading Knowland and Smith to the wisdom of his view. After an hour and a half of discussion, Knowland and Smith were still bitter and called Truman's statement "a policy of grave danger to the American people." To add to the turmoil Amb. Philip Jessup, in Japan to meet with Gen. MacArthur as part of his tour of the Far East for Acheson, stated on Jan. 5 that the U.S. "[would] not abandon" China and would continue to oppose Communist efforts to overthrow established governments by force. He repeated his remarks the next day. On top of all this, as the *NYT* observed, what Truman was saying and what the U.S. was doing seemed confusing if not contradictory. Truman said the U.S. would not provide either military assistance or advice to the Nationalists, but the U.S. already had military advisers on Taiwan training Nationalist forces. Moreover, the president had not moved to stop the Nationalists from continuing to draw on the unexpended $9 million left from the $125 million granted in the 1948 China Aid Act. McFall memo, meeting of Acheson and Kee, Jan. 4, Battle memo, Jan. 5, Acheson memo, meeting with Knowland and Smith, all in Acheson Papers, HST, box 65, memos of conversations, 1/50; Elsey memo, "Concerning Statement by the President on January 5, 1950, concerning China," Jan. 6, Elsey Papers, box 59; *NYT*, Jan. 5, pp. 1, 18, Jan. 6, pp. 1, 3, Jan. 7, p. 5.

48. Acheson testimony, Jan. 10, 1950, U.S., Senate Committee on Foreign Relations, *Reviews*, Jan. 10, pp. 133–34. Acheson also made clear to the committee that he did not see U.S. recognition of the Communist regime on the horizon. He said, as he had in the past, that no "hasty" administration action would be taken. He added a new point, however, saying, "We think no step should be taken until it has been thoroughly threshed out with the committees of both the House and the Senate, until we reach, if we ever do reach, a fairly united view in the United States about it." Given the strong feelings on the China question in the country, Acheson's promise effectively deferred recognition of Beijing indefinitely.

49. Stevenson to FO, Sept. 27, Oct. 3, War Office to FO, Dec. 8, 1949, PRO, FO371/75832/F14609, FO371/75832/F14890, FO371/75835/ F18615.

50. Hillenkoetter memo, Nov. 21, 1949, Truman Papers, PSF, box 249, Central Intelligence Memos 1949; McConaughy to Acheson, Dec. 16, 1949, *FRUS* 1949, 8: 618; Scarlett to Gascoigne, Jan. 30, 1950, PRO, FO371/83313/F.

51. Wu Xiuquan, *Zai waijiaobu banian de jingli*, pp. 3–4.

52. Kirk to Acheson, Dec. 18, Clubb to Acheson, Dec. 23, Dec. 24, 1949, *FRUS* 1949, 8: 637–38, 643–45, 9: 243–44; NA, minutes of Jan. 11, 1950, meeting, RG 59, PPS, box 32, Minutes of Meetings 1950, Clubb to SD, Jan. 26, 1950, RG 59, 661.93/1-2650. The State Dept.

also received several reports of supposed splits among Chinese Communist leaders. Chen Yi, mayor of Shanghai, was allegedly fed up with Soviet influence in China and encouraged U.S. officials to pursue possible overtures. McConaughy to Acheson, Jan. 5, 21, Acheson to McConaughy, Jan. 25, 1950, *FRUS* 1950, 6: 265–69, 289–93, 294. Nothing came of these efforts. McConaughy was keen to pursue Titoism in early 1950, but after his return to the U.S., he discouraged hopes of Titoism. See Ogburn memo, report by McConaughy to interdepartmental meeting on June 1, 1950, June 2, 1950, *FRUS* 1950, 6: 352–56.

53. Wu Xiuquan, *Zai waijiaobu*, p. 10. Nuclear weaponry may also have been discussed. The memoirs of one Chinese participant in the negotiations notes there was controversy over the inclusion of the phrase "by all the means at its disposal," referring to mutual assistance in the event of aggression. See Wu Xiuquan, "Sino-Soviet Relations," p. 18. A Soviet TV documentary in 1988 went so far as to claim that Mao asked Stalin for the atomic bomb; but Nikolai Fedorenko, Stalin's interpreter for the Stalin-Mao talks, pronounces the claim an "absurdity" and a "fantasy." Fedorenko recalls that Mao "did not raise the question of nuclear weapons during the negotiations with Stalin." *Foreign Broadcast Information Service*, Soviet Union, Aug. 3, 1988, p. 48; Nikolai Fedorenko, "Night Conversations," *Pravda*, Oct. 23, 1988, p. 4.

54. Wu Xiuquan, "Sino-Soviet Relations," pp. 20–21; Moscow to FO, Feb. 17, 1950, PRO, FO371/88315/FC10338/60; Mao quote from Martin, *Divided Counsel*, p. 118. See also the interesting accounts of Mao's interpreter during the Moscow talks, Shi Zhe, "I Accompanied Chairman Mao," and of the Soviet interpreter, N. Fedorenko, "The Stalin-Mao Summit in Moscow," *Far Eastern Affairs* (Moscow), 1989, no. 2, pp. 125–33, 134–48.

55. NA, Schwinn to Jessup, Sept. 9, 1949, and attachment, "U.S. Propaganda Policies and Objectives in the Far East," Aug. 22, 1949, RG 59, 890.00/11-1849.

56. Acheson to Bruce, Jan. 25, Feb. 11, 1950, *FRUS* 1950, 6: 294–96, 308; *DSB*, Jan. 23, 1950, pp. 114–15.

57. *Declassified Documents Reference System*, R-360B, R-360D; comments on Acheson's Jan. 12, 1950, speech, PRO, FO371/83314/FC10338/36; *NYT*, Jan. 13, 1950, p. 22.

58. Webb to Truman, Jan. 10, 1950, Truman Papers, WHCF, Confidential Files, box 37, SD correspondence.

59. NA, Acheson to Truman, Jan. 27, 1950, RG 59, 793.00/1-1050; Donovan, *Tumultuous Years*, p. 85.

60. *DSB*, March 27, 1950, pp. 467–72.

61. Graves to FO, Feb. 13, 1950, PRO, FO371/83320/FC10345/1G;

Bevin memo, "China," April 20, 1950, C.P. (50) 73, pp. 9–10, CAB 129/39; NA, SD to Amconsul, Peiping, March 14, 1950, RG 59, 793.00/2-2750.

62. Statement, March 17, 1950, and comment on James Reston's article of March 17, 1950, Judd Papers, box 104, Statements (1); NA, McConaughy to SD, Feb. 23, 1950, RG 59, 793.00/2-2350.

63. Peking to FO, May 20, FO to Peking, May 23, 1950, PRO, FO371/ 83290/FC 1022/352, FO371/83290/FC1022/366/G; memo, meeting with Herod and Hopkins, March 24, 1950, Acheson Papers, HST, box 65, Memos of Conversations, 3/50.

64. NA, Merchant to Acheson, March 2, 1950, RG 59, 693.00/3-250.

65. NSC-68, April 14, 1950, *FRUS* 1950, 1: 234–92; Henderson quote from Graebner, *National Security*, p. 31.

66. Gaddis, *Strategies*, pp. 98–99; Acheson testimony, March 29, 1950, U.S., Senate Committee on Foreign Relations, *Reviews*, pp. 276, 272.

67. NA, Bradley to Johnson, April 27, 1950, RG 330, OSD, box 73, CD 14-1-36.

68. NA, Bradley to Johnson, May 2, 1950, RG 330, OSD, China 008-901.3, 1949–50, entry 18B, box 48, Defense-ISA 1950–52; NA, Lemnitzer to Johnson, May 5, 1950, RG 330, CD 6-3-30, box 30.

69. Clubb to Kennan, April 25, 1950, quoted in Schaller, *American Occupation*, p. 253, and in Schaller, "Consul General Clubb."

70. NA, Clubb to Rusk, June 16, 1950, RG 59, OCA, box 17, Policy Toward China 1950; NA, minutes of interdepartmental meeting of June 8, 1950, RG 59, box 4210, 793.001/6-850.

71. NA, [Lemnitzer?] memo on joint State-Defense meetings on Formosan situation, [April or May 1950,] RG 330, China 008-091.3, 1949–50, entry 18B, box 48, Defense-ISA 1950–52.

72. Buhite, "Major Interests," 439; Blum, *Drawing the Line*, p. 195; memo, meeting with Rusk, April 20, 1950, Koo Papers, box 180, Notes of Conversation 1950.

73. Dulles to Rusk, Nitze, and Webb, May 18, 1950, *FRUS* 1950, 1: 314–16.

74. Howe to Armstrong, May 31, 1950, with annex, Rusk to Acheson, May 30, 1950, *FRUS* 1950, 6: 347–51; NA, Rusk to Acheson, June 9, 1950, RG 59, OCA, box 17, Policy Toward China 1950; Schaller, *American Occupation*, pp. 260–66.

75. Franks to Bevin, Dec. 17, 1949, PRO, Bevin Papers, FO800/462, pp. 220–21, FO800/517, pp. 66–69; minutes of bipartite ministerial talks, May 7, 1950, PRO, Bevin Papers, file 449, quoted in Leary and Stueck, "Chennault Plan," p. 362; U.S. delegation at the tripartite foreign ministers' meeting to Acting SecState, May 11, 1950, *FRUS* 1950,

3: 1036–1037; FO to Peking, May 23, 1950, PRO, FO371/83290/FC1022/366/G. Also see NA, "Agreed Anglo-American Report Summarising Discussion on China, May 2, 3, 1950," RG 59, 793.00/5-450.

76. Franks to Dening, June 7, 1950, PRO, FO371/83320/FC10345/9.

77. ConGen Tamsui to FO, June 5, 1950, PRO, FO371/83320/FC10345/7; NA, Burns to Davis and others, May 29, 1950, with attachment, Burns to Rusk, "Notes on State-Defense Conference held 25 May 1950," May 29, 1950, RG 330, OSD, CD6-3-30, box 30, 9/47–6/50.

78. Memo, meeting with Dulles, June 12, 1950, Koo Papers, box 180, Notes of Conversation 1950; Schaller, "Consul General Clubb," pp. 151–52.

79. MacArthur memo, June 14, Soule report through McConaughy to Acheson, Feb. 1, 1950, *FRUS* 1950, 7: 161–65, 6: 302–4; NA, interdepartmental meeting on Far East, June 22, 1950, RG 59, 793.00/6-2650.

80. Acheson to Bevin, July 10, 1950, *FRUS* 1950, 7: 348–50.

81. Office of Intelligence Research, IE 7, Korea, June 25, 1950, ibid., pp. 148–53.

82. NA, Jessup to Rusk, July 11, 1950, RG 59, 793.00/7-1150; memo, meeting with Truman, July 31, 1950, Acheson Papers, HST, box 65, Memos of Conversations, 8/50; minutes of meeting of representatives of France, UK, and U.S. in Paris, Aug. 4, 1950, *FRUS* 1950, 6: 419–20; Mayers, *Cracking the Monolith*, p. 96. On the U.S. consideration of the Sino-Soviet relationship during the Korean War, see Foot, *Wrong War*.

83. Bernstein, "Policy of Risk"; Foot, *Wrong War*, pp. 75–81.

84. Bernstein, "Policy of Risk," p. 17; Stueck, *Road to Confrontation*, pp. 230–31.

85. Gaddis, "Truman Doctrine," p. 397; Cohen, "Acheson," pp. 51–52.

86. Mayers, *Cracking the Monolith*, p. 99.

87. Lewis and Xue, *China Builds the Bomb*, pp. 7–10.

88. Nogee and Donaldson, *Soviet Foreign Policy*, pp. 92–94; Jervis, "Impact of the Korean War."

89. NA, "General U.S. Policy Respecting Formosa," [1951?], RG 59, OCA, box 18, Formosa, 8/50–12/28/50, p. 13; Mayers, *Cracking the Monolith*, pp. 87, 100.

Chapter Three

EPIGRAPH: U.S. minutes of 2d meeting of President Truman and Prime Minister Clement Attlee, Dec. 1950, *FRUS* 1950, 6: 1402.

1. Memo, meeting with Chiang, May 18, 1953, Rankin Papers, box

20, Chiang Kai-shek; diary entries, Sept. 9, 1952, May 31, 1953, Rankin Papers, box 20, Chiang Kai-shek, and box 1.

2. Diary entries, Sept. 5, 9, 1952, memo, meeting with Chiang, July 1, 1953, p. 2, ibid., box 1 and box 20, Chiang Kai-shek; Rankin, *China Assignment*, p. 164.

3. Radford oral history, May 1965, p. 36.

4. Diary entry, June 4, memo, meeting with T. F. Tsiang, June 10, 1953, Koo Papers, box 219, diary for 1/17/53–6/24/83, and box 187, Notes of Conversation 1953; Barnard to Nitze, April 3, 1953, Eisenhower Papers, WHCF, Confidential File, 1953–61, box 67, SD through 9/53 (7).

5. NA, Taipei to SD, July 25, 1952, 793.00/7-2552, RG 59, box 4201.

6. Dulles speech, SD press release, May 17, 1951, no. 407, Dulles Papers, Princeton, box 52, PRC 1951.

7. Private and confidential memo, March 31, Dulles memo, meeting with Yeh and Koo, Nov. 19, 1952, Dulles Papers, Princeton, box 60, Formosa, and box 58, PRC 1952. Wellington Koo's notes on the same conversation give a slightly different picture. Koo records the lengthy discussion about splitting China from the Soviet Union, including Dulles's belief that there must be Chinese leaders on the mainland who "could be expected to throw off the Soviet yoke." Koo's memo, however, does not have Dulles describing the different strategies of division. See memo, meeting with Dulles and Yeh, Nov. 19, 1952, Koo Papers, box 187, Notes of Conversation 1952. The Nationalists interpreted some of the secretary of state's early speeches as implying that the main problem with the Chinese Communists was their alliance with the Soviet Union, not the existence of Mao's regime itself. See NA, Rankin to SD, Jan. 30, 1953, RG 59, 793.00/1-3053.

8. Bowles to Dulles, March 10, 1952, Dulles Papers, Princeton, box 58, Bowles.

9. Bowles to SecState, Nov. 7, Dec. 6, 1951, July 7, 1952, *FRUS 1951*, 6: 2186–2191, 2191–2201, 1952–54, 14: 73–76.

10. Dulles to Bowles, March 25, 1952, Dulles Papers, Princeton, box 58, Bowles. Dulles made a similar point on "Meet the Press" on Feb. 10, 1952. Transcript, ibid., box 65, Meet the Press.

11. Bowles to Dulles, April 23, Dulles to Bowles, May 1, 1952, ibid., box 58, Bowles.

12. Kennan, *American Diplomacy*, pp. 105–6. For other views of Dulles and his "wedge strategy," see Gaddis, *Long Peace*, pp. 147–94; Gardner, *Approaching Vietnam*, pp. 130–32; and Immerman, "In Search of History."

13. NA, Bowles to Acheson, March 6, Acheson to Bowles, March 27, 1952, RG 59, 793.00/3-2750, box 4201; Foot, *Wrong War*, pp. 194–95.

14. BD [William Diebold?] to HFA, April 28, Bowles to Armstrong, March 26, Armstrong to Bowles, June 3, 1952, Armstrong Papers, box 10, Bowles FA 1952–55; Bowles, "New India," p. 80.

15. Harlan Cleveland used the term "closed door" to characterize U.S. China policy after the start of the Korean War in a *Reporter* article (Sept. 1, 1953). The aim of this policy, he wrote, was to prevent "China's aggrandizement at the expense of its neighbors," and it was necessary as long as China insisted on expanding its power. He did not refer to the Sino-Soviet alliance. Cleveland had been in China twice, first in 1937 at the start of the Sino-Japanese War and then in 1947–48, when he headed the U.N. Relief and Rehabilitation Administration.

16. Betts, *Nuclear Blackmail*, pp. 31–47; Keefer, "President Dwight D. Eisenhower."

17. Interviews with Chinese officials, 1985. Also see Friedman, "Nuclear Blackmail." Recent scholarship sustains the view that Eisenhower's nuclear threat was not decisive in ending the Korean War. See Dingman, "Atomic Diplomacy During the Korean War"; and Foot, "Nuclear Coercion."

18. Goodpaster memo, meeting with Eisenhower, Feb. 17, 1965, Johnson Papers, Special Files, Meeting Notes, box 1, p. 4.

19. Pickett, "Eisenhower Solarium Notes"; Kennan oral history, March 1967, p. 38; Task Force "A," report to NSC, July 16, 1953, Eisenhower Library, WHO OSANSA: NSC, Subjects box 9, Project Solarium TFA, folders 3–7, pp. 111–19, 131, and box 10, Project Solarium, folder 1.

20. Kennan, *Memoirs*, pp. 374–75; Task Force "A," report to NSC (as cited in note 19), p. 150.

21. NSC 166/1, "U.S. Policy Toward Communist China," "NSC Staff Study on U.S. Policy Toward Communist China," both Nov. 6, 1953, *FRUS* 1952–54, 14: 278–306.

22. NSC, "Basic U.S. Objectives Toward Communist China," April 6, 1953, ibid., pp. 175–79.

23. Memo on NSC's 169th meeting, Nov. 5, 1953, ibid., pp. 265–66.

24. "Meet the Press" transcript, Feb. 10, 1952, Dulles Papers, Princeton, box 65, Meet the Press, p. 3.

25. NSC 166/1 (as cited in note 21, above), pp. 296–97.

26. Cabinet meetings, April 8, Oct. 29, Dec. 4, 1952, June 15, 1954, PRO, C.C. (52) 39th Conclusions, p. 27, CAB 128/24; C.C. (52) 91st Conclusions, pp. 61–62, 102d Conclusions, p. 136, both CAB 128/25, C.C. (54) 40th Conclusions, pp. 4–5, CAB 128/27.

27. "Second Restricted Tripartite Meeting. . . ," Dec. 7, 1953, *FRUS* 1952–54, 5: 1808–1818. CIA analysts already noted latent ideological differences between Soviet leaders and Mao. See Bridgham,

Cohen, and Jaffe, "Mao's Road," a 1972 reprint of a secret 1953 CIA report.

28. "Second Restricted Tripartite Meeting. . . ," Dec. 7, 1953, *FRUS* 1952–54, 5: 1808–1818.

29. Cutler memo, meeting with Eisenhower and others, May 28, Cutler to Dulles, June 2, memo on NSC's 200th meeting, June 3, 1954, *FRUS* 1952–54, 12: 521–37; Foot, *Wrong War*, pp. 232–43.

30. "Second Restricted Tripartite Meeting. . . ," Dec. 7, 1953, *FRUS* 1952–54, 5: 1817–1818.

31. See Robert Bowie's comments on Dulles's San Francisco speech of 1957, Dulles Papers, Princeton, box 114, Bowie.

32. NSC's 135th meeting, March 4, 1953, Eisenhower Papers (AW), NSC Series, box 4.

33. Memo on NSC's 136th meeting, March 11, 1953, ibid.; NA, Bohlen, "Policy Implications of Stalin's Death," March 10, 1953, RG 59, PPS 1947–53, box 23, USSR 1953; Stassen to Psychological Strategy Board, March 10, 1953, Eisenhower Library, Jackson Records 1953–54, box 1, PSB Plans for Psychological Exploitation of Stalin's Death.

34. Ambrose, *Eisenhower*, p. 91; Ulam, *Expansion*, pp. 545–50; Eisenhower, *White House Years*, 1: 144–45.

35. Quote from Hoopes, *Devil and John Foster Dulles*, p. 205.

36. J. F. Dulles, "Statement at Berlin," Jan. 26, 1954, *DSB*, Feb. 8, 1954, p. 181.

37. Dulles to SD, Jan. 30, 1954, *FRUS* 1952–54, 14: 353–54; Dulles to SD, Feb. 1, 1954, Eisenhower Papers (AW), Dulles-Herter, box 2, Dulles 2/54 (2).

38. Memo, Eisenhower to Jackson, March 4, 1954, "Post Berlin Thoughts on the Current Russian Psyche," Feb. 22, Eisenhower Library, Jackson Papers, General File, box 41, Eisenhower.

39. Dulles to Eisenhower, Feb. 16, 1954, and editorial note, *FRUS* 1952–54, 14: 361–62, 366; Jackson, "Post Berlin Thoughts" (as cited in preceding note).

40. NSC 5412/2, March 15, 1954, Eisenhower Library, WHO OS-ANSA, NSC, Policy Papers, box 10; Gray memo of meeting with Eisenhower, Sept. 25, 1959, and list of classified material, both in ibid., Special Assistants, Presidential subseries, box 4, Meetings with the President, 12/58–1/59.

41. Dulles to SD, April 30, 1954, *FRUS* 1952–54, 16: 621; Mayers, *Cracking the Monolith*, pp. 132–34; U. Alexis Johnson, *Right Hand*, p. 204; Eleanor L. Dulles to author, May 22, 1986. Two contrasting incidents occupy prominent places in the imagery of U.S.-China relations: Dulles rejecting Zhou Enlai's hand during the Geneva Confer-

ence of 1954, and President Richard Nixon, a politician who built his career on anticommunism, warmly grasping Zhou's hand at the Beijing airport when the two met in 1972. Nixon wanted his gesture to symbolize the beginning of a new relationship between the two countries, just as Dulles's insult had marked the era of animosity toward the People's Republic. However, some doubt has been cast on the authenticity of the original Dulles slight of Zhou Enlai. According to one of Zhou's longtime associates, Wang Bingnan, a ranking member of the Chinese delegation to Geneva and the subsequent chief negotiator for the Chinese in nine years of Sino-American talks, the slight is a myth. In my interview with him in Dec. 1985, he claimed that he was with Zhou the entire time at Geneva and never witnessed any such encounter. Moreover, in his memoirs Wang asserts that there was neither the "objective nor [the] subjective" possibility for the alleged meeting. The U.S. and Chinese delegations sat far removed from each other and exited and entered the meeting hall through different doorways. During the 15-minute break in sessions, the two delegations never gathered together in the lounge. What is more, Zhou was "extremely cautious and serious" and did not give a thought to shaking the hand of the "determinedly anticommunist chieftain." Wang accuses Western journalists of fabricating the story to embarrass Zhou. (Wang Bingnan, *Zhong-mei*, p. 22.) Wang's account seems strange, since Zhou himself frequently referred to the incident to dramatize U.S. intransigence and Chinese flexibility. Wang does not try to explain why Zhou would spread a story meant to embarrass him, as he did after Geneva.

But, curiously, Wang's version is not so easily dismissed. The origin of the Dulles-Zhou incident is obscure, and the specifics vary with different accounts, each of which raises questions about what actually happened. There are no contemporary accounts of the incident. One of the first versions in print was provided by Edgar Snow in 1961 in *The Other Side of the River*, pp. 94–95. Snow interviewed Zhou, who recalled that Dulles was already in a lounge of the conference room when Zhou entered. The premier advanced, extended his hand, and was rebuffed by Dulles, who folded his hands behind his back, shook his head, and left the room. This account is odd because Zhou told Snow that no one else was in the room at the time, and it seems unlikely that either the Chinese premier or the U.S. secretary of state would have ever been left alone during the conference, let alone both at once. *Time* magazine reported observing Zhou Enlai in the lounge followed by "platoons of bodyguards with bulging shoulder holsters." (May 10, 1954, p. 28.)

Townsend Hoopes, *Devil and John Foster Dulles*, p. 222, quotes an unnamed source as saying that Dulles "quite brusquely" refused to shake hands with Zhou. Hoopes may have based his information on Herbert Parmet. In *Eisenhower and the American Crusades*, published a year earlier, Parmet draws a relatively detailed picture (p. 222), but one that varies considerably from the account Zhou gave to Snow. Parmet says the incident took place during a break in the first session. Zhou, not Dulles, supposedly was already in the room, along with Anthony Eden, Molotov, and a number of photographers. Zhou saw Dulles and approached. "Just as Chou Enlai extended his hand, the Secretary 'quite brusquely'—according to a member of the American delegation standing nearby—turned his back." Parmet listed a "confidential source" in his note for this account.

Dick Wilson describes the incident in somewhat similar terms in his biography of Zhou Enlai, even having Dulles utter, "I cannot," as he strolled away. Wilson cites Anthony Eden's 1960 work, *Full Circle*, as a source. But Eden, who according to Parmet was present at the encounter, makes no mention at all of the event, even though he describes the proceedings of the conference in detail, including the many contacts he had with Dulles, Zhou, and Molotov. Eden's description of Zhou's actual attitude during the first days of the conference is more consistent with Wang's statement that Zhou was not interested in shaking hands with Dulles. According to Eden, Zhou was "bitterly anti-American" and cold.

Apparently the only firsthand account other than Zhou's is that of U. Alexis Johnson, a member of the U.S. delegation, who claims to have witnessed the entire encounter. In *Right Hand of Power*, p. 204, he says that during a break in the first session, Dulles entered the lounge and Zhou, who was already there, walked across the room "with a broad smile and his usual air of urbane familiarity." Zhou extended his arm. Dulles, noting the "press photographers poised" for a story, quickly turned his back.

Johnson may have been the source for Parmet, for their two stories are quite similar. But this version also is perplexing. The first session lasted only 30 minutes, hardly time enough for a rest break. Moreover, the *NYT*'s report on it (April 27, 1954, p. 3) explicitly noted that both Dulles and Zhou ignored each other during the session. The major problem is that we have no journalistic accounts of the story. If eager photographers were milling about, one certainly would have recorded the incident, if not on film, at least in print. The press corps was extremely curious about any possible contact between the U.S. and China, but none of the American news accounts refers to a Dulles affront to Zhou, an event that would have certainly made headlines. Indeed, according to the *NYT*, during the whole of his one-week stay in Geneva, Dulles never came into contact with the Chinese.

Eleanor Dulles seems to provide the final word. In her letter to me of May 22, 1986, she states: "I am sure that the event . . . took place. As I understand it from conversations I had with my brother what he had in mind was the use by the Soviets of photographs of President Eisenhower seated with—probably Khrushchev—possible Bulganin. These were cropped taking out the other participants—western statesmen—blown up to large size and widely posted throughout the Warsaw Pact countries. Similar treatment of photographs of him shaking hands with Chou En-lai would in his view give a false impression of our national policy towards China and lead to undesirable confusion."

42. Gardner, *Approaching Vietnam*, pp. 248–314; *People's Daily* quote from Mayers, *Cracking the Monolith*, pp. 133–34.

43. Report of the Van Fleet Mission to the Far East, April 26–Aug. 7, 1954, submitted Oct. 5, 1954, Eisenhower Library, WHO OSANSA, Special Assistants, Presidential subseries, box 2, President's Papers 1954 (8).

44. "Background paper" for Bowie nomination hearings, clipping, Drew Pearson column, *Washington Post and Times Herald*, Jan. 28, 1956, p. 43, Knowland Papers, box 283, Patronage—State—Bowie 1956, and box 247, Dulles, 1954–58; Anderson oral history, June 1966, pp. 19–20.

45. Halle to Dulles, July 28, 1954, Herman Phleger Papers, box 4, SD, pp. 5–7. As early as 1952 Halle predicted that Beijing would become a major problem for Moscow. *Civilization and Foreign Policy*, pp. 150–57.

46. "Does New Look at China Mean Recognition?" *U.S. News and World Report*, Jan. 29, 1954, pp. 66–69.

47. Dulles to Knowland, Jan. 12, 1954, Knowland Papers, box 247, Dulles 1954–58; Dean, "United States Foreign Policy."

48. See CFR, Study Group on Soviet-American Relations no. 1, 1953–55, Groups, vols. 50–53, 59.

49. Working papers nos. 11 and 12, "The Far East" and "The Far East (continued)," March 30, April 27, 1954, "Report of the Third Subgroup," Feb. 4, 1955, all in ibid. The chief researcher for the study group, Henry L. Roberts of Columbia University, published his own findings in 1956. For his discussion of China and the Sino-Soviet alliance, see *Russia and America*, pp. 212–20.

50. SD, "The Sino-Soviet Relation and Its Potential Sources of Differences," April 6, 1954, *FRUS* 1952–54, 14: 401–7.

51. Memos on NSC's 169th and 193d meetings, Nov. 6, 1953, April 13, 1954, *FRUS* 14: 268–69, 408–12.

52. Memo on NSC's 193d meeting, ibid., pp. 409–11.

53. Ibid., p. 412.

54. Ibid., 12: 693–703.

55. Robertson to SD, Aug. 10, Ogburn to Robertson, Aug. 11, memo on NSC's 210th meeting, Aug. 12, 1954, ibid., pp. 696–703, 716–17, 718–19, 724–33.

56. JCS to SecDefense, Aug. 11, 1954, ibid., pp. 719–23 (emphasis in original). Also see Ridgway, *Soldier*, p. 279.

57. Memo on NSC's 211th meeting, Aug. 18, 1954, *FRUS* 1952–54, 14: 526–40.

58. Ibid.; Merchant memo, meeting of Dulles, Radford, et al., May 9, memo, meeting with Eisenhower and Anderson, May 25, 1954, Dulles Papers, DDE, Subjects, box 8, Indochina 5/53–5/54 (2), White House Memoranda, box 1, Meetings with President 1954 (3).

59. Memo on NSC's 211th meeting, Aug. 18, 1954, *FRUS* 1952–54, 14: 526–40.

60. Grantham to Sung, Feb. 10, 1954, Sung Papers, box 4, Grantham; memo on NSC's 177th meeting, Dec. 23, 1953, Eisenhower Papers, (AW), NSC, box 5, pp. 13–15.

61. Memo on NSC's 211th meeting, Aug. 18, 1954, *FRUS* 1952–54, 14: The "hard-headed detente" with the Soviet Union that Nixon advocated years later sounded much like this "tough coexistence policy." See *Los Angeles Times*, July 1, 1984, p. 6.

62. Memo on NSC's 211th meeting, Aug. 18, 1954, *FRUS* 1952–54, 14: 538–40. The administration's heightened aggressiveness toward China was part of a larger U.S. response to a perceived favorable shift in the world balance of power in 1953–54. See Trachtenberg, "Wasting Asset," especially pp. 35–44.

63. Memo on NSC's 226th meeting, Dec. 1, Robertson to Dulles, Dec. 30, 1954, *FRUS* 1952–54, 14: 968–77, 12: 1078–1079.

64. NSC 5429/5, Dec. 22, 1954, ibid., 12: 1062–1072.

65. Memo on NSC's 226th meeting, Dec. 1, 1954, ibid., 14: 968–77.

66. Memo on NSC's 211th meeting, Aug. 18, NSC 5429/3, Nov. 19, 1954, ibid., pp. 534, 911–19.

67. Memo on NSC's 226th meeting, Dec. 1, Allen Dulles, "Comments on Review of Basic National Security Policy," Nov. 18, 1954, ibid., pp. 968–77, 2: 776–81.

68. Dulles memo, meeting with Eisenhower, Dec. 22, memo on NSC's 229th meeting, Dec. 21, 1954, ibid., 14: 1048, 2: 836.

Chapter Four

EPIGRAPH: NA, Meyer memo, meeting of Dulles and Chiang Kai-shek, March 18, 1956, RG 59, 611.93/3-1856.

1. Anderson to Eisenhower, Sept. 3, 1954, Eisenhower Papers (AW), Dulles-Herter, box 3, Dulles 9/54 (2); Eisenhower, *White House Years*, 1: 459.

2. George and Smoke, *Deterrence*, pp. 266–74; Stewart Alsop, "The Story Behind Quemoy: How We Drifted Close to War," *Saturday Evening Post*, Dec. 13, 1958, pp. 26–27, 86–88; NA, memo of conversation, Yu Ta-wei, Walter Robertson, and others, Dec. 6, 1955, and J. F. Dulles, "Preliminary Draft of Possible Statement of Position for Communication to the Republic of China," April 4, 1955, both in RG 59, OCA 1948–56, box 53, Offshore Islands 1955.

3. NA, Bradley to Johnson, July 13, 1950, RG 330, OSD, box 177, CD 092 China, 7/50–12/50; memo, meeting with Eisenhower, Radford, et al., May 22, 1954, Dulles Papers, DDE, White House Memoranda, box 1, Meetings with President 1954 (3); Kalicki, *Pattern*, pp. 126–28; Stolper, *China*, pp. 20–25.

4. NA, ConGen Hong Kong to SD, Dec. 28, 1954, RG 59, 793.00/12-2854.

5. Lewis and Xue, *China Builds the Bomb*, pp. 20–26; Wang Bing-nan, *Zhong-mei*, pp. 41–42; Mao quote from He Di, "Evolution of the PRC's Policy," p. 7; CIA, "The Chinese Offshore Islands," Sept. 8, 1954, Eisenhower Papers (AW), International, box 9, Formosa (1).

6. NA, USAIRA, Taipei, to CSAF, Sept. 3, 1954, RG 59, OCA 1948–56, box 48. The British representative in Beijing later told London confidentially that he was not certain who was actually responsible for the fighting in the area, since both the Communists and the Nationalists had engaged in hostile actions during the summer of 1954. Trevelyan to Allen, Jan. 22, 1955, PRO, FO371/115038/FC1041/445.

7. CIA, "Chinese Offshore Islands" (as cited in note 5), pp. 18, 25. Publicly the KMT said it anticipated an imminent invasion of Jinmen, but in private top military officers, including Chief of Staff Chou Chih-jou, disagreed. They believed the Communists were probing U.S. intentions. NA, ALUSNA, Taipei, to SecState, Sept. 3, 1954, RG 59, 793.00/9-354.

8. Memo on NSC's 213th and 214th meetings, Sept. 9, 12, 1954, *FRUS* 1952–54, 14: 583–95, 613–24.

9. Radford to Wilson, Sept. 11, 1954, ibid., pp. 598–610.

10. Memo on NSC's 214th meeting, Sept. 12, 1954, ibid., pp. 613–24.

11. NA, memo on meeting of McConaughy and Joy, Nov. 6, Con-Gen, Hong Kong, to SD, Dec. 28, 1954, RG 59, 793.00/11-654, 793.00/12-2854.

12. Dulles memo, Sept. 12, memo on NSC's 215th meeting, Sept. 24, Dulles to Robertson, Oct. 7, Dulles memo, meeting with Eisenhower, Oct. 18, Dulles report to NSC, Oct. 28, 1954, *FRUS 1952–54*, 14: 611–13, 658–60, 708, 770, 809–12; Mutual Defense Treaty Between the United States of America and the Republic of China, Dec. 2, 1954, *DSB*, Dec. 13, 1954, p. 899.

13. Goodpaster memo, meeting of Dulles, Radford, and others, Oct. 29, Radford memo, Oct. 29, memo on NSC's 221st meeting, Nov. 2, 1954, *FRUS 1952–54*, 14: 814–16, 817–19, 827–39.

14. Sheldon to Goodpaster, Jan. 31, 1955, Eisenhower Library, WHO OSANSA, NSC, Briefing Notes, box 17, Taiwan and Offshore Islands. Seven of the eight U.S. personnel were evacuated before Yijiang fell. According to a historian who cites previously closed Chinese sources, Beijing employed limited military means as a political instrument to draw attention to the Taiwan question. Beijing wanted to take only Yijiang, not Jinmen or Mazu, and did not want to confront the U.S. After Yijiang was taken, in fact, Defense Min. Peng Dehuai and the Central Military Commission ordered Chinese forces to postpone their attack on the Dachens to avoid a clash with the U.S. He Di, "Evolution of the PRC's Policy."

15. Dulles memo, meeting with Eisenhower and Radford, Jan. 19, 1955, McConaughy memo, meeting of Dulles, Yeh, and others, Jan. 19, Cutler memo, meeting of Dulles, Hoover, and others, Jan. 19, 1955, *FRUS 1955–57*, 2: 41–44, 46–52. Eisenhower, *White House Years*, 1: 466.

16. Memo on NSC's 232d meeting, Jan. 20, 1955, Eisenhower Papers (AW), NSC, box 6, Summaries of Discussion.

17. A draft message for Congress that Dulles wrote for Eisenhower following the NSC meeting specifically mentioned Jinmen and Mazu as territories the U.S. would help defend. The draft was not used. Dulles, "Draft message from the President to the Congress," Jan. 20, 1955, *FRUS 1955–57*, 2: 83–85.

18. Memo on NSC's 233d meeting, Jan. 21, 1955, Eisenhower Papers (AW), NSC, box 6, Summaries of Discussion.

19. Public Law 4, Jan. 29, 1955, *FRUS 1955–57*, 2: 162–63; *NYT*, April 7, 1955, p. 13. A top secret unsigned State Dept. memo to Eisenhower explicitly warned of the danger of a vague U.S. position. If the Communists "are left in ignorance of our intentions as to Quemoy and Matsu," it read, "they might stumble into a war with us, not be-

lieving that we would react. They could then allege with some plausibility that we had failed to state our position in advance and that if we had done so hostilities could have been avoided." NA, "Draft Memorandum for the President," Feb. 1955, RG 59, OCA 1948–56, box 53, Offshore Islands 1955.

20. Goodpaster memo, meeting of Eisenhower, Hoover, and others, Jan. 30, 1955, Eisenhower Library, WHO OSANSA, NSC, Briefing Notes, box 17, Taiwan and Offshore Islands; Offshore Islands Chronology, June 3, 1955, Rankin Papers, box 28, Offshore Islands; Hoover to Rankin (cable), Jan. 31, 1955, *FRUS* 1955–57, 2: 182–84; NA, Briscoe to Eisenhower, Feb. 12, 1955, RG 218, JCS, box 6, 091 China 2/55–3/55. Wellington Koo, the Nationalists' ambassador to the U.S., also received the U.S. promise. See diary entries, Jan. 27, 29, 31, Feb. 3, 1955, Koo Papers, box 220, diaries, no. 34, 1/1/55–8/31/55.

21. Rankin to SD (cable), Jan. 30, Scott memo, meeting of Hoover, Radford, and others, Jan. 30, 1955, *FRUS* 1955–57, 2: 167–68, 168–72; NA, Ogburn, "U.S. Commitments to GRC," Feb. 1, 1955, RG 59, OCA 1948–56, box 51, Offshore Islands 1955. Dulles and Charles Bohlen, the U.S. ambassador in Moscow, were uneasy with the continuing public vagueness of the U.S. position, and at one point Dulles thought it would be necessary to inform the Chinese Communists about the American commitment through confidential channels. This was never done. There seem to be several reasons for Dulles's and Eisenhower's change of mind about making a public commitment to Jinmen and Mazu. Pressure from the British was one. The British threatened to scuttle the U.N. effort, if an announcement was made. But Eisenhower also personally seemed to favor a vague public policy. See Dulles to Bohlen (cable), Jan. 22, Bohlen to Dulles (cable), Jan. 23, Merchant memo, meeting of Dulles, Makins, and others, Jan. 20, and MacArthur memo, meeting of Eisenhower, Hoover, and others, Jan. 30, 1955, *FRUS* 1955–57, 2: 111–12, 114–15, 86–89, 173–76.

22. Memo on NSC's 242d meeting, Feb. 24, 1955, Eisenhower Papers (AW), NSC, box 6, Summaries of Discussion.

23. Dulles to SD, Feb. 21, 1955, *FRUS* 1955–57, 2: 299–300; memo on NSC's 237th meeting, Feb. 17, 1955, Eisenhower Papers (AW), NSC, box 6, Summaries of Discussion.

24. Lawrence Freedman, "The First Two Generations of Nuclear Strategists," in Paret, *Makers of Modern Strategy*, pp. 740–43.

25. Dulles to Hoover, Feb. 25, 1955, Eisenhower Papers (AW), Dulles-Herter, box 3, Dulles 2/55 (1); Dulles to SD, Feb. 25, Minnich minutes of cabinet meeting, March 11, 1955, *FRUS* 1955–57, 2: 307–10, 352–53.

26. Memo on NSC's 242d meeting, Feb. 24, Eisenhower Papers (AW), NSC, box 6, Summaries of Discussion; memo, meeting with Eisenhower, March 6, 1955, Dulles Papers, DDE, White House Memoranda, box 3, Meetings with the President 1955 (4).

27. Memo on NSC's 240th meeting, March 10, 1955, Eisenhower Papers (AW), NSC, box 6, Summaries of Discussion; unsigned memo for the record of NSC's March 10 meeting, Eisenhower Papers (AW), International, box 9, Formosa Visit to CINCPAC 1955 (1).

28. JCS quote from Brands, "Testing Massive Retaliation," p. 141; NA, CINCPAC to CNO (cable 012155Z), Feb. 2, 1955, RG 218, JCS, CCS 381 Formosa (11/8/93) (sec. 19).

29. Cutler memo, March 11, 1955, Eisenhower Library WHO OSANSA, NSC, Briefing Notes, box 17, Taiwan and the Offshore Islands.

30. Brands, "Testing Massive Retaliation," p. 149.

31. Ambrose, *Eisenhower*, p. 239; Stolper, *China*, pp. 89–90.

32. AP article, *San Jose Mercury News*, March 26, 1988, p. 6A. The British were appalled by Eisenhower's and Dulles's public statements about nuclear and conventional weapons. See Eden, "Distinction Between Large and Tactical Nuclear Weapons," April 5, 1955, PRO, CAB 129/74, C(55) 95.

33. Hsieh, *Communist China's Strategy*, pp. 32–33; Trevelyan to FO, Feb. 5, 1955, PRO, FO371/115032/FC1041/282.

34. Eisenhower, *White House Years*, 1: 480; NA, Bohlen to SecState, Oct. 2, 4, 9, Dulles to Bohlen, Oct. 8, 1954, RG 59, 793.00/10-254, 793.00/10-454, 793.00/10-954, 793.00/10-454.

35. Clubb, *China and Russia*, p. 403; NA, SD to all American diplomatic and consular posts, Nov. 23, Bureau of Far Eastern Affairs, briefing paper, Dec. 12, 1954, RG 59, 661.93/11-2354, 793.00/12-1354.

36. Memo on NSC's 234th meeting, Jan. 27, 1955, Eisenhower Papers (AW), NSC, box 6, Summaries of Discussion.

37. FO to Makins, March 12, 1955, PRO, FO371/115042/FC1041/557.

38. Press and radio background news conference, Jan. 24, 1955, Dulles Papers, Princeton, box 96, Quemoy and Matsu, p. B-2; U.S., House Committee on Foreign Affairs, *U.S. Policy in the Far East*, p. 394; editorial note, *FRUS 1955–57*, 2: 202–3.

39. Kirkpatrick, "Situation in the Far East," Feb. 26, 1955, PRO, PREM11/869/PM/IK/55/13.

40. Memo, meeting with Dulles, Robertson, and Yeh, Feb. 10, 1955, Koo Papers, box 195, Notes of Conversation, Offshore Islands.

41. *NYT*, Feb. 17, 1955, p. 1.

42. Harry Schwartz, "Moscow and Peiping: Can West Drive a Wedge?," *NYT*, March 27, 1955, sec. IV, p. 3.

43. Eisenhower to Churchill, Feb. 10, 1955, Eisenhower Papers (AW), International, box 17, President-Churchill, 1/1/55–4/7/55 (4); Eisenhower to Gruenther, Feb. 1, 1955, ibid., Diaries, box 9, Diary 2/55 (1); memo on NSC's 234th meeting, Jan. 27, 1955, ibid., NSC, box 6, Summaries of Discussion.

44. Betts, *Nuclear Blackmail*, p. 59; memo, meeting with the president at 10:45 A.M., March 11, 1955, Dulles Papers, DDE, White House Memoranda, box 3, Meetings with the President 1955 (6).

45. Cutler memo, meeting with Eisenhower, Dulles, and others, March 11, 1955, Eisenhower Library, WHO OSANSA, NSC, Briefing Notes, box 17, Taiwan and Offshore Islands; Goodpaster memo, meeting with Eisenhower, Dulles, and others, March 11, 1955, Eisenhower Papers (AW), International, box 9, Formosa, Visit to CINCPAC 1955 (1).

46. *NYT*, April 22, 1955, p. 1 (emphasis added).

47. Eisenhower and Dulles (phone call), March 28, 1955, Eisenhower Papers (AW), Diaries, box 9, Phone Calls 1/55—7/55 (2); Eisenhower news conference, March 30, 1955, U.S., *Public Papers: Eisenhower*, pp. 368–81; Eisenhower quote from Ambrose, *Eisenhower*, pp. 240–41. Although he did not expect imminent war, Eisenhower commented in his diary on March 26 that members of the cabinet thought hostilities would break out within the month. Entry for March 26, 1955, Eisenhower Papers (AW), Diaries, box 10, Diary 3/55 (1).

48. Pacific Command, "Ma-tsu Island Group," *Weekly Intelligence Digest*, March 11, 1955, pp. 9, 11, CINCPAC/CINCPACFLT Intelligence Estimate, "Chinese Communist and Chinese Nationalist Capabilities and Probable Courses of Action. . . ." Feb. 18, 1955, pp. 10, 12, 15, 17, both in Eisenhower Papers (AW), International, box 9, Formosa, Visit to CINCPAC 1955 (3).

49. LeMay to Twining, March 31, 1955, Twining Papers, box 100, Office File Messages, Ja-Mr 1955.

50. *NYT*, April 1, 1955, p. 1.

51. Hanes memo, meeting of Dulles and others, March 28, 1955, Dulles Papers, DDE, White House Memoranda, box 2, Formosa Strait (1). References to the use of atomic weapons are deleted from the version appearing in *FRUS* 1955–57, 2: 409–15.

52. Dulles memo, conversation with Eisenhower, April 4, 1955, *FRUS* 1955–57, 2: 444–45; Eisenhower to Dulles, April 5, 1955, Dulles Papers, DDE, White House Memoranda, box 2, Position Paper on Offshore Islands 4/55–5/55 (5).

53. Chase to Stump, Stump to Carney, April 8, 1955, *FRUS* 1955–57, 2: 465–66, 471–73; Scott to FO, April 18, 1955, PRO, FO371/115047/FC1041/732G.

54. Bowie to Dulles, April 9, 1955, *FRUS* 1955–57, 2: 473–75.

55. Memo, meeting with Eisenhower, April 17, 1955, Dulles Papers, DDE, White House Memoranda, box 3, Meetings with President 1955 (5).

56. Ibid.; *NYT*, April 18, 1955, p. 1.

57. Memo on the Robertson and Radford mission, April 24–27, 1955, April 29, 1955, Rankin Papers, box 26, Chiang Kai-shek. The Navy immediately began planning the implementation of the blockade. See Carney to Radford, April 22, 1955, *FRUS* 1955–57, 2: 504. Dulles also had his adviser Herman Phleger develop a "legal" rationale for the move. Phleger suggested that a "zone of defense" was acceptable under international law and could be imposed as part of the protection of Taiwan against the "threat of armed aggression." A "blockade," though, he cautioned, was "permissible only in time of war, or when authorized by the UN," and thus the use of the term was to be avoided. Admiral Carney, head of the Navy, advised Eisenhower and Radford that if the Communists challenged the proposed evacuation of Jinmen and Mazu, the U.S. could probably not maintain air superiority over the area solely with the use of conventional weapons. NA, Anderson to Radford (cable), Carney to Radford, both April 22, 1955, RG 218, JCS, Chairman's File, Radford 1953–57, box 7, 091 China 4/55.

58. Rankin memo on Robertson and Radford mission (as cited in preceding note); Offshore Islands chronology, June 3, 1955, Rankin Papers, box 28, Offshore Islands; Robertson to Dulles, April 25, 1955, *FRUS* 1955–57, 2: 510–17; Goodpaster draft memo, meeting of Eisenhower, Robertson, and Radford, May 3, May 7, 1955, Eisenhower Library, WHO OSANSA, Special Assistants, Chronological Subseries, box 1, 5/55 (2).

59. Wang Bingnan, *Zhong-mei*, pp. 44–45.

60. CFR, digest of 5th meeting, March 7, 1956, Groups, vol. 61, Group on Sino-Soviet Relations, 1955–56, p. 1.

61. Nogee and Donaldson, *Soviet Foreign Policy*, p. 112; Hoopes, *Devil and John Foster Dulles*, p. 293; *NYT*, April 15, 1955, p. 1.

62. Memo on NSC's 245th meeting, April 21, 1955, Eisenhower Papers (AW), NSC, box 6, Summaries of Discussion.

63. Schurmann, *Logic*, p. 249.

64. NA, "Reassessment of Chinese Communist Activities in the Taiwan Strait," Aug. 24, 1955, RG 59, SD Office of Intelligence Research.

65. Robert Divine, *Eisenhower and the Cold War*, cited by Ambrose, *Eisenhower*, p. 245.

66. Memo on NSC's 243d meeting, March 31, 1955, Eisenhower Papers (AW), NSC, box 6, Summaries of Discussion.

67. Chiang Kai-shek and Mme Chiang Kai-shek oral history, Sept. 24, 1964, p. 14.

68. Dulles memo, conversation with Eisenhower, April 25, Eisenhower to Dulles, April 26, 1955, *FRUS 1955–57*, 2: 517, 522–23. Also see Hoover to Robertson and Radford, April 22, 1955, and notes, pp. 501–2.

69. The Indonesian ambassador to the U.S. explicitly warned Washington about the dangers of its policy. In April he told a leading State Dept. official that Asian and European diplomats in Washington appeared "completely confused" about the administration's position on Jinmen and Mazu. Urging Washington "to announce clearly that it would resist or that it would not," the ambassador expressed his fear that "in this 'confusion' . . . the Chinese Communists may become reckless and decide to launch an assault on the offshore islands." Young memo, meeting with Notowidigdo, April 5, 1955, *FRUS 1955–57*, 2: 451–52.

70. Lewis and Xue, *China Builds the Bomb*, pp. 35–39.

71. Dulles, draft statement, April 8, 1955, *FRUS 1955–57*, 2: 455–63.

72. James Shepley, "How Dulles Averted War," *Life*, Jan. 16, 1956, pp. 70–80. There is considerable evidence to show that Beijing's actions had been limited and restrained during the crisis. Much of this information had been available to American officials in 1955. See Stolper, *Offshore Islands*, pp. 86–87; Lewis and Xue, *China Builds the Bomb*, pp. 22–24; and He Di, "Evolution of the PRC's Policy."

Chapter Five

1. Acheson to Johnson, June 19, 1957, Acheson Papers, DDE, box 17, folder 217; Gaddis, *Strategies of Containment*, p. 194.

2. NIE-43-54, "Probable Developments in Taiwan Through Mid-1965," Sept. 14, 1954, *FRUS 1952–54*, 14: 627–45.

3. *NYT*, Jan. 20, 1955, pp. 1, 3. In mid-1956 the editor of the *NYT* predicted that European pressures would force the U.S. to alter its relations with China after the November election. Sulzberger, *Giants*, p. 327.

4. Dulles draft statement, Jan. 8, Dulles to Debevoise, Jan. 13, top secret memo, May 18, Dulles to Acheson, Nov. 30, 1950, all in Dulles Papers, Princeton, box 47, PRC 1950; NA, Dulles to Webb, May 19, 1950, RG 59, OCA, box 17, Policy Toward China 1950, 306.001; NA,

Dulles memo on Formosa, Oct. 25, 1950, RG 59, OCA, box 18, Formosa 8/50–12/50 (28).

5. Macmillan memo, June 20, Makins to FO, Jan. 29, 1955, PRO, FO371/115054/FC1041/943, FO371/115029/FC1041/185.

6. Memo, meeting with advisers on June 7, 1953, memo, meeting with Eisenhower, Aug. 17, 1954, Dulles Papers, DDE, Subjects, box 1, Bermuda Conference Foreign Ministers Meeting, White House Memoranda, box 1, Meetings with President 1954 (1).

7. Dulles memo, Sept. 12, 1954, *FRUS* 1952–54, 14: 611–13 (emphasis in original). Also see Bowie memo, meeting of Dulles, Eden, and others, Sept. 29, 1954, pp. 667–69.

8. McConaughy memo, meeting of Chiang and others, Oct. 13, Goodpaster memo, meeting of Eisenhower, Yeh, and others, Dec. 20, 1954, ibid., pp. 728–53, 1040–1041.

9. Memo, meeting with Chiang and Dulles, Sept. 9, 1954, Rankin Papers, box 23, Chiang Kai-shek 1954; memos, meeting with Dulles and Yeh, Feb. 10, meeting with Robertson, July 28, 1955, Koo Papers, box 195, Notes of Conversation, Offshore Islands.

10. Dulles to Hoover, March 4, 1955, Eisenhower Papers (AW), International, box 9, Formosa 1952–57 (4); memo on NSC's 216th meeting, Oct. 6, 1954, *FRUS* 1952–54, 14: 700; memo on NSC's 231st meeting, Jan. 13, 1955, Eisenhower Papers (AW), NSC, box 6, Summaries of Discussion; cabinet meeting, Oct. 22, 1954, PRO, C.C. (54) 69th Conclusions, pp. 3, 4, CAB 128/27.

11. Wilson to Cutler, Oct. 5, 1954, memo on NSC's 216th meeting, Oct. 6, 1954, *FRUS* 1952–54, 14: 687–701.

12. Memo on NSC's 242d meeting, March 24, 1955, Eisenhower Papers (AW), NSC, box 6, Summaries of Discussion.

13. Memo, meeting with Eisenhower, April 17, 1955, Dulles Papers, DDE, White House Memoranda, box 3, Meetings with President 1955 (5); Goodpaster memo, meeting of Eisenhower and Wilson, July 9, 1955, Eisenhower Papers (AW), Whitman Diary, box 5, ACW Diary 7/55 (5).

14. Operations Coordinating Board, "Progress Report on U.S. Objectives and Courses of Action with Respect to Formosa and the Chinese National Government," July 16, 1954, "Progress Report," Feb. 18, 1955, Eisenhower Library, WHO OSANSA, NSC, Policy Papers, box 4, NSC 146/2, Formosa and Chinese Nationalist Government (1); R. C. memo, Aug. 8, 1957, ibid., Special Assistants, Chronological Subseries, box 5, 8/57 (2).

15. Dulles, summary of remarks at Canadian cabinet meeting, March 18, 1955, Eisenhower Papers (AW), Dulles-Herter, box 4, Dulles 3/55; memo, Far East presentation, May 10, 1955, Dulles Papers,

Princeton, box 96, NATO Ministerial Meeting Paris 5/6/55–5/13/55; Eisenhower to Churchill, March 29, 1955, Eisenhower Papers (AW), International, box 17, President-Churchill 1/1/55–4/7/55 (3). Also see Walter LaFeber, *America*, p. 177.

16. NIE 11-3-55, "Soviet Capabilities and Probable Soviet Courses of Action Through 1960, May 17, 1955, Eisenhower Library, WHO OSANSA, NSC, Subjects, box 11, pp. 1–6, 9.

17. Rostow to Rockefeller, June 10, 1955, Eisenhower Papers, WHCF Confidential File, Subjects, box 63, Russia (6).

18. Quantico Report, annex.

19. Ibid., tab 4, "Straining the Sino-Soviet Alliance," pp. 1–3, and annex to tab 4, "Chinese Political Behavior."

20. Ibid., annex to tab 4, "Chinese Political Behavior." Also see Gittings, *World and China*, p. 201; and Gittings, "Review," p. 479.

21. Jackson to Dulles, June 13, Dulles to Jackson, July 5, Eisenhower to Jackson, June 14, 1955, Eisenhower Library, Jackson Papers, General File, box 40, Dulles, box 41, Eisenhower—Correspondence through 1965 (1).

22. Nelson Rockefeller, memo on psychological strategy at Geneva—no.10, July 11, 1955, Eisenhower Papers (AW), International Meetings, box 2, Geneva Conference 7/18/55–7/23/55 [2] (1).

23. *NYT*, July 5, 1955, p. 1.

24. Memos on conversations, Eisenhower and Zhukov, July 20, July 23, 1955, Eisenhower Papers, General Correspondence and Memoranda, box 3, Strictly Confidential U-Z (2). In his memoirs Eisenhower refers to a talk with Zhukov, but does not mention the lengthy discussions about China (*White House Years*, 1: 524–25). Eisenhower generally neglects discussing U.S. interest in disrupting the Sino-Soviet relationship in his memoirs, even though that was a prominent goal of his administration. The omission is consistent with the U.S. effort in the early 1960's to avoid saying anything that could hinder the emergence of the Sino-Soviet split. Confirmation that the U.S. had sought early accords with the Soviets about China would have been incendiary and sustained China's accusation that the USSR capitulated to U.S. imperialism. Indeed, in light of the widespread interest in the Sino-Soviet split in the 1960's, Eisenhower's memoirs are conspicuously short of references to the Sino-Soviet relationship, a fact that helped perpetuate the belief that his administration was oblivious to the possibilities of encouraging a Communist split. His neglect of the topic actually may indicate the opposite.

It is not yet clear how vigorously the U.S. pursued the idea of a two-China policy with the Soviets, but talk of a U.S.-Soviet deal greatly disturbed the Nationalists. In October 1955 Ambassador Koo asked

Dulles about a rumor that Molotov was considering recognizing the Taiwan regime if Washington would recognize Communist China. Dulles, to the undoubted shock of the Nationalist envoy, said that idea sounded interesting (memo, meeting with Dulles, Oct. 4, 1955, Koo Papers, box 195).

25. Memos on conversations, Eisenhower and Zhukov, July 20, July 23, 1955 (as cited in note 24).

26. Macmillan, *Tides of Fortune*, pp. 619, 622; Eden, notes of talk with Marshal Bulganin and Khrushchev in Geneva on July 19, 1955, PRO, FO371/114974/F1071/13.

27. Gittings, *World and China*, pp. 198–201; digest of 1st meeting, Oct. 24, 1966, Study Group on Sino-Soviet Relations 1955–56, CFR, Groups, 41: 5; N. Khrushchev, *Khrushchev Remembers* (1970), pp. 466–67. Also see memo, meeting with Adenauer, Nov. 21, 1961, Acheson Papers, HST, box 85, SD 10/61–12/61.

28. Memo on NSC's 256th meeting, July 28, 1955, Eisenhower Papers (AW), NSC, box 7, Summaries of Discussion.

29. Dulles memo, "Estimate of Prospect of Soviet Union Achieving Its Goals," July 6, 1955, Eisenhower Papers (AW), International Meetings, box 1, Geneva Conference 7/18/55–7/23/55 (1); "Geneva Meetings with Chinese Communists," Aug. 30, 1955, Dulles Papers, DDE, Subjects, box 10, Wang-Johnson Talks, Prisoners of War 1955 (1).

30. Memo on Geneva meeting with Chinese Communists, Aug. 30, memo, meeting with Eisenhower, Aug. 5, 1955, Dulles Papers, DDE, Subjects, box 10, Wang-Johnson Talks, Prisoners of War 1955 (1), White House Memoranda, box 3, Meetings with President 1955 (3); U. Alexis Johnson, *Right Hand*, p. 239.

31. "Ambassadorial Talks at Geneva with Chinese Communists," *DSB*, Jan. 30, 1956, pp. 164–67; Gittings, *World and China*, p. 204. For more on the bilateral talks, see U. Alexis Johnson, *Right Hand*, pp. 228–65; Young, *Negotiating*; and Wang Bingnan, *Zhong-mei*, pp. 58–60.

32. *NYT*, Feb. 29, 1956, p. 4.

33. *Historical Experience*, p. 16 (the original Chinese version was first published on April 5, 1956); Mao Tsetung, "Speech at the Second Plenary Session of the Eighth Central Committee of the Communist Party of China," Nov. 15, 1956, in *Selected Works*, 5: 341–42.

34. Memo on NSC's 280th meeting, March 22, 1956, Eisenhower Papers (AW), NSC, box 7, Summaries of Discussion.

35. Dulles news conferences, April 3, July 11, Dulles speech at AP meeting, April 23, *DSB*, April 16, 1956, pp. 637–38, July 23, 1956, pp. 145–50, April 30, 1956, pp. 707–8; U.S., *Public Papers: Eisenhower*, pp. 417, 423.

36. Allen Dulles, "Soviet Challenges to U.S. Foreign Policy," speech at the annual World Affairs Conference, April 13, 1956, Knowland Papers, box 282, Secretary of State 1954–56.

37. Goodpaster memo, meeting of Eisenhower, Hoover, Allen Dulles, and others, May 28, 1956, Eisenhower Papers (AW), Diaries, box 15, Goodpaster 5/56; Dulles to Hoover, Dec. 18, 1956, Dulles Papers, DDE, White House Memoranda, box 4, Meetings with President 8/56–12/56 (2); Eisenhower, *White House Years*, 1: 530.

38. Dulles, speech at Kiwanis convention, June 21, *DSB*, July 2, 1956, p. 5; meeting with Humphrey and Wilson on April 19, 1956, Dulles Papers, DDE, General Correspondence and Memorandums, box 1, Memos of Conversation—General, E–I (3).

39. Chiang to Eisenhower, April 16, Eisenhower to Chiang, May 17, 1956, Eisenhower Library, WHO Office of the Staff Secretary, Subjects, State Department, box 1, 4/56–6/56 (3); report, Sept. 22, 1957, Eisenhower Library, WHO OSANSA, Special Assistants, Chronological Subseries, 9/57 (3).

40. Schurmann, *Logic*, pp. 271–72; Johnson to SD, May 15, 1957, *FRUS* 1955–57, 3: 522–23; Dulles, speech at international convention of Lions International, June 28, 1957, "Our Policies Toward Communism in China," pp. 7–9, Dulles, speech at CFR dinner, "Concerning the Conduct of Foreign Relations," p. 28, June 7, 1957, Dulles Papers, Princeton, box 122. Also see Dulles to Goodpaster, Feb. 24, 1957, Eisenhower Papers (AW), Administration, box 13, Allen Dulles (3).

41. See Cohen, *New Frontiers*, pp. 151–55; Kalicki, *Pattern*, pp. 159–67; Sutter, *China-Watch*, pp. 4–7, 49–62; Allen Whiting, "Mao, China and the Cold War," in Nagai and Iriye, *Origins*, pp. 252–76; and Barnett, *China and the Major Powers*, pp. 186–89.

42. See, for example, Hoopes, *Devil and John Foster Dulles*; and F. Dulles, *American Policy*, pp. 165–66.

43. Memo, meeting with Eisenhower, Oct. 11, 1956, Dulles Papers, DDE, White House Memoranda, box 4, Meetings with President 8/56–12/56 (4); Dulles to Eisenhower, Nov. 7, 1955, Eisenhower Papers (AW), Dulles-Herter, box 5, Dulles 11/55 (2); Phleger to James McCargar, March 18, 1966, Phleger personal papers.

44. Rushkoff, "Eisenhower"; Divine, *Eisenhower and the Cold War*, pp. 33–70; Ambrose, *Eisenhower*, chaps. 9–11. Townsend Hoopes says that by 1957 Eisenhower's dislike of Beijing may have even exceeded Dulles's; *Devil and John Foster Dulles*, pp. 417, 423.

45. Makins to FO, Aug. 6, 1955, FO371/115009/FC10345/57; Dulles to Blum, May 28, 1965, Allen Dulles Papers, box 139, PRC 1965; Hoopes, *Devil and John Foster Dulles*, p. 423.

46. Memo, meeting with Eisenhower, Aug. 5, 1955, Dulles Papers,

DDE, White House Memoranda, box 3, Meetings with President 1955 (3).

47. Stevenson to Bowles, Aug. 10, 1956, Bowles Papers, box 157, folder 627; Acheson to Johnson, June 19, 1957, Acheson Papers, Yale, box 17, folder 215; Kusnitz, *Public Opinion*, pp. 68–78.

48. Youde to Mayall, July 14, 1956, PRO, FO371/120896/FC10345/88; speech by Henry Ford II, Jan. 28, 1957, PRO, FO371/127239/FC1071/5/; Kusnitz, *Public Opinion*, pp. 76–77.

49. American Assembly, *United States and the Far East*, p. 223.

50. "Latest Opinion Trends on Big Four Meeting," July 1, 1955, Eisenhower Papers, WHCF, Confidential File, Subjects, box 29, Geneva Conference 7/55 (3).

51. U.S., Dept. of Defense, *United States–Vietnam*, book 7, sec. V.B-10.

52. Ibid., book 1, sec. IV.A.3, pp. 23–39; Herring, *America's Longest War*, pp. 43–72.

53. NSC 5612/1, "U.S. Policy in Mainland Southeast Asia," Sept. 5, 1956, U.S., Dept. of Defense, *United States–Vietnam*, book 10, pp. 1082–1095, and sec. IV.A.4, pp. 11–12.

54. Transcript of background conference at San Francisco Press and Union League Club, June 28, 1957, Dulles Papers, Princeton, box 118, Japan and the Girard Case 1957, pp. 8–10. Concern for the bordering countries was also the reason Dulles gave to justify his refusal to grant American newsmen permission to travel to China in 1957. Dulles, speech at the CFR, "Concerning the Conduct of Foreign Relations," June 7, 1957, ibid., box 122, pp. 28–29.

55. Transcript of tape no. 2 of speech to Harvard Business School Residency Program, March 31–April 2, 1965, Allen Dulles Papers, box 239, Speeches, Discussions Re CIA, Communism, etc., p. 49.

56. CIA, "Communist China's Role in Non-Communist Asia," Dec. 3, 1957, p. 3, in Kesaris, *CIA Research Reports*, reel 1; Eisenhower to Wallace, June 8, 1957, Eisenhower Papers (AW), Diaries, box 24, June 1957 Misc. (2); Kahin, *Intervention*, p. 92.

57. Herring, *America's Longest War*, p. 39.

58. Goodpaster oral history, Jan. 1966, p. 7; Bowie oral history, Aug. 1964, pp. 11–12; Dulles, speech at CFR, June 7, 1957, p. 15 (as cited in note 54).

59. Bowie oral history, pp. 18–20; Dulles, speech at International Convention of Lions International, "Our Policies Toward Communism in China," June 28, news conference of July 2, 1947, Dulles Papers, Princeton, box 122.

60. News conference of July 2, and background news conference,

June 28, 1957, Dulles Papers, Princeton, box 122, speech, "Our Policies. . . ," box 118, Japan and the Girard Case 1957.

61. Sinclair Weeks to Joseph M. Dodge, July 21, and attachment, "Review of Economic Defense Policy and Program," Jan. 20, 1955, Eisenhower Library, U.S. Council on Foreign Economic Policy Records, Policy Papers, box 1, CFEP 501 (Action Papers 1955) (3); "Report on Foreign Economic Policy Discussions Between U.S. Officials in Europe and Clarence B. Randall and Associates," Sept. 1956, and brief notes for Bermuda meeting, March 21–23, 1957, "East-West Trade," n.d., Eisenhower Papers, WHCF, Confidential File, Subjects, box 18, Council on Foreign Economic Policy (2), and box 9, Bermuda Meeting—March 21–23, Folder for President (4).

62. See, for example, F. Dulles, *American Policy*, p. 136; Hinton, *Bear at the Gate*, p. 85; and Ulam, *History*, p. 239.

63. Mao Tsetung, "Talks at a Conference of Secretaries of Provincial, Municipal and Autonomous Region Party Committees," Jan. 1957, in *Selected Works*, 5: 362–64.

64. Quoted in editor's note, *FRUS* 1952–54, 14: 521–22; Minnich handwritten notes of cabinet meetings, C-18(2) Nov. 5, 1954, Eisenhower Library, WHO, Office of Staff Secretary, Cabinets, box 2, pp. 45–47; Eisenhower, *White House Years*, 2: 369.

65. Anderson oral history, DDE, Dec. 1969, p. 101.

66. For a study of popular attitudes toward China and India in the mid-1950's, see Isaacs, *Scratches on Our Minds*; on racism in American foreign policy, see Hunt, *Ideology and American Foreign Policy*.

67. Divine, *Eisenhower*, p. 33; transcript of Eisenhower remarks to Menon, June 14, 1955, Eisenhower Papers (AW), Whitman Diary, box 6, ACW Diary 6/55 (4).

68. Eisenhower to Churchill, March 29, memo on NSC's 237th meeting, Feb. 17, 1955, Eisenhower Papers (AW), International, box 17, President-Churchill 1/1/55–4/7/55 (3), NSC, box 6, Summaries of Discussion. Eisenhower expressed the same view to British Lt. Gen. Sir Archibald Nye; memo of conversation, May 5, 1955, ibid., Whitman Diary, box 5, ACW Diary 6/55 (7). Also see Ambrose, *Eisenhower*, p. 102.

69. F. Dulles, *American Policy*, p. 133; E. Dulles, *John Foster Dulles*; memo, meeting with Dulles, Nov. 29, 1951, Koo Papers, box 184, Notes of Conversation 1951.

70. Memo on NSC's 242d meeting, March 24, 1955, Eisenhower Papers (AW), NSC, box 6, Summaries of Discussion.

71. Quantico Report, annex to tab 4, "Chinese Political Behavior."

72. Eisenhower, *White House Years*, 2: 369; Dulles, summary of

remarks, March 18, 1955, Eisenhower Papers (AW), Dulles-Herter, box 4, Dulles 3/55.

Chapter Six

1. Providence *Journal*, Jan. 3, 1954, p. 1; *U.S. News and World Report*, Jan. 29, 1954, pp. 66–69; Dean, "U.S. Foreign Policy and Formosa," pp. 360–75; CFR, digest of meeting with Arthur H. Dean, March 15, 1955, Meetings, 20: tab B, p. 3.

2. CFR, list of members, Study Group on Sino-Soviet Relations, 1955–56, Groups, 61.

3. CFR, digest of 1st meeting, Oct. 24, 1955, ibid., pp. 1–3. Boorman's essay was revised on the basis of the discussion in the study group and published as the lead essay in Boorman et al., *Moscow-Peking Axis*, pp. 1–53.

4. CFR, digest of the 1st meeting, Oct. 24, 1955, Study Group on Sino-Soviet Relations, 1955–56, Groups, 61: 8–11.

5. CFR, digest of the 5th meeting, March 7, 1956, ibid., pp. 1–13; Arthur H. Dean, "Foreword," in Boorman et al., *Moscow-Peking Axis*, p. vii.

6. The final reports of the project were published collectively as *Prospect for America*.

7. SSP, minutes of 3d meeting, Subpanel I, Jan. 8, 1957, pp. 14–16, box 1, Meetings 3 and 4.

8. Ibid., pp. 16–17.

9. Ibid., p. 18.

10. Ibid., pp. 18–19. Also see SSP, minutes of 6th meeting, Subpanel I, April 26, 1957, box 1, Meetings 5–6, p. 16, and "General Objectives," April 26, 1957, box 1, Subpanel I Meetings—Issues 1957, pp. 8–10.

11. SSP, minutes of 3d meeting of Overall Panel, May 6–8, 1957; box 19, Overall Panel—Meeting 3, pp. 48–50, 52, 62, 64–65.

12. All SSP: outline of report of Subpanel I, March 12, 1957, box 1, Subpanel I Meetings—Issues 1957; report outline, May 5, 1957, ibid., box 4, Subpanel I—Report Drafts: Cooke, notes of Sub-Subgroup I, Far East, etc., May 10, 1957, box 4; 2d draft: "U.S. International Objectives and Strategy," July 12, 1957, Box 4, Subpanel I—Report Drafts; draft, "Foreign Policy: The Mid-Century Challenge," July 27, 1959, box 4, Subpanel I—Report Drafts: Heckscher; comments of Dean Rusk, Sept. 17, 1959, pp. 1–4, box 19, Overall Panel—Meeting 10; Heckscher to Rusk, Sept. 28, 1959, box 1, Subpanel I—Membership, Rusk 1956–61.

13. *Prospect for America*, pp. 36–48.

14. See Gittings, *World and China*, pp. 217–19; Hinton, *Peking-Washington*; Zagoria, *Sino-Soviet Conflict*, pp. 200–217; Hsieh, *Communist China's Strategy*, pp. 165–72; and Ulam, *Expansion*, pp. 613, 628–29.

15. Lewis and Xue, *China Builds the Bomb*, pp. 60–72; He Di, "Evolution of the PRC's Policy," pp. 21–30; Operations Coordinating Board, "Report on U.S. Policy Toward Taiwan and the Government of the Republic of China," April 16, 1958, Eisenhower Library, WHO OSANSA, NSC, Policy Papers, box 23, NSC 5723—Policy Toward Taiwan and ROC.

16. NA, CINCPAC to Cmdr. U.S. Taiwan Defense Command, June 29, 1956, RG 218, JCS, Geographic File 1957, CCS 381 Formosa (11-8-48), sec. 33.

17. Eisenhower, *White House Years*, 2: 292–93; memo, meeting with Eisenhower, Aug. 12, 1958, Dulles Papers, DDE, White House Memoranda, box 7, Meetings with President 7/1/58–12/31/58 (8); U.S., *Air Operations*, pp. 13–14.

18. Goodpaster to Aurand, Aug. 31, 1958, Eisenhower Papers (AW), International, box 10, Formosa [1958] (3).

19. Goodpaster memo, meeting of Eisenhower and others on Aug. 25, 1958, ibid.; Ambrose, *Eisenhower*, p. 482; U.S., *Air Operations*, p. 24; Drumwright to SecState, Aug. 26, 1958, Eisenhower Library, WHO, Office of Staff Secretary, Subjects, SD, box 3, 5/58–8/58 (6).

20. Dulles to Macmillan, Sept. 4, 1958, Eisenhower Papers (AW), International, box 10, Formosa [1958] (2).

21. Eisenhower, *White House Years*, 2: 295; Goodpaster memo as cited in note 19.

22. Memo, meeting with Eisenhower, Sept. 23, Greene to Eisenhower, Sept. 29, 1958, Dulles Papers, DDE, White House Memoranda, box 7, Meetings with President 7/1/58–12/31/58, respectively, (6) and (5).

23. Wang Bingnan, *Zhong-mei*, p. 69.

24. Lewis and Xue, *China Builds the Bomb*, pp. 69–72; Joseph C. Harsch, "Sino-Soviet Split," *Christian Science Monitor*, Feb. 25, 1988, p. 14.

25. Historians presenting the Soviet view single out 1958 as the year differences over foreign policy began to separate China and the Soviet Union. One major account accuses the "Mao group" of deliberately provoking the Strait crisis to sabotage the Soviet Union's efforts to achieve détente with the West. See Borisov and Koloskov, *Soviet-Chinese Relations*, pp. 152–54. A similar view is given in Sergeichuk,

Through Russian Eyes, p. 79. The Chinese likewise cite 1958 as a turning point in their relations with Moscow. In one of the CCP's early polemics with the CPSU, it accused the Soviets of unfaithful support during the 1958 Jinmen crisis. "Statement by the Spokesmen of the Chinese Government, September 1, 1963," *Peking Review*, Sept. 6, 1963, p. 13. American specialists are divided on the point. Among those who argue that China and the Soviet Union had serious differences over the Jinmen crisis are Barnett, "1958 Quemoy Crisis"; Hsieh, *Communist China's Strategy*, pp. 121–30; Kalicki, *Pattern*, pp. 184–202; Stolper, *China*, pp. 114–30; Thomas, "Soviet Behavior"; Young, *Negotiating*, pp. 138–98; and Zagoria, *Sino-Soviet Conflict*, pp. 206–21. But authors like Morton H. Halperin and Tang Tsou, "The 1958 Quemoy Crisis," in Halperin, *Sino-Soviet Relations*, pp. 265–303, and Segal, *Defending China*, pp. 129–30, strongly disagree.

26. Eisenhower, *White House Years*, 2: 293.

27. Goodpaster, synopsis of intelligence and SD items reported to the president, Aug. 8, 15, 19, Eisenhower Papers (AW), Diaries, box 35, Goodpaster Briefings 8/58; Ulam, *Rivals*, p. 292 (Ulam calls the reversal of the Soviet decision the "first clear cut case of a Soviet political move being reversed at the behest of China"); Bundy to author, Aug. 6, 1985 (emphasis added). For more on the Chinese view of the Khrushchev visit to China, see Nie Rongzhen, *Huiyilu*, p. 804.

28. *Khrushchev Remembers: The Last Testament*, pp. 261–63.

29. Goodpaster memo, meeting of Eisenhower and others, Aug. 29, 1958, Eisenhower Papers (AW), International, box 10, Formosa [1958] (3).

30. U.S., *Air Operations*, pp. 20–27; Eisenhower, *White House Years*, 2: 297.

31. Goodpaster memo, meeting of Eisenhower, Radford et al., May 24, 1956, Eisenhower Papers (AW), Diaries, box 15, Goodpaster 5/65.

32. JCS to CINCPAC, [Sept. 3, 1958?], ibid., International, box 10, Formosa [1958] (3); conversation with Twining, Sept. 2, 1958, Dulles Papers, DDE, Telephone Calls, box 9, Telephone Conversations—General 8/1/58–10/31/58 (4).

33. U.S., *Air Operations*, pp. 27–30; Ambrose, *Eisenhower*, pp. 482–83. The services were divided on the question, with the Army favoring a greater reliance on conventional weaponry than the Navy and Air Force, both of which strongly advocated the early use of nuclear weapons. Memo on JCS meeting, Sept. 2, 1958, Eisenhower Papers (AW), International, Formosa [1958] (2).

34. U.S., *Air Operations*, pp. 28–30, 34–36.

35. Cited in Whiting, "New Light on Mao."

36. Dulles quote from Young, *Negotiating*, pp. 147–48.

37. Barnett, "1958 Quemoy Crisis"; *NYT*, Feb. 22, 1988, p. 1. The Chinese government officially denied Gromyko's allegation. *Ta Kung Pao*, March 3–9, 1988 (no. 1123), p. 3.

38. Goodpaster memo, meeting of Eisenhower and Dulles, Sept. 6, 1958, Eisenhower Papers (AW), International, box 10, Formosa [1958] (2); NA, Herter to Beam, Sept. 19, 1958, RG 59, 611.93/9—1958.

39. Memo, meeting with Eisenhower, Aug. 12, 1958, Dulles Papers, DDE, White House Memoranda, box 7, Meetings with President 7/1/58–12/31/58 (8).

40. Jacobson and Stein, *Diplomats*, p. 80.

41. Zagoria, *Sino-Soviet Split*, pp. 200–205; Hsieh, *Communist China's Strategy*, pp. 116–23.

42. Divine, *Blowing on the Wind*, pp. 228–29.

43. Young, *Negotiating*, pp. 154–55.

44. Telephone call to Eisenhower, Sept. 8, 1958, Dulles Papers, DDE, Telephone Calls, box 13, Telephone Conversations—White House 8/1/58–12/5/58 (3); Eisenhower, *White House Years*, 2: 301, n. 6; Goodpaster to Dulles, Sept. 11, memo, meeting with Eisenhower, Sept. 11, 1958, both in Dulles Papers, DDE, White House Memoranda, respectively, boxes 6 and 7, Meetings with President, 7/1/58–12/31/58 (6).

45. Howe, *Multicrises*, pp. 223, 252.

46. *DSB*, Nov. 3, 1958, p. 696.

47. *DSB*, Nov. 10, 1958, p. 724.

48. U.S., *Air Operations*, pp. 41–43.

49. Telephone call, Dulles to Eisenhower, Sept. 8, 1958 (as cited in note 44); Goodpaster memo, meeting of Eisenhower and McElroy, Sept. 11, 1958, Eisenhower Papers (AW), Diaries, box 36, Staff Notes 9/58.

50. Telephone call, Max Krebs and Mr. Greene, Sept. 16, 1958, Dulles Papers, DDE, Telephone Calls, box 9, Telephone Conversations—General 8/1/58–10/31/58 (3); Eisenhower, *White House Years*, 2: 303; U.S., *Air Operations*, pp. 41–43; Stolper, *China*, p. 118.

51. NA, Office of Intelligence and Research, "Peiping's Present Outlook on the Taiwan Strait Situation," report no. 7799, Sept. 18, 1958, General Records of SD.

52. *DSB*, Sept. 29, 1958, p. 482; Eisenhower to Green, Oct. 2, 1958, quoted in Howe, *Multicrises*, pp. 254–55. Also see Dulles speech at meeting of the Far East–America Council of Commerce and Industry, Sept. 25, 1958, *DSB*, Oct. 13, 1958, p. 566.

53. Transcript of background conference for the press, Sept. 17,

1958, Dulles Papers, Princeton, box 127, Chiang Kai-shek 1958, pp. 11–15. Dulles was similarly speculative in a talk during the crisis with Andrew H. Berding, who worked with him in State. Berding, *Dulles on Diplomacy*, p. 64.

54. Young, *Negotiating*, pp. 173–74.

55. Hoopes, *Devil and John Foster Dulles*, pp. 452–53; Young, *Negotiating*, pp. 188–89; Zagoria, *Sino-Soviet Split*, pp. 215–17.

56. Young, *Negotiating*, pp. 193–94; Stolper, *China*, p. 118.

57. Memo to Eisenhower, Sept. 27, 1958, Dulles Papers, DDE, White House Memoranda, box 6, White House—General Correspondence 1958 (2); telephone call, Dulles and Eisenhower, Sept. 26, 1958, Eisenhower Papers (AW), Diaries, box 36, Telephone Calls.

58. "Offshore Islands Chronology," n.d., Kennedy Papers, POF, Box 113a, China, Security 1962–63.

59. Goodpaster memo, meeting of Eisenhower and Twining, Sept. 30, 1958, Eisenhower Papers (AW), Diaries, box 36, Staff Notes 9/58; Eisenhower to Dulles, Oct. 7, 1958, ibid., Dulles-Herter, box 8, Dulles 10/58; telephone call, Eisenhower and Twining, Oct. 9, 1958, Twining Papers, Telephone Log, box 6, Daily Log Oc 1958; Goodpaster memo, meeting of Eisenhower and Twining, Oct. 13, 1958, Eisenhower Library, WHO, Office of the Staff Secretary, Subjects, Dept. of Defense, box 4, JCS (5) 9/58–1/59.

60. Memo, conversation with Eisenhower, Oct. 6, 1958, Herter Papers, box 9, Misc. Memos 1958 (1); Dulles to Eisenhower, Oct. 23, 1958, Eisenhower Papers (AW), Dulles-Herter, box 8, Dulles 10/58; memo, meeting with Eisenhower, Oct. 24, 1958, Dulles Papers, DDE, White House Memoranda, box 7, Meetings with President 7/1/58–12/31/58 (4).

61. Macomber memo, meeting of Dulles and Green, Oct. 12, 1958, Dulles Papers, DDE, General Correspondence and Memos, box 1, Memos of Conversations—General E–I (1).

62. Allen Dulles, "An Intelligence Review of the Communist Bloc," Oct. 28, 1958, Allen Dulles Papers, box 229, pp. 1–4; CFR, digest of meeting, Oct. 28, 1958, Meetings, 29: 1.

63. Allen Dulles, "An Intelligence Review" (as cited in preceding note), pp. 3–4.

64. Ibid., pp. 13–14.

65. Ibid., p. 15.

66. CFR, digest of meeting, Oct. 28, 1958, Meetings, 29: 4.

67. Bundy to author, Aug. 6, 1985.

68. Goodpaster memo, meeting of Eisenhower, Foster, and others, Nov. 5, 1958, Eisenhower Papers (AW), Diaries, box 37, Staff Notes 11/58, p. 3.

69. Gray to Herter, Jan. 14, 1959, Eisenhower Library, WHO OSANSA, Special Assistants, Chronological Subseries, box 6, 1/59.

70. CFR, digest of 7th Meeting, March 18, 1959, Study Group on China and U.S. Policy in Asia, 1958–59, Groups, vols. 78–79. Liberals outside the administration were pessimistic about dividing the Sino-Soviet alliance. Edmund Clubb told a CFR study group in January 1959 that relations between China and the Soviet Union were "at their closest at the present" (digest of 5th meeting, Jan. 14, 1959, 78–79: 7). Doak Barnett argued that the Sino-Soviet alliance was perhaps stronger than "it was in Stalin's lifetime" and criticized the view "that the best way to promote increased tensions or frictions within the Peking-Moscow axis is to isolate the Chinese Communist regime as much as possible from the outside world, forcing it into a position of maximum dependence on Moscow." "It is difficult to say," Barnett wrote in *Communist China and Asia* (1960), p. 382, "that this kind of pressure has brought significant results over the past decade." Edwin Martin, chief of the OCA under the diehard Walter Robertson, also minimized the importance of trying to encourage divisions and the effectiveness of U.S. efforts to produce discord between the two powers (CFR, digest of 5th meeting, 78–79: 7).

Chapter Seven

EPIGRAPH: McGeorge Bundy summarizing the conclusion of a CIA report for President Kennedy, Weekend Reading, July 19, 1963, Kennedy Papers, NSF, box 318, Index of Weekend Papers 7/63–11/63.

1. Medvedev, *China and the Superpowers*, pp. 27–28.

2. On Soviet aid to the Chinese nuclear weapons program, see Lewis and Xue, *China Builds the Bomb*, pp. 35–72.

3. Khrushchev, *Khrushchev Remembers* (1970), p. 466.

4. Chinese source cited in Lewis and Xue, *China Builds the Bomb*, p. 265, n. 103.

5. Mori, "Sino-Soviet Relations."

6. Cited in Lewis and Xue, *China Builds the Bomb*, p. 7.

7. On the evolution of Soviet thinking about nuclear weapons, see Holloway, *Soviet Union and the Arms Race*, pp. 29–64.

8. Zagoria testimony, Nov. 19, 1975, U.S., House Subcommittee on Future Foreign Policy, *Great Power Triangle*, part I, p. 62.

9. Makins to FO, Feb. 7, 1955, PRO, FO371/115033/FC1041/307.

10. Embassy, Moscow, to SecState, Dec. 4, 1958, Kennedy Papers, POF, box 126, USSR Vienna Meeting—Background Telegrams; Goodpaster briefings, Dec. 8, 17, 1958, Eisenhower Papers (AW), Diaries, box 37, Goodpaster 12/58.

11. "Highlights of Dulles-Mikoyan Conversation," Jan. 16, notes of Jan. 17, 1959, Merchant Papers, box 5, Mikoyan 1959 Visit to Washington 1/16–1/17; CFR, digest of meeting with Mikoyan, Jan. 15, 1959, Meetings, 31: 3–4; Cousins, *Improbable Triumvirate*, p. 163.

12. Ambrose, *Eisenhower*, pp. 541–44; Ulam, *Expansion*, pp. 626, 628–29; Ulam, *Rivals*, pp. 305–6; Eisenhower, *White House Years*, 2: 445. President Kennedy was advised on the eve of his summit with Khrushchev in 1961 that the subject of China had been discussed "in considerable detail" by the Soviet leader and Eisenhower at Camp David in 1959. Position Papers: "Communist China," May 25, 1961, Kennedy Papers, POF, box 126, USSR–Vienna Meeting—Background Documents 1956–61 (G2), p. 3.

13. "U.S. Objectives in Khrushchev Visit and Suggested Tactics for Conversation with Him," n.d., "Major Themes of Khrushchev's Public and Private Statements and U.S. Counter-Arguments," Sept. 8, 1958, Eisenhower Papers (AW), International, box 48, Khrushchev Visit 9/59 (1). On Ambassador Llewellyn Thompson's speculation that Khrushchev might even propose a secret deal against China, see Sulzberger, *Last of the Giants*, pp. 571–72.

14. Wallace to Eisenhower, Aug. 10, Eisenhower to Wallace, Aug. 15, 1959, Wallace Papers, nos. Ia52-380, Ia52-382.

15. Memo of conversation with Khrushchev, Sept. 27, 1959, Eisenhower Library, WHO, Office of Staff Secretary, International Trips and Meetings, box 9, Khrushchev Visit 9/59 (3).

16. Herter to Eisenhower, Sept. 28, 1959, and attached draft letter, Herter Papers, box 7, Chronological File 9/59 (1).

17. Embassy, Moscow to SecState, June 24, 1959, Eisenhower Papers (AW), Dulles-Herter, box 9, Herter 6/59 (1).

18. CIA, "The Tenth Anniversary Celebration of the People's Republic of China," Sept. 1, 1959, Eisenhower Library, WHO OSANSA, NSC, Briefing Notes, box 5, [Report on Communist China's Anniversary Celebration], pp. 4, 22. The State Dept. also underestimated tensions in the Sino-Soviet relationship. See NA, "Recent Developments in Sino-Soviet Relations," March 27, 1959, RG 59, SD Office of Intelligence Research Papers.

19. Statement by spokesmen of the Chinese Government, Sept. 1, 1963, *Peking Review*, Sept. 6, 1963, p. 13; Nie Rongzhen, *Huiyilu*, p. 805; Griffith, *Sino-Soviet Rift*, p. 400; interviews in China, 1985. Khrushchev quote from Han Nianlong, chief editor, *Dangdai Zhongguo waijiao* [Contemporary China's foreign affairs] (Beijing, 1987), p. 115.

20. Minnich handwritten notes of Nov. 6, 1959, Eisenhower Library, WHO, Office of Staff Secretary, Cabinets, box 5, C-52(2); Schur-

mann, *Logic*, pp. 302–10; Lewis and Xue, *China Builds the Bomb*, pp. 71–72.

21. Memo, meeting with Kishi, Jan. 19, 1960, Eisenhower Papers (AW), Diaries, box 47, Staff Notes 1/60 (2).

22. "Long Live Leninism!," in Editorial Board of *People's Daily* and *Red Flag*, comp., *Long Live Leninism*, 3d ed. (Peking, 1960), pp. 1–55.

23. Interviews in China, 1985.

24. Ulam, *Expansion*, pp. 633–35; LaFeber, *America*, pp. 213–15; Kennan to Kennedy, Aug. 17, 1960, letter attached to Kennan oral history. Harrison Salisbury also linked the failure of the Paris summit to the Sino-Soviet rift. See *NYT*, May 26, 1960, pp. 1, 7.

25. Hudson et al., *Sino-Soviet Dispute*, pp. 132–40; Schurmann, *Logic*, pp. 311–12; Nogee and Donaldson, *Soviet Foreign Policy*, p. 227. On Dec. 4 the *People's Daily* reported that the Soviets withdrew 1,390 experts, "tore up 343 contracts," annulled 257 items of scientific and technical cooperation, and slashed the supply of equipment and parts.

26. For a sense of some of the early debate, see Zagoria, "Strains"; and Brzezinski, "Patterns."

27. "Bear and Dragon: What Is the Relation Between Moscow and Peking?," *National Review*, Nov. 5, 1960, pp. S1–S48.

28. For a survey of the Western literature on the split, see Donald W. Treadgold, "Alternative Western Views of the Sino-Soviet Conflict," in Ellison, *Sino-Soviet Conflict*, pp. 325–55. The most comprehensive account of the original doctrinal differences between the CCP and the CPSU remains Zagoria's *Sino-Soviet Conflict*. One of the most recent interpretations of the sources of the discord is found in Bialer, *Soviet Paradox*, pp. 232–56. Recent Chinese historical perspectives are considerably less vitriolic than the past polemics. They stress the Soviets' domineering attitude and efforts to subordinate China to their interests. The ideological differences are de-emphasized. See Nie Rongzhen, *Huiyilu*; Wang Bingnan, *Zhong-mei*; and Wu Xiuquan, *Zai waijiaobu*. Available Soviet histories like Sergeichuk, *Through Russian Eyes*, and Borisov and Koloskov, *Sino-Soviet Relations*, use a broad brush, blaming the "nationalism" of a "Maoist clique" for the decline in relations. Medvedev, *China and the Superpowers*, presents a more balanced Soviet view.

29. F. Dulles, *American Policy*, p. 189; Kennedy, "Democrat."

30. Thomson to Read, Sept. 1, 1960, Thomson Papers, box 7, Far East and Middle East; Bowles, "'China Problem' Reconsidered."

31. Bowles to Archibald Cox, Aug. 15, 1960, Bowles Papers, box 205, folder 0056.

32. Bowles to Kennedy, Oct. 6, 1960, "Some Requirements of American Foreign Policy," July 1, 1961, ibid., box 210, folder 164, box 297, folder 495. See also Bowles speech, "The Soviet–United States Conflict in the 1960's, Oct. 21, 1960, Thomson Papers, box 7.

33. Stevenson, "Putting First Things First"; Cohen, *Dean Rusk*, pp. 86, 168.

34. Kennan to Kennedy, Aug. 17, 1960, letter attached to Kennan oral history.

35. Bohlen to Bundy, Feb. 16, Bowles to Kennedy, March 29, 1961, Kennedy Papers, POF, box 106, Sino-Soviet Relations, box 88, State 4/61–5/61.

36. "The Sino-Soviet Dispute and Its Significance," April 1, 1961, ibid., NSF, box 22, China—General; notes on NSC meeting, Nov. 15, 1961, Johnson Papers, VPSF, NSF, box 4, NSC (11); CIA, SNIE 13-2-61, "Communist China in 1971," "The Sino-Soviet Conflict and U.S. Policy," and "Summary," Dec. 19, 1961, all in Thomson Papers, box 14.

37. Kaysen to Schlesinger, Aug. 23, 1961, Schlesinger Papers, box 16, Subjects—1961–64, NSC 5/5/61–10/30/61.

38. See Kennedy press conference, Nov. 8, 1961, *Public Papers: Kennedy 1961*, p. 705; draft paper, "Guidelines for Co-Ordinated Information Policy Re: The Sino-Soviet Dispute," May 16, 1962, Hilsman Papers, box 1, Communist China—Sino-Soviet Dispute, U.S. Overt Attitude, 5/62; and Hilsman, *To Move a Nation*, p. 344.

39. *DSB*, July 31, 1961, p. 179.

40. Thomson quote from Hilsman, *To Move a Nation*, p. 344.

41. "The Sino-Soviet Conflict and U.S. Policy" and "Summary," Dec. 19, 1961, Thomson Papers, box 14.

42. Thomson to Harriman, Jan. 12, 1962, ibid., box 15, General 1/62–3/62.

43. Hilsman made the first official public report on the Sino-Soviet split on Nov. 8, 1962. See *DSB*, Nov. 26, 1962, pp. 807–11.

44. SD, "1962 Public Attitudes Toward U.S. Policy on China," Sept. 18, 1962, Thomson Papers, box 15, General 7/62–12/62.

45. Operations Coordinating Board, "Report on U.S. Policy Toward Taiwan and the Government of the Republic of China," May 18, 1960, Eisenhower Library, WHO OSANSA, NSC, Policy Papers, box 22, NSC 5723, Policy Toward Taiwan and ROC.

46. Ibid.

47. Sorensen, *Kennedy*, pp. 661–62; Chiang quote from Hilsman, *To Move a Nation*, pp. 310–11.

48. Handwritten notes, meeting with Hilsman, March 14, 1963, Thomson Papers, box 15, General 1/62–3/62.

49. Drumright to Rusk, Jan. 11, Feb. 13, Rusk to Drumright, Jan. 8, 17, 1962, Kennedy Papers, NSF, box 23, China—General–Return to the Mainland 1/1/62–3/6/62; Hilsman, *To Move a Nation*, pp. 310–320.

50. Hilsman, *To Move a Nation*, p. 311; notes, meeting of Bowles and Harriman, Jan. 8, 1962, Thomson Papers, box 7, General 1962.

51. Hilsman, *To Move a Nation*, pp. 315–16; notes, meeting of Bowles and Harriman, June 8, INR/RSB, "Chinese Communist Food Deficits and U.S. Policy," Jan. 5, Harriman to Rusk, April 13, Bowles to Kennedy, May 23, Kohler to Rostow, March 8, 1962, all in Thomson Papers, box 7, General 1962 (Bowles-Harriman meeting), box 15, Food for China 1/62–2/62, 3/62–5/62.

52. Burris to Johnson, June 5, 1962, Johnson Papers, VPSF, Col. Burris, box 5, Memos to Vice President 1/61–6/62; Bundy, Weekend Reading 4/20/62, Kennedy Papers, NSF, box 318, Index of Weekend Papers, 1/62–6/62; Hilsman, *To Move a Nation*, pp. 314, 317–18.

53. Notes, meeting of Kennedy et al., June 20, memo, meeting of Harriman and Dobrynin, June 22, 1962, both in Hilsman Papers, box 1, China—Offshore Island Crisis 6/62; Hilsman, *To Move a Nation*, pp. 318–19.

54. Harriman to Kennedy, Aug. 8, 1962, Harriman to Kirk, n.d., Kennedy Papers, POF, box 88, State 8/62–12/62.

55. Clough to State, March 13, 1963, Johnson Papers, VPSF, Government Agencies, box 13, SD—Misc. Cables 1961–63; Hilsman, *To Move a Nation*, p. 319.

56. Chiang to Kennedy, Sept. 5, 1963, plus attachment, Kennedy Papers, POF, box 113a, China—General 1963.

57. Embassy, Taipei, to SecState, June 19, 1960, Eisenhower Library, WHO Office of Staff Secretary, International Trips and Meetings, box 12, Far East Trip 1/60.

58. Chiang to Kennedy, April 1, 1961, Kennedy Papers, POF, box 113a, China—General 1/61–4/61.

59. Handwritten notes of March 9, 1965, P.M., Thomson Papers, box 19, Baguio 2, 3/65. By 1967 Chiang seems to have had a change of heart about using nuclear weapons against the mainland. He is said to have warned Dean Rusk against using the bomb against his countrymen. See Schoenbaum, *Waging Peace and War*, p. 454.

Chapter Eight

1. "Should We Bomb Red China's Bomb?," *National Review*, Jan. 12, 1965, pp. 8–10. *National Review* repeated its call for the bombing of China in June 1, 1965, pp. 449–50. I thank Benjamin Loeb for his help with this chapter.

2. NA, Commander-in-Chief Pacific, "Pacific General War Plan (U)," Jan., p. D-9, Ciro E. Zoppo and Alice L. Hsieh, "The Accession of Other Nations to the Nuclear Test Ban," March 8, 1961, p. 57, both in RG 218, JCS 1961, respectively, box 44, CCS 3146, CINCPAC-CNUNC 1/26/61, sec. 1, box 23, CCS 3050, Disarmament 3/8/61, sec. 1; Hsieh, *Communist China's Strategy*, p. 154; interview with Rostow, 1985; Rostow to Stevenson, May 31, 1960, Stevenson Papers, box 797, Rostow 1960; *DSB*, Sept. 18, 1961, p. 487.

3. Bundy, "Notes on Discussion of the Thinking of the Soviet Leadership, Cabinet Room, Feb. 11, 1961," pp. 1–6, Kennedy Papers, NSF, CF, box 176, USSR—General 2/2/61–2/14/61; Harriman to Kennedy, Nov. 12, 15, 1960, Kennedy Papers, POF, countries, box 1254, USSR—General; Kennan to Kennedy, Aug. 17, 1960, p. 7, attached to Kennan oral history. Bohlen concluded early in the administration that the "Soviet Union's great fear was not United States nuclear power, it was China's possession of the atomic bomb." *Witness to History*, p. 475.

4. President's Meeting with Khrushchev Position Papers: "Progress Toward a Viable World Order," May 26, "Communist China," May 25, 1961, Kennedy Papers, POF, box 126, USSR–Vienna Meeting—Background Documents 1953–61 (G-2); President's Meeting with Khrushchev Position Papers: "Soviet Aims and Expectations," "Soviet Positions on Various Disarmament Questions," pp. 5–7, both May 25, 1961, ibid. (G-3).

5. Sorensen, *Kennedy*, pp. 548–49; Schlesinger, *Thousand Days*, p. 344.

6. Bohlen to SecState, March 23, 1961, Kennedy Papers, NSF, CF, box 180, USSR—General 3/23/61–5/8/61.

7. Memo 393, Krock Papers, Memoranda, book 3, 10/61; memo, meeting of Rusk, McNamara et al., April 29, 1961, Kennedy Papers, NSF, CF, box 130, Laos—General 6/1/61–6/26/61; "Summary of the President's Remarks to the National Security Council Jan. 18, 1962," Kennedy Papers, NSF, box 313, NSC Meetings 1962. Dean Rusk's biographer contends that it was Kennedy himself who was responsible for the rigid China policy of the early 1960's, not the secretary of state. See Schoenbaum, *Waging Peace and War*, p. 388.

8. Sorensen, *Kennedy*, p. 518.

9. For background on arms negotiations during the Eisenhower years, see Divine, *Blowing on the Wind*; Bloomfield et al., *Khrushchev*; U.S., National Academy of Sciences, *Nuclear Arms Control*, pp. 187–90.

10. Jacobson and Stein, *Diplomats*, pp. 381–416; Seaborg, *Kennedy*, pp. 162–71.

11. Dean, *Test Ban*, pp. 90–91; Jacobson and Stein, *Diplomats*, pp. 397–413.

12. Hilsman to Rusk, Nov. 20, 1962, Hilsman Papers, box 1, India—Sino-Indian Border Clash, 1962; cover memo, Ray S. Cline, "Sino-Soviet Relations," Jan. 14, CIA, "Sino-Soviet Relations at a New Crisis," both in Kennedy Papers, NSF, CF, box 180, USSR—General 1/9/63–1/14/63. Kennedy himself linked the worsening of Sino-Soviet relations with the U.S. stand during the Cuban missile crisis in a TV interview on Dec. 17, 1962. *Public Papers: Kennedy: 1962*, pp. 901–2.

13. CIA, "Sino-Soviet Relations at a New Crisis" (as sited in preceding note), p. 6.

14. Tyler oral history, March 7, 1964, pp. 37–39, and attachment: Tyler to LaFeber, Dec. 10, 1971.

15. Foster oral history, pp. 36–37; "Mr. Hilsman's Remarks at Director's Meeting," Jan. 22, 1963, Hilsman Papers, box 5, National Security—Hilsman Summary of President's Views 1/22/63. Parts of Foster's oral history relating to China and the test ban are still sanitized, including several paragraphs in which he describes Kennedy's "willingness to consider politically dangerous moves" against China (p. 37).

16. Seaborg, *Kennedy*, p. 188. Arthur Dean, an architect of the Limited Test Ban Treaty, also admits that the treaty was based on the acceptance of the possibility of Soviet cheating. *Test Ban*, p. 82.

17. U.S., Senate Preparedness Investigating Subcommittee, *Military Aspects*, pp. 7–11. McGeorge Bundy writes that, like Glenn Seaborg, he has never been clear about Kennedy's reasons for thinking that the test ban treaty might impede the Chinese nuclear weapons program (*Danger and Survival*, p. 461). On the eve of Harriman's departure for Moscow, William Foster, replying to a request from the president, submitted an ACDA memorandum on the "Political Implications of a Nuclear Test Ban." Foster pointed to reduced tensions with the Soviet Union and a controlled arms race as possible consequences. He also stressed that a treaty would enhance the U.S. ability to deal with China. "The U.S. might be able to develop something approaching a community of interest with the Soviet Union," Foster wrote, "at least insofar as Communist China's external conduct is concerned." Foster to Kennedy, July 12, 1963, Kennedy Papers, NSF, box 265, ACDA Disarmament—Harriman Trip.

18. CIA, "Growth of Chinese Influence Among World Communists," May 17, 1963, cited by Bundy in Kennedy Papers, NSF, box 318, Index of Weekend Papers.

19. Kohler to SD (cable), March 16, 1963, Johnson Papers, VPSF, box 4, Government Agencies, SD—Misc. Cables 1961–63; cover

memo, Hilsman to Rusk, March 7, cited by Bundy, and Hilsman to Rusk, research memo, March 7, 1963, Kennedy Papers, NSF, box 318, Index of Weekend Papers 1/63–3/63.

20. U.S., Arms Control and Disarmament Agency, *Documents*, p. 194; *NYT*, May 30, 1963, p. 1.

21. Hughes to Rusk, June 14, 1963, pp. 1, 4, Embassy Moscow to SD, "Motivations for Moscow's Signature of the Test Ban Agreement," Sept. 6, 1963, FOIA releases in author's possession.

22. Embassy, Moscow, to SD, "Motivations" (as cited in preceding note), pp. 4–5. For a different point of view, see Jonsson, *Soviet Bargaining Behavior*.

23. Rusk to SD (cable), June 25, 1963, FOIA release in author's possession.

24. *NYT*, June 25, 1963, pp. 1, 10.

25. Barr memo, meeting of Harriman and Kield Gustav Knuth-Winterfeldt, July 1, 1963, Stackhouse memo, meeting of Rusk and Mongi Slim, July 15, 1963, FOIA releases in author's possession.

26. Harriman to Kennedy, Nov. 12, 15, 1960, Kennedy Papers, POF, box 125, USSR—General; Thompson oral history, March 25, 1964, pp. 25–28; Bloomfield et al., *Khrushchev*, p. 190; SD, "Elements for a Package Deal with Moscow," July 3, Rostow memo, July 5, Foster, "Memo for the President: Political Implications of a Nuclear Test Ban," July 12, 1963, all in Kennedy Papers, NSF, box 265, ACDA Disarmament—Harriman Trip to Moscow Part III; Col. Jackson to Johnson, July 9, 1963, and unsigned, undated "personal & confidential" memo to Johnson, Johnson Papers, PSF, box 5, Col. Burris—NSC 1962–63; Seaborg, *Kennedy*, p. 228; Schlesinger, *Thousand Days*, p. 825.

27. *Time*, July 19, 1963, pp. 24–25; *NYT*, July 14, pp. 1, 3, July 15, p. 1, July 16, 1963, pp. 1, 3; *Peking Review*, July 19, 1963, p. 10.

28. Sorensen, *Kennedy*, pp. 734–35; Read oral history, Feb. 22, 1966, p. 3.

29. Kennedy to Harriman (cable), July 15, 1963, FOIA release in Benjamin Loeb's possession (italics added).

30. Rusk to SD (cable), June 25, 1963, FOIA release in author's possession. Former AEC Chairman Glenn Seaborg agrees that the July 15 cable indicated a possible interest in a joint preemptive strike against Chinese nuclear facilities. *Kennedy*, p. 239.

31. Hsieh, *Communist China's Strategy*, p. 154; memo, meeting of Harriman and Penn Nouth, Aug. 19, Rusk to ambassador, Bonn (cable), July 24, and Barr memo, meeting of Harriman and Knuth-Winterfeldt, July 1, 1963, FOIA releases in author's possession. After the withdrawal of Soviet technicians in 1960, China's trade with the Eastern

bloc plummeted, to stand at only about 30% of the total by 1963. See Gittings, *Survey of the Sino-Soviet Dispute*, pp. 129–34.

32. SecDefense to President, draft memo, Feb. 12, 1963, Johnson Papers, VPSF, box 7, Disarmament Proposals 2/63.

33. Defense Dept., "Harriman Trip to Moscow—Briefing Book," June 20, 1963, Kennedy Papers, NSF, box 265, ACDA Disarmament, 2: tab D.

34. Arthur Barbar, "Briefing Book on US-Soviet Non-Diffusion Agreement for Discussion at the Moscow Meeting," June 12, 1963, ibid., 1: 1–7.

35. Herken to Thelen, March 4, 1987, in author's possession (I am grateful to Gregg Herken for sharing the information about a possible preemptive strike); Joseph Alsop, "Thoughts," pp. 30–31, 100–105. In 1988 McGeorge Bundy wrote that though there had been talk in Washington about the possibility of a preemptive strike against China, plans never approached an operational level. *Danger and Survival*, p. 532. See also Stewart Alsop, "The Real Meaning of the Test Ban," *Saturday Evening Post*, Sept. 28, 1963, p. 20.

36. Rusk to ambassador, Bonn (cable), July 18, Kohler to Bundy (cable), July 21, 1963, FOIA releases in Benjamin Loeb's possession; *NYT*, July 20, July 21, 1963, pp. 1, 2 in both.

37. Rusk to Harriman (cable), July 24, 1963, FOIA release in author's possession; Harriman to Kennedy (cable 277), July 23, Kohler to Rusk (cable 294), July 23, 1963, FOIA releases in Benjamin Loeb's possession. George Bunn, ACDA general counsel, was struck by the attention Harriman's cables from Moscow gave to the Soviets' concern about China. Interview with Bunn, 1987.

38. Rusk to Harriman (cable), July 23, 1963, FOIA release in Benjamin Loeb's possession; Schlesinger, *Thousand Days*, p. 829. For other interpretations of the Kennedy administration's possible military response to China's nuclear acquisition, see Schurmann, *Logic*, pp. 385–95; and Segal, *Great Power Triangle*, pp. 124–25.

39. *National Review*, Aug. 20, 1963, p. 6.

40. Rusk to ambassador, Bonn (cable), July 24, 1963, FOIA release in author's possession.

41. NA, Senate Committee on Foreign Relations, "Declassified Portions of *Nuclear Test Ban Treaty*," Aug. 28, 1963, p. 71, RG 46, Senate Records.

42. U.S., Senate Preparedness Investigating Subcommittee, *Military Aspects*, pp. 300–305, 376; Seaborg, *Kennedy*, pp. 228–29.

43. U.S., Senate, Committee on Foreign Relations, *Nuclear Test Ban Treaty*, pp. 274–75, 397, Preparedness Investigating Subcommit-

tee, *Military Aspects,* pp. 676–77, 707, 738. On Aug. 13, 1963, Rusk personally met with the JCS to discuss the test ban treaty. In reply to General LeMay's question about the political advantages of the treaty, Rusk mentioned aggravating the Sino-Soviet split; he also thought the treaty might "lead to further favorable developments in our relations with the Soviets." Memo for the record, Aug. 15, 1963, FOIA release in author's possession.

44. CINCPAC to DIA, July 13, 1964, Johnson Papers, NSF, CF, China, box 237–38, Cables (1) 12/63–9/64. CINCPAC still urged Washington to take "action" to impede the Chinese nuclear program.

45. Bundy, memo for the record, Sept. 15, 1964, ibid., NSF, Aides, box 2, Bundy—Memos to President (6) 7/1/64–9/30/64. Stewart Alsop and L. Mendel Rivers, chairman of the House Armed Services Committee, publicly called for U.S. strikes against China's nuclear facilities at about this time. See F. Dulles, *American Policy,* pp. 222–23. After the Chinese test explosion a panel headed by Under Secretary of Defense Roswell Gilpatric considered recommending a "surgical strike," among other options, to stop China's further nuclear development. See Segal, *Great Power Triangle,* p. 127.

46. Hilsman, "Remarks to the Council on World Affairs," Nov. 18, 1964, Thomson Papers, box 16, General 11/64–12/64 and undated. Nikita Khrushchev's son Sergei confirms that China policy was involved in Khrushchev's ouster. "My Father Nikita's Downfall," p. 44.

47. Cohen, *Dean Rusk,* p. 169; *DSB,* Nov. 26, 1962, pp. 807–11; CIA, "Possibilities of Greater Militancy by the Chinese Communists—SNIE 13-4-63," July 31, 1963, Johnson Papers, VPSF, Nations and Regions, container 11; U.S., Senate Committee on Foreign Relations, *Nuclear Test Ban,* pp. 337, 342; M. Graeme Bannerman, staff director, Senate Committee on Foreign Relations, to author, 1986, with some declassified deletions from *Nuclear Test Ban.* Several years later Mao pointedly denied that he had ever claimed China would benefit from a nuclear war. See Edgar Snow, "Interview with Mao."

48. All of the following are from Kennedy Papers, NSF: Bundy, no. 7, misc. papers for Hyannisport, July 21–23, 1961, box 318, Index of Weekend Papers 1/61–12/61; CIA, "The Signs of Chinese Communist Friendliness," July 17, 1961, box 22, China—General 7/15/61–7/24/61; Bundy, Weekend Reading (2), July 21, 1962, box 318, Index of Weekend Papers; Hilsman to McConaughy, July 7, 1961, box 22, China—General 8/1/61–8/10/61; Cabot to Rusk, (cable nos. 255, 258), Aug. 8, Forrestal to Kennedy, Aug. 10, 1963, all in box 153, CF, Poland, Subjects—Beam-Wang talks/ Cabot-Wang talks.

49. Hilsman to Harriman, Aug. 13, 1963, Hilsman Papers, box 5,

Test Ban Treaty 7/63; Bundy, Weekend Reading, July 19, 1963, Kennedy Papers, NSF, box 318, Index of Weekend Papers 7/63–11/63.

Chapter Nine

EPIGRAPH: Palmerston speech in British House of Commons, 1848.

1. "Comments on China Policy, 1948 [1949?]," Judd Papers, box 96, China 1950–60 (italics in original). Judd fully supported the American intervention in Vietnam in the 1960's. Though he acknowledged that differences divided Moscow and Beijing, he stressed their common hostility toward the West and opposed any reduction of hostility toward China. See his testimony of March 28, 1966, in U.S., Senate Foreign Relations Committee, *U.S. Policy with Respect to Mainland China*, pp. 437–95.

2. See Schurmann, *Logic*, p. 460.

3. F. Dulles, *American Policy*, pp. 211–12.

4. CIA, "Trends in the World Situation," June 9, 1964, Johnson Papers, NSF, Agency, box 5, 8–10, pp. 13, 39.

5. Ibid., p. 43.

6. Geyelin, *Lyndon B. Johnson*, p. 197; Goldman, *Tragedy*, p. 223; memo, meeting with Rusk, McNamara, and others on Sept. 9, 1964, Sept. 14, 1964, Johnson Papers, Special Files, Meeting Notes, box 1.

7. Interview with Walt W. Rostow, 1985.

8. Rostow to Allen Dulles, Sept. 18, Oct. 7, 1953, Rostow reply to questions from Project Gossard, Jan. 8, 1954, Eisenhower Library, Jackson Papers, 1953–54, box 6, Rostow.

9. Rostow to Jackson, March 29, 1955, ibid., General File, box 75, Rostow to 1956.

10. Luce to Jackson, Aug. 9, 1955, Rostow to Luce, June 22, 1956, ibid., box 58, Luce (2), box 75, Rostow to 1956.

11. Rostow to Kennedy, June 17, 1961, Kennedy Papers, POF, box 65, Rostow 6/61–12/61; Rostow to Stevenson, May 31, 1960, Stevenson Papers, box 797, Rostow 1960.

12. Rostow, "Basic National Security Policy," March 26, 1962, Johnson Papers, VPSF, National Security Policy, box 7, pp. 166, 176, 190–96.

13. Ibid., pp. 197–99; Rostow, "Some Reflections on National Security Policy," March 5, 1965, Johnson Papers, box 1, NSF, Agency File—State, Policy Planning (4).

14. Gittings, *Survey*, pp. 212–17; U.S., *China and U.S. Far East Policy*, p. 137.

15. Dean Rusk testimony, Jan. 28, 1966, cited in Fulbright, *Vietnam Hearings*, pp. 4–5, 18, 21.

16. William B. Ballis, "Relations Between the USSR and Vietnam," in Rupen and Farrell, *Vietnam*, pp. 43–56; Kolko, *Anatomy of a War*, pp. 157–58, 401–11.

17. Memo for Bundy, "The US and Communist China in the Months Ahead," Oct. 28, 1964, quoted in SD, *Administrative History*, chap. 7, part C, Johnson Papers, NSC, CF, China, box 244–45; L. Grant, "Visit of Prime Minister Harold Wilson: China Problem, December 4, 1964," Johnson Papers, NSF, CF, Europe and USSR, UK, box 213, UK PM Wilson Visit Briefing Book.

18. Bundy to Johnson, Dec. 16, 1964, Johnson Papers, NSF, Aides, box 2, Bundy—Memos to president (6) 7/1/64–9/30/64.

19. Cleveland to Ball, Oct. 31, 1964, ibid., NSF, CF, UN, box 290, UN—Chinese Representation.

20. Memo, ConGen Hong Kong, Nov. 6, 1964, ibid., CF, China, box 237–38, Memos (1) 12/63–9/64.

21. *New York Post*, Feb. 6, 1964; notes of March 9, 1965, P.M., Thomson Papers, box 19, Baguio 2, March 1965.

22. U.S., House Subcommittee on the Far East, *Report on the Sino-Soviet Conflict*, pp. 76–79, 89, 106.

23. See Zagoria testimony, Nov. 19, 1975, U.S., House Subcommittee on Future Foreign Policy, *Great Power Triangle*, part I, p. 62.

24. U.S., House Subcommittee on the Far East, *Report on the Sino-Soviet Conflict*, pp. 112–16, 146–47, 150.

25. Green testimony, March 23, Rusk testimony, March 31, 1965, ibid., pp. 337–38, 354–57, 364–65; declassified security deletion included in a letter from Helen C. Mattas to the author, March 9, 1988.

26. *Refutation of the New Leaders*, p. 10; Gittings, *Survey*, pp. 254–58.

27. Bundy to Johnson, April 20, SD to Embassy, Paris, July 2, Bundy memo on NSC's meeting of July 27, 1965, all in Johnson Papers, respectively: NSF, Aides, box 3, Bundy Memos to President (10) 4/15/65–5/31/65; CF, France, box 171, Cables (7) 6/65–8/65; Special File, Meeting Notes, box 1, NSC meeting, joint leadership meeting.

28. CIA, SNIE 10-9-65, "Communist and Free World Reactions to a Possible US Course of Action," July 20, Bundy to Johnson, Nov. 27, and memo, meeting with advisers on bombing pause, Dec. 18, 1965, all in Johnson Papers, respectively: NSF, NSC History, box 43, Deployment of Major U.S. Forces to Vietnam, July 1965, 6: tabs 384–400; NSF, Aides, box 5, Bundy Memos to President (17) 11/20/65–12/31/65; Special Files, Meeting Notes, box 1.

29. Kahin, *Intervention*, p. 417.

30. Segal, *Great Power Triangle*, pp. 100–101.

31. R. B. Smith, *International History*, p. 17.

32. Gaddis, *Strategies*, pp. 241–42; Kahin, *Intervention*, pp. 403–32; Kolko, *Anatomy*, pp. 176–78.

33. Zagoria, *Vietnam Triangle*, p. 78. Cohen, *Dean Rusk*, pp. 285–86.

34. Bundy to Johnson, Dec. 3, 1965, memo on meeting with advisers on resumption of bombing, Jan. 27, 1966, Johnson Papers, NSF, Aides, box 5, Bundy Memos to President (17) 11/20/65–12/31/65, Special Files, Meeting Notes, box 1. For a perceptive analysis of Lin Biao's essay, see Mozingo and Robinson, *Lin Piao on "People's War."* In February 1965 Mao told Edgar Snow that China had no intention of directly involving itself in Vietnam unless its border was threatened. Snow, "Interview with Mao."

35. Craig and George, *Force and Statecraft*, p. 127.

36. SD, *Administrative History*, chap. 7, Part C, Johnson Papers, n.p.

37. *DSB*, Jan. 6, 1964, pp. 11–17.

38. Beaman memo, chiefs of mission meeting, Thomson Papers, box 19, Baguio 3, Feb. 1966, Highlights—Chiefs of Mission Conference 2/27/66–3/2/66, pp. 6–8, 11–12, 36–38; Thomson to Bundy, Aug. 21, 1965, Johnson Papers, NSF, CF, China, box 237–38, Memos (4) 7/65–10/65; Johnson Papers, NSF, Aides, Bundy Memos to President as follows: Dec. 16, 1964, box 2, vol. 7, 10/1/64–12/31/64; Aug. 24, 1965, box 4, vol. 13, 8/65; Dec. 2, 1965, box 5, vol. 17, 11/20/65–12/31/65.

39. Bundy quote from Beaman memo, chiefs of mission meeting (as cited in preceding note); Jenkins to Rostow, Aug. 3, 1966, Johnson Papers, NSF, CF, China, box 239, Memos (6) 3/66–9/66.

40. W. P. Bundy, "The United States and Communist China," *DSB*, Feb. 28, 1966, pp. 310–18. See also Rogers, "Sino-American Relations."

41. Rogers, "Sino-American Relations," pp. 306–9; Kahin, *Intervention*, pp. 340–41; René Dabernat, "How a French Authority Sees U.S. Role in Asia," *U.S. News and World Report*, Jan. 23, 1967, pp. 93–97.

42. Lyndon Johnson, "The Essentials for Peace in Asia," speech at American Alumni Council, July 12, 1966, U.S., *China and U.S. Far East Policy*, p. 331; Jenkins to Rostow, Sept. 1, 1966, Johnson Papers, NSF, CF, China, box 240, Memos (7) 9/66–11/66; S/P 66-71-2a, "China—Communist China: Long-Range Study by the Special State-Defense Study Group," June 1966, p. 19, quoted in SD, *Administrative History*, chap. 7, part C (the long study is still classified), Johnson Papers; Gittings, *Survey*, pp. 259–60.

43. Thomson to Jenkins, July 25, 1966, Johnson Papers, NSF, CF, China, box 239, Memos (6) 3/66–9/66; U.S., Senate Committee on Foreign Relations, *U.S. Policy with Respect to Mainland China*.

44. For more on the CFR project, see Allen Dulles Papers, "Council on Foreign Relations 1962–66." For a representative volume, see Blum, *United States and China in World Affairs*.

45. "China—Communist China: Long Range Study by the Special State-Defense Study Group," June 16, 1966, Johnson Papers, NSF, CF, China, boxes 244–45; Thomson to Rostow et al., April 2, 1966, Thomson Papers, box 17, Far East—Communist China 4/66–6/66; SecState to Johnson, n.d., draft memo, "New Approach to Trade and Transaction Controls with Communist China," quoted in SD, *Administrative History*, chap. 7, part C, Johnson Papers, n.p.

46. *NYT*, Nov. 22, 1966, p. 1; U.S., *China and U.S. Far East Policy*, p. 208; various memos by John Roche, Nov. 1966, Johnson Papers, NSF, CF, China, box 241, Memos (7) 9/66–11/66.

47. Memo on meeting with advisers on resumption of bombing, Jan. 28, 1966, CIA cable, July 3, 1967, Johnson Papers, Special Files, Meeting Notes, box 1, NSF, CF, USSR, box 7, Cables (15) 4/67–5/67; U.S., *China and U.S. Far East Policy*, p. 209.

48. U.S., *China and U.S. Far East Policy*, p. 219; Medvedev, *China and the Superpowers*, pp. 40–47; Denny to Rusk, March 15, 1967, Johnson Papers, NSF, CF, China, box 241, Memos (9) 3/67–6/67.

49. Sutter, *China-Watch*, p. 69; Quested, *Sino-Russian Relations*, p. 139.

50. See Segal, *Great Power Triangle*, p. 96; Schurmann, *Logic*, pp. 512–17.

51. *NYT*, Sept. 10, 1966, p. 1.

52. Rusk to Embassy, Paris, "Soviet External Policy," July 1, 1965, Johnson Papers, NSF, CF, France, box 171, Cables (7) 6/65–8/65.

53. Interview with Rostow, 1985.

54. Kissinger, *White House Years*, pp. 57–58.

55. Mansfield to Johnson, April 29, 1967, Bromley Smith to Johnson, with Reischauer cable of Aug. 13, 1966, Jenkins memo, China Experts Meeting, Feb. 2, 1968, all in Johnson Papers: NSF, Names, box 5–6, Mansfield; WHCF, Formosa, box 7, CO 50-1; Special Files, Meeting Notes, box 2.

56. Rostow to Johnson, April 30, 1967, Feb. 22, 1968, ibid., NSF, Names, box 5–6, Mansfield, and WHCF, box 22, CO 50-2, 5/17/66–.

57. U.S., Senate Committee on Foreign Relations, *Communist World in 1967*, pp. 7–15. Fulbright to Bowles, March 19, 1968, Bowles to Johnson, May 18, 1967, Bowles Papers, box 330, folder 0075, box 332, folder 0112.

58. Goodpaster memo, meeting with Eisenhower, April 7, 1967, Johnson Papers, NSF, Names, box 2, Eisenhower.

59. Kissinger, *White House Years*, pp. 164—65.

60. Nixon, "American Policy Abroad," pp. 486—90.

61. Robert Scheer, "Nixon Urges Sharing Data on 'Star Wars,'" *Los Angeles Times*, July 1, 1984, part 1, p. 6; Nixon, *Memoirs*, pp. 280—81.

62. Bowles to Rusk, April 27, 1967, Bowles Papers, box 336, folder 0187.

63. Nixon, "Asia After Viet Nam," pp. 122, 123.

Epilogue

1. Shevchenko, *Breaking with Moscow*, pp. 164—66.

2. Ibid. Also see Sulzberger, *Coldest War*. According to Kissinger, a Soviet embassy official on Aug. 18, 1969, surprised a middle-level State Dept. specialist in Soviet affairs when he asked what the U.S. reaction would be to a Soviet attack on China's nuclear facilities. The encounter was reported to the highest levels of the U.S. government. *White House Years*, p. 183.

3. See Lo, *Three Kingdoms*.

4. The story of Sino-American rapprochement is well told in Nixon, *Memoirs*; Kissinger, *White House Years*; and Szulc, *Illusion of Peace*. A Soviet view is found in Medvedev, *China and the Superpowers*.

5. NA, National Security Study memos 14 and 63, Feb. 5, July 3, 1969, RG 273, NSC; Kissinger, *White House Years*, p. 182; Richard C. Thornton, "Strategic Change and American Foreign Policy: Perceptions of the Sino-Soviet Conflict," in Kim, *Strategic Triangle*, pp. 57—58.

6. For a study of the theory of triangular politics and Sino-Soviet-American relations, see Dittmer, "The Strategic Triangle." On Kissinger's awareness of the potential of triangular politics, see Hyland, *Mortal Rivals*, pp. 24—35.

7. See Caldwell, *American Soviet Relations*, chap. 3 and pp. 249—60.

8. NA, handwritten comments on Harlow to Nixon, June 23, 1969, POF, box 2, President's Handwriting 6/69; NA, Nixon to Kissinger, Sept. 22, 1969, Parker to Haldeman, March 13, 1972, Nixon Presidential Materials Project, WHSF, Subjects, box 6, [CF], China, CO 34; marginal comments on Nixon's 1967 *Foreign Affairs* article, clipping from *Washington Daily News*, Feb. 16, 1972, Judd to Nixon, Sept. 15, 1971, Radford to Judd, Jan. 27, 1972, all in Judd Papers: box 137, Nixon 1964—68, 1970—72+, box 101, Committee for a Free China 1971—72 (clipping).

9. Kissinger, *White House Years*, p. 1093.

10. U.S., House Subcommittee on Future Foreign Policy Research, *United States–Soviet Union–China*, part 1, p. 2.

11. See Whiting, "Use of Force."

12. Acheson to Eden, May 8, 1971, Acheson Papers, Yale, box 9, folder 119.

13. See Gordon Chang, "The Evolution of Triangular Politics and the Security of Northeast Asia," in *Peace, Security, and Cooperation*, a conference report of the Center for International Security and Arms Control, Stanford University (Stanford, Calif., Jan. 1989), pp. 67–77.

Sources

Archival Materials

Dean G. Acheson Papers, Sterling Memorial Library, Yale University; Harry S. Truman Library

Joseph and Stewart Alsop Papers, Library of Congress

Dillon Anderson Oral Histories, Dwight D. Eisenhower Library; Seeley G. Mudd Library, Princeton University

Hamilton Fish Armstrong Papers, Mudd Library, Princeton

Joseph W. Ballantine Papers, Hoover Institution on War, Revolution, and Peace

Robert W. Blum Papers, Sterling Library, Yale

Robert Bowie Oral History, Mudd Library, Princeton

Chester W. Bowles Papers, Sterling Library, Yale

Arleigh Burke Oral History, Mudd Library, Princeton

John M. Cabot Diplomatic Papers, Edwin Ginn Library, Fletcher School of Law and Diplomacy, Tufts University. Microfilm

John M. Cabot Oral Histories, Eisenhower and Truman Libraries

Chiang Kai-shek and Mme Chiang Kai-shek Oral Histories, Mudd Library, Princeton

Clark M. Clifford Papers, Truman Library

Matthew J. Connelly Papers, Truman Library

Council on Foreign Relations Papers, CFR Archives, New York City

Myron M. Cowen Oral History, Truman Library

Department of Defense, Record Groups 218, 330, National Archives

Department of State, Record Group 59, Records of the Policy Planning Staff (1947–53), Records of Charles E. Bohlen, National Archives

Allen Dulles Papers, Mudd Library, Princeton

John Foster Dulles Papers, Mudd Library, Princeton; Eisenhower Library

Dwight D. Eisenhower Papers, Eisenhower Library
George M. Elsey Papers and Oral History, Truman Library
William C. Foster Oral History, John F. Kennedy Library
Lord Oliver Franks Oral History, Truman Library
Andrew Goodpaster Oral History, Mudd Library, Princeton
W. Averell Harriman Oral History, Kennedy Library
Christian Herter Papers, Eisenhower Library
Roger Hilsman Papers, Kennedy Library
Stanley K. Hornbeck Papers, Hoover Institution
C. D. Jackson Papers, Eisenhower Library
Philip C. Jessup Papers, Library of Congress
Lyndon B. Johnson Papers, Lyndon B. Johnson Library
U. Alexis Johnson Oral History, Mudd Library, Princeton
Walter S. Judd Papers, Hoover Institution
George F. Kennan Oral History, Kennedy Library
George F. Kennan Papers, Mudd Library, Princeton
John F. Kennedy Papers, Kennedy Library
William F. Knowland Papers, Bancroft Library, University of California, Berkeley
Wellington V. K. Koo Papers, Butler Library, Columbia University
Arthur Krock Papers, Mudd Library, Princeton
Roger Lapham Oral History and Papers, Bancroft Library, UC-Berkeley
Tsung-ren Li Papers, Butler Library, Columbia
Edwin Martin Oral History, Truman Library
John J. McCloy Oral History, Eisenhower Library
John F. Melby Papers, Truman Library
Livingston Merchant Oral Histories, Mudd Library, Princeton, and Truman Library
Livingston Merchant Papers, Mudd Library, Princeton
National Security Council, Record Group 273, National Archives
Herman Phleger Papers, Bancroft Library, UC-Berkeley
Herman Phleger personal papers in possession of Atherton Phleger
Public Record Office, England, Ernest Bevin Papers, CAB, DEFE, FO, PREM files, Cabinet Minutes and Meetings, 1946–52 (microfilm)
Arthur W. Radford Oral History, Mudd Library, Princeton
Karl Lott Rankin Papers, Princeton
Benjamin Read Oral History, Kennedy Library
Harrison Salisbury Oral History, Eisenhower Library
Arthur Schlesinger Papers, Kennedy Library
John Service Oral History and Papers, Bancroft Library, UC-Berkeley
Theodore Sorensen Oral History, Kennedy Library
Philip Sprouse Oral History, Truman Library
John Sumner Papers, Truman Library

T. W. Sung Papers, Hoover Institution
Llewellyn E. Thompson Oral History, Kennedy Library
James C. Thomson Oral History, Johnson Library
James C. Thomson Papers, Kennedy Library
Harry S. Truman Papers, Truman Library
Nathan Twining Papers, Library of Congress
William R. Tyler Oral History, Kennedy Library
U.S. Council on Foreign Economic Policy Papers, Eisenhower Library
Henry Wallace Papers, University of Iowa. Microfilm

Correspondence and Interviews

M. Graeme Bannerman to author, Feb. 3, 1986
William P. Bundy to author, Aug. 6, 1985
George Bunn interview, Sept. 17, 1987
Chinese researchers interviews, Oct.–Nov. 1985, Beijing
Eleanor Lansing Dulles to author, May 22, 1986
Gregg Herken to David Thelen, March 4, 1987
Huang Hua interview, Nov. 29, 1985, Beijing
Helen C. Mattas to author, March 9, 1988
Walt Whitman Rostow interview, June 6, 1985, Austin, Tex.
Wang Bingnan interview, Nov. 25, 1985, Beijing
Wu Xiuquan interview, Nov. 28, 1985, Beijing
Zhang Wenjin interview, Nov. 29, 1985, Beijing

Other Sources

Acheson, Dean. *Present at the Creation: My Years at the State Department.* New York, 1969.
Alsop, Joseph. "Thoughts Out of China—Go Versus No Go," *New York Times Magazine,* March 11, 1973.
Ambrose, Stephen E. *Eisenhower: The President.* New York, 1984.
———. *Rise to Globalism: American Foreign Policy, 1938–1976.* New York, 1976.
American Assembly. *The United States and the Far East.* New York, 1956.
Avedon, John F. *In Exile from the Land of Snows.* New York, 1984.
Bachrack, Stanley D. *The Committee of One Million: "China Lobby" Politics, 1953–1971.* New York, 1976.
Barnett, A. Doak. *China and the Major Powers in Asia.* Washington, D.C., 1977.
———. *Communist China and Asia: A Challenge to American Policy.* New York, 1960.

———. "The 1958 Quemoy Crisis: The Sino-Soviet Dimension," *Problems of Communism*, July–Aug. 1976.

Beam, Jacob D. *Multiple Exposure: An American Ambassador's Unique Perspective on East-West Issues.* New York, 1978.

Beijing daxue guoji zhengzhixi [Dept. of International Politics, Beijing University]. *Zhonghua renmin gongheguo duiwai guanxi shi* [History of the foreign relations of the People's Republic of China], Beijing, 1985.

Berding, Andrew H. *Dulles on Diplomacy.* Princeton, N.J., 1965.

Bernstein, Barton J. "The Policy of Risk: Crossing the 38th Parallel and Marching to the Yalu," *Foreign Service Journal*, March 1977.

Betts, Richard K. *Nuclear Blackmail and Nuclear Balance.* Washington, D.C., 1987.

Bialer, Seweryn. *The Soviet Paradox: External Expansion, Internal Decline.* New York, 1986.

Bloomfield, Lincoln P., et al. *Khrushchev and the Arms Race: Soviet Interest in Arms Control and Disarmament, 1954–1964.* Cambridge, Mass., 1966.

Blum, Robert. *The United States and China in World Affairs.* New York, 1966.

Blum, Robert M. *Drawing the Line: The Origin of the American Containment Policy in East Asia.* New York, 1982.

———. "Surprised by Tito: The Anatomy of an Intelligence Failure," *Diplomatic History*, Winter 1988, pp. 39–57.

Boardman, Robert. *Britain and the People's Republic of China, 1949–1974.* London, 1976.

Bohlen, Charles E. *Witness to History, 1929–1969.* New York, 1973.

Boorman, Howard L., et al. *Moscow-Peking Axis: Strengths and Strains.* New York, 1957.

Borden, William S. *The Pacific Alliance: United States Foreign Economic Policy and Japanese Trade Recovery, 1947–1955.* Madison, Wis., 1984.

Borg, Dorothy, and Waldo Heinrichs, eds. *Uncertain Years: Chinese-American Relations, 1947–1950.* New York, 1980.

Borisov, O. B., and B. T. Koloskov. *Soviet-Chinese Relations, 1945–1970*, ed. and tr. Vladimir Petrov. Bloomington, Ind., 1975.

Bowles, Chester. *Ambassador's Report.* New York, 1954.

———. "The 'China Problem' Reconsidered," *Foreign Affairs*, April 1960.

———. "New India," *Foreign Affairs*, Oct. 1952.

Brands, Henry W., Jr. "Redefining the Cold War: American Policy Toward Yugoslavia, 1948–60," *Diplomatic History*, Winter 1987.

———. "Testing Massive Retaliation: Credibility and Crisis Management in the Taiwan Strait," *International Security*, Spring 1988.

Bridgham, Philip, Arthur Cohen, and Leonard Jaffe. "Mao's Road and Sino-Soviet Relations: A View From Washington, 1953," *China Quarterly*, Dec. 1972.

Brzezinski, Zbigniew. "Patterns and Limits of the Sino-Soviet Dispute," *Problems of Communism*, Sept.–Oct. 1960.

Buhite, Russell D. "'Major Interests': American Policy Toward China, Taiwan, and Korea, 1945–1950," *Pacific Historical Review*, Aug. 1978.

———. "Missed Opportunities? American Policy and the Chinese Communists, 1949," *Mid-America*, 61 (1979).

Bundy, McGeorge. *Danger and Survival: Choices About the Bomb in the First Fifty Years.* New York, 1988.

———. "The Presidency and Peace," *Foreign Affairs*, April 1964.

Cabot, John M. *First Line of Defense: Fifty Years' Experiences of a Career Diplomat.* Washington, D.C., [1979?].

Caldwell, Dan. *American-Soviet Relations: From 1947 to the Nixon-Kissinger Grand Design.* Westport, Conn., 1981.

Caplow, Theodore. "Further Development of a Theory of Coalitions in the Triad," *American Journal of Sociology*, March 1959.

———. "A Theory of Coalitions in the Triad," *American Sociological Review*, Aug. 1956.

———. *Two Against One: Coalitions in Triads.* Englewood Cliffs, N.J., 1968.

The China White Paper. Reissue of *United States Relations with China, with Special Reference to the Period 1944–49*, with Introduction by Lyman P. Van Slyke. 2 vols. Stanford, Calif., 1967.

Chiu, Hungdah. "Communist China's Attitude Toward Nuclear Tests," *China Quarterly*, Jan.–March 1965.

Clemens, Walter C., Jr. *The Arms Race and Sino-Soviet Relations.* Stanford, Calif., 1968.

Cleveland, Harlan. "The Closed Door in China," *The Reporter*, Sept. 1, 1953.

Clubb, O. Edmund. *China and Russia: The "Great Game."* New York, 1971.

———. "Formosa and the Offshore Islands in American Policy, 1950–1955," *Political Science Quarterly*, 74 (1959).

———. "'Titoism' and the Chinese Communist Regime: An American View," *World Today*, Dec. 1952.

Cohen, Warren I. "Acheson, His Advisers, and China, 1949–50," in Dorothy Borg and Waldo Heinrichs, eds., *Uncertain Years*, pp. 13–53.

———. "Ambassador Philip D. Sprouse on the Question of Recognition of the People's Republic of China in 1949 and 1950," *Diplomatic History*, Spring 1978.

———. *America's Response to China: An Interpretative History of Sino-American Relations*. 2d ed. New York, 1980.

———. "Consul General O. Edmund Clubb on the 'Inevitability' of Conflict Between the United States and the People's Republic of China, 1949–50," *Diplomatic History*, Spring 1981.

———. *Dean Rusk*. Totowa, N.J., 1980.

———, ed. *New Frontiers in American–East Asian Relations: Essays Presented to Dorothy Borg*. New York, 1983.

Congressional Quarterly Service, ed. *China and U.S. Far East Policy, 1945–1967*. Washington, D.C.: 1967.

Cousins, Norman. *The Improbable Triumvirate: John F. Kennedy, Pope John, Nikita Khrushchev*. New York, 1972.

———. "Notes on a 1963 Visit with Khrushchev," *Saturday Review*, Nov. 7, 1964.

Craig, Gordon A., and Alexander George. *Force and Statecraft: Diplomatic Problems of Our Time*. New York, 1983.

Crankshaw, Edward. *The New Cold War: Moscow Versus Peking*. Harmondsworth, Eng., 1965.

Dalleck, Robert. *The American Style of Foreign Policy: Cultural Politics and Foreign Affairs*. New York, 1983.

Davies, John Paton, Jr. *Dragon by the Tail: American, British, Japanese, and Russian Encounters with China and One Another*. New York, 1972.

Dean, Arthur. *The Test Ban and Disarmament: The Path of Negotiation*. New York, 1966.

———. "United States Foreign Policy and Formosa," *Foreign Affairs*, April 1955.

Dingman, Roger. "Atomic Diplomacy During the Korean War," *International Security*, Winter 1988–89.

Dittmer, Lowell. "The Strategic Triangle: An Elementary Game-Theoretical Analysis," *World Politics*, July 1981.

Divine, Robert. *Blowing on the Wind: The Nuclear Test Ban Debate, 1954–1960*. New York, 1978.

———. *Eisenhower and the Cold War*. New York, 1981.

Donovan, Robert J. *Eisenhower: The Inside Story*. New York, 1956.

————. *Tumultuous Years: The Presidency of Harry S Truman, 1949–1953*. New York, 1982.

Dulles, Eleanor Lansing. *John Foster Dulles, the Last Year*. New York, 1963.

Dulles, Foster Rhea. *American Policy Toward Communist China, 1949–1969*. New York, 1972.

Dulles, John Foster. "Far Eastern Problems: Defense Through Deterrent Power," *Vital Speeches*, June 1952.

————. "Policy for Security and Peace," *Foreign Affairs*, April 1954.

————. *War or Peace?* London, 1950.

Eden, Anthony. *Full Circle*. Cambridge, Mass., 1960.

Eisenhower, Dwight D. *White House Years*. Vol. 1: *Mandate for Change, 1953–1956*. Vol. 2: *Waging Peace, 1956–1961*. Garden City, N.Y., 1963–65.

Ellison, Herbert J., ed. *The Sino-Soviet Conflict: A Global Perspective*. Seattle, 1982.

Etzold, Thomas H., ed. *Aspects of Sino-American Relations Since 1784*. New York, 1978.

Etzold, Thomas H., and John L. Gaddis, eds. *Containment: Documents on American Foreign Policy and Strategy, 1945–1950*. New York, 1978.

Fairbank, John K. *The United States and China*. 4th ed. Cambridge, Mass., 1979.

Finlay, David J., et al. *Enemies in Politics*. Chicago, 1967.

Floyd, David. *Mao Against Khrushchev: A Short History of the Sino-Soviet Conflict*. New York, 1963.

Foot, Rosemary. "Nuclear Coercion and the Ending of the Korean Conflict," *International Security*, Winter 1988–89.

————. *The Wrong War: American Policy and the Dimensions of the Korean Conflict, 1950–1953*. Ithaca, N.Y., 1985.

Friedman, Edward. "Nuclear Blackmail and the End of the Korean War," *Modern China*, Jan. 1975.

Friedman, Edward, and Mark Selden, eds. *America's Asia: Dissenting Essays on Asian-American Relations*. New York, 1971.

Fulbright, J. William, ed. *The Vietnam Hearings*. New York, 1966.

Gaddis, John Lewis. "The Emerging Post-Revisionist Synthesis of the Origins of the Cold War," *Diplomatic History*, Summer 1983.

————. *The Long Peace: Inquiries into the History of the Cold War*. New York, 1987.

————. *Strategies of Containment: A Critical Appraisal of Postwar American National Security Policy*. New York, 1982.

———. "Was the Truman Doctrine a Real Turning Point?," *Foreign Affairs*, Jan. 1974.

Gallicchio, Marc S. *The Cold War Begins in Asia: American East Asian Policy and the Fall of the Japanese Empire*. New York, 1988.

Gardner, Lloyd C. *Approaching Vietnam: From World War II Through Dienbienphu, 1941–1954*. New York, 1988.

Gati, Charles, ed. *Caging the Bear: Containment and the Cold War*. Indianapolis, 1974.

George, Alexander L., and Richard Smoke. *Deterrence in American Foreign Policy: Theory and Practice*. New York, 1974.

Geyelin, Philip. *Lyndon B. Johnson and the World*. New York, 1966.

Gittings, John. "The Great Power Triangle and Chinese Foreign Policy," *China Quarterly*, July 1969.

———. "New Light on Mao," *China Quarterly*, Dec. 1974.

———. "Review of *The Logic of World Power*," *Modern China*, Oct. 1975.

———. *Survey of the Sino-Soviet Dispute: A Commentary and Extracts from the Recent Polemics, 1963–1967*. London, 1968.

———. *The World and China, 1922–1972*. New York, 1974.

Goldman, Eric F. *The Tragedy of Lyndon Johnson*. New York, 1969.

Goldman, Leonard H. D. "United States Opposition to Use of Force in the Taiwan Strait, 1954–1962," *Journal of American History*, Dec. 1985.

Gottlieb, Thomas M. *Chinese Foreign Policy Factionalism and the Origins of the Strategic Triangle*. RAND study R-1902-NA. Santa Monica, Calif., 1977.

Graebner, Norman A., ed. *The National Security: Its Theory and Practice, 1945–1960*. New York, 1986.

Grasso, June. *Truman's Two-China Policy, 1948–1950*. Armonk, N.Y., 1987.

Greene, Fred. *U.S. Policy and the Security of Asia*. New York, 1968.

Griffith, William E. *Peking, Moscow and Beyond*. Washington, D.C., 1973.

———. *The Sino-Soviet Rift*. Cambridge, Mass., 1964.

———. *World Communism Divided*. New York, 1964.

Guhin, Michael A. *John Foster Dulles: A Statesman and His Times*. New York, 1972.

———. "The United States and the Chinese People's Republic: The Non-Recognition Policy Reviewed," *International Affairs*, Jan. 1969.

Gurtov, Melvin, and Byong-moo Hwang. *China Under Threat: The Politics of Strategy and Diplomacy*. Baltimore, 1980.

Gwertzman, Bernard. "The Hostage Crisis: Three Decades Ago," *New York Times Magazine*, May 4, 1980.

Halle, Louis J. *Civilization and Foreign Policy*. New York, 1952.

———. *The Cold War as History*. London, 1967.

Halperin, Morton H. *China and the Bomb*. New York, 1965.

———, ed. *Sino-Soviet Relations and Arms Control*. Cambridge, Mass., 1967.

Halperin, Morton H., and Dwight H. Perkins. *Communist China and Arms Control*. New York, 1965.

Hartmann, Frederick H. *The Conservation of Enemies: A Study in Enmity*. Westport, Conn., 1982.

He Di. "Evolution of the CCP's Policy Towards the United States: 1944–1949." Unpublished paper, 1987.

———. "The Evolution of the People's Republic of China's Policy Toward the Offshore Islands (Quemoy and Matsu)." Unpublished paper, 1987.

Herring, George C. *America's Longest War: The United States and Vietnam, 1970–1975*. 2d ed. Philadelphia, 1986.

Hess, Gary R. "The First American Commitment in Indochina: The Acceptance of the 'Bao Dai Solution,' 1950," *Diplomatic History*, Fall 1978, pp. 331–50.

Hilsman, Roger. *To Move a Nation: The Politics of Foreign Policy in the Administration of John F. Kennedy*. Garden City, N.Y., 1967.

Hinton, Harold. *The Bear at the Gate: Chinese Policymaking Under Soviet Pressure*. Washington, D.C., 1971.

———. *Peking-Washington: Chinese Foreign Policy and the United States*. Washington, D.C., 1976.

———. *The Sino-Soviet Confrontation: Implications for the Future*. New York, 1976.

The Historical Experience of the Dictatorship of the Proletariat, ed. *People's Daily* and *Red Flag*. Peking, 1961.

Holloway, David. *The Soviet Union and the Arms Race*. 2d ed. New Haven, Conn., 1986.

Hoopes, Townsend. *The Devil and John Foster Dulles*. Boston, 1973.

Hornbeck, Stanley K. "Which Chinese: Diplomatic Recognition and Official Representation," *Foreign Affairs*, Oct. 1955.

Horowitz, David. "The Making of America's China Policy," *Ramparts*, Oct. 1971.

Howe, T. Jonathan. *Multicrises: Sea Power and Global Politics in the Missile Age*. Cambridge, Mass., 1974.

Hsieh, Alice Langley. *Communist China's Strategy in the Nuclear Era*. Englewood Cliffs, N.J., 1962.

———. "The Sino-Soviet Nuclear Dialogue: 1963," *Journal of Conflict Resolution*, June 1964.

Hudson, G. F., et al. *The Sino-Soviet Dispute*. New York, 1961.

Hunt, Michael H. *Ideology and U.S. Foreign Policy*. New Haven, Conn., 1987.

Hyland, William G. *Mortal Rivals: Superpower Relations from Nixon to Reagan*. New York, 1987.

Immerman, Richard H. "In Search of History—and Relevancy: Breaking Through the 'Encrustations of Interpretation,'" *Diplomatic History*, Summer 1988.

Iriye, Akira. *The Cold War in Asia: A Historical Introduction*. Englewood Cliffs, N.J., 1974.

Isaacs, Harold. *Scratches on Our Minds: American Images of China and India*. New York, 1958.

Isaacson, Walter, and Evan Thomas. *The Wise Men: Six Friends and the World They Made*. New York, 1986.

Ivanov, O. *Soviet-Chinese Relations Surveyed*. Moscow, 1975.

Jacobson, Harold, and Eric Stein. *Diplomats, Scientists and Politicians: The United States and the Nuclear Test Ban Negotiations*. Ann Arbor, Mich., 1966.

Jervis, Robert. "The Impact of the Korean War on the Cold War," *Journal of Conflict Resolution*, Dec. 1980.

Jessup, Philip C. *The Birth of Nations*. New York, 1974.

Johnson, Lyndon B. *Vantage Point: Perspectives of the Presidency, 1963–1969*. New York, 1971.

Johnson, U. Alexis. *Right Hand of Power*. Englewood Cliffs, N.J., 1984.

Jonsson, Christer. *Soviet Bargaining Power: The Nuclear Test Ban Case*. New York, 1979.

Kahin, George McT. *Intervention: How America Became Involved in Vietnam*. New York, 1986.

Kalicki, J. H. *The Pattern of Sino-American Crises: Political-Military Interactions in the 1950s*. London, 1975.

Keefer, Edward C. "President Dwight D. Eisenhower and the End of the Korean War," *Diplomatic History*, Summer 1986.

Kennan, George F. *American Diplomacy, 1900–1950*. New York, 1951.

———. *Memoirs, 1925–1950*. Boston, 1967.

———. *Memoirs, 1950–1963*. Boston, 1972.

Kennedy, John F. "A Democrat Looks at Foreign Policy," *Foreign Affairs*, Oct. 1957.

Kesaris, Paul, ed. *CIA Research Reports: China, 1946–1976*. Frederick, Md., 1982. Microfilm.

Khrushchev, N. S. *Khrushchev Remembers*, tr. and ed. Strobe Talbott. Boston, 1970.

———. *Khrushchev Remembers: The Last Testament,* tr. and ed. Strobe Talbott. Boston, 1974.

Khrushchev, Sergei. "My Father Nikita's Downfall," *Time,* Nov. 14, 1988.

Kim, Ilpyong J., ed. *The Strategic Triangle: China, the United States and the Soviet Union,* New York, 1987.

Kissinger, Henry A. *Nuclear Weapons and Foreign Policy.* Cambridge, Mass., 1971.

———. *White House Years.* Boston, 1979.

Kistiakowsky, George B. *A Scientist at the White House: The Private Diary of President Eisenhower's Special Assistant for Science and Technology.* Cambridge, Mass., 1976.

Kolko, Gabriel. *Anatomy of a War: Vietnam, the United States, and the Modern Historical Experience.* New York, 1985.

Kolko, Joyce, and Gabriel Kolko. *The Limits of Power: The World and United States Foreign Policy, 1945–1954.* New York, 1972.

Kusnitz, Leonard A. *Public Opinion and Foreign Policy: America's China Policy, 1949–1979.* Westport, Conn., 1984.

Labedz, Leopold, and G. R. Urban, eds. *The Sino-Soviet Conflict: Eleven Radio Discussions.* London, 1964.

LaFeber, Walter. *America, Russia, and the Cold War, 1945–1966.* New York, 1967.

Leary, William M., and William Stueck. "The Chennault Plan to Save China: U.S. Containment in Asia and the Origins of the CIA's Aerial Empire, 1949–1950," *Diplomatic History,* Fall 1984.

Lees, Lorraine M. "The American Decision to Assist Tito, 1948–1949," *Diplomatic History,* Fall 1978.

Levine, Steven I. *Anvil of Victory: The Communist Revolution in Manchuria, 1945–1948.* New York, 1987.

Lewis, John W. "Quemoy and America China Policy," *Asian Survey,* March 1962.

Lewis, John W., and Litai Xue. *China Builds the Bomb.* Stanford, Calif., 1988.

Li Changjiu, ed. *Zhong-mei guanxi erbainian* [Two hundred years of Sino-American relations]. Beijing: Xinhua chubanshe, 1984.

Lilienthal, David E. *The Journals of David E. Lilienthal,* Vol. 2: *The Atomic Energy Years.* New York, 1964.

Lin Piao [Lin Biao]. *Long Live the Victory of People's War!* Peking, 1965.

Lo, Kuan-chung. *Three Kingdoms: China's Epic Drama,* tr. Moss Roberts. New York, 1976.

Lowenthal, Richard. "Diplomacy and Revolution: The Dialectics of a Dispute," *China Quarterly,* Jan. 1961.

MacFarquhar, Roderick, ed. *Sino-American Relations, 1949–71.* New York, 1972.

Macmillan, Harold. *Riding the Storm, 1956–59.* London, 1971.

———. *Tides of Fortune, 1945–1955.* New York, 1965.

Mao Tsetung [Mao Zedong]. *Selected Works.* Vols. 1–5. Peking, 1961–77.

Marshall, Charles Burton. "Three Powers—Two Oceans," *Naval War College Review,* Winter 1978.

Martin, Edwin W. *Divided Counsel: The Anglo-American Response to Communist Victory in China.* Lexington, Ky., 1986.

May, Ernest R. *The Truman Administration and China, 1945–1949.* Philadelphia, 1975.

May, Ernest R., and James C. Thomson, Jr., eds. *American–East Asian Relations: A Survey.* Cambridge, Mass., 1972.

Mayers, David Allan. "American Policy Toward the Sino-Soviet Alliance, 1949–1955." Ph.D. dissertation, University of Chicago, 1979.

———. *Cracking the Monolith: U.S. Policy Against the Sino-Soviet Alliance, 1949–1955.* Baton Rouge, La., 1986.

McLean, David. "American Nationalism, the China Myth, and the Truman Doctrine: The Question of Accommodation with Peking, 1949–50," *Diplomatic History,* Winter 1986.

Medvedev, Roy. *China and the Superpowers,* tr. Harold Shukman. Oxford, 1986.

Mehnert, Klaus. *Peking and Moscow,* tr. Leila Vennewitz. New York, 1963.

Melby, John F. *The Mandate of Heaven: Record of a Civil War: China 1945–1949.* Toronto, 1968.

Miscamble, Wilson D. "Encouraging Chinese Titoism? George F. Kennan, John Paton Davies and the Limits of America's China Policy, 1947–50." Unpublished paper, June 1987.

Moorsteen, Richard, and Morton Abramowitz. *Remaking China Policy: U.S.-China Relations and Government Decisionmaking.* Cambridge, Mass., 1971.

Morgenthau, Hans J., and Kenneth W. Thompson. *Politics Among Nations: The Struggle for Power and Peace.* 6th ed. New York, 1985.

Mori, Kazuko. "Sino-Soviet Relations: From Confrontation to Cooperation," *Japan Review of International Affairs,* Vol. 2, No. 1 (Spring/Summer 1988).

Mozingo, D. P., and T. W. Robinson. *Lin Piao on "People's War": China Takes a Second Look at Vietnam.* RAND memo. RM-4814-PR, Nov. 1965.

Nagai, Yonosuke, and Akira Iriye, eds. *The Origins of the Cold War in Asia.* New York, 1977.

Newman, Robert P. "The Self-Inflicted Wound: The China White Paper of 1949," *Prologue*, Fall 1982.

Nie Rongzhen. *Nie Rongzhen huiyilu* [Memoirs of Nie Rongzhen]. Beijing, 1984.

Nixon, Richard M. "American Policy Abroad: Analysis and Recommendations," address to the American Society of Newspaper Editors, Washington, D.C., April 20, 1963, *Vital Speeches*, July 1, 1963.

——. "Asia After Viet Nam," *Foreign Affairs*, Oct. 1967.

——. *Memoirs*. New York, 1978.

——. *Six Crises*. Garden City, N.Y., 1962.

Nogee, Joseph L., and Robert H. Donaldson. *Soviet Foreign Policy Since World War II*. New York, 1984.

North, Robert C. *Moscow and Chinese Communists*. 2d ed. Stanford, Calif., 1963.

On Khrushchev's Phoney Communism and Its Historical Lessons for the World, ed. *People's Daily* and *Red Flag*. Peking, 1964.

Oppose U.S. Occupation of Taiwan and "Two Chinas" Plot. Peking, 1958.

Paret, Peter, ed. *Makers of Modern Strategy: From Machiavelli to the Nuclear Age*. Princeton, N.J., 1986.

Parmet, Herbert S. *Eisenhower and the American Crusades*. New York, 1972.

Paterson, Thomas G. "If Europe, Why Not China? The Containment Doctrine, 1947–1949," *Prologue*, Spring 1981.

People of the World Unite for the Complete, Thorough, Total and Resolute Prohibition and Destruction of Nuclear Weapons. Peking, 1963.

Peterson, Sophia. *Sino-Soviet-American Relations: Conflict, Communication and Mutual Threat*. Denver, 1979.

Pickett, William B. "The Eisenhower Solarium Notes," *Newsletter of the Society for Historians of American Foreign Relations*, June 1985.

Porter, Brian. *Britain and the Rise of Communist China: A Study of British Attitudes, 1945–1954*. New York, 1967.

Prospect for America: The Rockefeller Panel Reports. Garden City, N.Y., 1961.

Pruessen, Ronald W. *John Foster Dulles: The Road to Power*. New York, 1982.

Purifoy, Lewis McCarroll. *Harry Truman's China Policy: McCarthyism and the Diplomacy of Hysteria, 1947–1951*. New York, 1976.

Quested, R. K. I. *Sino-Russian Relations, a Short History*. Sydney, 1984.

Rankin, Karl Lott. *China Assignment*. Seattle, 1964.

Reardon-Anderson, James. "Yenan: The Foreign Policy of Self-Reliance." Ph.D. dissertation, Columbia University, 1975.

Refutation of the New Leaders of the CPSU on "United Action," ed. *People's Daily* and *Red Flag*. Peking, 1965.

Reischauer, Edwin O. *Wanted: An Asian Policy*. New York, 1955.

Ridgway, Matthew B. *Soldier: The Memoirs of Matthew B. Ridgway, as told to Harold H. Martin*. New York, 1956.

Roberts, Henry L. *Russia and America: Dangers and Prospects*. New York, 1956.

Rogers, Frank E. "Sino-American Relations and the Vietnam War, 1964–66," *China Quarterly*, June 1976.

Rostow, Walt Whitman. *Diffusion of Power: An Essay in Recent History*. New York, 1972.

———. *Prospects for Communist China*. Cambridge, Mass., 1954.

Rotter, Andrew J. "The Big Canvas: The United States, Southeast Asia and the World: 1948–1950." Ph.D. dissertation, Stanford University, 1981.

———. *The Path to Vietnam: Origins of the American Commitment to Southeast Asia*. Ithaca, N.Y., 1987.

Rupen, Robert A., and Robert Farrell, eds. *Vietnam and the Sino-Soviet Dispute*. New York, 1967.

Rushkoff, Bennett C. "Eisenhower, Dulles and the Quemoy-Matsu Crisis, 1954–1955," *Political Science Quarterly*, Fall 1981.

Rusk, Dean. "Chinese-American Friendship: Peiping Regime Not Chinese," *Vital Speeches*, June 15, 1951.

Salisbury, Harrison E. *War Between Russia and China*. New York, 1969.

Saran, Vimla. *Sino-Soviet Schism: A Bibliography, 1956–1964*. London, 1971.

Schaller, Michael. *The American Occupation of Japan: The Origins of the Cold War in Asia*. New York, 1985.

———. "Consul General O. Edmund Clubb, John P. Davies, and the 'Inevitability' of Conflict Between the United States and China, 1949–50: A Comment and New Documentation," *Diplomatic History*, Spring 1985.

———. "Securing the Great Crescent: Occupied Japan and the Origins of Containment in Southeast Asia," *Journal of American History*, Sept. 1982.

———. *The U.S. Crusade in China, 1938–1945*. New York, 1979.

Schlesinger, Arthur M. *A Thousand Days: John F. Kennedy in the White House*. Boston, 1965.

Schoenbaum, Thomas J. *Waging Peace and War: Dean Rusk in the Truman, Kennedy, and Johnson Years*. New York, 1988.

Schurmann, Franz. *The Logic of World Power: An Inquiry into the Origins, Currents, and Contradictions of World Politics.* New York, 1974.

Seaborg, Glenn T. *Kennedy, Khrushchev, and the Test Ban.* Berkeley, Calif., 1981.

Seaborg, Glenn T., with Benjamin Loeb. *Stemming the Tide: Arms Control in the Johnson Years.* Lexington, Mass., 1987.

Segal, Gerald. *Defending China.* New York, 1985.

―――. *The Great Power Triangle.* London, 1982.

―――, ed. *The China Factor: Peking and the Superpowers.* New York, 1982.

Sergeichuk, S. *Through Russian Eyes: American-Chinese Relations,* tr. Elizabeth Cody-Rutter. Arlington, Va., 1975.

Service, John. *The Amerasia Papers: Some Problems in the History of U.S.-China Relations.* Berkeley, Calif., 1971.

Shaw, Yu-ming. "John Leighton Stuart and U.S.-Chinese Communist Rapprochement in 1949: Was There Another 'Lost Chance in China'?," *China Quarterly,* March 1982.

Shevchenko, Arkady N. *Breaking with Moscow.* New York, 1985.

Shewmaker, Kenneth E. *Americans and Chinese Communists, 1925– 1945: A Persuading Encounter.* Ithaca, N.Y., 1971.

Shulman, Marshall D. *Stalin's Foreign Policy Reappraised.* Cambridge, Mass., 1963.

Simon, Nancy S. "From the Chinese Civil War to the Shanghai Communique: Changing U.S. Perceptions of China as a Security Threat." Ph.D. dissertation, Johns Hopkins University, 1982.

Smith, Gaddis. *Dean Acheson.* New York, 1972.

Smith, R. B. *An International History of the Vietnam War,* Vol. 1: *Revolution Versus Containment, 1955–61.* Vol. 2: *The Struggle for South-East Asia, 1961–65.* London, 1983–85.

Snow, Edgar. "Interview with Mao," *New Republic,* Feb. 27, 1965.

―――. *The Other Side of the River: Red China Today.* New York, 1962.

―――. "Will China Become a Russian Satellite?," *Saturday Evening Post,* April 9, 1949.

Sorensen, Theodore C. *Kennedy.* New York, 1965.

Stevenson, Adlai. "Putting First Things First," *Foreign Affairs,* Oct. 1959.

Stolper, Thomas E. *China, Taiwan, and the Offshore Islands.* Armonk, N.Y., 1985.

Stuart, Douglas T., and William T. Tow, eds. *China, the Soviet Union, and the West: Strategic and Political Dimensions in the 1980's.* Boulder, Colo., 1982.

Stueck, William Whitney, Jr. *The Road to Confrontation: American Policy Toward China and Korea, 1947–1950.* Chapel Hill, N.C., 1981.

Sulzberger, C. L. *The Coldest War: Russia's Game in China.* New York, 1974.

———. *The Last of the Giants.* New York, 1970.

———. *A Long Row of Candles.* New York, 1969.

Sun-tzu. *The Art of War,* tr. Samuel B. Griffith. London, 1963.

Sutter, Robert C. *China-Watch: Toward Sino-American Reconciliation.* Baltimore, 1978.

Szulc, Tad. *The Illusion of Peace: Foreign Policy in the Nixon Years.* New York, 1978.

Tatu, Michel. *The Great Power Triangle: Washington-Moscow-Peking.* Paris, 1970.

Terchek, Ronald. *The Making of the Test Ban Treaty.* The Hague, 1970.

Thomas, John R. "Soviet Behavior in the Quemoy Crisis of 1958," *Orbis,* Spring 1962.

———. "Soviet Policy Toward Communist China and the 1958 Taiwan Straits Crisis." Ph.D. dissertation, George Washington University, 1970.

Thomson, James C., Jr. "Dragon Under Glass: Time for a New China Policy," *The Atlantic,* Oct. 1967.

Trachtenberg, Marc. "A 'Wasting Asset': American Strategy and the Shifting Nuclear Balance, 1949–1954," *International Strategy,* Winter 1988/89.

Trevelyan, Humphrey. *Living with the Communists: China 1953–5, Soviet Union, 1962–5.* Boston, 1971.

Truman, Harry S. *Memoirs: Years of Trial and Hope.* Garden City, N.Y., 1956.

Tsou, Tang. *America's Failure in China, 1941–1950.* Chicago, 1964.

———. "The Quemoy Imbroglio: Chiang Kai-shek and the United States," *Western Political Quarterly,* Dec. 1959.

Tuchman, Barbara. "If Mao Had Come to Washington: An Essay in Alternatives," *Foreign Affairs,* Oct. 1972.

Tucker, Nancy B. *Patterns in the Dust: Chinese-American Relations and the Recognition Controversy.* New York, 1983.

Ulam, Adam B. *Expansion and Coexistence: The History of Soviet Policy, 1917–67.* New York, 1968.

———. *A History of Soviet Russia.* New York, 1976.

———. *The Rivals: America and Russia Since World War II.* New York, 1971.

[The place of publication for all the following U.S. sources is Washington, D.C.]

United States, Arms Control and Disarmament Agency. *Documents on Disarmament, 1963.* 1964.

——, Department of Defense. *Air Operations in the Taiwan Crisis of 1958.* 1962.

——, ——. *United States–Vietnam.*

——. Department of State. *Bulletin.* 1948–68.

——, ——. *Foreign Relations of the United States.* 1948–57.

——, ——. *Transcript of the Round Table Discussion on American Policy Toward China Held in the Department of State, October 6, 7, 8, 1949.*

——, House of Representatives, Committee on Armed Services. *Pentagon Papers.* 12 books. 1971.

——, ——, Committee on Foreign Affairs. *U.S. Policy in the Far East,* vol. 2: *Developments in Southeast Asia: The China Question.* 1980.

——, ——, Subcommittee on the Far East and the Pacific of the Committee on Foreign Affairs. *Report on the Sino-Soviet Conflict and Its Implications,* and *Hearings on the Sino-Soviet Conflict,* 89: 1, 1965.

——, ——, Subcommittee on Future Foreign Policy Research and Development of the House Committee on International Relations. *United States–Soviet Union–China: The Great Power Triangle. Hearings,* 94, 1976.

——, National Academy of Sciences, Committee on International Security and Arms Control. *Nuclear Arms Control: Background and Issues.* 1985.

——. *Public Papers of the Presidents: Dwight D. Eisenhower, 1956.* 1958. *John F. Kennedy, 1961,* and *1962.* 1962–63. *Harry S. Truman, 1949.* 1964.

——, Senate, Committee on Armed Services and Committee on Foreign Relations. *Military Situation in the Far East. Hearings,* 82: 1, 1951.

——, ——, Committee on Foreign Relations. *The Communist World in 1967. Hearings,* 90: 1, 1967.

——, ——, ——. *Disarmament and Foreign Policy. Hearings,* 86: 1, 1957.

——, ——, ——. *Economic Assistance to China and Korea: 1949–50. Hearings.* Historical Series, 1974.

——, ——, ——. *The North Atlantic Treaty. Hearings*, 81: 1, 1973.

——, ——, ——. *Nuclear Test Ban Treaty. Hearings*, 88: 1, 1963.

——, ——, ——. *Reviews of the World Situation: 1949–1950. Executive Session Hearings*, 81: 1, 2. Historical Series, 1974.

——, ——, ——. *The United States and Communist China in 1949 and 1950: The Question of Rapprochement and Recognition*, by Robert M. Blum. Staff study, 1973.

——, ——, ——. *U.S. Policy with Respect to Mainland China. Hearings*, 89: 2, 1966.

——, ——, ——. *The Vandenberg Resolution and the North Atlantic Treaty. Executive Session Hearings*, 80: 2, 81: 1. Historical Series, 1973.

——, ——, Preparedness Investigating Subcommittee of the Committee on Armed Services. *Military Aspects and Implications of Nuclear Test Ban Proposals and Related Matters. Hearings*, 88: 1, 1963.

——, ——, Subcommittee of the Committee on Foreign Relations. *Nomination of Philip C. Jessup to Be United States Representative to the United Nations. Hearings*, 82: 1, 1951.

——, ——, Subcommittee to Investigate the Administration of the Internal Security Act of the Committee on the Judiciary. *The Institute of Pacific Relations. Hearings*, 82: 1, 1951.

Van Slyke, Lyman P. *Enemies and Friends: The United Front in Chinese Communist History*. Stanford, Calif., 1967.

Wang Bingnan. *Zhong-mei huitan jiunian huigu* [Looking back on nine years of Sino-American talks]. Beijing, 1985.

Wang Jisi. "1947–1950 nian meiguo dui zhongguo gongchandang tong sulian guanxi de kanfa he meiguo dui hua zhengce" [The U.S. view of the relationship of the Communist Party of China and the Soviet Union, and U.S. China policy, 1947–1950], *Shijieshi yanjiu dongtai* [World History Research Trends], no. 8, 1984.

Whelan, Joseph G. "The United States and Diplomatic Recognition: The Contrasting Cases of Russia and Communist China," *China Quarterly*, March 1961.

Whiting, Allen S. *China Crosses the Yalu: The Decision to Enter the Korean War*. Stanford, Calif., 1960.

——. *The Chinese Calculus of Deterrence: India and Indochina*. Ann Arbor, Mich., 1975.

——. "Communist China and Big 'Brother,'" *Far Eastern Survey*, Oct. 1955.

————. "Contradictions in the Moscow-Peking Axis," *Journal of Politics*, Feb. 1958.

————. "Quemoy 1958: Mao's Miscalculations," *China Quarterly*, June 1975.

————. "The Use of Force in Foreign Policy by the People's Republic of China," *Annals of the American Academy of Political and Social Science*, July 1972.

Wiesner, Jerome B., and Herbert F. York. "The Test Ban and Security," *Survival*, Jan. 1965.

Wilcox, Francis O., ed. *China and the Great Powers: Relations with the United States, the Soviet Union, and Japan*. New York, 1974.

Wilson, Dick. *Zhou Enlai*. New York, 1984.

Wolf, David C. "To Secure a Convenience: Britain Recognizes China—1950," *Journal of Contemporary History*, April 1983.

Wu, Fu-mei Chiu. *Richard M. Nixon, Communism and China*. Washington, D.C., 1978.

Wu Xiuquan. "Relations Between China and Yugoslavia: Memoirs of a Veteran Diplomat," *Beijing Review*, Dec. 5, 1983.

————. "Sino-Soviet Relations in the Early 1950s," *Beijing Review*, Nov. 21, 1983.

————. *Zai waijiaobu banian de jingli* [Eight years of experiences in the Ministry of Foreign Affairs]. Beijing, 1981.

Yasuhara, Yoko. "Japan, Communist China, and Export Controls in Asia, 1948–52," *Diplomatic History*, Winter 1986.

Yost, Charles P. *History and Memory*. New York, 1980.

Young, Kenneth T. *Negotiating with the Chinese Communists: The United States Experience, 1953–1967*. New York, 1968.

Zablocki, Clement J., ed. *Sino-Soviet Rivalry: Implications for U.S. Policy*. New York, 1966.

Zagoria, Donald S. "Mao's Role in the Sino-Soviet Conflict," *Pacific Affairs*, Summer 1974.

————. *The Sino-Soviet Conflict, 1956–1961*. Princeton, N.J., 1962.

————. "Strains in the Sino-Soviet Alliance," *Problems of Communism*, May–June 1960.

————. *Vietnam Triangle: Moscow, Peking, Hanoi*. New York, 1967.

Zhou Enlai. *Selected Works*. Vol. 1. Beijing, 1981.

Zi Zhongyun. "US Policy Towards Taiwan (1948–50)," *Beijing Review*, 2 parts, July 5, July 12, 1982.

Index

In this index an "f" after a number indicates a separate reference on the next page, and an "ff" indicates separate references on the next two pages. A continuous discussion over two or more pages is indicated by a span of page numbers, e.g., "57–59." *Passim* is used for a cluster of references in close but not consecutive sequence.

Library of Congress Cataloging-in-Publication Data

Chang, Gordon H.
  Friends and enemies : the United States, China, and the
Soviet Union, 1948–1972 / Gordon H. Chang.
      p.   cm.—(Modern America)
    ISBN 0-8047-1565-3 (alk. paper) :
      1. United States—Foreign relations—China. 2. China—
Foreign relations—United States. 3. United States—For-
eign relations—Soviet Union. 4. Soviet Union—Foreign
relations—United States. 5. United States—Foreign rela-
tions—1945– 6. World politics—1945– 7. Soviet
Union—Foreign relations—China. 8. China—Foreign relations—Soviet Union. I. Title. II. Series: Modern America
(Stanford, Calif.)
E183.8.C6C47   1990   89-21865
327.73047—dc20   CIP

  ∞   This book is printed on acid-free paper